THE DECLINE OF

THE ANCIENT WORLD

A. H. M. JONES

LONGMAN
LONDON AND NEW YORK

Longman Group Ltd

Longman Group Ltd, London
Associated companies, branches and
representatives throughout the world

© A. H. M. Jones 1966

First published 1966
Second impression 1968
Third impression and first appearance in
paperback, 1975

SBN 0 582 48309 3

Set in Plantin Series 110
and printed in Great Britain
by Whitstable Litho Ltd, Whitstable, Kent

A GENERAL HISTORY OF EUROPE

EDITED BY DENYS HAY

Contents

List of Maps

Preface

My special interest in the later Roman Empire began before World War II, and this book represents some twenty-five years of labour and thought—in the intervals of war work and my regular academic duties. The full fruits of my labours have already been published in *The Later Roman Empire* (Blackwell, 1964), which is a very long book (three volumes) and correspondingly dear (14 guineas). This book is a shortened and simplified version of that work, without its notes and appendices, which fill one of its volumes. Any reader who wants to know on what evidence I base my conclusions should consult the larger work, where he will find controversial issues argued in detail and the supporting texts cited.

I owe a debt of gratitude to Professor Hay and to my wife, who read this book in typescript in the capacity of 'intelligent but non-specialist readers', and suggested many omissions, additions and alterations. I hasten to add that they are not responsible if such readers find any part of the book dull or obscure, particularly as I rejected much of their advice, taking a higher view than they did of the intelligence of my public and their general knowledge.

In deference to Professor Hay, I should perhaps add that in calling the bishop of Rome the pope I imply no theological overtones, nor do I imply that he was commonly so called in the period of which I write—any more than the emperor was called *imperator*. The title *papa* was sometimes applied to him, and also to the bishop of Alexandria, and indeed by some authors to any bishop, but he was usually styled the bishop, or archbishop, of Rome; to use this title today would, however, savour of aggressive protestantism.

I also owe a debt of gratitude to Sir Basil Blackwell, who raised no objection to the publication of a book which he might reasonably fear as a rival to the *Later Roman Empire*. Finally I must thank Messrs Longmans Green & Co. for the courteous persistence with which they prodded me to produce my manuscript, their patience in waiting for it and their prompt efficiency in printing it when they at last received it.

Jesus College, Cambridge   A. H. M. JONES
October 1965

I

The Sources

As compared with the preceding and following ages, the period from the accession of Diocletian in 284 to the death of Phocas in 610 is well documented. In the first place, historiography was a popular form of literature in the Greek East, and a series of authors wrote histories of their own times. If all of them had survived we should be very well informed, but though most have perished the works of a few outstanding historians have survived and from the rest there are summaries and fragments. The first historian of the age whose work has been preserved in bulk is Ammianus Marcellinus, a Greek of Antioch who, in order to bring his writings to the notice of the senatorial aristocracy of Rome, wrote in Latin. He was an admirer of Tacitus and took up his tale where Tacitus stopped, at the death of Domitian. The surviving books of his work begin with A.D. 351 and he closes with the battle of Adrianople in 378. Ammianus is not so great a stylist as Tacitus, but he is one of the greatest of Roman historians. He knew the empire well, having served as a *protector* or officer cadet on the staff of Ursicinus, master of the soldiers on the eastern front, moved with his chief to the imperial court, and subsequently served under Julian in Gaul and in Persia. He was a remarkably fair-minded man, a pagan who could appreciate the virtues of the Christian clergy and criticize his hero Julian. His narrative is full and vivid and his character sketches of the emperors and their ministers are penetrating.

The next historian who has survived in full is Procopius, a barrister of Caesarea in Palestine, who served as *assessor* or judicial adviser to Justinian's great general Belisarius, accompanying him on his eastern, African and Italian campaigns. He was an admirer and imitator of Thucydides, and wrote an exhaustive history of Justinian's wars down to 554. He also wrote a short work giving a very full account of Justinian's building activity throughout the empire. These works are accurate and impartial. The same cannot be said of his *Secret History*, a scurrilous attack on Justinian, his empress Theodora and all his principal ministers. Many of the statements made in this work are demonstrably untrue and many obviously malicious gossip. The history of Justinian's wars was continued by Agathias, a barrister of Myrina in Asia. The last of the surviving contemporary historians is Theophylact Simocatta, who wrote the story of the reign of Maurice (582–602). Both these last are competent if not inspired. History was popular not only among the educated classes but also among the masses, for whose benefit John Malalas of Antioch wrote a chronicle of the world from Adam to Justinian, describing the personal appearance of the emperors, which party they favoured in the games, the circus riots and the intrigues of the court.

A good deal has survived in one way or another of the historians who filled the gaps between the surviving authors. Some, like Eunapius of Sardis and Olympiodorus of Egyptian Thebes, who covered the periods 270–404 and 407–25 respectively, have been pirated by historians (in this case Zosimus) who wrote in the middle of the fifth century. Others again have been copied by medieval Byzantine chroniclers—and often garbled in the process. Others have been summarized by medieval Byzantine scholars, notably the omnivorous reader Photius. In this way we have some knowledge of the works of Candidus the Isaurian or John of Epiphaneia. Large fragments survive from several, thanks to the emperor Constantine Porphyrogenitus, who ordered that all passages of ancient historians bearing on diplomacy, strategy and other political topics should be excerpted for the instruction of present-day statesmen and generals. To him we owe the fascinating account by Priscus of Panium of his embassy to Attila and the full details of Justinian's negotiations and treaties with Persia as told by Menander the *protector*.

In addition to the secular, there are the ecclesiastical historians. Eusebius of Caesarea gives a most valuable and detailed narrative of the Great Persecution under Diocletian and his successors. Thereafter no historians of the church survive until the middle of the fifth century, when Socrates, Sozomen and Theodoret wrote the story from the conversion of Constantine. At the end of the sixth century Evagrius of Antioch carried on the history of the church from 431 to his own day. We also possess in Syriac translations substantial portions of the church histories of the monophysite bishops Zacharias of Mitylene and John of Ephesus, the former covering the period from 450 to 491, the latter the reigns of Justin II and Tiberius. The ecclesiastical historians do not confine themselves to the affairs of the church and fill many gaps in secular history.

Unlike the secular historians, who in obedience to the stylistic canons of the day never quote original documents, the church historians reproduce *in extenso* many encyclicals and imperial letters; to them we owe a letter of Constantine inviting Arius to court, and the full text of Zeno's edict of union, the Henoticon.

The Latin west produced few historians. Aurelius Victor wrote thumbnail biographies of the emperors down to Constantius II, Eutropius a brief summary of the history of Rome from its foundation to 364, Orosius another brief history down to 417; in this by recounting all the disasters that the Roman people had undergone in its long history, he endeavoured to prove that the triumph of Christianity had not brought disaster on the empire. Ecclesiastical historians are as meagre. Rufinus at the end of the fourth century translated Eusebius and added two books carrying on the story to his own day. Optatus' history of the Donatist controversy is chiefly valuable for its appendix of documents, which include several letters of Constantine and the official record of two trials, those of Silvanus, bishop of Cirta, who was alleged to have lapsed in the Great Persecution, and of Ingentius, who falsely accused Felix, bishop of Aptungi, of the same offence. Sulpicius Severus wrote a world chronicle whose chief point of interest is his description of the Priscillianist movement in Spain and Gaul and its ruthless suppression. For the history of the west we are often reduced to bare annalists who give lists of the consuls with occasional notes of battles and church councils.

Biographies are abundant and a most useful source of information. They vary of course in quality from contemporary records by friends to mere legend. Eunapius' *Lives of the Sophists* gives a vivid picture of the pagan intellectuals of the fourth century. The rest are lives of saints, from great figures like Ambrose and Augustine to humble hermits. They are of particular value as depicting the life of all sorts and conditions of men and women. The life of Melania the Younger, written by her secretary, gives a vivid picture of the wealth and luxury of the great senatorial families of Rome, with their villas and estates scattered throughout the provinces. The life of Porphyry, bishop of Gaza, written by Mark, one of his deacons, depicts the pagan city of Gaza in the reign of Arcadius, and the intrigues at the court of Constantinople whereby Porphyry ultimately obtained an imperial order to demolish its temples and build a church. Daniel the Stylite, who stood on a column in an Asiatic suburb of Constantinople for thirty-three years (460–93), also saw much of the court, being consulted by many great men of the day, including the emperors Leo and Zeno. On the other hand Theodore, the illegitimate son of an innkeeper's daughter at the Galatian village of Syceon, spent all his life—in the late sixth and early seventh centuries—exorcizing the countless devils which plagued the peasantry of the area. With the biographies of saints may be included collections of anecdotes about holy men, such as the *Lausiac History* of Palladius, or the *Spiritual Meadow* of John Moschus, which include stories of merchants, craftsmen, peasants, soldiers, actors and all manner of people.

Large numbers of speeches have survived. Most are panegyrics and contain little useful information, but Libanius, a fourth-century professor of rhetoric at Antioch, has left a large number of speeches dealing with the social problems of the day. Sermons also survive in vast numbers: most are trite but they illustrate the ethical ideas of the period. Another abundant source of information is letters. We possess great collections of letters from many of the leading figures of the age, lay and clerical, from the emperor Julian and the Roman senator Symmachus to Basil, bishop of Caesarea, and Severus, patriarch of Antioch. Epistolography was esteemed as an art and many of the collections were edited for publication. A great number of the letters are literary trifles written only to display the wit and elegance of the author, some are theological dissertations, but many contain historical information of high value, especially for social and economic affairs.

Miscellaneous sources include the *de Magistratibus* of John Lydus, who served for forty years as a clerk in the praetorian prefecture of the East under Anastasius, Justin I and Justinian, and devotes most of his space to the great office in which he passed his working life. Substantial fragments survive from the work of Peter the Patrician, master of the offices of Justinian, on the ceremonies of the court. We also possess a few technical manuals, such as Palladius on agriculture and Vegetius on the art of war.

In verse we have panegyrics and invectives like Claudian's praises of Stilicho and denunciations of Rufinus and Eutropius, historical epics like the *Johannid* of Corippus, which recounts at vast length the exploits of John, master of the soldiers in Africa under Justinian, autobiographies like those of Gregory of Nazianzus and Paulinus of Pella, occasional verse and hymns.

By far the most important source is the legal codes. In the Theodosian

Code we have a record of imperial legislation from the accession of Constantine in 312 to 437. The laws are not reproduced in full, the preambles being omitted, and for the first fifty years the record is not complete. We also possess eighty novels or new laws issued by Theodosius II and Valentinian III after 437, and a few of Majorian and Anthemius and Severus in the west and of Marcian in the east. Of these we have the full text including the preambles, which often give interesting information on the motives of the ministers who drafted them. The Code of Justinian contains in slightly abbreviated form all laws from Hadrian to 531 still in force in the latter year. Over 180 novels or new laws of Justinian survive, and half a dozen from his three successors. The Digest comprises the private law as current in Justinian's day. We also possess a small collection of edicts of the praetorian prefects of the East, in a very abbreviated form, dating from the late fifth and early sixth century; the official dispatches of Symmachus, prefect of the city of Rome in 384; and the *Variae* of Cassiodorus, which comprise the official letters which he wrote as quaestor on behalf of Theoderic, king of Italy, and his immediate successors, and as praetorian prefect of Italy. Other official documents include the *Notitia Dignitatum*, a list of all administrative and military posts in the empire from provincial governors upwards, including a complete army list, drawn up in 408, and in the west corrected down to 423; a list of the cities of Gaul at the same period; and a list of all the cities of the eastern empire from the reign of Theodosius II.

In ecclesiastical law we have canons of scores of church councils, from that of Arles in 314 to the second Ecumenical Council of Constantinople in 553, and the full records of several major councils, including those of Ephesus in 431 and 449, the latter in a Syriac translation, and Chalcedon in 453. We also possess official letters of the popes from Siricius (385–99) onwards. Of particular value is the complete register of Gregory the Great (590–604), which illuminates all sides of his activity from the combating of the Donatist schism in Africa to the management of the papal patrimony.

To supplement the documents handed down by the manuscript tradition we have the papyri. A few of these of the fifth and sixth centuries survive in the church archives of Italy and France, a few have been found in southern Palestine, the vast majority, numbering many thousands, come from Egypt. They illustrate every aspect of life. There are the minutes of town councils, official correspondence, military archives, tax records, wills, divorces, marriages, records of legal proceedings, leases, sales, private accounts and private letters. Of particular value for social history are groups of documents belonging to one family or person. Thus we possess an important group of estate accounts illustrating the management of the great properties of the Apion family, who provided one of the last consuls at Constantinople; the papers of Flavius Abinnaeus, who rose from a private soldier to the rank of *praefectus alae* in the reign of Constantius II; a collection of contracts, settlements and other legal documents concerning the family of Flavius Dios, a soldier of the garrison of Syene in the late sixth century; and a voluminous group of sixth-century documents from the village of Aphrodito, including tax registers, petitions to the imperial government, leases, and documents concerned with the administration of the village, together with the poems of Dioscorus, the local notary to whom this collection belonged.

Coins are in two ways a valuable source of information. By their types and legends they illustrate imperial propaganda, by their weight and fineness the stability or depreciation of the currency. Inscriptions, though rarer than under the principate, add substantially to our knowledge. Many Roman inscriptions record the official careers of senators, and a few preserve imperial enactments not preserved in the codes. The most notable of these is Diocletian's edict on prices of 302, which specifies the maximum price for many thousands of articles and fixes the wages of all kinds of workers. Copies of this huge document or portions of it have been found in many cities of the empire.

Lastly there is the archaeological evidence. The museums of Europe and the United States treasure many masterpieces of early Byzantine art, engraved silver plate, crystal chalices, and ivory diptychs sent to their friends by the consuls as invitation cards to their games. Vast quantities of pottery, glass and metalwork survive. Finally, there are buildings, from Diocletian's huge palace near Salona, which contains half the modern town of Split in Yugoslavia—the emperor's tomb is the cathedral—to Justinian's masterpiece, the church of Santa Sophia in Constantinople. Throughout north Africa and all along the desert fringe of Syria and Palestine, and on the eastern and southern coasts of Asia Minor, countless fortresses, monasteries, villas, villages and entire cities survive, as they stood when they were abandoned after the Arab invasion in the seventh century, except for damage by earthquake and the weather. Many wall mosaics and innumerable floor mosaics not only illustrate the art of the period but sometimes also give vivid pictures of the age. Particularly noticeable are the recently excavated floors

of Piazza Armerina, a sumptuous villa near Enna in Sicily, which probably belonged to the great senatorial family of the Symmachi. They
depict many mythological scenes, the chariot races of the Circus
Maximus, the hunting of wild beasts for the arena and their transport to
Italy and, most curious of all, a group of female athletes clad in bikinis.
Even more famous is the group of Justinian, Theodora and their court
in the church of San Vitale at Ravenna.

The evidence which we possess, full though it is, has some gaps.
Owing to the absence of western historians important events in that
area cannot be precisely dated. Dispute has raged whether Britain was
lost to the empire towards the end of the reign of Theodosius I, when
Roman coins cease to be found in the island, or a generation later, when
the *Notitia Dignitatum* still records troops stationed there. There is a
similar uncertainty as to the date when Spain was occupied by the
Visigoths.

In the second place we possess virtually no statistical information.
We can only make a plausible guess at the population of the empire.
The population of Constantinople in Justinian's reign was, to judge by
the amount of corn annually imported to feed it, about two-thirds of a
million, and that of Rome about the same in the fourth century.
Alexandria, judging again by its corn supply, was about half this size, and
Antioch, according to Libanius, numbered 150,000. There were a few
other cities of comparable size, such as Carthage and Milan. The population of Egypt excluding Alexandria was $7\frac{1}{2}$ million in the first century
A.D. and is not likely to have altered appreciably in the next few centuries. The western provinces were more sparsely peopled. The population of Gaul, the area between the Rhine and the Atlantic and the
Pyrenees, can be estimated at about three million.

On the other hand, thousands of tombstones provide adequate
statistical material for the age distribution of the population. Women
had a shorter expectation of life than men, and the inhabitants of big
cities than those of small towns and villages. What is, however, most
significant is the universally high rate of mortality. The figures closely
resemble those of India early in this century. As children were not given
tombstones we have no figures for infant or child mortality, but they
must have been very high. We have no adequate evidence for the size of
families or for the birth rate.

We have similarly no statistics for the numbers of Christians and
pagans at any date: we can only say that Christians were an insignificant
minority at the beginning of Constantine's reign, and pagans by that of

Justinian. We have a reliable figure for the army at the end of the fourth century, 635,000. The civil servants can be calculated to have numbered about 30,000. We lack global figures of revenue. Egypt in the reign of Justinian produced wheat to the value of 800,000 *solidi* and perhaps as much again in money taxes. The taxes of Numidia and Mauretania Sitifensis before the Vandal invasion in 429 came to 78,200 and 41,600 *solidi*: we have no figures for the remaining ninety provinces, nor for other periods. Three documents reveal the rate of the land tax, one in Italy and one in Africa under Valentinian III, the third in Egypt under Justinian.

The *Edictum de Pretiis* gives the price and wage structure of the empire as laid down by Diocletian in 302, but unfortunately in a currency which was depreciating rapidly. For prices, wages and rents in Egypt, reckoned in *denarii* and in gold, we have, thanks to the papyri, an adequate body of evidence, but only occasional figures for the rest of the empire. What figures there are reveal no significant variations either regional or in time, reckoning in gold. From this information we can roughly estimate the purchasing power of the *solidus*. Bread for one year (3 lb a day) cost rather over a *solidus*, meat (1 lb a day) and wine (1 pint a day) rather under two *solidi* each, oil about three quarters of a *solidus*. The cheapest clothing cost two-thirds to one *solidus* per garment. A common soldier received a ration allowance of four or five *solidi* a year, but we hear of poor men who lived on three *solidi* a year.

The abundant legal evidence is difficult to interpret and assess. Since laws are usually prohibitions of abuses they give, like police-court news, a perhaps unduly gloomy picture of the condition of the empire. But the main difficulty is to judge how far they were actually enforced. Most modern historians have consciously or unconsciously assumed that they were, and drawn a picture of a regulation-ridden empire. This is very improbable. It must be remembered that the Roman government had no police force and relied for the enforcement of the laws on its ordinary administrators and their officials, who had other things to do, and upon private informers, who acted only when they would profit financially. There is moreover abundant evidence in the laws themselves that they were, to say the least, laxly enforced, and often virtually ignored. The same prohibition is repeated again and again, decade after decade, and past breaches of the law are at intervals condoned wholesale. The emperors often complain of the slackness or disobedience of the officials and of the provincial governors and even of their own ministers, and threaten them with heavy penalties if they connive at breaches of the law. It is clear that they were generally susceptible to social pressure and to bribes. The laws are in fact evidence only of the policy of the government and of the existence of the abuses which they attempt to correct. From Constantine to Justinian there is an almost continual stream of penal legislation against heretics, but there were still in the sixth century active communities of ancient sects like the Marcionites and the Montanists, which dated from the second century A.D.

II

Background: The Principate

When Diocletian was proclaimed emperor in A.D. 284 the empire was already more than three centuries old: it was in 27 B.C. that Augustus had founded the monarchical system of government known as the principate. For many of the provinces Roman rule was older still. Sicily and Sardinia had been annexed after the First Punic War in 242 B.C., Spain after the Second Punic War in 202 B.C., Africa (that is the modern Tunisia) after the fall of Carthage in 146 B.C. In the same year Macedonia and Greece had become a province, in 129 B.C. Asia (western Asia Minor); southern Gaul had been annexed in 118 B.C. In 66–63 B.C. Pompey had added the rest of Asia Minor and Syria to the empire and in 58–48 B.C. Julius Caesar had conquered northern Gaul. Augustus himself had annexed Egypt and the Danubian provinces of Pannonia and Moesia. The only important subsequent additions to the empire were Britain, conquered by Claudius in A.D. 43; Dacia, north of the lower Danube, subdued by Trajan in A.D. 102; and Mesopotamia (that is the area between the upper Euphrates and the upper Tigris west of the river Chaboras), annexed by Septimius Severus in A.D. 199. But of these provinces Dacia had been evacuated by Aurelian shortly before Diocletian's accession.

So long had the empire endured that its subjects could not conceive that it should ever come to an end. Pagans believed that the rule of the Eternal City would last for ever, and Christians that it would endure until the coming of Antichrist and the Last Judgment.

On the west the empire was bounded by the Atlantic Ocean, on the north by the Rhine, the Danube and the Black Sea, on the south by the Sahara, and on the east by the Syrian desert and the upper course of the Euphrates. On the south and south-east its neighbours were the nomad Moorish and Arab tribes of the desert, who were from time to time a nuisance but never a serious menace until Islam united the Arabs and inspired them with an aggressive spirit. In the north of Britain the

Picts and Scots occasionally crossed Hadrian's Wall, but were not a serious danger.

On the north, beyond the Rhine and the Danube, the German tribes presented a greater danger, and it was along the two great rivers that the bulk of the Roman army was stationed. Germany at this period was largely covered with forests and marshes, and the Germans were a primitive people. They were a settled folk who practised agriculture, though they still supplemented their diet by hunting. Politically they were divided into tribes and clans, ruled by kings and lesser chieftains supported by councils of nobles; for important decisions a general assembly of the warriors of the tribe was convoked. The Germans were a warlike people, and the tribes and clans were constantly engaged in raiding one another for slaves and cattle and other booty. Those who bordered on the empire were naturally particularly tempted by the rich booty to be obtained from the provinces, but the imperial government was normally able to hold them in check, partly by military force, partly by diplomacy. Treaties were made with the kings of the neighbouring tribes, guaranteeing them protection against their enemies on condition that they prevented their subjects from raiding Roman territory, and loyal kings were paid subsidies, while those who broke their treaties were chastised by punitive expeditions.

Such was the general state of affairs in the first two centuries of the empire. The Roman army along the Rhine and the Danube was normally occupied in police duties, checking and rounding up local raiders, and only occasionally resisting a larger-scale attack or conducting a punitive expedition. But in the latter part of the second century A.D. the Marcomanni and other tribes on the Danube made a massive irruption into the empire, even penetrating into northern Italy, and Marcus Aurelius (161–80) had to fight a long series of wars to beat them back and restore the frontier defences. From this time onwards the pressure of the German tribes all along the Danube frontier, and on the Rhine also, increased very greatly, and the Roman armies in the middle decades of the third century were unable to prevent massive raids into Gaul and the Balkans.

We know very little of the causes of these aggressive movements, but it would appear that they were, in part at any rate, due to pressure on the tribes bordering the empire from others in the interior. From the traditional legends of the Goths and from other fragments of information it would seem that a number of tribes, the Goths, the Vandals, the Burgundians, the Lombards, who had in the first century lived around the Baltic, began to trek southwards, whether because their numbers had outgrown the means of subsistence in their northern homes, or because they were excited by stories of richer lands to the south. In their movements they drove other tribes from their homes, and set in action a general drift southwards and westwards until it broke upon the line of the Roman frontier. By the middle of the third century the Goths had reached the lower Danube and were invading the Balkan provinces *en masse*.

The main movement of the German tribes was southwards, but the western tribes along the Rhine no doubt felt some pressure from the rear. During the third century these tribes banded themselves into two loose confederations, the Franks in the north and the Alamans in the south, and these groups frequently broke through the defences on the Rhine and ravaged Gaul and even raided Spain.

It was only on the east that the Roman faced a civilized power comparable to itself, Persia. Down to 226 Persia was ruled by the Parthian dynasty of the Arsacids, and as long as they reigned Rome had little to fear. The Arsacid dynasty was feeble and unstable and frequently weakened by civil wars between rival claimants to the throne, or between kings and their rebellious satraps. The main bone of contention between the empires was the kingdom of Armenia which bordered Roman Asia Minor on the west, and Parthian Mesopotamia and Assyria on the south. In 226 Artaxerxes, a Persian, overthrew the Arsacids and founded the Sassanian dynasty which ruled the Persian empire until the Arab conquest in the seventh century.

The Sassanids created a strong central government which kept the satraps under control and revived the national Persian religion, Zoroastrianism, and with it the Persian national spirit. They claimed, as successors to the Achaemenid dynasty which had ruled the Persian Empire before Alexander the Great, all the provinces which Darius and his successors had ruled, including Egypt, Syria and Asia Minor, and in the middle of the third century they endeavoured to make good their claim by war. Persia was probably a more formidable enemy to the Roman Empire than all the German tribes, but fortunately its kings were not normally aggressive, and they usually observed their treaties of peace with the Roman Empire with scrupulous fidelity.

Augustus in 27 B.C. had ostentatiously restored the republican constitution, but this was merely a political manœuvre designed to placate the republican sentiment of the Roman senatorial aristocracy and the educated classes of Italy. The emperor was in theory invested by the senate and people with certain magisterial powers, but in virtue of these powers he was from the beginning an absolute monarch in fact. He was the commander-in-chief of all the Roman armies, governed through his delegates a great group of provinces, which covered some three-quarters of the empire, with authority to control the ten or a dozen provinces which were still governed by annual proconsuls in the old way. Judicially he was the supreme appellate judge of the empire, and in practice the supreme source of law. He likewise controlled, directly or indirectly, all the finances of the empire.

One problem was never quite satisfactorily solved, the succession to the principate. In strict constitutional theory the powers which made up the principate were voted by the senate and people to an individual for life, and on each emperor's death the principate expired. The people never played more than a formal role in the creation of an emperor, and the senate from an early date tended to be overshadowed by the army. Claudius (A.D. 41–54) was first proclaimed by the praetorian guard, and the senate had to confirm their choice; proclamation by the army was thereafter a regular part of the accession ceremony, though it did not always play a decisive role.

Popular sentiment, and in particular the feeling of the army, was strongly in favour of an hereditary succession. Senators on the other hand did not like the hereditary principle. It was, they felt, undignified that the empire should pass from father to son like a private estate. The emperor should, according to philosophic principles, be the best man in the state, by which they meant a leading and senior senator. Sons of emperors, born and bred in the purple, were in fact very often quite unsuitable to rule, and were always liable to be disrespectful to senatorial advice.

In effect the empire was governed for the first century of its existence by the descendants (actually all adopted) of Augustus. Several of the emperors were highly unsatisfactory, but at least the devotion of the army to the family of Caesar maintained political stability. The mechanical problem of transmitting the imperial powers was, by provident emperors, solved by getting the senate and people to invest their heirs with the principal imperial powers during their own lifetime.

When Nero fell the weakness of the system became apparent. There was no surviving member of Caesar's family, and the armies had no figure to focus their loyalty. The result was that rival claimants, mostly army commanders in the provinces, got their troops to proclaim them, and civil war ensued. After the year of the four emperors (A.D. 69)

Vespasian, the victor in the struggle, founded a dynasty. This dynasty ended with the assassination of his younger son Domitian in A.D. 96, but the senate (in co-operation with the conspirators) elected a new emperor, Nerva. He started a new system, which proved equally satisfactory to the senate and the army. He and the next three emperors selected their successors from the senate and adopted them as their sons. The senate could believe that the best man had been chosen to rule, the army accepted the fiction of an hereditary succession. This compromise depended however on each successive emperor having no son, and unfortunately Marcus Aurelius (A.D. 161–80) had one, and a very unsatisfactory one, Commodus. On his assassination in 192 there was another round of civil wars between rival claimants until Septimius Severus established another dynasty which lasted until 238. Thereafter no dynasty succeeded in rooting itself and no orderly succession was maintained. Until the accession of Diocletian in 284 there was a continuous series of military proclamations and civil wars. No less than twenty legitimate emperors, acknowledged by the senate, reigned, and countless usurpers ruled parts of the empire for longer or shorter periods.

The senate was, as under the republic, a body of about six hundred men. Admission to the senate was gained, as under the republican system, by election to the quaestorship; normally a licence had to be obtained by an outsider to stand for the quaestorship. The emperor could also nominate—the technical term is 'adlect'—older men to the senate, giving them appropriate seniority as ex-aediles, ex-praetors, or rarely ex-consuls. The emperors used their powers to widen the narrow oligarchy which the old senatorial order had been. Men were brought in first from the cities of Italy and then from the more Romanized provinces of the west, Narbonensis (southern Gaul), Spain and later Africa. Very few came from the more recently conquered and more barbarous provinces of the west, such as northern Gaul and Britain, or from Pannonia and Moesia (the northern Balkans), and very few too from the Greek-speaking provinces of the east. The men enrolled were of course Roman citizens, either of Italian descent from the Roman colonies in the provinces, or provincials whose ancestors had been granted the franchise. Socially most of them came from the landed gentry, though poor men could sometimes rise to the top by service in the army.

The senate had virtually no powers. It elected to the old magistracies, but these were empty honours only. It could pass resolutions (*senatus consulta*) which had the force of law, but it never did so except upon the initiative of the emperor. It was a court which passed judgment in criminal cases against senators, but its members were also amenable to the jurisdiction of the emperor, and the emperor found no difficulty in swaying the senate's vote. The senate was nominally a council of state which the emperor consulted on important issues. But in fact the emperor discussed and formed policy in a small privy council (his *consilium*) chosen by himself, and the senate applauded his decisions.

In view of its changing composition the senate might have been expected to become a body of subservient placemen, but in fact it always retained a memory of its ancient authority and a certain tradition of independence. The infiltration of new members was gradual, and they mostly came from a class which had been educated in the old traditions. The new members quickly absorbed the traditions of the house, and often became more zealous champions of its privileges than the surviving aristocrats.

The senate seems at first sight to have been a powerless and helpless body. A resolute emperor could easily defy it, and could cow it into submission by accepting charges of treason against its members and either trying them himself or bullying the senate into condemning them. But emperors who thus defied the senate rarely died in their beds, and prudent emperors treated it with respect and conciliated its goodwill. The reasons for the survival of the senate as a political force are difficult to discern. Its members were the social cream of Italy and the Romanized western provinces. They were moreover immensely rich. There was a substantial property qualification for membership, a million sesterces, but most entrants owned considerably larger fortunes, while the hereditary members had accumulated vast wealth by marriages with the heiresses of extinct families, or by being adopted into the old families and thus inheriting their wealth. Wealth thus accumulated in the hands of the senatorial order from generation to generation. Above all the senate still enjoyed an immense prestige not only among the upper classes but among the general public throughout the empire and even in the army. It included among its members the army commanders, both active and retired, and the commanders of the individual legions. An emperor who quarrelled with the senate might fear that his own generals and other higher officers might be more influenced by their loyalty to the senate than by their allegiance to himself.

It was for this reason that Augustus had entrusted certain key military posts, the prefecture of Egypt and the command of his own bodyguard, the praetorian cohorts, to non-senators. Septimius Severus (193–211), who was on bad terms with the senate, entrusted the newly conquered province of Mesopotamia with its two legions to a non-senatorial commander. Finally Gallienus (260–68) excluded senators from all military commands. The effect of this ruling was that senators were confined to the governorships of the ungarrisoned provinces as proconsuls or imperial legates, and to a number of administrative and judicial posts in Rome and Italy. The senior of these was the prefecture of the city of Rome, a post awarded for life to a very senior senator. He still commanded the three or four urban cohorts who formed the city *gendarmerie*—they were far outnumbered by the nine or more praetorian cohorts.

Up to this date the emperor had employed senators as governors of all the important provinces, except Egypt and Mesopotamia, and of the armies which they contained, and as commanders of the legions, except those stationed in Egypt and Mesopotamia. For other posts, military, administrative, and particularly financial, he employed men of equestrian grade. These men were free-born citizens who possessed a property qualification of 400,000 sesterces. Equestrian rank was not hereditary, and all equestrian officers were appointed by the emperor and served during his pleasure. Most of them were recruited from the civil population, but a special avenue of promotion was provided for ex-centurions from the army. Men of equestrian rank served in the lower officer posts of the army, as military tribunes in the legions—each legion had six tribunes, five of whom were equestrian and the sixth a young man of senatorial birth—and as prefects and tribunes of the auxiliary regiments. The normal opening of an equestrian career was three officer posts in the army, as prefect of an auxiliary cohort, tribune of a legion, and prefect of an auxiliary cavalry regiment (*ala*). Some served fewer or more numerous posts, and some, in particular lawyers who had risen to the rank of counsel to the treasury (*advocatus fisci*), omitted the military posts altogether. Then followed a variety of administrative, mainly financial, posts with the title of *procurator*. Every province had its procurator, the imperial finance officer, who in the provinces governed by imperial legates handled all the financial business, collecting the taxes and paying the troops, and in the provinces governed by proconsuls handled the emperor's financial interests, in particular the imperial estates. Other procurators governed a few small provinces; others supervised the collection of the indirect taxes; others managed important groups of imperial estates; others imperial establishments such as the gladiatorial schools. The prefects of the fleets were also officers of equestrian rank, and so were the heads of the central ministries in Rome. These included the secretaries of state who handled the emperor's official correspondence in Latin and Greek (*ab epistulis, ab epistulis Graecis*), the minister of petitions (*a libellis*), who dealt with judicial appeals and other petitions from private citizens, the finance minister (*a rationibus*), who handled the imperial department of the *fiscus*, the revenues which the emperor controlled and the outgoings for which he was responsible, and the manager of the imperial patrimony (*a patrimonio*), the vast accumulation of landed property which had been formed from the private fortunes of successive emperors, from the great number of bequests which they received, and from the confiscated property of felons. The patrimony gradually came to be regarded as crown property rather than the personal property of the emperor, and Septimius Severus founded a new department, the *res privata*, into which he put the estates of the numerous senators whom he convicted of treason. Later the *res privata* absorbed the patrimony, and the two chief financial ministers were known as the *a rationibus* or *rationalis summae*, who managed the tax revenues, the mints and the mines, and the *magister* or *rationalis rei privatae*, who managed all imperial lands.

The summit of the equestrian carrier was the four great prefectures. These were the posts of the *praefectus vigilum*, the commander of the fire brigade and night watch of Rome, the *praefectus annonae*, who was responsible for the food supply of Rome, and in particular for the shipment of corn from Africa and Egypt to feed the capital, the prefect of Egypt, and finally the praetorian prefect, the commander of the praetorian guard. The praetorian prefecture gradually grew in importance and acquired new functions. When the emperor went on a campaign the prefect served as his chief of staff, and sometimes, but rarely, took over the command. He was also on such occasions the emperor's quartermaster general, seeing to the supply of the troops. From the Severan period the emperor normally delegated to his praetorian prefect or prefects—for the office was often shared between two holders—much of his appellate jurisdiction, and from this time a number of eminent lawyers held the prefecture.

All equestrian posts above the junior military commissions were graded in four salary classes, the *sexagenarii*, who received 60,000 sesterces a year, and the *centenarii*, *ducenarii* and *trecenarii*, who received 100,000, 200,000 and 300,000 respectively. There was a regular ladder of promotion from grade to grade—several posts might be held in each—and equestrian officials, unlike senators, who only occupied imperial governorships at intervals, seem to have served the government continuously, passing directly from one post to another. The service, which was rudimentary in the first century of the empire, expanded to comprise, apart from the junior military commissions, about 110 posts in the middle of the second century A.D. and about 175 under the Severi. From the time of Gallienus it was equestrians who filled the higher officer posts in the army also.

All these officers of state, and military officers also, had their staffs of officials, clerks, accountants and orderlies. Those who served provincial governors and military officers were technically soldiers, seconded from their regiments, but soldiers who once entered the government offices seem to have served their whole career there. The officials who served the procurators and in the central ministries, the treasury and the secretariats, were imperial slaves and freedmen. The service was hereditary, as the sons of imperial slaves (who were not normally manumitted until the age of thirty or later) were slaves until they in their turn were manumitted, having produced a number of slave sons. Imperial slaves received salaries and ranked socially as free persons, normally marrying citizen wives.

The Roman army had been since Augustus' day a standing professional force. Men usually joined at the age of eighteen and served for twenty-five years, receiving, if they were legionaries, an allotment of land or a substantial cash bonus on discharge. Recruitment was normally voluntary, but on occasions of crisis conscription was enforced. Apart from the praetorian and urban cohorts, which occupied a specially privileged position with higher pay and a shorter term of service, the army consisted of legions of Roman citizens, and of cohorts and *alae* recruited from the provincials. The legions were 6,000 strong, mainly infantry with a small cavalry element. Cohorts (infantry) and *alae* (cavalry) were normally 500 strong, some 1,000 strong. All these regiments were permanent institutions; some were destroyed by enemy action, others disbanded for rebellion, but the majority retained their identity for over four centuries and a few even into the sixth century A.D.

The strength of the army rose from twenty-five legions under Augustus to thirty-three under Septimius Severus. The number of auxiliary units is more difficult to calculate, but they probably added 50 per cent to the total strength. In the early third century the army would have comprised some 300,000 men. Nearly all the forces were disposed on the northern and eastern frontiers. There was one legion in Spain, one in

Italy, one in Africa, one in Egypt, two in Palestine and one in Arabia. Eight guarded the eastern front from the Black Sea to the middle Euphrates, four garrisoned the Rhine, and the remaining fourteen were disposed along the most dangerous front, the Danube. All units were static, normally occupying fortified camps. When a special concentration of troops was required at any point detachments were sent by the legions elsewhere and auxiliary units temporarily moved.

The auxiliaries of the cohorts and *alae* received lower pay than the legionaries, but apart from this the distinction was more formal than real and became increasingly nominal. From an early period provincial recruits were accepted by the legions and unofficially deemed to be Roman citizens and given Roman names. Recruitment came to be increasingly local and hereditary. Officially soldiers were not allowed to marry while on service, but they nearly always did so, and their sons, usually of provincial status since their mothers were provincials, could acquire citizenship by joining the army.

Recruitment of the auxiliaries was also normally local. A cohort of Spaniards stationed in Syria received Syrian recruits, and the racial titles of the units soon became formal. Auxiliaries received the Roman citizenship with their children on discharge, and as the sons often joined their fathers' regiments, many of the auxiliaries came to be Roman citizens. These distinctions were finally abolished in A.D. 212 when all the inhabitants of the empire became Romans.

The higher officers of the Roman army would seem to have been its weakest point. The senators who commanded legions at the age of about thirty had had no previous experience except as military tribunes at the age of about twenty. Senators tended, however, to specialize on either a civil or a military career, and those who wished to become generals served longer terms as military tribunes in youth. By the time they became generals they would have a good many years of service behind them. The prefects of cohorts were taken straight from civilian life, but by the time an equestrian officer retired he would often have served ten years.

The discipline and training of the Roman army depended on the centurions, of whom there were sixty to a legion: they also officered the auxiliary cohorts, and corresponding officers served in the *alae*. They were career officers who often served for more than the twenty-five years for which a private served. Some were commissioned from the ranks, but these usually started their officer career too late to rise high. Most were directly commissioned from civilian life. They were frequently transferred from legion to legion, and seem by all accounts to have been a not very pleasant type of man. They used the rod freely on their men, and made money out of the privates by accepting tips for exemption from fatigues and for grants of leave. In a mutiny the centurions were the first victims of the troops.

The empire consisted of cities. By this term is meant not merely a town, but a town and the surrounding rural area with its villages. Cities varied greatly in size and character in the different parts of the empire and even within the same province. Some were small towns with large territories, some were small and had small territories. There were great cities with small rural areas, which lived mainly by commerce and industry. There were great cities which ruled extensive territories. The average city in the Roman empire was not a great port or manufacturing town. The vast majority were centres of government and markets for the surrounding countryside, and possessed a few minor industries which supplied local and regional needs. Their leading citizens were not merchants or manufacturers but the landlords of the area.

They were self-governing. The citizens, who might be the towns-people or all the inhabitants of the territory, elected the annual magistrates, but they had no governing powers. The governing body was a council, consisting either of ex-magistrates or of members elected by the people. These councillors, the decurions, sat for life and they had to possess a substantial property qualification, which in antiquity meant land. Since landed estates normally passed from father to son, the councils tended to become hereditary bodies.

The councils not only administered the municipal services of the towns, the street paving, the drains, the water supply, the temples and their cult, the periodical games—theatrical shows, concerts, athletic events and chariot racing—the gymnasium or athletic club and the baths, but also policed both the town and the territory. They furthermore performed very important services for the central government. When conscription was ordered they selected and sent up the recruits. When government couriers or other persons armed with a warrant demanded, they supplied post horses and lodging. Above all they collected the imperial taxation. It was because so much detailed work was delegated to the city councils that the imperial machine could be as modest in numbers as it was. The governor's main function was the administration of justice; otherwise he only had to supervise the cities. The procurator had only to collect the sums due in taxes from the civic authorities and settle disputed claims.

Towards the end of the second century and even more in the third the system of local government began to break down. The cities had very slender financial resources, and it was the decurions and especially the magistrates who were expected to foot the bill. During the first and second centuries civic spirit was strong, and the decurions and magistrates subscribed lavishly, especially to municipal games and splendid buildings. There was much inter-city rivalry, and each tried to outbid the other in such civic amenities. The result was that the normal expenditure expected of decurions and magistrates grew so large that even the wealthy found office more of a burden than an honour, and soon the local notables were no longer standing for office. Popular election lapsed for lack of candidates, and the council became a co-optative body and chose magistrates from itself. When moral suasion failed it had to fall back on legal compulsion. It had always been a legal principle that duly qualified citizens must perform appropriate services for their cities, and the rule was now enforced: a qualified person duly nominated as a decurion must join the council and hold a magistracy unless he could prove legal immunity.

The filling of the vacancies on the council and the magistracies naturally involved many legal disputes, and the provincial governor found himself more and more involved in adjudicating claims and enforcing service. The work was essential since not only did the cities maintain all the amenities of civilized life, but the imperial government depended on them for its revenues.

The fiscal system of the empire was on the whole equitable and the taxes moderate. There were customs duties at 20 per cent on the frontiers of the empire, at much lower rates (2 or 2½ per cent) at certain inter-provincial boundaries and at some ports. There was an inheritance tax of 5 per cent payable by Roman citizens only; this became applicable to all inhabitants of the empire in 212 but it was paid only on fairly substantial inheritances (over 100,000 sesterces) and direct heirs such as sons and daughters did not pay.

The main taxes were two. There was a poll tax (*tributum capitis*) levied at varying rates in different provinces and according to different rules; in Egypt males only paid, from the age of fourteen to sixty-five; in Syria both sexes. Roman citizens did not pay this tax before 212. More important was the land tax (*tributum soli*). It was a percentage on the assessed capital value of the land; in Syria, where alone we have a figure, it was one per cent. It would appear that other forms of property, such as houses and ships, were entered under this schedule. Regular censuses of population and property were held to keep the registers of taxable persons and property up to date. The land of Italy was exempt from land tax, so that Roman citizens who owned Italian land paid only the inheritance tax.

From the point of view of the taxpayer there were two main flaws in this system. For an agricultural economy a fixed tax which is the same every year causes occasional difficulties, particularly in Mediterranean countries, where the rainfall is barely adequate and is irregular, and in some years the crops may fail in some districts. In the second place the taxation system was not progressive. The peasant paid at the same rate on his tiny holding as the great landlord on his wide estates. The system was indeed regressive, since Roman citizens, usually better off than their neighbours, paid no poll tax.

From the point of view of the government the system was too inflexible. The revenue was the same whether expenses were normal or whether a war called for more money. Surpluses (in actual coin) accumulated in peacetime, but in times of difficulty it was impossible to borrow, and the government had to sell imperial property or confiscate the estates of wealthy senators on false charges of treason. A last resort was to debase the currency by mixing copper with the silver *denarius*. Severus and his son Caracalla greatly increased the military budget by raising the pay of the troops, and the latter debased the *denarius* to 50 per cent of copper and issued a new double *denarius*, the *antoninianus*, which weighed only 50 per cent more than the *denarius*. An inflationary spiral was started in which prices rose astronomically, but the taxes were not adjusted to the new value of money. In the middle of the third century the government was collecting taxes whose real value was perhaps one per cent of their second-century value, and despite minting vast issues of small copper coins washed with silver, supposed to be five or two *denarii*, found difficulty in feeding and clothing the army. Clothes and food for the troops had always been obtained by compulsory purchase, and in the old days the prices had been fair. Now the old prices were still paid, and the compulsory purchase became practically requisition without payment.

Legally all free inhabitants of the Roman empire were from the year 212 Roman citizens. Citizenship by this time did not mean much, but it did mean that everybody was now subject to the same body of law and judged in the same courts. It also meant that the old distinction between the ruling class of Romans and the subject class of provincials was swept away, and that men from any province, according to their wealth and social status, could join the legions, obtain posts in the equestrian service, or even become senators. From this time onwards the distinction was no longer regional between Italians and provincials, but social, between *honestiores*, that is senators, equestrians, decurions and members of the professions, and *humiliores*. The latter were liable to be tortured in the courts of law and could be condemned to unpleasant penalties if found guilty of crime; execution, penal servitude in the mines, or even burning alive or being devoured by wild animals in the arena. The former suffered only loss of property and forced residence on some lonely island.

The culture of the upper classes was extremely uniform throughout the empire. There was, it is true, a linguistic cleavage between the Latin-speaking west and the Greek-speaking east, and there were certain divergences between these areas. The Greeks were more devoted to athletics and to music and the drama. The popular amusements favoured in the Latin west were gladiatorial combats and fighting with wild beasts. But the type of education, based on the study of the ancient poets and orators, and in particular the study of rhetoric, was the same throughout the empire. Art and architecture were similar everywhere, and so were the things of everyday life, the clothes, the food and the furniture, and the customs of social life; everywhere going to the baths occupied much of the day.

We know very little of the urban workmen and shopkeepers, or of the peasants, but they certainly had no share in the culture of the upper class. In many provinces they still spoke their old native languages, Celtic in Britain and Gaul, Punic or Berber in Africa, Coptic and Syriac in Egypt and Syria, and sundry now extinct tongues in Asia Minor and the Balkans. These languages were spoken dialects only and none existed in written form.

The religion of the empire was a chaotic amalgam of local and regional cults. In Italy and in the Roman colonies in the provinces the gods of the Roman pantheon were worshipped, and in Greece and Macedonia, and in the old Greek cities of the coasts of Asia Minor, the Greek pantheon. The Greek and Roman gods had for centuries been identified, and shared a common mythology. In Britain and Gaul the Celts worshipped the spirits of sacred springs and trees. In Africa the chief deity was the Semitic Heavenly Goddess of Carthage, in Asia Minor various forms of the Great Mother and her youthful son and lover. In Syria there were numerous local Baals, for the most part fertility gods; in some cities their cult included ritual prostitution. The

Egyptians worshipped their beast-headed deities and reverenced their sacred animals, and in the ancient temples hundreds of shaven priests in their white linen robes carried on the age-old rituals. Except in Egypt full-time paid professional priests were rare. Priesthoods were normally held as an honour by prominent citizens, usually decurions, either for life or on an annual basis.

A superficial unity was given to this amalgam by the practice of giving Greek and Roman names to the local deities. The identifications were often very arbitrary. There was little resemblance between Artemis, the virgin huntress of Greece, and Artemis of Ephesus, a many-breasted goddess of fertility, or between Zeus and Elagabal, the meteoric black stone of Syrian Emisa. Moreover except in Egypt, where the Pharaonic style was still maintained, temples were everywhere built in the Greco-Roman style, and in the city temples at any rate the Greek and Roman rituals of sacrifice seem to have been practised.

Besides the local cults, which were maintained by the city governments, there was the empire-wide cult of Rome and Augustus. This was celebrated in the capital of each province by a federal council of representatives from all the provincial cities. It seems to have had little or no religious content, and its chief function was magnificent games, usually including gladiatorial combats, provided at the expense of the High Priest of the province, a wealthy provincial notable elected for the occasion by the federal council.

There were also a number of international cults maintained by private societies of devotees. The most popular were those of the Phrygian Ma, the Egyptian goddess Isis and the Persian god Mithras. They are often called mystery religions, because their rites were, in part at any rate, secret, and worshippers were admitted to successive degrees of initiation. They had a wide appeal because they promised their initiates purification from sin and a blessed life hereafter.

In the first centuries B.C. and A.D. many upper-class people, though they conformed to the established religion of their community, were sceptics or agnostics, and the more serious-minded among them guided their lives by one of the Greek philosophies, especially Stoicism. From the second century onwards the tone of high society became slowly more religious. Cultured people did not believe literally in the myths of the Greek and Roman gods. They tended to be rather vague pantheists or monotheists, regarding the popular gods as various emanations or manifestations of one supreme god, sometimes symbolized by the sun, sometimes more philosophically conceived as the Prime Cause or the

Platonic Idea of the Good. In the third century there was a considerable revival and development of Platonism, initiated by the great Egyptian philosopher Plotinus; the movement has been labelled Neoplatonism by modern scholars. The philosophers of this age, so far from deriding the popular cults and legends, regarded them as divinely inspired allegories whereby simple people could gain some understanding of the ultimate truths.

Philosophy and the innumerable cults of the empire were thus tolerant and respectful of one another except for two sects. The Jews refused to worship any god save their own, and declared all others to be false. Jews were much disliked by their pagan neighbours, but the Roman government steadily protected their cult and their right to follow their own religious law; a Jew could not be summoned or sued on the sabbath, nor be conscripted into the army, where he obviously could not obey the Mosaic law. Not that most members of the Roman governing class had any sympathy with this peculiar sect; but it was a principle of the imperial government that every community should be allowed to worship its own gods in its own way, and the Jewish community had received guarantees dating back to Julius Caesar.

The other intolerant sect, which declared that the gods were alternatively graven images or maleficent demons, was Christianity. Christians were even more unpopular than the Jews. It was commonly believed that they practised ritual infanticide—it no doubt leaked out that at their secret meetings they ate the flesh and blood of a son of man; and incestuous orgies—they were known to hold Love Feasts at which men and women who called themselves brothers and sisters did something which they did not care to reveal. But the main charge against the Christians was that they were atheists, who denied and insulted all the gods. Ordinary people naturally thought that the gods were angered by such impiety and might visit their wrath on the empire which tolerated it. Whenever there was an earthquake or a famine the people called for the Christians to be thrown to the lions to appease the angered gods.

The emperor Nero threw the blame for the great fire of Rome in A.D. 64 on this unpopular sect, and it may well have been from this date that the profession of Christianity became a capital crime. The Jews were excusable because they were following their ancestral national cult, but the Christians had of their own choice abandoned the worship of the gods. Christianity was, however, treated with great leniency. The emperor Trajan instructed Pliny, governor of Bithynia, that he was not to hunt for Christians; he was only to take action if informers made formal accusations. A Christian moreover was pardoned if he renounced the forbidden religion and proved his sincerity by cursing Christ and sacrificing to the gods: only obstinate recusants were executed. Persecutions in fact were local and sporadic in the first and second centuries and the first half of the third, and were usually due to popular agitation.

Christianity gradually spread among the middle and lower classes in the towns, mainly in the Greek-speaking east. There were Christian communities from an early date in the great cities of the west, but they were mainly confined to the local Levantine population; at Rome the language of the church was Greek until the early fourth century. The peasantry were hardly touched, and there were few conversions among the upper classes. A few intellectuals, however, were won over to the new faith, notably at Alexandria, where in the late second and early third centuries a succession of philosophers and scholars, Pantaenus, Clement and the great Origen, laid the foundations of Christian theology by interpreting the traditional and scriptural beliefs of Christianity in the terminology of Greek philosophy.

As Christianity spread the disasters of the empire increased and the emperor Decius apparently became convinced that the popular view was correct. In 250 he ordered that all citizens—that is all free inhabitants of the empire—should sacrifice to the gods and obtain a certificate that they had done so from the local authorities. Many Christians, probably the majority, lay low; this was not difficult unless their pagan neighbours were spiteful and denounced them. Many bribed the inspectors to give them certificates. Large numbers, particularly among the upper classes, who found it difficult to evade the order, performed their sacrifice. A very few were executed.

Decius was killed in battle against the Goths a year later and the persecution lapsed. In 257 Valerian renewed the attack on different lines, confiscating the churches, forbidding services in private houses, and banishing the bishops and clergy. A few courageous bishops who defied the order were executed. But Valerian was shortly taken prisoner by the Persians, and his son Gallienus not only lifted the persecution but restored their buildings and cemeteries to the churches. Thenceforward the church enjoyed peace for forty years and its numbers steadily increased and Christianity penetrated more into upper-class society. Popular feeling against the Christians seems to have waned; people were growing used to them and they were perhaps less peculiar in their habits.

It has often been asked if there was any national feeling in the provinces against Roman rule. The Jews still cherished Messianic hopes and broke out into formidable risings, against Nero in A.D. 66–70, against Trajan in 115–16, and against Hadrian in 133–35. These rebellions were ruthlessly crushed, but the government nevertheless continued to tolerate Judaism. Apart from this there is virtually no sign of nationalist unrest. There was an attempt by some of the Gallic cities to set up an 'empire of the Gauls' in A.D. 70, but the movement petered out ingloriously. There was a popular rebellion in Egypt under Marcus Aurelius, which was led by a priest and may have been of a nationalist character; the quiescence of Egypt is all the more remarkable in that the natives had frequently led serious rebellions against the later Ptolemies in the second and first centuries B.C. This is all that there is to record, and it is clear from the literary record that the upper classes, both Greek and Latin speaking, were content and passively loyal. We cannot hope to know what the illiterate masses thought, but they gave no signs of discontent.

III

Diocletian

On 20 November 284 the army proclaimed as emperor Valerius Diocletianus, a man of humble origins—a freedman, it was alleged—who had risen to be commander of the imperial guard of *protectores*. This remarkable man has been chiefly remembered by posterity as the author of the final and most severe persecution of the Christians. His achievement was to restore stability to the empire, to reorganize the administration, to double the army, and to put the finances in a sound condition.

Perhaps his most remarkable achievement was that he reigned twenty-one years and then abdicated in favour of successors of his own choice. During all this time he was challenged by only two revolts, that of Carausius and his successor Allectus, who held Britain for nine years (287–96), and that of Domitius Domitianus in Egypt, which lasted less than a year (297–8). Diocletian's success in stopping the riot of military *pronunciamentos* has been attributed to various measures. He enhanced

BIBLIOGRAPHY. The main narrative sources are Lactantius, *De Mortibus Persecutorum* and for the Great Persecution Eusebius, *Ecclesiastical History*, VIII and IX and his *Martyrs of Palestine*. The most important papyri are *Papyri from Panopolis in the Chester Beatty Library, Dublin* (ed. T. C. Skeat, Dublin, 1964) and the documents collected in *The Archive of Aurelius Isidore* (ed. A. E. R. Boak and H. C. Youtie, Ann Arbor, 1960). Among the inscriptions the Edict on Prices is translated in Tenney Frank, *Economic Survey of Ancient Rome* (Oxford, 1933–40), vol. v, pp. 305–421. The most important of Diocletian's laws is in *Collatio Mosaicarum et Romanorum Legum* xv, 3. Acts of the Martyrs are to be found in Ruinart, *Acta Sincera*.

There is no full-scale modern biography of Diocletian. W. Seston has never completed his *Dioclétien et la Tétrarchie* (Paris, 1946) of which only the first volume has appeared. There are exhaustive and useful articles by G. Costa in *Dizionario Epigrafico* and by W. Ensslin in Pauly-Wissowa (s.v. Valerius Diocletianus). Apart from the general works mentioned on p. 371, there is a full account of the reign in the *Cambridge Ancient History*, XII, chapters ix, x, xi and xix.

the dignity of the imperial office by adopting Persian royal robes and introducing the Persian practice of prostration (*adoratio*), and by living in seclusion, making only ceremonial public appearances. Like his predecessors he was worshipped as a god, adopting the style of 'Iovius'. Such trifles can hardly have made much practical difference. Secondly, he greatly increased the number and diminished the size of the provinces thus, it is claimed, reducing the power of provincial governors to rebel. The only potential rebels were, however, the governors of garrisoned provinces, and Diocletian did not increase the number of army commanders. He moreover left untouched the power of the praetorian prefects, who were the commanders in chief of the armies.

A more important contribution to the stability of the empire was his division of it into two and later four parts. Shortly after his accession he chose a colleague, Maximian, to rule the western parts. Maximian was technically his equal as Augustus, but he was in practice a junior partner. His position was symbolized by his style of 'Herculius'; he was the representative of the hero who cleared the world of monsters at the behest of Jupiter. In 293 Diocletian appointed two Caesars or junior emperors, Constantius to assist Maximian in the west, and Galerius as his own subordinate in the east. Constantius took over the charge of Gaul and the task of suppressing Carausius in Britain. Galerius was normally in command of the Danube armies but when war broke out with Persia in 298 was summoned to the eastern command. With a team of four emperors the chances of a successful rebellion were greatly reduced.

Each Caesar was adopted by his Augustus and married to his daughter. They were thus marked out for the succession and when in 305 Diocletian abdicated and compelled his colleague to do likewise, Constantius and Galerius were proclaimed Augusti and two new Caesars were appointed, Severus in the west and Maximin in the east. This attempt to ignore the hereditary principle proved a failure. When Constantius died prematurely in 306 his army promptly declared his son Constantine Augustus at York, and in the same year Maxentius, Maximian's son, rebelled at Rome, recalled his father to the throne and defeated and killed Severus. Galerius accepted Constantine as Caesar of Gaul and Britain, but appointed Licinius as Augustus of the west. Licinius was however unable to dislodge Maxentius and had to content himself with Illyricum. Next Alexander, the vicar of Africa, proclaimed himself Augustus. There were thus seven Augusti ruling various parts of the empire, Constantine, Maximian, Maxentius, Alexander, Licinius,

Galerius and Maximin. All except two were rapidly eliminated. Maxentius conquered Alexander; his father Maximian, who had quarrelled with his son and taken refuge with Constantine, raised a revolt against the latter and was killed; Galerius died in 311 and his dominions were partitioned between Licinius and Maximin. In 313 Constantine conquered Maxentius and Licinius Maximin. Constantine and Licinius shared the empire from 313 to 324, when Constantine eliminated his last rival. The orgy of civil wars which followed Diocletian's abdication shows that it was no system, but Diocletian's personality, which gave peace to the empire for twenty years.

Diocletian's dominance over his colleagues is all the more remarkable because he was not a notable general, and preferred to leave the conduct of wars to them. After the defeat of Carinus he conducted some campaigns on the Danube and later suppressed the rebellion of Domitius Domitianus in Egypt. In the west he left to Maximian and Constantius the tasks of subduing the widespread peasant risings of the Bacaudae in Gaul, of beating back the incursions of the Franks and Alamans, of suppressing the rebellious Moorish tribes of Africa, and of recovering Britain from Carausius and Allectus. In his own half of the empire, he put his Caesar Galerius in charge of the Danube front, where there was constant fighting, and when war broke out with Persia in 297 he summoned him to the eastern front. After an initial defeat Galerius won a resounding victory in 298, and the Persian king not only accepted a Roman nominee as king of Armenia, but surrendered to Rome seven satrapies north of the upper Tigris and adjacent to Roman Mesopotamia.

Diocletian found the empire divided into fifty provinces and left it divided into a hundred. Some small provinces were left untouched, but many were bisected and some of the largest, like Asia, were divided into six. The object was to increase administrative efficiency. The governor was the sole judge in his province and in the larger provinces business in his court was hopelessly congested. Under the principate moreover it had been possible to keep the imperial administration small because the routine work of collecting the taxes, repairing the roads, raising recruits and maintaining the post had been delegated to the cities. Constant interference by the provincial governor was now needed to keep the wheels of the administration moving. In some frontier provinces Diocletian separated the civil government from the military command, but this was not universally done and the military commander (*dux*) often commanded the armies of several provinces.

In order to increase the efficiency of the administration yet further,

Diocletian divided the provinces into thirteen large circumscriptions called dioceses, the Britains, the Gauls, Viennensis (the southern half of Gaul), the Spains, Italy (the northern half), the City of Rome (southern Italy and the islands), Africa, Pannonia, Moesia and Thrace (covering the Balkans), Asiana and Pontica (Asia Minor) and Oriens (Syria and Egypt). Each was governed by a deputy (*vicarius*) of the praetorian prefects, and each had two financial officers, the *rationalis* and the *magister rei privatae*.

Finally each emperor had his central administration, which accompanied him wherever he might be, his *comitatus*. It comprised his praetorian prefect, his *rationalis summarum* and *magister rei privatae*, his secretariats and his corps of couriers (*agentes in rebus*). The praetorian prefect was by far the most important minister. Judicially he was a supreme judge of appeal, co-ordinate with the emperor. In the military sphere he was the emperor's chief of staff, sometimes commanding in his stead, adjutant general, controlling recruitment and discipline, and quartermaster general, providing rations and levying the foodstuffs required. He was thus in practice the chief finance minister, since the revenue and expenditure of the empire were largely in kind. He also maintained the roads and the post and the arms factories. The *rationalis rei summae* controlled the money taxes, the mines and the mints, and also levied and distributed uniforms and managed the state weaving and dyeing works which produced part of the army's requirements. The *magister rei privatae* collected the rents of the vast complex of imperial estates. Of the secretaries, the most important was the *magister memoriae*, who was the emperor's legal adviser and drafted legislation, and also served as foreign secretary.

It had been the practice under the principate to employ senators as provincial governors, and therefore as army commanders, and men of equestrian rank in financial and secretarial posts. Owing to the hostility which often prevailed between the emperor and the senate, Gallienus had excluded senators from all military posts. Diocletian excluded them also from all but a handful of provincial governorships. They served only as proconsuls of Africa and Asia and *correctores* of Sicily and Achaea, and of the provinces into which Italy was now divided. The only important office left to them was the prefecture of the city of Rome.

All administrative and military officers had their staffs or *officia*. Provincial governors had one hundred officials and vicars three hundred. The staffs of the central offices were naturally larger. The officials of the praetorian prefects, vicars, governors and military officers, were technically soldiers seconded from their regiments. Those in the financial offices were imperial slaves and freedmen whose service was hereditary.

Under the Severi the army had consisted of thirty-three legions of infantry of 6,000 men each and of auxiliary infantry cohorts and *numeri* and cavalry *alae*, normally 500 strong, sometimes 1,000. The precise number of units is unknown but the gross strength of the auxiliaries was probably roughly half that of the legionaries, and the army thus numbered about 300,000 men. During the third quarter of the third century the numbers of the cavalry had been increased by an unknown number of squadrons known as *vexillationes*, each 500 strong. The old legionary cavalry were also detached and became *vexillationes* of *equites promoti*. The entire army was distributed in permanent camps along the frontiers and when a field force was required it was formed by concentrating auxiliary units and detachments, usually 1,000 strong, from the legions from other parts of the frontier.

Diocletian was conservative in his military ideas and clung firmly to the conception of a continuous line of defence. He greatly strengthened the frontier by building forts and roads. Above all he vastly increased the size of the army. A contemporary Christian pamphleteer declared that each of the four emperors had an army larger than the whole army of the past. This is a wild exaggeration, but a study of the army lists in the *Notitia Dignitatum* strongly suggests that Diocletian doubled the number of legions, and he no doubt increased the other units proportionally. Some of the new troops were barbarians from beyond the frontiers but the vast majority were, it would seem, Roman citizens. The army had hitherto been recruited from sons of soldiers and veterans, and by other volunteers; conscription was rarely applied. To raise the vast numbers now required, Diocletian made hereditary service a legal obligation and instituted a new system of conscription. As conscripts were assessed on the same schedule as the land tax, the burden fell exclusively on the agricultural populations.

Diocletian and his colleagues had small field armies which accompanied them (*comitatus*). These included the cohorts of the praetorian guard, until they were disbanded in 312, and *protectores*, a corps of officer cadets. Diocletian probably also raised a new imperial guard, the *scholae*, consisting of regiments 500 strong of *Scutarii* (Roman citizens) and *Gentiles* (barbarians). In addition to these units, the *comitatus* included three or four legions and vexillations. For any serious operation the *comitatus* was supplemented by contingents from the frontier armies, as under the principate.

During the great inflation, silver had ceased to be issued and very little gold was minted—only, it would seem, to provide accession donatives for the troops. The bullion reserves of the empire disappeared into hoards or were converted into plate and jewellery. Diocletian attempted to restore a sound coinage, issuing gold coins (*aurei*) at sixty to the pound and silver *denarii* at ninety-six to the pound. Twenty-four silver *denarii* went to an *aureus*. He secured the necessary bullion by levies assessed on land and by compulsory purchase, paid in copper, from the cities, but he was unable by these means to secure enough for anything like an adequate currency. He continued to issue vast quantities of copper *nummi* in two denominations, a larger washed with silver, tariffed at five *denarii communes*, and a smaller (of the same size as the *antoninianus*) worth two *denarii*. This was a deflationary measure as Aurelian had rated the *antoninianus* at five *denarii*. Five large *nummi* were supposed to go to the silver *denarius*. The inflation continued and Diocletian was compelled to re-rate the smaller *nummus* at twenty-five *denarii*. He then tried to reduce prices by halving its nominal value, and finally in 302 issued his famous edict, in which he endeavoured to fix all prices, prescribing and inflicting the death penalty for any infringement. The edict was a total failure, goods disappearing from the market, and the inflation of the copper currency continued unchecked, reaching astronomical proportions. For any large transaction sealed bags (*folles*) of one thousand small *nummi*, now worth 12,500 *denarii*, were used. The relation between gold and silver on the one hand and copper on the other hand was governed by the market. By 324 the pound of gold, rated in 302 at 50,000 *denarii*, fetched over 300,000.

If Diocletian failed to stabilize the currency, he successfully organized the requisitions (*indictiones*) on which the state now depended. These had hitherto been irregular (*extraordinariae*), levied when and where they were required, and therefore most inequitably distributed. As Aristius Optatus, prefect of Egypt, proclaimed in 297:

Our most providential emperors, Diocletian and Maximian Augusti and Constantius and Maximian (Galerius), most noble Caesars, having seen that the levies of the public taxes take place in such a way that some people get off lightly and some are overburdened, have determined to root out this most evil and pernicious practice in the interest of their provincials and to lay down a salutary rule whereby the levies shall be made. I have therefore publicly given notice how much has been assessed for each *arura* according to the quality of the land and how much on each head of the peasants, and from what age and to what age, according to their published divine edict and the schedule annexed thereto, and I have issued copies of them in my edict. So the provincials, seeing that they have received great benefits, must take care that they make their payment with all speed according to the divine regulations and do not wait to be compelled. All must fulfil their obligations with the greatest zeal, and if anyone be found doing otherwise after such great benefits he will be punished.[1]

The first necessity was a census of the empire, and this was gradually carried out, diocese by diocese. The process was not completed until after Diocletian's death, and was carried out on different systems in the various dioceses. The most perfect system of assessment was that used in the diocese of Oriens (excluding Egypt), where Diocletian himself directed the census. The land was assessed in fiscal units called *iuga*, of equal value, different categories and qualities of land being assigned different values. Thus twenty *iugera* (five-eighths of an acre) of first-class arable, forty *iugera* of second-class arable, sixty *iugera* of third-class arable were assessed at one *iugum* and so also were five *iugera* of vineyard or 220 *perticae* of good olives or 450 *perticae* of mountain olives. In Asiana the *iuga* were of a much smaller value and less accurately assessed, only pasture, arable, vineyard and olive-yard being distinguished, without regard to quality. In Egypt the traditional unit, the *arura* (two-thirds of an acre), was preserved with the same distinctions of land use. In Africa the fiscal unit was the traditional *centuria* (200 *iugera* or 125 acres) without any distinction of use or quality, and in southern Italy another traditional unit of area, the *millena* (twelve and a half *iugera* or seven and a half acres), was used. This meant of course that in these dioceses the incidence of levies was inequitable.

The rural population was also counted and assessed in fiscal units (*capita*), and here again different systems were followed in different areas, according to local custom. In Egypt males only were counted from the ages of fourteen to sixty-five. In Syria both sexes were counted, females from twelve, males from fourteen. In Pontica females were rated at half a *caput*. Stock was also rated in fractions of a *caput*.

Each farm and each village and every holding within it was thus assessed at so many *iuga* or equivalent units (or fractions thereof, down

[1] *P. Cairo Isid.* 1.

to figures as precise as one-half, one-third, one-thirty-second, one-128th) and so many *capita*. From these data were built up figures for cities, provinces and dioceses. It was the task of the praetorian prefects to estimate each year how much wheat, barley, wine, meat and oil were required to feed the army and the civil service and the population of Rome, how many uniforms, horses and recruits were needed for the army, how many horses, mules and oxen for the post, how many labourers for public works, and then to divide the numbers by the number of *iuga*. The resultant rate of levy was published in the annual indiction and it only remained for the *tabularii* of the cities to make out the demand notes and for the civic collectors to extract the due amounts from the taxpayers. The schedule of *capita* seems to have been used in Diocletian's reign for levying a cash poll tax, but very soon afterwards the *iuga* and *capita* of each farm were added together and the total was used as the basic assessment.

The indiction is the first example in history of an annual budget whereby the taxes were adjusted each year to the estimated needs of government. The system was too convenient. In the old days when the rate of the taxes was fixed the government had to cut its coat according to its cloth. Now if it wanted to spend more it could raise the rate of the indiction. In fact we are told by Themistius that in the forty years between 324 and 364 it was doubled.

It may be noted that the whole burden of taxation, apart from customs dues, which were insignificant, fell on agriculture. Galerius imposed the poll tax on the urban population in the east but this measure was revoked on his death. In the west the position is not clear, but it is improbable that townspeople paid poll tax except in Africa.

It has already been mentioned that Diocletian compelled the sons of soldiers to serve in the army. It was left to Constantine to apply a similar rule to officials, who were technically soldiers, and later we find the workers in the state arms factories which Diocletian established also ranked as soldiers, and therefore as a hereditary caste. The workers in the mints and the weaving and dyeing factories which Diocletian created were state slaves and their service also was hereditary. Gold miners and washers too were later a hereditary caste. Decurions, or town-councillors, were already in Diocletian's time *de facto* a hereditary class, since all citizens and residents who possessed the requisite property qualification were obliged to serve unless they could claim a legal exemption: the most important of these was the service of the imperial government, past or present. Diocletian forbade decurions or other qualified persons to join the army, but he allowed them to hold commissions as officers and administrative posts. He could hardly do otherwise since the curial class (decurions and their families) comprised the educated stratum of the population. The result was a considerable leakage of the wealthier decurions from the councils, for commissions and administrative posts were more and more numerous and were usually held for a year or two only. Moreover, despite imperial prohibitions, decurions often obtained codicils of equestrian rank without holding any post.

Other hereditary classes which probably already existed in Diocletian's day were the guilds of bakers, butchers, bargees, carters, and so forth at Rome, and the diocesan guilds of shippers (*navicularii*), who carried corn and other public cargoes to Rome and the base ports of the army. Membership of these guilds was not strictly hereditary, falling on all who acquired land subject to the service, whether by inheritance, gift, dowry, or purchase.

Diocletian's great contribution to the growing caste-system of the empire was that, in order to facilitate the collection of the poll tax and the levies in kind, he enacted that all peasants must remain in the places in which they were registered in the census. As infants were registered, though they paid no tax, the agricultural population was thus hereditarily tied to the soil.

Diocletian appears to have been a man of sincere old-fashioned piety. He did not favour the popular gods of the day, such as Mithras or the Unconquered Sun, but gave his devotion to Jupiter Optimus Maximus, the traditional patron of Rome. In a law of which the full text has been preserved he shows strong religious feeling, prohibiting incest under the severest penalties on the ground that it might alienate the immortal gods from the empire. Nevertheless, for the first dozen or more years of his reign, he tolerated the Christians.

Diocletian's change of policy, according to Lactantius, professor of Latin at Nicomedia, the imperial residence, was caused by a failure to obtain omens at a state sacrifice. The priests reported that the livers of the slaughtered beasts had no markings, and when asked the reason said that the Christian soldiers on parade, by making the sign of the cross, were offending the gods. Furious at this gratuitous sabotage of a state ritual, Diocletian ordered all Christians to be expelled from the army and civil service unless they sacrificed. Still he took no general move against the Christians and it was probably, as Lactantius states, the Caesar Galerius, a rabid pagan, who eventually badgered him into acting.

On 23 February 303 an edict was posted at Nicomedia ordering that all churches should be closed and the Scriptures surrendered and burnt. Religious meetings were forbidden and Christians of any official rank deprived of it. As the result of two fires in the imperial palace, started, according to Lactantius, by Galerius himself, a second edict was issued ordering the arrest of all the clergy. They were held in prison until November, when they were forcibly compelled to go through the motions of sacrifice and released. Finally, a fourth edict ordered a general sacrifice.

The first edict was promulgated and enforced in Maximian's dominions. His Caesar, Constantius, closed the churches but took no further action. There were no martyrdoms in Gaul and Britain. The other three edicts do not seem to have been promulgated in the west and on Maximian's abdication on 1 May 305 the persecution ceased. Maxentius even restored their property to the churches. In the east Galerius and Maximin carried on the campaign with fervour. Another general sacrifice was ordered in 305, precautions being taken to see that no one slipped through the net. In 311 Galerius, who was dying of a painful and disgusting disease, became convinced that this was the vengeance of the Christian God and revoked the persecution. It had been the emperors' wish, he stated, to recall the Christians to the worship of their ancestral gods, but the only result had been that they worshipped neither their own nor the other gods. He accordingly urged them to pray for the empire to their own god. Galerius died in a few days but his deathbed edict was respected by Licinius and, for the time being, Maximin.

The latter, however, was a determined pagan and soon renewed the attack in a more constructive way. He gave paganism the organization which it had hitherto lacked by appointing an official high priest for each city and a superior high priest for each province. He published spurious Acts of Pilate and ordered them to be taught in the schools. He obtained and publicized confessions from prostitutes that they had participated in Christian orgies. He graciously acceded to petitions from Nicomedia, Tyre and other large cities and even from entire provinces that Christians should be expelled from their boundaries. After these preliminaries the persecution began again in earnest. Maximin was opposed to executions and preferred to condemn recusants to the mines and quarries after blinding one eye and ham-stringing one leg, but there were a few martyrdoms. This persecution was revoked by Maximin after his defeat by Licinius in 313, shortly before his death.

We possess a number of authentic Acts of martyrs; we also possess the official record of the proceedings of the *curator* of Cirta, the capital of Numidia, when the first edict was received. He assembled the clergy at the church and ordered them to produce all their movables and the Scriptures. The clergy produced the other property but declared that the Scriptures were held by the readers, who were not present. A list of them was however obtained and they meekly surrendered the Scriptures. Our most valuable document is Eusebius' *Martyrs of Palestine*. In all, eighty-three persons were executed between 303 and 313, of whom thirty-two were natives of Palestine and fifty-one were Egyptian convicts. Most of the local martyrdoms were the result of deliberate provocation. One young man, for instance, interrupted the governor at a sacrifice, and another group of six presented themselves with their hands bound, shouting that they were Christians. There is no reason to think that Palestine was exceptional and the number of martyrdoms must have been small except in Egypt and Africa. These were the only areas where Christianity had spread among the peasantry and they proved far more stubborn than the townspeople. Undoubtedly the vast majority of Christians either escaped detection or lapsed. Many practised various forms of evasion. The clergy surrendered heretical texts instead of the Scriptures and laymen got their pagan friends (or less creditably compelled their Christian slaves) to impersonate them at sacrifices. Confessors were far more numerous than martyrs, for the government was not out to kill, and preferred to inflict prolonged tortures on recusants in order to make them sacrifice. Altogether the suffering inflicted in the eastern provinces over ten years must have been immense. The result was to strengthen the church, for the lapsed clamoured for readmission when the ordeal was over and many pagans were impressed by the courage of the confessors and martyrs. There seems to have been very little popular animosity against the Christians by this date, and the action of the local authorities was often very lax. The mayor of Tigisis in Africa begged the bishop to surrender *some* books to burn if he wanted to keep the Scriptures.

IV

Constantine

Constantine was the eldest son of Constantius by a barmaid named Helena. He was born at Naissus (Nish, in Yugoslavia) on 17 February in about 290. When Constantius became Caesar he had to divorce Helena in order to marry Maximian's daughter Theodora, and little Constantine was sent to be educated at the court of Diocletian. Here he rose to be a tribune and witnessed the great persecution. In one of his later edicts he recalls priests from the oracle of Apollo at Branchidae reporting that the oracle was dumb 'because of the just upon the earth' and Diocletian's asking what this phrase meant and receiving the reply: 'The Christians, of course.' On his father's accession as Augustus he asked Galerius for leave to join him, but Galerius repeatedly put him off until Constantine at last gave him the slip. He rejoined his father at Boulogne, preparing to embark for a campaign in Britain. On 23 July 306 Constantius died and the army proclaimed his son Augustus.

Constantine's next ambition was to conquer his neighbour Maxentius. There is no reason to doubt the story which he told to Eusebius many years later under oath, that while marching with his army somewhere in

BIBLIOGRAPHY. The latest scholarly work on Constantine is J. Vogt, *Constantin der Grosse und sein Jahrhundert* (Munich, 1960), which contains a bibliography of the abundant modern literature; cf. the same author's article 'Constantinus der Grosse' in the *Reallexicon für Antike und Christentum* (1956). I have set out my own view of Constantine in full in my popular work, *Constantine and the Conversion of Europe* (New York, 1963), which though it gives no references cites the major documents in translation *in extenso*. See also A. Piganiol, *L'empéreur Constantin* (Paris, 1932).

The main narrative sources are the pagan Zosimus and the Christian Eusebius, *Ecclesiastical History*, x, and the *Life of Constantine*. For ecclesiastical history there are Socrates, Sozomen, Theodoret and Rufinus, and for the Arian controversy the historical works of Athanasius. For secular affairs there is also the first Anonymus Valesianus (usually printed with Ammianus Marcellinus).

The most important group of documents is Optatus of Mileve, *Appendix*.

Gaul and meditating on his chances in attacking Maxentius he saw a cross of light superimposed on the sun: the phenomenon is rare but well attested. We may reasonably doubt that he saw the words *Hoc signo vince* written in stars about the cross, but this was the interpretation which he put upon the heavenly sign. Constantine had probably been hitherto a worshipper of the Unconquered Sun. He now seems to have formed the belief that the Sun was identical with the Christian God, who had taken him under his protection. Despite great numerical inferiority he boldly invaded Italy and before the final battle at the Milvian Bridge just outside Rome ordered his soldiers to paint the symbol ☧ (a monogram of Christ) on their shields. Maxentius was killed and Constantine was proclaimed senior Augustus by the senate.

He forthwith showered gifts of money on the churches and gave the clergy immunity from curial duties 'so that they may not be diverted by any sacrilegious error or mistake from the service which is owed to the Divinity but may rather without any disturbance serve their own law, since the conduct of the greatest worship of the Divinity will in my opinion bring immeasurable benefits to the commonwealth'.[1] He soon found that there were complications. Hosius, bishop of Corduba, whom he had adopted as his spiritual adviser, warned him that there were certain false Christians in Africa who were highly displeasing to the Highest Divinity and that he must confine his gifts to those called Catholics. Constantine obeyed but shortly received a petition from a group of African bishops stating that they had a dispute with Caecilian, bishop of Carthage, and requesting him to appoint bishops from Gaul to settle it. He instructed Miltiades, bishop of Rome, to investigate the case with three Gallic bishops.

The dispute was between the rigorist and charitable wings of the African church. Many African Christians, especially in the rural province of Numidia, held that those who had surrendered the Scriptures (*traditores*) were for ever damned and even condemned those who had evaded the edict. Others, led by Mensurius, bishop of Carthage, denounced those who deliberately incurred martyrdom. Mensurius himself had surrendered books to be burned and Anullinus, the proconsul of Africa, had refused to take any action when it was alleged that these books were not the Scriptures. When Mensurius died his archdeacon Caecilian was hastily consecrated by Felix, the bishop of the little town of Aptungi, before the Numidian bishops, who normally had a voice in the election, could arrive. They countered by declaring that Felix was a

[1] Eusebius, *Hist. Eccl.* x. 7.

traditor and Caecilian's consecration thus invalid, and elected a rival bishop of Carthage, Majorian, who was shortly succeeded by Donatus, who gave his name to the movement.

Miltiades, having added fifteen Italian bishops to the court, pronounced in favour of Caecilian, but the Donatists alleged that the case had not been fairly tried and appealed. Constantine was annoyed, but in 314 summoned a council of thirty-three bishops from all the western provinces to Arles. This council again condemned the Donatists, who now appealed to Constantine himself. The dispute was actually never healed but raged with increasing bitterness until the Arab invasion if not later. Constantine tried every method to reconcile or suppress the schismatics. He succeeded in proving that the charge of *traditio* brought against Felix was a malicious falsehood, but the Donatists remained intransigent. He tried persecution, but they welcomed martyrdom. Eventually he abandoned them to the judgment of God.

A large dossier of original documents on the dispute has survived, including several letters of Constantine which clearly reveal his attitude. In a postscript to Aelafius, a high official in Africa, he writes:[1] 'Since I have been informed that you too are a worshipper of the Highest God I will confess to your gravity that I consider it absolutely contrary to the divine law that we should overlook such quarrels and contentions whereby the Highest Divinity may perhaps be roused to wrath, not only against the human race but also against myself, to whose care He has by His celestial will committed the government of all earthly things.' In a later letter to Domitius Celsus, vicar of Africa, he writes:[2] 'What higher duty have I in virtue of my imperial office and policy than to dissipate errors and repress rash actions and so cause all to offer to Almighty God true religion, honest concord and due worship?' He thus clearly reveals his belief that his own victories and the salvation of the empire were dependent on the goodwill of the *summa divinitas* whom the Christians worshipped, and that this divinity would be bitterly incensed if there was division in his church. It had been a traditional duty of the emperor to maintain the *pax deorum*, and Constantine considered it his duty to maintain the *pax dei*. He took the advice of bishops as experts, but he took the final decisions himself and himself executed them. But though he believed himself to be God's servant he was singularly ill-instructed in his faith. He apparently still believed that Christ and the sun were identical, for he issued coins with the legend *Sol Invictus Comes Augusti* down to 318, and from the wording of an edict enforcing Sunday

[1] Optatus of Mileve, *App.* III.   [2] Optatus of Mileve, *App.* VII.

rest appears to have believed that the Christians observed the first day of the week in honour of the sun.

Constantine and Licinius held a meeting at Milan in 313, at which Licinius married Constantine's half-sister Constantia and was apparently persuaded to accept the Christian God. At any rate, in the war with Maximin which followed immediately, he ordered his army to use a monotheistic prayer identical with that later prescribed by Constantine for his soldiers, and on entering Nicomedia in triumph he issued an edict (the so-called Edict of Milan) which guaranteed absolute toleration for the Christians and made full restitution of all their confiscated property. He later reverted to paganism and in the early 320s initiated a rather half-hearted persecution. This was the signal for Constantine to launch a crusade and, led by the Labarum, the imperial banner with the ☧ monogram on its stave, his army triumphed.

Constantine had hoped that the eastern bishops would solve the Donatist controversy. He was aghast to find that the east was ridden by even more embittered disputes. One, the Melitian, was exactly parallel to the Donatist and was confined to Egypt. The other, the Arian, was more abstruse and involved the whole eastern church. Arius was a priest of Alexandria, a pupil of Lucian of Antioch, a famous Origenist theologian who had suffered martyrdom. Starting from the neoplatonic dogma that God was an indivisible monad, he argued that the Son must be in some sense posterior to the Father—he would not say there was a time when He was not, since the Son came into being before all time, but asserted that 'there was when He was not'. He also asserted the Son must have been begotten or created out of nothing since the substance of the Father was indivisible. Alexander, bishop of Alexandria, condemned these doctrines and called a council of Egyptian bishops which confirmed his verdict. Arius went abroad and enlisted the support of a number of prominent theologians, including Eusebius, bishop of Nicomedia and the historian Eusebius, bishop of Caesarea in Palestine. A war of pamphlets ensued.

Constantine's first reaction was that of the plain man. He wrote a long letter to Alexander and Arius jointly, protesting that such subtleties should not have been raised and that if there was a difference of opinion the disputants should, like pagan philosophers, agree to differ. Hosius, who took this letter to Alexander, advised Constantine that the conflict could not be so simply healed, and Constantine resolved to summon a general council of all the eastern bishops and issued invitations for next year to Ancyra in Galatia. But in the meanwhile Hosius, who had taken

Alexander's side, took advantage of the death of Philogonius, bishop of Antioch, to call a large council from Cilicia, Syria, Mesopotamia and Palestine to elect a successor. The council elected Eustathius, a violent opponent of Arius, provisionally condemned the latter's doctrines and excommunicated Eusebius of Caesarea and Narcissus of Neronias, pending the verdict of the emperor's great council. It circularized its decision not only throughout the east but also to Rome. Since the west was now involved, Constantine decided to make his council universal or ecumenical, changing its place to Nicaea, which would be more convenient for the western bishops and for himself, as he intended to preside.

On 20 May 325 the Council of Nicaea opened. About 275 bishops attended, of whom only four and two deacons representing the pope came from the west. Constantine delivered a short opening speech in Latin (not that he did not know Greek, but Latin was the official language of the empire). His object was to secure a unanimous decision and he called on the recently condemned Eusebius of Caesarea to propose a statement of belief. Eusebius, greatly flattered, read out the traditional creed of Caesarea, which closely resembled the Apostles' Creed. No one could object, for it was a statement of impeccable orthodoxy. Its one disadvantage was that Arius could accept it. The debate continued. Violent controversialists on either side were reproved by Constantine. Various amendments were suggested, such as inserting 'the power of God' as a description of the Son, in the hope that the Arian bishops would find it unacceptable. But the Arians smilingly agreed, remarking that according to the Scriptures grasshoppers were also 'the power of God'.

Finally Constantine intervened and produced his bombshell. Would Eusebius accept the insertion of the phrase 'of one substance with the Father'? Eusebius was horrified. The phrase was heretical, it had been condemned by the great Council of Antioch in 268, and meant in the contemporary acceptation of the word *homoousios* that the Father and the Son were identical. He weakly objected that the word was unscriptural, and Constantine replied that the truth might be expressed in new words. Under the emperor's eye Eusebius' courage failed, and he agreed. All the other bishops, to the more educated of whom the phrase was equally obnoxious, eventually agreed, except two, Secundus of Ptolemais and Theonas of Marmarice, both in Libya, Arius' native province. They were excommunicated, together with Arius and a tiny band of his disciples, and also Eusebius of Nicomedia and Theognis of Nicaea, who while accepting the creed protested that Arius' doctrines had been misrepresented. There can be little doubt that Constantine's action had been suggested by Hosius and Alexander. The word *consubstantialis*, the Latin equivalent of *homoousios*, had long been considered orthodox in the west and Dionysius, one of Alexander's predecessors, had on the insistence of Pope Dionysius accepted it. On the other hand, Arius had publicly declared that it was absolutely heretical.

The council offered generous terms for reunion to the Melitians and the Novatians, an earlier rigorist sect which dated from Valerian's persecution. It endeavoured to determine the date of Easter, which Constantine found to his distress was celebrated on different days in the various churches. There was a small sect, the Quartodecimans, who observed 14 Nisan, the first full moon after the vernal equinox, the Jewish Passover. Most churches observed the following Sunday, some, if 14 Nisan fell on a Sunday, kept the 21st. There was finally doubt about the exact date of the vernal equinox; some churches thus kept the feast a month later than others. The council ordered that the rule of Rome and Alexandria should prevail, which was not very helpful, as these two churches followed different systems for calculating the equinox.

The council also settled some points of church discipline. Clergy were forbidden to migrate from their original city without their bishop's permission. Bishops were absolutely forbidden to move from one city to another. The bishops of the provincial capitals, or metropolitans, were instructed to hold two councils each year of all the bishops of their provinces. The consecration of a new bishop had to be approved by the metropolitan and a majority of the provincial bishops. In the sixth canon the superior authority of certain great churches was recognized: 'Let the ancient customs in Egypt and Libya and Pentapolis prevail, so that the bishop of Alexandria has authority over all these, since this is the custom for the bishop of Rome also, and similarly at Antioch and in the other provinces let the churches keep their prerogatives.' It was the custom in Egypt that the bishop of Alexandria should consecrate all other bishops, either personally or by proxy, there being no metropolitan except that of Ptolemais of Libya. The second clause refers, as the Latin version of the canon shows, to the similar position of the pope in the Suburbicarian diocese (south Italy and Sicily) where there were likewise no metropolitans. The primacy of Antioch over the diocese of Oriens (less Egypt) was less well defined. It is curious that the council, although Caecilian was present, did not confirm the primacy of Carthage in the diocese of Africa. Here the other provinces had no metropolitans, but the senior bishop, whatever his see, acted as primate in each province. The see of Jerusalem was accorded particular honour, but remained subject to the metropolitan of Caesarea, the provincial capital.

Constantine next issued an edict confiscating the churches of the various heretical sects in the east and forbidding them to hold services. A year later he lifted the ban on the Novatians, by whose stern piety he was apparently impressed. His next ambition was to reconcile Arius and his handful of adherents to the church. He invited Arius to court and induced him to write out a vague confession of faith which seemed to him satisfactory. He then appears to have reassembled the Council of Nicaea, which received back Arius and his friends, including Eusebius of Nicomedia and Theognis of Nicaea. Alexander however refused to take Arius back, and so did Athanasius, who shortly succeeded him as bishop of Alexandria.

If Constantine hoped for peace in the church after Nicaea, he was disappointed. The Melitians in Egypt, after a momentary reconciliation, again quarrelled with the Catholics. The bishops who abhorred the *homoousios* did not dare to attack it openly while Constantine lived. He believed it to be divinely inspired, 'for the decision of 300 bishops must be considered as no other than the judgment of God, especially as the Holy Spirit dwelling in the minds of so many men of such character brought to light the Divine will'.[1] They managed, however, to secure the condemnation of its principal supporters. Marcellus of Ancyra was condemned for heresy and Eustathius of Antioch for immorality, and many attacks were made on Athanasius.

There were two major charges against him, that Macarius, one of his clergy, had broken up the communion service and smashed the chalice in a village church in Mareotes near Alexandria, served by a priest called Ischyras, and that his agents had murdered Arsenius, the Melitian bishop of Hypsele. It was proved that Macarius could not have interrupted a communion service, as he had not arrived on a Sunday, when alone the communion was celebrated. Athanasius however as good as admits that Macarius broke a cup, purporting to be a chalice, in a house which purported to be a church. Ischyras was a schismatic. The truth about Arsenius was apparently that Athanasius' bullies had tied him up in his house and set fire to it. He escaped and emigrated to Tyre, where he was some years later identified and produced as a refutation of the murder charge. Athanasius was cleared by Constantine and his brother Dalmatius on both these charges, but his enemies brought others, and

[1] Socrates, *Hist. Eccl.* I. 9.

eventually in 335 Constantine ordered that a council be held in Caesarea to investigate them. Athanasius refused to attend, alleging that it was packed against him, but next year consented to stand trial before a council at Tyre, held under the presidency of Dionysius, an imperial commissioner. This council was in fact packed with Athanasius' enemies and sent a commission of enquiry to Mareotes which reported that the charge of the broken chalice was true. Athanasius was condemned and set sail to Constantinople, where he convinced the emperor of his innocence. In the next few days however delegates from the council at Tyre arrived and Constantine changed his mind and banished Athanasius to Trier in Gaul.

Constantine forthwith summoned a universal council to Jerusalem to celebrate the dedication of the Church of the Holy Sepulchre, which he had just completed, and solemnly to admit Arius to communion. The heresiarch died shortly afterwards in a public latrine at Constantinople, an event which the orthodox acclaimed as the judgment of God.

Constantine built a number of magnificent churches at Rome and Constantinople, at Jerusalem, Bethlehem and Hebron in the Holy Land, and at Cirta, Nicomedia and Antioch. He endowed these churches with vast estates. Those given to the Roman churches brought in rents amounting to over 30,000 *solidi* a year. He also bestowed allowances of corn on every church in the empire, to feed the clergy and the poor. These were so large that the pious Jovian when he restored them after Julian's reign reduced them to a third of the original amount. The emperor also expressly legalized bequests to the church, gave bishops the power, hitherto reserved to provincial governors, to make slaves Roman citizens, and, strangest of all, gave them inappellable jurisdiction. Either party to a suit might transfer it to a bishop's court, whose judgment was final. The immunity from curial obligations which Constantine had granted to the clergy proved embarrassing, for decurions flocked into holy orders; the emperor was obliged to rule that clergy might be ordained only to fill vacancies caused by death, and decurions and their sons and others qualified to serve on the city councils might not be ordained.

Constantine naturally favoured the Christians in his service. Ablabius, his greatest praetorian prefect, was a Christian of very humble origin, the son of a provincial official in Crete. The emperor showered gifts and titles on highly placed converts, with the result, as Eusebius was bound to admit, that there were many interested conversions. He also favoured communities which were predominantly Christian. Maiuma, the Christian port of Gaza, was given the rank of a city, and Orcistus, a village of Nacoleia, was also accorded city rank 'because all the inhabitants of the said place are said to be followers of the most holy religion'.[1]

In his edict on the date of Easter Constantine used the most violent antisemitic language, but his bark was worse than his bite. He allowed the Jewish clergy immunity from curial duties and only forbade Jews to circumcise their Christian slaves or molest their co-religionists if they were converted to Christianity. The last law was provoked by an assault on Joseph, an apostle or counsellor of the hereditary patriarch at Tiberias, who was head of the whole Jewish community in the empire. Joseph was given the title of *comes* and a pension by Constantine, and built churches at Sepphoris and Tiberias, but failed to convert the Jewish population of Galilee.

Towards the pagans Constantine was at first tolerant. He apparently enacted a severe law against divination in 324 and, encouraged by this, zealous Christians tried to stop all sacrifices. Constantine accordingly issued an edict in which he urged his pagan subjects to adopt his faith but allowed them to worship the old gods and forbade Christians to molest them. He later destroyed three famous temples, that of Asclepius at Aegae, renowned for its cures, and those of Heliopolis and Apheca in Phoenice, notorious for their ritual prostitution. In 331 he confiscated the temple lands and treasures, even stripping the cult images of their gold plating, leaving only the wooden armatures. Finally, shortly before his death, he banned sacrifices.

Constantine made a major change in the organization of the army, creating a substantial field force or *comitatus*. It was formed in part by removing vexillations and legionary detachments from the frontier, partly by raising new vexillations of cavalry and infantry units styled *auxilia*, many of them recruited from Germans. The *comitatenses* received higher pay and privileges, and the regiments who garrisoned the banks of the Rhine and Danube (*riparienses*) and the other frontiers (*limitanei*) became second-class troops, receiving recruits of inferior quality. He greatly increased the German element in the army and favoured German generals. To command the *comitatus* he created a master of the foot (*magister peditum*) and a master of the horse (*magister equitum*) who had authority over the *duces* of the frontier. The praetorian prefects thus lost their military functions but still furnished rations, recruits and arms to the army. From Constantine's day, the military and administrative careers were entirely separated.

[1] Dessau, *Inscr. Lat. Sel.* 6091.

In the civil administration, Constantine made few changes. Unlike Diocletian, he favoured the senate, changing the title of the governor in many provinces from *praeses* to *consularis* and reserving these posts for senators. He also often appointed senators as vicars and freely granted senatorial rank to equestrian officials and their sons. He furthermore revived the old patriciate as a personal and very select honour and created a new order of nobility in the *comites*. Those who accompanied the emperor had always been called his companions (*comites*). Now the *comites* became an official order, divided into three grades, to which both senators and others were eligible. Select *comites* (*intra palatium*) served on the imperial council or consistory. Others (*comites provinciarum*) were appointed instead of vicars with a special mission of investigating the complaints of the provincials: this institution did not outlive Constantine except in the diocese of Oriens, where the vicar was permanently replaced by a *comes Orientis*. Others again (*comites rei militaris*) were given special commands in the field army. The ministers of the *comitatus* also received the title, and *rationalis rei summae* came to be known as the *comes sacrarum largitionum* and the *magister* as the *comes rei privatae*. Constantine also created the office of *quaestor sacri palatii*, who replaced the *magister memoriae* as legal adviser and draughtsman, and the master of the offices. This minister had general control over the secretarial departments and the lesser offices of the *comitatus* and commanded the corps of couriers, the *agentes in rebus*; he later acquired disciplinary control of the *scholae*. He regulated audiences with the emperor and received foreign envoys and supplied interpreters for them. Zosimus states that Constantine created the four territorial praetorian prefectures which existed in his own day, the Gauls, Italy, Illyricum and the East. This is untrue. It can be proved that the emperor instituted a special praetorian prefecture of Africa, presumably to cope with the Donatist problem. In the latter part of his reign he divided the empire between his sons and nephew, whom he successively created Caesars, Crispus and Constantine in 317, Constantius in 324, Constans in 333 and his nephew Dalmatius in 335. Crispus ruled Gaul between 318 and 324 but was executed in 325, according to later legend for adultery with his stepmother the empress Fausta, who was also executed in the same year. After this, the younger Constantine and Constantius and then Constantine again successively ruled the Gauls, Constans ruled Italy, Constantine followed by Dalmatius Illyricum and Constantius the East. These Caesars all had their own praetorian prefects.

In the last twelve years of his reign Constantine was grossly extravagant. He first ran through the reserve which the parsimonious Licinius had accumulated. He then acquired vast quantities of bullion from the temple treasures. This windfall enabled him to establish an abundant gold and silver coinage. The gold coin which he issued, the *solidus*, at 72 to the pound, remained unchanged in weight and purity until the Middle Ages. The silver coin, the *milliarensis*, was less successful. It was struck at 96 to the pound and tariffed at one carat or *siliqua* (one-twenty-fourth of a *solidus*.) The relative value of gold and silver however fluctuated violently and after various adjustments the silver issues were virtually abandoned in 395.

Despite these two windfalls, Constantine was obliged to raise the rate of the indiction substantially and also instituted two new taxes. The first, the *gleba* or *follis*, was a very modest impost on senators, who were graded according to their property in three classes which paid eight, four and two *folles*, equivalent apparently to approximately 40, 20 and 10 *solidi*. The other tax was the *collatio lustralis* or *chrysargyron*, a levy of gold and silver made every five years on all traders in the widest sense of the word, including craftsmen who sold their own products, money-lenders, and even prostitutes. This tax seemed just in principle, since the urban population was otherwise immune, but the classes it affected were very poor and it inflicted great hardship and brought in an insignificant revenue. Constantine seems also to have appropriated to the central government the *octroi* dues and other local taxes levied by the cities.

One of Constantine's greatest titles to fame is Constantinople. He states in one of his laws that he founded the city by God's command and he probably intended it as a memorial of the victory over Licinius which God had granted to him at Byzantium. As such, the city was never sullied by pagan cult and was richly endowed with churches. It appears that Constantine gave it the title of 'the new Rome', but it had none of the constitutional prerogatives of Rome, no prefect of the city, consuls, magistrates or senate. The city councillors were given the title of *clari*, not *clarissimi*. The city took six years to build, being dedicated on 11 May 330. It was nevertheless according to Julian jerry-built and until the reign of Valens inadequately supplied with water. Constantine despoiled the cities of the east of their artistic treasures to adorn its streets and squares; the bronze serpent column from Delphi which commemorated the victory of the Greeks over the Persians in 479 B.C. still stands in the Hippodrome. He encouraged wealthy settlers to build houses by granting them state lands and stimulated the influx of population by instituting upon 18 May 332 a free daily distribution of 80,000 bread rations.

Constantinople was strategically well placed mid-way between the Danube and Euphrates fronts, with easy communications both by road and by sea with either, and it was no doubt for this reason that Constantine chose it for the administrative capital of the eastern parts: Diocletian had for similar reasons made Nicomedia his habitual residence. Constantinople, as the imperial capital, was strongly defended and effectually sealed Asia Minor and the east against the barbarian invaders of Europe. It was moreover in itself a wellnigh impregnable fortress, and stood unconquered even when all the rest of the empire had fallen to the Persians and the Avars in 626.

Constantine's conversion was a profoundly important event. It is sometimes assumed that eventually some emperor must have been converted and Christianity would have triumphed. In fact Christians were at this time a tiny minority and belonged predominantly to the urban lower classes. The senatorial aristocracy was pagan almost to a man and the vast majority of the educated classes were pagan. The peasantry and therefore the army were universally pagan except in Africa and Egypt. The chances of a Christian emperor were remote and without a Christian emperor the conversion of the empire would have been indefinitely postponed. Christians were numerous in Persia but no Persian king was converted and Christianity always remained a minority sect.

Constantine's conversion also profoundly influenced relations between church and state. As the servant of God, responsible to Him for the good order of the church, he felt no qualms in intervening decisively in ecclesiastical affairs. He established the precedent that only an emperor could summon an ecumenical council. The church accepted his domination without question. Not only the Donatists but Athanasius himself appealed to the emperor against an ecclesiastical council.

In 337 Constantine fell seriously ill. Knowing that he was very near his end he received baptism from Eusebius, bishop of Constantinople. It may seem strange that the servant of God, who had presided at an ecumenical council, should still have been a catechumen, but it was at this stage common for pious Christians to postpone baptism until they were on their deathbeds and could sin no more.

V

The House of Constantine

After the death of Constantine there was a curious interregnum of three months. Then the army at Constantinople mutinied and, declaring that they would have no emperors but Constantine's sons, massacred the Caesar Dalmatius, another nephew, Hannibalianus, the late emperor's two half-brothers, Constantius and Dalmatius, and two elder statesmen, Optatus and Ablabius. Constantine, Constantius and Constans were then proclaimed Augusti, the first ruling the Gauls with Britain and Spain, the second the East with Thrace from Dalmatius' portion, the third Italy and Africa with Illyricum, which had belonged to Dalmatius. Constantine, as the eldest, was apparently given some titular primacy, and when Constans ignored it invaded Italy to be defeated and killed. Constantius succeeded to a Persian war which had broken out shortly before his father's death. The Persian king had ejected the pro-Roman and Christian king of Armenia, and Constantine had responded by declaring his nephew Hannibalianus king of Armenia. The war was bitterly fought and exhausting to both sides but indecisive. It continued with intervals of quiescence during the whole of Constantius' reign.

When Constantine II fell Constans still kept a praetorian prefect in his former dominions and from now on the prefecture of the Gauls, comprising Britain, the two Gallic dioceses and Spain, became a standing institution. From now onwards also there was always a prefecture of the East, comprising the dioceses of Thrace, Asiana, Pontica and Oriens,

BIBLIOGRAPHY. The sons of Constantine have not attracted biographers, but Julian has inspired many, the best of whom is J. Bidez, *La vie de l'empereur Julien* (Paris, 1930). There is also a useful collection of sources for his reign, J. Bidez and F. Cumont, *Iuliani Imperatoris epistulae et leges* (Paris, 1922).

The main narrative source is Zosimus until we reach Ammianus Marcellinus in 351, and the four ecclesiastical historians; Athanasius' and Hilary's works continue to be useful for the Arian controversy. For Julian the main sources are his own works, Gregory of Nazianzus, *Orationes contra Julianum*, and Libanius' Funeral Speech for Julian.

which Constantius II ruled. Constans' original dominions—Italy, Africa, Pannonia, Dacia and Macedonia (Moesia had been divided into these two dioceses by Constantine)—were normally governed by one prefect, sometimes by two. It was not until 395, when Dacia and Macedonia became part of the eastern empire, that the prefecture of Illyricum became a standing institution.

The three brothers naturally divided the *comitatus* between them and each had a *magister peditum* and a *magister equitum*. In practice the field army came to be yet further subdivided. In 342, when Constantius was at Antioch with the bulk of his army, Hermogenes, his *magister equitum*, was in command of a considerable force in Thrace, and in 350, when Constans was in Gaul, Vetranio was *magister peditum* of the armies of Illyricum. It soon became the practice for each emperor to have part of the field army, styled the *palatini*, immediately attached to him, commanded by a *magister peditum* and a *magister equitum praesentales*. The rest of the *comitatenses* were distributed in regional reserves on the eastern, Thracian, Illyrian and Rhine fronts under the command of *magistri equitum* or *comites rei militaris*. In the east the more logical title 'commanders of both services' (*magister utriusque militiae*) came to be applied to all the major commands. Small detachments of the field army were sometimes stationed in turbulent provinces under *comites rei militaris* and some of these commands, like that of the *comes Africae*, became permanent.

Early in his reign Constantius II, jealous no doubt of his younger brother who ruled Rome and the senate, instituted a senate at Constantinople. Henceforth the old Roman magistrates, quaestors, aediles, tribunes of the plebs and praetors, were elected at Constantinople also, and the last gave games. The emperor prescribed how much they must spend on them. Only the ordinary consuls who gave their names to each year were not duplicated. One was nominated by the western emperor, the other by the eastern. The president of the new senate was at first a proconsul, probably the governor of Europe, the province in which Constantinople lay. On 11 December 359 the first prefect of the city took office and the constitutional parity of the old and the new Rome was complete.

Constantius naturally enrolled in his senate such Roman senators as were domiciled in his dominions, but they were few and not very distinguished. For the rest he created new senators, enrolling men of birth, wealth or literary fame from the eastern provinces. Proconsuls and consulars of the provinces automatically received a seat in the senate and vicars and praetorian prefects, masters of the soldiers and ministers of the court were normally granted them. Constantius was chary of honouring military men, who were often barbarians and mostly uneducated, and in his day *duces* were still of equestrian rank only.

The Constantinopolitan senate initially numbered 300 only, but after a generation had increased to 2,000. The Roman senate, which had traditionally numbered 600 under the principate, underwent a similar inflation. The extension was partly due to the large annual intake of office-holders but more to the lavish grant of senatorial rank to aspiring members of the provincial aristocracy and also to palatine civil servants.

The Constantinopolitan senate never acquired the prestige of the old senate of Rome. As Libanius[1] somewhat unkindly put it, 'the whole senate of Constantinople did not consist of nobles whose ancestors for four generations back had held offices and been ambassadors and performed public services'. It fell far behind the Roman senate in riches also. Though it contained many very wealthy men, its richest families did not own a tithe of the vast estates which the old Roman houses had accumulated over many generations. In tone it was very different. The Roman senate still retained memories of the old days when it had ruled the empire. It had traditions of independence and even of hostility to the emperors and was jealous of its privileges. Since the emperor rarely resided at Rome, it was often out of touch with the imperial government. The senators of Constantinople were an aristocracy of service who owed their position to imperial favour and the emperor and his court were normally resident at Constantinople. The eastern senate thus never developed any spirit of independence.

Many of the new senators were of very humble origin. There were masters of the soldiers who, like Arbetio, had risen from the ranks. In civilian offices Constantius II greatly favoured palatine civil servants, especially the imperial notaries who kept the minutes of the consistory. Libanius maliciously cites many examples of men of working-class origin who had risen from shorthand clerks to become praetorian prefects and ordinary consuls: Philippus, the son of a sausage-seller, consul in 361; Datianus, the son of a cloakroom attendant, consul in 358; and half-a-dozen others. These men founded noble families which supplied praetorian prefects and consuls in the east for generation after generation, down to the sixth century. In the west such cases were rare, for Constans, surrounded by the old Roman aristocracy, tended to appoint senators to high offices of state.

[1] Oration XLII, 22.

The influx of wealthy provincials into the senates of Rome and Constantinople exacerbated the problem of the curial order. Hitherto decurions had aspired only to equestrian offices which gave them personal immunity for life but left their sons members of the city councils, unless, as often, they secured posts or codicils for them individually. Senators possessed hereditary immunity from curial status and every new senator therefore meant a whole family lost to the council for ever. Early in his reign Constantius II, while confirming existing curial senators in their position, absolutely forbade acquisition of senatorial rank by decurions for the future. This law, like all others on this topic, proved a dead letter. He also in 341 forbade decurions to enter the palatine civil service, while confirming in their posts those who had served for five years. Similar laws were issued later from time to time and with only temporary effect. Towards decurions who took holy orders Constantius was more indulgent. His father's prohibition was relaxed and instead he ruled that decurions who became clergy must surrender their property to their sons, who would replace them on the council, or, if they had no sons, consign a third of their property to a relative who would take their place or, if they had no relative, to the council itself. In 361 Constantius greatly relaxed these rules, allowing bishops to keep their property in all cases and priests and deacons if they were ordained with the approval of the city council.

The sons of Constantine had been brought up as pious Christians and continued their father's policies. The ban on pagan sacrifices was reiterated and many temples were demolished. Constans had to issue a law protecting the historic temples of Rome from destruction. Constantius II even removed from the senate house the altar of Victory which Augustus had placed there. The privileges of the clergy were confirmed and extended. They were immune from the poll tax (*capitatio*) and the poorest among them, the grave-diggers, who often earned their living by trade or handicrafts, were excused the *collatio lustralis*. Constantius II, however, refused a petition from the Council of Ariminum in 359 that the clergy should be excused the land tax and quickly withdrew the immunity which he granted on the request of the same council to the lands corporately owned by the churches. Bishops were exempted from the jurisdiction of the secular courts in criminal cases and could be tried by councils of their fellow bishops only. The clergy were placed under the jurisdiction of their bishops in criminal cases.

In doctrinal matters Constantine II and his brother faced very different situations. In the west, where the term *consubstantialis* was traditional, the creed of Nicaea commanded almost unanimous assent and indeed devotion, and one of Constantine II's first actions was to release Athanasius, its great champion, from his exile at Trier and to send him back to the east, where he entered Alexandria in triumph on 28 October 338. In the east, on the other hand, opinion was greatly divided and most bishops who had any knowledge of theology were bitterly opposed to the Nicene formula. There was a strong party of Arians, but a still larger body which, while rejecting Arius' views, still objected to the heretical and unscriptural term *homoousios*, 'of one substance'. They were divided into many schools of thought, some willing to stomach *homoiousios*, 'of like substance', a difference of one *iota* which nevertheless marked a radical difference in theology. Constantius naturally followed the view of his theologians, in particular of Eusebius, formerly bishop of Nicomedia and now, contrary to the Nicene canon, of Constantinople.

One of the main objectives of the anti-Nicene group was to unseat Athanasius. By accepting restoration by the emperor when he had been condemned by a council of bishops Athanasius had taken a false step, and Eusebius and his friends took advantage of this to declare him deposed and elect a new bishop of Alexandria, Gregory, who was installed with the aid of imperial troops. Athanasius fled to Italy and appealed to Pope Julius, who took up his case and asked the eastern bishops to send representatives to Rome to bring their charges against Athanasius. The eastern bishops denied the pope's jurisdiction and Julius in 340 tried the case in their absence and declared Athanasius innocent. The eastern bishops now held a series of councils in which they endeavoured to hammer out a creed which would satisfactorily express their views. Meanwhile the pope persuaded Constans to bring pressure on his brother to hold a general council of the whole church to settle Athanasius' case. In 342 or 343 (the date is disputable) a council was summoned to Sardica, a city on the eastern border of Constans' dominions, but it never met as one body. The western delegation insisted that Athanasius should be invited as a member of the council, the eastern that he should be summoned as an accused person. The westerners duly acquitted Athanasius at Sardica and issued a number of canons conferring an appellate jurisdiction on the pope. The easterners met at Adrianople and condemned Athanasius and also issued a new creed. In 345, however, on Gregory's death, Constantius, under pressure from his brother, allowed Athanasius to return as bishop to Alexandria.

On 18 January 350 Constans was assassinated at Helena by his *comes sacrarum largitionum* Marcellinus, and Magnentius, the officer commanding the crack regiments of the Ioviani and Herculiani, was proclaimed Augustus. Shortly afterwards on 1 March Vetranio, the elderly master of the soldiers in Illyricum, was proclaimed Augustus by his troops and on 3 June Nepotianus, a nephew of Constantine the Great, was proclaimed at Rome. Magnentius rapidly dealt with Nepotianus and both he and Vetranio sent envoys to Constantius II requesting his recognition of their titles. It would appear that Vetranio's proclamation was collusive and designed to hold the loyalty of the Illyrian armies until Constantius could arrive on the scene from Antioch. When he arrived Vetranio allowed him to address the troops and they forthwith acclaimed him. Vetranio was pardoned and pensioned off. Constantius now had only Magnentius to deal with. To hold the east while he moved west he on 15 March appointed a Caesar, his nephew Gallus, who with his younger half-brother Julian was the only surviving member of Constantine's family. On 28 September 351 Constantius defeated Magnentius at Mursa. Magnentius retreated into Gaul where he was finally defeated and killed at Mons Seleuci (summer 353).

In Gaul Constantius received very unfavourable reports of Gallus. The young man was utterly inexperienced, having been brought up in seclusion in a remote Cappadocian fortress together with Julian. Both brothers had been trained for the church and received minor orders. Suddenly placed in supreme power, he proved an unbalanced character, violent and cruel. He suppressed a Jewish revolt in Galilee with unnecessary severity, destroying the city of Sepphoris, and in a bread shortage at Antioch he created a reign of terror over the decurions and allowed the provincial governor to be lynched. Constantius acted cautiously, changing his ministers one by one and gradually withdrawing his troops. Finally Gallus was brought under arrest to Pola and executed (winter 354).

Despite this discouraging experience Constantius on 6 November 355 proclaimed Gallus' half-brother Julian Caesar. He was assigned Gaul and Britain where, during the civil war, the barbarians had burst in and created havoc. Like Gallus, Julian was given limited powers. Constantius appointed his praetorian prefect, his master of the soldiers and all his ministers, and allowed him no *comes sacrarum largitionum* or *comes rei privatae*. For cash he was dependent on Constantius' treasury and in fact he received very inadequate supplies.

Julian proved a complete contrast to his half-brother. By sharing their hardships and dangers he made himself the idol of the troops, and he became overnight a brilliant general, defeating the German invaders in several battles and successfully rounding them up and pushing them back behind the Rhine, where they were glad to observe the peace and contribute recruits to the Roman army. He also proved a conscientious and able administrator and financier. He refused to sign the supplementary indiction which Florentius, his praetorian prefect, declared was necessary and by cutting down unnecessary expenditure and reforming the revenue collection succeeded during his five years as Caesar in reducing the rate of tax from twenty-five to seven *solidi* per *caput*.

Constantius II, though a well-meaning and conscientious man, was weak, timid and suspicious. He was dominated by ministers, courtiers and favourites, especially by Eusebius, his chief eunuch (*praepositus sacri cubiculi*). After Magnentius' revolt he lived in fear of conspiracies and rebellions, and his fears were exploited by his court, who profited greatly by grants of land and money from the property of condemned traitors, real or supposed. The supporters of Magnentius were mercilessly hunted down and new plots constantly reported. In this sinister work the *curiosi* or inspectors of the post appointed from the *agentes in rebus* played a prominent role, and the corps has obtained an evil reputation, which it does not deserve, as a kind of secret police.

In one instance the suspicions of Constantius almost had disastrous results. After Magnentius' defeat he had appointed as master of the soldiers in Gaul Silvanus, a Frankish officer, who had deserted Magnentius at the battle of Mursa with the regiment of the guard which he commanded. An informer forged a treasonable letter over Silvanus' name and produced it to the emperor. The Frankish officers at the court protested that Silvanus was innocent, but that if he got wind of the emperor's suspicion he might well rebel in self-defence, and asked that he be honourably recalled. Nevertheless Apodemius, a notorious *agens in rebus*, was sent to summon him to court, and the predicted result followed. Silvanus, after thinking of taking refuge with his tribesmen, decided that they would surrender him to the emperor or kill him and appealed to his Roman troops, who proclaimed him Augustus. The position was now very dangerous and Constantius decided to try guile. Ursicinus, master of the soldiers in the East, who had been recalled to court, was ordered to proceed to Cologne and to pretend to Silvanus that the news of his revolt had not yet reached the emperor and that he had been sent to replace him in the ordinary course. Silvanus, who had no imperial ambitions, fell into the trap and was arrested and executed.

The rebellion was thus repressed without fighting, but it need never have occurred.

Constantius desired to keep taxation down and enacted that supplementary indictions were not to be levied by the praetorian prefects or by lower authorities without his signature, but he was extravagant and lax in controlling expenditure. He was lavish in bestowing state lands on his *entourage*, and allowed the domestic personnel of the palace and the palatine ministries to swell in numbers inordinately, and increased their emoluments. As a result, taxation continued to rise.

Having reconquered the west, Constantius was able to fulfil his long-cherished ambition of restoring unity to the church. He summoned councils of bishops in Gaul and Italy, which obediently condemned Athanasius. He eventually wore down the resistance of his chief champions, Pope Liberius and Bishop Hosius, by sentences of exile. On 6 February 356 Athanasius was expelled from Alexandria for the third time and an Arian, George, was forcibly installed in his place. Finally in 359 Constantius called a general council of the western bishops to Ariminum. Taurus, the praetorian prefect of Italy, who presided, was instructed not to let the bishops disperse until they had signed a creed acceptable to the emperor, and at length the bishops gave in. Simultaneously an eastern council was held at Seleucia on the Calycadnus, which signed a similar creed, and shortly afterwards a small council at Constantinople confirmed the work of Ariminum and Seleucia.

Constantius' ecclesiastical policy has been judged by the writings of Athanasius and Hilary of Poitiers, his leading opponents, and posterity has condemned him as a tyrant who imposed his heretical views on the church. But he acted correctly according to the standards of the time. It was the duty of the emperor to ensure that the church was united in the true faith, and some measure of compulsion was inevitable. Constantius was not to know which version of the faith would in the end be accepted as true, and accepted the best theological advice available to him.

Julian's victories and growing popularity could not but disturb Constantius' suspicious mind and in the winter of 359–60 he dispatched a notary to Gaul, ordering Julian to send to the eastern front four of his best regiments and three hundred men from each of his other units. Julian announced the emperor's orders to the army and a mutiny ensued. They were already discontented that Constantius had sent them no money pay or donatives during Julian's reign. They strongly objected to leaving their homelands to be ravaged by the Germans and going to the distant east, and they were devoted to their leader who they no doubt rightly suspected was destined for Gallus' fate. In February 360 they proclaimed Julian Augustus and after a brief hesitation he accepted the title. He wrote to his uncle explaining the situation and offering to him what troops he could spare. He only asked the right to nominate his own ministers, except for the praetorian prefect, whose choice he left to Constantius. But Constantius refused all compromise. Julian marched east with lightning speed and had already reached Naissus (Nish) when news came that Constantius, proceeding slowly westward from Antioch, had died at Mopsucrene in Cilicia (3 November 361). Like his father, Constantius was baptized on his deathbed.

As sole Augustus, Julian could now put into action his religious views, which he had only made public after his proclamation. From childhood he had been passionately devoted to Greek literature and to the civilization of which it was the expression. He had detested the uncouth and illiterate scriptures which he had been forced to learn and their condemnation of all that he held good and beautiful. He had loathed his uncle, his father's murderer, and the religion which he professed. As a young man he had been allowed to attend the courses of the professors of rhetoric and philosophy at Athens, who were nearly all pagans, and he had conceived a profound devotion for the philosopher Maximus, who was noted for his miracles. Julian's religion was a mixture, common in that age, of philosophy, antiquarianism and superstition. He was philosophically a pantheist who believed that the divinity infused all nature, finding its highest symbol in the sun. At the same time he regarded all pagan rites and myths as divinely inspired allegories, and he believed implicitly in the oracles and in the miraculous powers of the great philosophers. Like many serious pagans of the age, he was an ascetic. He was scrupulously faithful to his wife, he refused the elaborate banquets which his uncle had carefully prescribed for the Caesar's table and contented himself with a private soldier's rations. He slept little, devoting many hours of the night to reading and meditation. He boasted proudly of the lice that swarmed in his uncombed philosophic beard.

Julian promptly revoked the laws against sacrifice, reopened the temples and returned their confiscated lands to them. He ordered that those temples which had been demolished should be rebuilt at the expense of those who had pulled them down. As no law had authorized the destruction of temples, this measure was legally justified, but caused some hardship to harmless citizens who had built themselves houses from the stones taken from temples and had either to pull their houses down and re-erect the temples or pay the heavy cost of new temples. Julian also naturally encouraged paganism by giving offices and titles to his co-religionists, and thereby produced a crop of apostasies. He devoted special attention to the army, frequently sacrificing hecatombs of oxen and feeding men with their meat, and placing altars at the pay-desks and encouraging the men to offer incense when they received their pay. Following Maximin's lead he appointed civic and provincial high priests. Several of his letters survive which give these pagan clergy instructions and advice: they are to lead exemplary and sober lives, never attending the theatre or the games; they are to maintain their dignity in face of the provincial governors; above all, they are to copy the Christians by organizing charity for the poor and strangers. Julian provided foodstuffs for the purpose from the imperial granaries. The allowance for the high priests of Galatia was 60,000 *sextarii* of wine and 30,000 *modii* of corn. He also urged the high priests to exhort wealthy pagans and pagan villages to contribute.

Though he cannot have approved of the Jews, who were as atheistic as the Christians, he favoured them as enemies of Christianity. He remitted the levies of gold to which they had been subjected, and made preparations for rebuilding the temple at Jerusalem.

He naturally cancelled the privileges fiscal, judicial and curial of the clergy, and stopped the government grants to the churches which Constantine had initiated, but he did not persecute. He proclaimed full toleration for all religions, thereby revoking the penal laws against heretics, and took malicious pleasure in the disputes which ensued.

This sudden reversal of policy naturally provoked sporadic disorders, and it must be admitted that Julian was not entirely impartial in punishing them. When the Alexandrians rose and lynched their hated bishop George, he merely wrote them a letter of mild rebuke: when the people of Caesarea in Cappadocia contumaciously demolished their one surviving temple, he imposed the poll tax on the whole urban population and enrolled the clergy in the provincial office, the lowest and very unpopular grade of the civil service. He imposed a severe fine on the church of Edessa for the destruction of a heretical conventicle. When the citizens of the strongly pagan city of Gaza lynched the men responsible for the destruction of a temple, he cashiered the provincial governor for his severity to the rioters.

One measure of Julian's excited not only the furious indignation of most Christians, but also the criticism of moderate pagans like Ammianus. He forbade Christians to be teachers of grammar and rhetoric, contemptuously recommending them 'to go off to their churches and expound Matthew and Luke'. His position was logical enough; a teacher should believe in what he teaches and a Christian could not honestly expound the stories of the pagan gods in Homer and Virgil. A small minority of Christians held the same view, but to the vast majority the traditional classical education was the passport to professional and official advancement and to cultivated society. Christian parents, if faced with the alternative of denying their children a classical education or of exposing them to the propaganda of pagan teachers, would certainly choose the latter, and the leaders of the church justifiably feared the wholesale apostasy of the younger generation. Two Christian scholars endeavoured to solve the problem by transposing the Scriptures into classical modes, rewriting them in the form of Homeric epics, Pindaric odes, Attic tragedies and comedies and Platonic dialogues; but their labour was wasted. Christians returned to the genuine pagan classics as soon as Julian was dead.

As Augustus Julian was as careful and hard-working an administrator as he had been as Caesar. He conducted a great purge of the palace staff and drastically reduced the numbers of the notaries, *agentes in rebus*, and *domestici et protectores*, favoured corps which had swollen unduly under Constantius II. He strictly regulated the issue of warrants for the public post, which was a heavy burden on the provincials. He restored to the cities the lands and taxes which provided their revenue and which his predecessors had confiscated. He brought the city councils up to strength, cancelling exemptions from membership.

His main preoccupation, however, was preparation for his projected Persian campaign. We are not told what his objectives were. A demonstration of strength was desirable in order to bring the long-drawn war to a conclusion with a favourable peace. But Julian was perhaps fired with greater ambitions of rivalling Alexander the Great. He collected the largest army which the Roman empire ever mustered for a single operation, 65,000 men, marched them down the Euphrates and defeated the Persian army at Ctesiphon, the capital. He did not, however, attempt to besiege the city and the Persians refused another battle, resorting to harassing tactics. Julian endeavoured to make his way home up the Tigris towards Armenia, where he had left a relieving force, but progress was slow and difficult and supplies ran short. The enemy constantly harassed the retreating army and in one of the engagements Julian was fatally wounded (26 June 363).

It is generally assumed by modern historians that Julian's pagan reaction was foredoomed to failure. In the fifty years since Constantine's conversion Christianity, it is true, had made much progress. Many of the new aristocracy were Christians by upbringing or conformed to the religion of the court, and the army seems to have accepted the official religion. But the old Roman aristocracy was still solidly pagan and so was the bulk of the educated classes. Paganism indeed showed a surprising vitality and hopes of a restoration of the old gods were still cherished a century later. Many of the converts, moreover, were not reliable; a number of the new nobility apostatized under Julian, and the army, Julian claimed and Gregory Nazianzen admitted, promptly returned to the old gods: which was not surprising, as the bulk of the men were drawn from the peasantry or from the barbarians, both of whom were still predominantly pagan. Contemporary Christian pamphleteers like Gregory Nazianzen betray not only hatred but fear of the emperor. What they professed to fear was that Julian on his return from Persia would start a persecution. But Julian was too intelligent to adopt such a policy; what they had more to fear was that he would continue his subtle campaign of propaganda and social pressure. In the fifteen months of his reign he achieved much. If after a victory over Persia, he had enjoyed a prosperous reign of thirty years, it seems possible that he could have reached his objective.

VI

The House of Valentinian

With Julian's death the house of Constantine became extinct and Julian had nominated no successor. A meeting of the generals and civilian ministers was hastily called and a division soon became apparent between the generals appointed by Constantius and those whom Julian had promoted. The two groups agreed to offer the crown to Salutius Secundus, the praetorian prefect, an elderly pagan who was generally respected. On his refusal they compromised on a nonentity, Jovian, the senior member of the corps of *domestici* and the son of a popular *comes domesticorum*. He was in his early thirties, a Pannonian and a Christian. Anxious to extricate his army and to establish his position at home, Jovian hastily signed a very unfavourable peace with Persia whereby he surrendered not only the satrapies across the Tigris conquered by Diocletian but the important frontier cities of Nisibis and Singara as well. On 17 February 364 he died at Ancyra in Galatia.

Once again the civil and military leaders met at Nicaea. The claims of a relative of Jovian, Januarius, who was *comes rei militaris* in Thrace, was canvassed, and Equitius, another Pannonian recently promoted *comes rei militaris*, was also proposed. These candidates were, however, rejected as too boorish, and the choice of the council fell on yet another Pannonian, Valentinian, a tribune of the *scholae*. Valentinian was acclaimed on 26 February by the army, which demanded that he appoint a colleague, and a month later he nominated his younger brother Valens to rule the eastern parts.

BIBLIOGRAPHY. The main narrative source is still Ammianus Marcellinus down to 378, and thereafter Zosimus again. For ecclesiastical affairs the three ecclesiastical historians, Socrates, Sozomen and Theodoret continue, and for western affairs Sulpicius Severus becomes important. The speeches of Themistius and Libanius give a valuable commentary on political and social affairs. For the election of Damasus and the subsequent disorders we have a very interesting file of letters in the *Collectio Avellana*. The Letters of Ambrose are important for the relations of church and state.

The brothers were sons of Gratian, a peasant who had risen from the ranks to be *comes rei militaris*, and were uncultivated military men. Valentinian showed a positive hostility to men of wealth and culture, and both were solicitous for the welfare of the lower classes. Valentinian was an able general, his brother had less talent, but both were conscientious administrators and Valens in particular showed his peasant origin in his careful and even parsimonious finance. Valentinian was a man of violent temper, prone to hasty decisions, and had an excessive confidence in his own judgment. His choice of ministers was often bad, but he placed implicit confidence in them. Valens was more cautious but as obstinate, and lacking in self-confidence. His rule was early challenged by a pretender, Procopius, a relative of Julian, and though he quickly suppressed the rebellion, he remained nervous and suspicious of possible pretenders.

Both the brothers were earnest Christians. Valentinian had even offered to resign his commission rather than participate in pagan rites under Julian. Their religious policy was quite different. Jovian had proclaimed toleration of paganism and all the sects of Christianity, and Valentinian and Valens did the same. The elder brother observed the edict both in letter and spirit. He refused to intervene in doctrinal controversy. On being asked to convoke a council on the faith, he replied: 'It is not right that I, a layman, should meddle in such matters. The bishops, whose business it is, may meet of their own accord if they wish.'[1] Magic and Manichaeism, which were reprobated by pagans and Christians alike, were banned, but the old Roman forms of divination were expressly permitted, and nocturnal sacrifices, normally forbidden as being used for magical purposes, were, on the request of Agorius Praetextatus, the pagan proconsul of Achaea, authorized in that province, where they formed part of the ancient cults of the mysteries.

Valens was tolerant of paganism but felt it his duty to suppress heresy. Since the official orthodoxy was the faith proclaimed by the councils of Ariminum, Seleucia and Constantinople, he ordered the banishment of all bishops who had been exiled by Constantius II and restored by Julian. Of the champions of Nicaea only Athanasius, who, having been allowed to return by Julian had subsequently been exiled by him and restored by Jovian, was allowed to retain his see. In 371 Valens instituted a regular persecution of surviving homoousians and in 373 he deposed Peter, Athanasius' brother, who had succeeded him as bishop of Alexandria, and deported eleven bishops who supported him.

[1] Sozomen, *Hist. Eccl.* VI. 7.

Valens' action, though correct, was unfortunate, since a substantial group of the eastern bishops, led by Basil of Caesarea, had by now worked out a reinterpretation of the term *homoousios*, which enabled them to accept the Nicene formula of faith, and were negotiating with Pope Damasus and Ambrose, bishop of Milan, for a renewal of communion with the western churches. As Basil's party won in the end, Valens, who dutifully maintained the orthodoxy of the day, has been, like Constantius II, condemned by the tradition of the church as a heretical persecutor.

Valentinian I showed a curious interest in the official precedence in the senate and consistory. His object was probably to fit the more recent palatine and military offices into the scheme, which was based on the offices normally held by senators. The list was headed by the ordinary consuls and ex-consuls followed by patricians. Next came the praetorian and urban prefects, or ex-prefects, with whom were equated the *magistri militum*. These were followed by the *comites consistoriani*, that is the quaestor, master of the offices, *comes sacrarum largitionum* and *comes rei privatae*. All these grades came to bear, at first unofficially and later officially, the title of *illustres*. The next grade was that of proconsuls and the next that of vicars. With these were equated *comites rei militaris*, *duces* and certain minor palatine officers. These came to be styled as *spectabiles*. Next came consulars of provinces, who were senators and therefore held the title of *clarissimi*, and finally *praesides* and *rationales*, who were not yet accorded senatorial rank and who were styled *perfectissimi*.

An interesting attempt to protect the poor was the institution of *defensores plebis*, or *civitatis*, in all the cities of the empire. Their function was to protect the lower classes from the extortion of officials and in general from the injuries of the powerful. They were armed with powers of jurisdiction in minor civil cases. They were to be selected by the praetorian prefects and their names to be personally approved by the emperor. They were to be drawn from ex-provincial governors, from retired *agentes in rebus* and other palatine civil servants and from barristers. They were not to be drawn from the officials of the praetorian prefects, vicars or governors, who were the oppressors of the poor, nor from decurions, who were probably excluded on the same ground. *Defensores* proved useful in providing inexpensive justice for the poor, but it may be doubted whether they otherwise fulfilled the role assigned to them.

Another reform was the transfer of the collection of the taxes and the superintendence of the post from the decurions to *honorati*—that is retired provincial governors and *comites* and holders of equivalent honorary rank—and to retired civil servants. The object of this reform was to secure more reliable collectors and superintendents. It proved abortive as the classes designated successfully evaded service and decurions were soon appointed again. If they were not individually reliable, their deficits were guaranteed by the council which nominated them.

Both brothers are said by Ammianus to have been careful and economical financiers. Valens, we are told by Themistius, not only stopped the indiction from increasing yearly, as it had done for the last forty years, but actually reduced it. Valentinian abolished the *tributum capitis*, which bore particularly hardly on the peasantry, in Illyricum, but he allowed his praetorian prefect, Petronius Probus, to use the most ruthless methods in extorting the land tax in the same area. Both brothers tried to increase the yield of the gold mines, rounding up miners who had abandoned them for agriculture and collecting the *chysargyron* in gold only. The regular issue of silver coins fell off and ceased altogether under their successors. They naturally resumed the lands of the temples which Julian had restored, and they also resumed the civic lands and taxes which Julian had given back to the cities. Later, however, they allowed the cities to keep one-third in order to maintain their walls and other public buildings.

Valentinian and Valens both took much interest in the army: they reformed the mechanism of conscription so as to equalize the burden upon the landowners, and increased the grants of land made to veterans. Valens was active in suppressing the peculation of officers, whereby they defrauded the men of their rations, clothing and equipment and allowed the numbers of their units to fall below the establishment. Valentinian was a great builder of frontier forts. Both waged a number of wars. Valentinian had to restore order in Britain, which the barbarians had overrun, and to suppress the rebellion of a Moorish chieftain, Firmus, in Africa. He also waged many campaigns against the Alamanni on the upper Rhine and in 376 was faced with an invasion of the Quadi and Sarmatians on the upper Danube. Here, enraged by the insolent demeanour of the barbarian envoys, he had a stroke of apoplexy and died. He was succeeded by his elder son Gratian, whom he had already proclaimed Augustus in 367 and who was at this time in Gaul. Gratian was a virtuous and cultured young man and a keen sportsman. He could, according to a contemporary[1] 'have been filled

[1] *Epit. Caes.* xlvii, 4–6.

with every virtue if he had put his mind to the art of government, for which he was alien by temperament and training'. Valentinian's younger son, Valentinian II, who was living with his mother Justina in the neighbourhood, was now also proclaimed Augustus by his late father's ministers though he was only a child of four. Their object was apparently to secure the loyalty of the Illyrian army to the dynasty.

Valens meanwhile had waged a punitive war against the Tervingi, or Visigoths, on the lower Danube, who had furnished support to the pretender, Procopius. He had then moved to Antioch and conducted inconclusive operations in Armenia and negotiations with Persia in order to restore Roman nominees to the thrones of Armenia and Iberia.

In 376 Valens was faced with a momentous choice. During the past few years the Huns had been driving westwards, creating havoc and terror. The king of the Gruthungi, or Ostrogoths, in south Russia committed suicide in despair, and the king of the Visigoths, north of the lower Danube, when he tried to organize the defence of his kingdom, was abandoned by his people, who petitioned Valens for asylum within the empire, promising to serve in his army. Such a request was not unprecedented; under Constantine a large group of Sarmatians, 300,000 souls it was alleged, defeated by their rebellious subjects, had been received within the empire and settled under Roman prefects in small groups scattered all over the Balkans and Italy. Such transplanted barbarians were known as *laeti* and in return for their land had to furnish recruits. Valens was attracted by the prospect of receiving such a large addition to the armed forces, which would enable him to commute the Roman conscripts for gold and thus increase his revenue as well. He granted permission and the Visigoths were ferried across the river.

It was evidently Valens' intention to deal with the Visigoths as Constantine had dealt with the Sarmatians. He enlisted many young Goths under Roman officers in the army of the East and promised deserted lands in Thrace to the remainder. But the situation was mismanaged: the Goths were not promptly dispersed and adequate supplies were not available, while the local *comes* and *dux* exploited the refugees by selling them food at exorbitant prices and buying their children as slaves in exchange. Disorders broke out, and in the confusion the Ostrogoths also managed to cross the Danube. The united tribes are said to have numbered 200,000.

Valens, who was at Antioch, marched west, reaching Constantinople on 30 May 378. Gratian was sending reinforcements to assist his uncle, but Valens, over-confident, joined battle with the Goths at Adrianople without awaiting them, and was utterly defeated and killed (9 August 378). Gratian appointed a Spaniard, Theodosius, son of a distinguished general, and himself a general of some experience despite his youth—he was only thirty-two—to take charge of the Gothic war, and on 19 January 379 proclaimed him Augustus at Sirmium, assigning to him the eastern parts and the two dioceses of Dacia and Macedonia.

It is impossible from our meagre sources to follow the confused fighting that followed. After over three years of indecisive warfare both sides were ready to make peace. The Ostrogoths were expelled from the empire, becoming subjects of the Huns. With the Visigoths Theodosius, on 3 October 382, made a treaty giving them lands between the Lower Danube and the Balkans in return for military service. This settlement differed in one vital point from that which Constantine made with the Sarmatians. The Goths were not dispersed under Roman prefects but allowed to retain their tribal cohesion under their own chieftain. In technical terms they were not *laeti*, subjects of the empire, but *foederati*, a foreign state bound by treaty to Rome.

A few years later the quarrel with Persia over Armenia was at last settled by partitioning the country. The Persians got the lion's share but the six satrapies acquired by Rome were strategically valuable, since they filled in the deep re-entrant between the upper Euphrates and the Tigris. These Armenian satrapies were not assimilated to the Roman provincial system, but retained their own law and were ruled by their hereditary satraps, who commanded the local levies.

Eventually Gratian forfeited the respect of the armies and when a Spanish officer, Magnus Maximus, was proclaimed emperor by the army in Britain and invaded Gaul, he was deserted by his troops and killed on 15 August 383. Maximus receives a good character from two of his subjects, Sulpicius Severus and Orosius, 'a vigorous and honest man, worthy to be Augustus if he had not risen by usurpation contrary to his own oath of allegiance'.[1] For the moment he contented himself with the Gauls and was in 384 recognized as Augustus by Valentinian II, or rather by his mother, Justina, who continued to rule Italy and Illyricum, and by Theodosius. In 387, however, Maximus invaded Italy. Valentinian and Justina took refuge at Thessalonica and appealed to Theodosius for aid. Next year Theodosius marched west and defeated and killed Maximus. He stayed three years in the west, leaving

[1] Orosius VII. xxxiv, 9, Sulp. Sev. *Dial.* III, 11.

the east under the nominal rule of his elder son, Arcadius, whom he proclaimed as Augustus in 383, and establishing Valentinian at Trier. He returned to Constantinople in 391 but next year Valentinian quarrelled with Arbogast, his Frankish *magister militum,* whose assumption of authority he resented. Arbogast accordingly secured his death and had proclaimed Augustus the *magister scrinii,* Eugenius. In 394 Theodosius again marched west and defeated and killed Eugenius (6 September). The house of Valentinian was now extinct and the empire reunited under Theodosius: five months later he died (17 January 395), leaving Arcadius to rule the east, and his other son, Honorius, proclaimed Augustus in 393, to rule the west.

In religious affairs Gratian had been at first neutral. As sole emperor in 378 he issued an edict of toleration, but acceded to a request of the pope to lend the aid of the secular arm to compel recalcitrant bishops to submit to the jurisdiction of the Roman see. Next year he revoked the edict of toleration, probably under the influence of Ambrose, bishop of Milan, and revived the persecution of heretics.

From 374 to 397 Ambrose played a dominating role in the affairs of both church and state. He was the son of a praetorian prefect and was actually consular of Aemilia when he was elected bishop of Milan by popular acclamation. He was temperamentally a strong-minded—not to say domineering—character, and his self-confidence was enhanced by his social rank as a senator; bishops in that period usually came from much humbler classes of society. He interfered without any canonical justification whatever in ecclesiastical disputes as far afield as Pannonia and even Dacia, and claimed to dictate its policy to the government in affairs of religion and morals. When Theodosius punished the bishop of Callinicum in Mesopotamia for burning down a Jewish synagogue, Ambrose by spiritual terrors compelled the emperor to retract his decree. Again, when Theodosius massacred the population of Thessalonica for lynching his *magister militum,* Butharic, Ambrose refused him communion until he did penance. It seems likely that Theodosius' campaign against paganism was also inspired by Ambrose.

Maximus' reign is chiefly notable for his persecution of Priscillian, a Spanish heretic, and his followers. Priscillian and several others were executed, technically on charges of magic but actually for their religious beliefs, and a general persecution was only averted by the protests of Martin, bishop of Tours.

Justina, who was an Arian, caused her son Valentinian II to issue a law declaring the faith of the Ariminum orthodox, and to demand the use of a church in Milan for the Arians. She was, however, forced to give way to Ambrose, who organized passive resistance among the Catholics.

Theodosius was by upbringing a convinced adherent of the Nicene Creed, and by temperament bigoted and authoritarian. A year after his accession he issued an edict (27 February 380) declaring the doctrines of Damasus of Rome and Peter of Alexandria to be the true Catholic faith, and a year later (10 January 381) he ordered that all churches should be surrendered to bishops who held the Catholic faith as he defined it. Having by state action imposed on the church his own beliefs, he summoned a council of 150 bishops to Constantinople (May 381). They naturally confirmed the emperor's decisions and issued two canons on the organization of the church, one giving a primacy of honour second only to Rome to the see of Constantinople, the new Rome, and the other declaring that in Egypt the bishop of Alexandria should have supreme authority and that in the other civil dioceses of the eastern parts the bishops of each diocese should manage their own affairs without external interference. The council was instructed by the emperor to draw up a list of suitable candidates, from whom he could choose the new bishop of Constantinople, and Theodosius selected Nectarius, a pious but as yet unbaptized senator.

Theodosius was a fanatical persecutor of heretics, issuing no less than eighteen penal laws against them. It was fortunate for his posthumous fame that his views happened to coincide with those of the majority of the eastern bishops, who had by now become reconciled to the *homoousion*. Arianism now rapidly dwindled in importance and in fact only survived on any large scale among the east German tribes. The Visigoths had been converted under Constantius, while a form of Arianism was the official faith of the empire, and they clung to the doctrine which they had learned from their first bishop, Ulphilas, who had translated the Scriptures into Gothic. The Ostrogoths, Vandals, Burgundians and other tribes seem to have derived their Christian beliefs from the Visigoths.

The altar of Victory which Constantius II had removed from the senate house had naturally been restored by Julian, and had been left in position by the tolerant Valentinian I. In 381 Gratian, under the influence of Ambrose, dropped the traditional pagan title of Pontifex Maximus, removed the altar of Victory once more and confiscated the funds of the Vestal Virgins and other ancient Roman priesthoods. The senate next year petitioned him to reverse this decision, but Pope

Damasus got up a counter-petition of Christian senators, who were, he declared, in a majority, and with Ambrose's moral support Gratian held to his decision. In 384 another petition was sent by Symmachus, prefect of the city, to Valentinian II, but Ambrose drew up a rebuttal of it and Valentinian decided to uphold his brother's decision.

Theodosius issued severe laws in 381 and 385 against sacrifice for the purpose of divination, and the effect seems to have been to prohibit all sacrifices, though prayers and offerings of incense continued. No general law for the demolition of temples was issued, but petitions for the destruction of individual temples, or their conversion to churches, were favourably received and the government connived at Christian fanatics who destroyed temples without authorization. There was fighting in many cities between Christians and pagans. At Apamea the bishop, Marcellus, who was a zealous destroyer of temples, using hired gladiators and Roman troops to overcome local resistance, was killed in one of his expeditions. At Alexandria the pagans, led by a spirited philosopher, Olympius, seized the Serapeum and from it conducted raids on the Christians, but an imperial order was obtained to demolish all the temples of Alexandria and pagan resistance collapsed.

It was not till 391, two years after Maximus' defeat, that Theodosius, who was then residing in Milan, formally ordered all the temples to be closed and abolished all forms of pagan cult. It may be suspected that this edict was due to the influence of the bishop of Milan. Eugenius, who was a nominal Christian, after some hesitation yielded to the pleas of the senate to restore the altar of Victory, and granted the lands of the Vestals to pagan senators. The pagan aristocracy of Rome, headed by Nicomachus Flavianus, the praetorian prefect of Italy, rallied enthusiastically to his cause. Flavianus and Arbogast the *magister militum*, who was also a pagan, boasted that after defeating Theodosius they would stable their horses in the churches. Christian authors in alarm issued pamphlets protesting against a pagan revival. The hopes of the pagans were dashed and the fears of the Christians were dispelled by Theodosius' victory.

During the two generations which followed Constantine's death, the proportion of barbarians, particularly Germans, who rose to high command in the army steadily increased. By Gratian's reign most of the *magistri militum* in the west were Franks and Alamans and in the east under Theodosius we know of two Goths, a Vandal, two other Germans, and two Persians, as against five Romans. The imperial guard, the *scholae*, were at this period largely recruited from Germans and it was mainly from officers of the guards that the *comites rei militaris* and *magistri militum* were chosen. Germans also were found among the *duces*, but Romans were more numerous in this grade. The military career was quite separate from the civil and there was often tension between the military officers, who were barbarians or peasants who had risen from the ranks, and the civil ministers.

In the civil ministries there was a marked contrast between the eastern and western parts. In the west the old senatorial aristocracy came more and more to the fore from Constantine's day onwards. Even under Valentinian I, who disliked senators, the great noble Petronius Probus, head of the Anician house, served many years as praetorian prefect of Italy, Africa and Illyricum and under Valentinian's successors he held three more prefectures. In the east, on the other hand, where there was no old aristocracy, new men had the field to themselves and many men of quite humble origins, imperial notaries and other civil servants and barristers, rose to the highest offices. It was not until the end of the fourth century that a new aristocracy began to form in the east from the sons and grandsons of men promoted under Constantine and his sons.

By the end of the fourth century not only *magistri militum* but *comites rei militaris* and *duces* ranked as senators and on the civilian side not only the praetorian and urban prefects, proconsuls and vicars and consulars of provinces but even *praesides*. The promotion of new men thus vastly expanded the senatorial order, all the more so as most posts were held for a brief period only, provincial governorships for about a year, the higher posts for two or three years as a rule. The senate was further increased by numerous grants of titular offices.

Many of the new senators came from the curial order and the flow of decurions into the senatorial order seriously weakened the city councils. The imperial government fought this movement, but with little success. Valentinian and Valens introduced the rule that not all sons of senators, but only those born after their fathers' promotion, should henceforth rank as senators, and insisted that no decurion should be admitted to the senate unless he had one son already, whom he had to leave in his city council. Theodosius went further and enacted that decurions who entered the senate were to retain their administrative and financial obligations to their native cities. This rule was difficult to enforce, as the expenses of senatorial rank were heavy and few decurions could bear both burdens simultaneously.

The growth of the clergy also depleted the city councils. Both Valentinian and Valens and Theodosius tried to combat this danger by insisting on the rule that curial ordinands must surrender their property to their sons, or if they had no sons, two-thirds of it to a relative or to the council itself. The rule was frequently disobeyed and the emperors had often to condone past breaches of it wholesale.

VII

The House of Theodosius

Both the sons of Theodosius the Great were young when they succeeded their father, Arcadius being seventeen or eighteen, Honorius only ten. Both proved feeble and lazy characters when they grew up. The government was as a result exercised in their name by others. In the west the actual ruler was for thirteen years the Vandal general Stilicho, who was in the last months of Theodosius' reign in supreme command of the bulk of the field army of the whole empire, both the eastern force which had subdued Eugenius and the defeated army of the west. He had married Serena, a niece of Theodosius, and had been appointed guardian of both his sons by the dying emperor. In the west Stilicho strengthened his position by centralizing the army command. He held both the posts

BIBLIOGRAPHY. For the first part of the period covered by this chapter there is a detailed study, E. Demougeot, *De l'unité à la division de l'empire Romain* (Paris, 1951), and for the relations of the empire with the Huns, E. A. Thompson, *A History of Attila and the Huns* (Oxford, 1948.)

The narrative of Zosimus continues down to 410. After this we possess only fragments of Olympiodorus of Thebes and Priscus of Panium, and are obliged to fall back on Orosius for western affairs (down to 417) and the ecclesiastical historians, Theodoret (down to 408), Sozomen (down to 425), and Socrates (down to 439). The ecclesiastical historians contain much purely secular matter. Church affairs are taken up again from 431 by Evagrius. The fall of John Chrysostom is recorded in detail in Palladius' *Dialogus*. The Acts of the Council of Ephesus (431) are published in full in E. Schwartz, *Acta Conciliorum Oecumenicorum* (Berlin and Leipzig, 1922), together with much official correspondence leading up to the council and following it. The Acts of the Second Council of Ephesus are translated from the Syriac in S. G. F. Perry, *The Second Council of Ephesus* (1881).

The *Notitia Dignitatum* was drawn up during this period. The poems of Claudian, the speeches, the letters and 'The Egyptian Tale' of Synesius contain much valuable historical information. For the ecclesiastical affairs of Africa Augustine's Letters are valuable, and for the condition of Asia Minor those of John Chrysostom. Salvian in his *De Gubernatione Dei* gives a vivid if exaggerated picture of the social evils of the west.

of *magister peditum* and *magister equitum praesentalis*, being styled *magister utriusque militiae*, and the other *magistri* were *de facto* if not *de iure* subordinate to him. All *comites rei militaris* and *duces* were put under his disposition and the chief clerks of their offices were supplied from the offices of the *praesentales*.

In the east, however, Stilicho's claims, based on the last words of Theodosius, were strongly resisted. Here the supreme power was at first wielded by the praetorian prefect of the East, Rufinus, a barrister from Aquitania, who had found high favour with Theodosius. The tension between the eastern and western parts was exploited by Alaric, recently elected king of the federate Visigoths in northern Thrace, who marched south and ravaged the neighbourhood of Constantinople. Rufinus persuaded him to turn west into Greece and Stilicho sent a large army to suppress him. This brought into the open two disputes between Stilicho and Rufinus. Rufinus demanded the return of the eastern troops which had suppressed Eugenius and claimed Illyricum (the dioceses of Dacia and Macedonia) as part of the eastern parts. Stilicho rather surprisingly yielded to both demands, but arranged that Gainas, the Gothic officer in charge of the returning eastern army, should kill Rufinus.

If he had hoped thereby to secure control of the east, Stilicho was disappointed. The man who succeeded to Rufinus' power was Eutropius, Arcadius' chief eunuch, and he proved as hostile to Stilicho's claims as Rufinus had been. When in 397 Stilicho sent a force by sea to round up Alaric in Greece, he was again ordered to withdraw, and Eutropius appointed Alaric *magister militum* of Illyricum. He also encouraged and gave moral support to Gildo, the *magister militum* in Africa, when he rebelled in 397, but Stilicho soon reduced Africa to obedience once more.

In 399 Gainas, who had been appointed one of the *magistri militum praesentales* in the east, put himself at the head of a rebellious body of Ostrogothic *laeti* and federates and demanded the execution of Eutropius. Eutropius was dismissed and killed but Gainas failed to make himself master of the east. A large number of his Goths whom he had brought into Constantinople were massacred by the townspeople and the reins of government were seized by Aurelian, who was appointed praetorian prefect. Aurelian was a son of Taurus, a man of humble origin who had been praetorian prefect and consul under Constantius II, and leader of a party among the aristocracy which wished to purge the high command and the army of Germans. For the moment he appointed as *magister militum* Fravitta, another Goth, who defeated Gainas and chased him out of the empire. Fravitta was shortly afterwards dismissed and for the next few years the generals were all Romans and control of the eastern parts rested in the hands of the praetorian prefects, Aurelian, followed in 405 by Anthemius, grandson of Philip, the sausage-seller's son, who had been consul under Constantius II.

In the west, meanwhile, Alaric, having sucked Illyricum dry, invaded Italy in 401. Stilicho managed to defeat him at Pollentia and Verona next year and to expel him from Italy, but did not attempt to crush the Visigoths completely. In 405 a mixed horde of Germans, mainly Ostrogoths, led by Radagaesus, poured into Italy. Stilicho was once more able to defeat the invaders at Faesulae and captured or killed vast numbers of them. Having fended off the barbarians, he next planned to establish his control over Illyricum and enrolled Alaric to help him, appointing him *magister militum* of Illyricum by anticipation. His plans were upset by another great barbarian invasion. In the winter of 406–07 swarms of Siling Vandals, Asding Vandals, Alans, Sueves and Burgundians swarmed over the Rhine, whose garrison had been depleted in order to reinforce the army of Italy, and created desolation in Gaul. What was in Roman eyes even more dangerous, the army of Britain proclaimed a usurper, Constantine, who crossed over to Gaul and tried to restore the situation. In the circumstances Stilicho decided to postpone his claims on Illyricum, but Alaric seized the opportunity to demand four thousand pounds of gold as compensation for his lost command. Stilicho bullied the senate into accepting Alaric's demand which, in the crucial situation, could not be resisted.

At this juncture Arcadius died (1 May 408), leaving as his heir his infant son Theodosius II, who had been proclaimed Augustus at his birth in 402, and both Honorius and Stilicho wished to seize the opportunity to assert their authority in the east. But Stilicho had by now lost Honorius' favour and become very unpopular with the aristocracy. His victories over Radagaesus and Alaric were forgotten and he was accused of collusion with the latter and of a plan to make his own son Eucherius Honorius' successor. The latter charge is certainly false and the former dubious. He had spared Alaric twice in Greece, in obedience to the orders of Arcadius. After the battle of Verona he may have allowed him to escape, hoping to use him, as he later did, but more probably was afraid to risk his forces in a desperate final struggle. Stilicho had also, by the favour he gave to Gothic and Hunnic federates, alienated the Roman troops, and Olympius, the master of the offices, was able to ferment a mutiny among them. All the holders of the high military and civic offices, who were Stilicho's men, were lynched, and Stilicho himself, though he might have resisted with the aid of his barbarian body-guard, surrendered and was executed.

The Roman troops next massacred the wives and children of the barbarian federates, and they promptly joined Alaric's Visigoths. Alaric demanded money and land for his tribesmen. Olympius haughtily refused but was helpless to resist him. Alaric marched on Rome and blockaded it, only relaxing his hold when the senate paid him 5,000 pounds of gold, 30,000 pounds of silver and 3,000 pounds of pepper, and promised to support his demands upon the emperor. Olympius still refused to treat and failed to take effective action. He fell from power and was succeeded as Honorius' chief minister by Jovius, the praetorian prefect of Italy. Jovius entered into negotiations with Alaric, but they again broke down. Alaric, losing patience, marched on Rome and compelled the senate to elect a rival emperor, Attalus, who duly appointed Alaric his *magister militum*. Attalus' rule was, however, not accepted in Africa, and Honorius, who had received reinforcements from the east, held out in Ravenna. Alaric deposed Attalus and entered once more into negotiations with Honorius. When these failed he again marched on Rome and captured and sacked it on 24 August 410.

The sack of Rome came as a terrible shock to Romans throughout the empire. In distant Bethlehem Jerome[1] cried: 'When the brightest light on the whole earth was extinguished, when the Roman empire was deprived of its head, when to speak more correctly, the whole world perished in one city, then "I was dumb with silence, I held my peace even from good, and my sorrow was stirred".' It had however little military significance. The next year Alaric died and in 412 his successor, his brother Athaulf, led the Visigoths, who had exhausted Italy, into Gaul. Here conditions were anarchic. The usurper Constantine had occupied Spain and put his son Constans as Caesar in charge of it. Next in 409 the Vandals, Alans and Sueves had invaded Spain. Constans had cashiered his *magister militum* Gerontius for his negligence, and Gerontius had proclaimed a rival emperor, Maximus, who defeated and killed Constans and besieged Constantine in Arles. The British and Armorican cities threw off the rule of the usurper and organized their own defence, and the Burgundians established themselves on the left bank of the Rhine. In 411 Constantius, a Roman from Sirmium who had been appointed *magister militum praesentalis* by Honorius, invaded Gaul with

[1] *Comm. in Ezech.* I, *praef.*

a powerful army and defeated both Constantine and Maximus, who were deserted by their troops in favour of the legitimate emperor. Another pretender, Jovinus, was now proclaimed by the Burgundians and Alans on the Rhine. Athaulf offered him the support of the Visigoths, but they quarrelled and Athaulf helped Constantius to subdue him.

The usurpers were now all eliminated, but the barbarians were still all at large in Gaul and Spain. The Burgundians were accepted as federates occupying the left bank of the middle Rhine, and after many quarrels the Visigoths also finally entered Roman service and under their king Wallia fought the other barbarians in Spain, almost exterminating the Siling Vandals and the Alans, whose remnants joined the Asding Vandals, who, with the Sueves, were penned into Gallaecia. This done, the Visigoths were withdrawn from Spain and settled as federates in Aquitania (418). Spain and Gaul were thus all more or less pacified and Britain was apparently brought back under Roman rule.

In the east, meanwhile, the government had been carried on by Anthemius, the praetorian prefect, who continued to hold the office until his death in 414. He appears to have been succeeded as chief minister by Helio, who became master of the offices in that year and held the post at least until 427, perhaps until 429. The little emperor, Theodosius II, was given a very strict and pious education by his elder sister Pulcheria, who was proclaimed Augusta in 414 and seems to have exercised much influence on the government of the empire. She continued to be powerful until the early 440s, though latterly her influence was rivalled by that of Eudocia, the wife whom she selected for Theodosius, the cultivated daughter of an Athenian philosopher. She was likewise proclaimed Augusta in 423.

The eastern empire during this period enjoyed a respite from major wars, being only troubled by the forays of the nomad tribes in Libya and upper Egypt and by the widespread raids of the Isaurians in southeastern Asia Minor. There was a brief war with Persia in 421–22 in which the Romans were victorious, and in the same year a Hunnic invasion of Thrace, after which it appears the eastern government promised to pay the Huns an annual subsidy of 300 pounds of gold.

On 8 February 421 Constantius, the *magister militum* or, as the commander-in-chief of the west was commonly from now onwards called, patrician, having married Galla Placidia, the half-sister of Honorius, was made his colleague as Augustus. He died the same year (2 September), but he and Placidia had a son, Valentinian, who, as Honorius had no children, was designated heir with the title of a *nobilissimus puer*. Placidia was at the same time proclaimed Augusta, but later she quarrelled with Honorius and withdrew with the little Valentinian to Constantinople. Thus when Honorius died on 15 August 423 there was no heir on the spot and Castinus, who had succeeded Constantius as *magister militum*, had John, the *primicerius* of the imperial notaries, proclaimed Augustus. Theodosius' government supported the little Valentinian's claims, and an expedition commanded by the Alan general Ardaburius defeated and killed John. Valentinian III was proclaimed Augustus at Rome on 23 October 423.

In 427 Boniface, *comes Africae*, was suspected of planning a revolt and recalled. He refused to obey and troops were dispatched to Africa to subdue him. Taking advantage of the confusion, the Vandals in 429 crossed the Straits of Gibraltar and ravaged the Mauretanian provinces. Galla Placidia hastily pardoned Boniface, but the united Roman troops, assisted by an expeditionary force from the east, were unable to withstand the Vandals, and in 435 the Mauretanias and Numidia were formally ceded to them. Meanwhile, by an obscure series of assassinations, mutinies and battles, Aetius, a Roman officer from Durostorum in Moesia, had succeeded in imposing himself on Galla Placidia, first as *magister equitum* in Gaul, then as second-in-command in Italy and finally in about 435 as commander-in-chief and patrician. He owed his success partly to his military talents but more to the fact that he had been a hostage for some years at the Hunnic court and formed a friendship with the king of the Huns; he was thus able to obtain large hordes of Hunnic troops from him at crucial moments. He ruled the west in Valentinian's name for twenty years and succeeded so long as he lived in keeping the barbarians in Gaul and Spain more or less in check, largely by means of his Huns. In 435 there was a peasant revolt in Gaul and both the Visigoths and the Burgundians took advantage of it to encroach. Next year the Burgundians were decimated by the Huns. Those who survived were a few years later transplanted to Savoy. Against the Visigoths Litorius, Aetius' commander, was less successful and he had to cede two cities to them. In 439 Gaiseric, king of the Vandals, captured Carthage and, after a war in which the western Romans were again assisted by the eastern, signed in 442 a treaty whereby he acquired the rich provinces of Africa Proconsularis and Byzacium and retroceded the exhausted provinces of Numidia and the Mauretanias to the empire. In the same year Britain was overrun by Saxons, but the Britons fought on, appealing in vain for aid to Aetius in or after 446, when he was consul for the third time.

Meanwhile in the east the Hunnic king Rua, complaining that the government of Constantinople was harbouring his rebel tribes, threatened to invade the empire (434). He died shortly afterwards and his successor Attila extorted a doubling of the subsidy, which became 700 pounds of gold per year. In 441, while a large eastern force was engaged in Africa, the Persian king attacked the empire. He was easily defeated, but Attila took advantage of the difficult situation to make further demands and, on failing to get satisfaction, crossed the Danube and destroyed a number of cities. Ultimately peace was bought by the empire in 443 at the price of an immediate payment of 6,000 pounds of gold and an annual subsidy of 2,100 of gold. In 447 Attila made a fresh invasion and only consented to make peace on condition that a strip of land along the south side of the Danube five days' journey in width should be evacuated by the Romans.

By this time the government of the eastern parts had got into the hands of Chrysaphius, one of the imperial eunuchs, who fomented a quarrel between Pulcheria and Eudocia and estranged Theodosius from both of them. He worked with Nomus, the master of the offices, who was apparently an able administrator. Chrysaphius tried to secure Attila's assassination, but the plot was given away by the Hunnic noble concerned and the Roman ambassadors who brought the money to reward him were exposed to Attila's wrath. Curiously enough, he did not exploit his opportunity but signed a relatively favourable treaty in which he promised to withdraw from the evacuated zone south of the Danube. He appeared to have decided that he could not bleed the eastern empire any more than he was already doing and turned his attention to the west. Here he was given an opportunity to intervene by the folly of Honoria, the sister of Valentinian III, who, furious at being made to marry a man she disliked, sent a letter with her signet ring to Attila appealing for his aid. He professed to take this as an offer of marriage, demanded half the empire as her dowry and, on receiving a refusal, marched westward into Gaul. Here he was met near Châlons by Aetius at the head of the Roman forces, together with the various federate barbarians of Gaul, the Visigoths, the Franks, Burgundians and Alans, and also the Armoricans from north of the Loire, who were by this time no longer under Roman rule. The Huns were defeated (451) and withdrew, but next year invaded and ravaged Italy. In 453 Attila died and the subject peoples of the Huns rose against them. The Hunnic empire dissolved.

During the fifty years that had elapsed since the death of Theodosius I the western empire had undergone some serious territorial losses. Africa Proconsularis and Byzacena, on which the corn supply of Rome depended, formed the independent kingdom of the Vandals; Britain and Armorica, that is, all Gaul north of the Loire, were no longer part of the empire. Within the remaining territory there were many enclaves occupied by barbarian tribes which were nominally in alliance with the empire and owed it military service, but which in fact were independent and often raided the neighbouring territory or conquered parts of it. The tribes included the Sueves in Gallaecia in north-west Spain, the Visigoths in Aquitania, the Burgundians in Savoy, the Franks on the lower Rhine and two groups of Alans at Valence and Orléans.

Even more serious were the losses in manpower. From the army lists of the *Notitia Dignitatum*, which in the west appear to date from the end of the reign of Honorius, it may be deduced that about half the regiments of the *comitatus* had perished in the civil wars at the end of Theodosius' reign and the barbarian invasions in that of Honorius. The *comitatus* had on paper been brought up to strength and perhaps increased and stood at about 115,000 men, but this had only been done by transferring large numbers of *limitanei* into it. About two-thirds of the losses were made good in this way. As a result some areas, notably Gaul and Africa, were virtually stripped of *limitanei*. In many areas the change was nominal only: the *limitanei* remained at their old stations or at any rate in their old provinces. Even in the reign of Theodosius the Great the proportion of barbarian federates to regular troops had already increased and by the time of Aetius federates were a majority, to judge by the composition of the army which fought Attila at Châlons.

The barbarian invasions also caused heavy losses of revenue. Not only were the taxes of such areas as Africa, Britain and Armorica lost in their entirety, but in the areas still under Roman control drastic remissions had to be made in view of the devastation that they had suffered from the barbarian invasions. In 413, when the Visigoths moved to Gaul, Honorius had to reduce the taxes of southern Italy to one-fifth of the existing figure, and when Numidia and Mauretania were evacuated by the Vandals and restored to the empire in 442 their taxes were reduced to one-eighth. Though the weight of the land tax was crushing the government was unable to feed its existing armies, much less to provide for much-needed reinforcements, and in 444 Valentinian III's government had to invent a new tax on trade, the *siliquaticum*, a payment of one-twenty-fourth on all sales, in the hope of replenishing its empty treasury.

The east by contrast had suffered little serious loss. Its Illyrican and Thracian provinces had, it is true, been severely ravaged, first by the Goths, later by the Huns, and brought in little revenue, but the rich lands of Asia Minor, Syria and Egypt were intact. The eastern government employed some barbarian federates but could raise adequate forces from its own subjects. The Balkan provinces continued to be good recruiting grounds and at the end of Theodosius II's reign eastern Asia Minor came to the fore. The government paid enormous sums in blackmail to Attila but showed no signs of financial exhaustion.

After the anti-barbarian reaction in the west which followed Stilicho's fall few Germans were employed as generals for the next fifty years and the commander-in-chief was always a Roman. The anti-barbarian movement in the east which followed the rebellion of Gainas had less lasting results. By 421 both the *magistri praesentales*, Areobindus and Ardaburius, were Germans, and twenty years later both were still Germans, Ardaburius having been succeeded by his son Aspar, who was still holding his command at the end of Theodosius II's reign. The *magister militum per Orientem* seems always to have been a Roman, but the generals in Thrace and Illyricum were frequently barbarians.

The praetorian prefecture was generally held by men of modest origins and administrative experience under Honorius, but under Valentinian III almost exclusively by grand nobles like Acilius Glabrio Faustus and Petronius Maximus, who often took office at an early age having held only one previous post. In the east on the other hand the prefecture was held either by the sons and grandsons of the new men of Constantius II's reign, men like Aurelian and Anthemius, or by new men. Both classes were expected to hold several posts and thus gained some experience before they attained to the prefecture. The result was that the finances of the eastern parts were more efficiently managed than those of the western. The young and inexperienced aristocratic prefects of the west could not control their officials and the latter's fees and perquisites grew inordinately and greatly increased the burden of taxation. These noble prefects were also lax in the grant of immunities to the wealthy taxpayers and in remissions of arrears, which mostly benefited the wealthy, since the humble citizen was compelled to pay promptly. In the east the officials were kept under control and remissions of arrears were sparingly granted, while the wealthy holders of immunities were compelled to refund a proportion of what they had gained in order to pay for Attila's subsidies.

In 438 the government of Theodosius II carried through a useful legal reform. A great part of the law was based on imperial constitutions, but there existed no official collection of them. In the reign of Diocletian a lawyer named Gregorius had published a private collection of constitutions ranging from the reign of Hadrian to 291, and four years later another lawyer, Hermogenianus, had published a supplement of subsequent legislation. These two private collections were generally recognized as authorititative, but since 295 nothing had been done. In 429 the eastern government, inspired it would seem by Antiochus, former quaestor and praetorian prefect, set up a commission to collect and publish all general laws from 312, when Constantine became senior Augustus, up to date. The resulting Theodosian Code was promulgated in the east on 15 February 438, and in the west on 23 December of the same year.

The western churches were in this period troubled by only one doctrinal controversy. Pelagius, a layman from Britain who delivered popular lectures in Rome, tended in his zeal to inculcate the rules of Christian morality to emphasize the importance of human will and to understress the necessity of divine grace for salvation. His views were well received in many western provinces, including his own, but excited opposition in Africa where, in 411, one of his disciples was condemned by a council held at Carthage. Pelagius himself, having migrated to Palestine on Alaric's sack of Rome, was attacked by one of Augustine's disciples, the Spanish priest Orosius, but was vindicated by a council of local bishops at Diospolis in 415. Alarmed by this, the Africans formally condemned his doctrines and asked Pope Innocent to confirm their verdict. Innocent did so, but his successor Zosimus changed sides. The Africans however got the support of the imperial government and Zosimus thought it wiser to retreat.

The main ecclesiastical development in the west during this period was the growing authority of the papacy. Bishops and councils in Spain, Gaul and Illyricum asked for the popes' rulings on their problems and disputes and on the whole accepted them. In Illyricum Pope Siricius asserted his supremacy in a more formal way by appointing the bishop of Thessalonica his vicar and giving him the power to consecrate all bishops in the two dioceses of Macedonia and Dacia. There was no canonical justification for this step, but the papal vicariate of Illyricum became a permanent institution and maintained the authority of Rome in this area, despite the fact that politically it came under Constantinople. An attempt of Pope Zosimus to found a similar papal vicariate of Arles, to control the three provinces of Viennensis and Narbonensis I and II, was however a failure because the metropolitans of the provinces concerned refused to accept the dominance of Arles. The attempt was abandoned by Zosimus' successors. The African church was even more independent. As we have seen, it compelled Zosimus to agree with its condemnation of Pelagius, and when an appeal from an African priest, Apiarius, was received by the same pope, successfully challenged his jurisdiction, proving that the alleged Nicene canons on which Zosimus relied were in fact only canons of Sardica. When Carthage came under Vandal rule the spirit of the African churches was broken and Pope Leo was able to dictate to the bishops of Mauretania.

In the east there was a similar growth of the authority of Constantinople. The see of Constantinople had been accorded a primacy of honour second only to Rome in 381. Its bishops moreover had the ear of the emperor and could enforce their claims by imperial rescripts. Many bishops, particularly in the adjacent dioceses of Thrace, Asiana and Pontica, submitted their problems to the see of the capital and invited and accepted its intervention. The growing power of Constantinople was, however, viewed with jealousy and suspicion by the bishops of Alexandria, which had hitherto been the leading see of the east, and they seized every opportunity to humble the pride of the new Rome.

John, an eloquent preacher of Antioch and hence called Chrysostom (of the golden mouth), was in 398 appointed bishop of Constantinople by the eunuch Eutropius, who then controlled the government. He was no theologian, but exceptional for his strong interest in social questions, vigorously denouncing the luxury of the rich (including the clergy) and inculcating charity to the poor. He became a popular idol, but made himself many enemies in high places, including at times the empress Eudoxia. In 401 Theophilus, bishop of Alexandria, condemned four monks for heresy and they went to Constantinople and appealed to John. Very properly he refused to accept the case, as it came from another diocese, but the monks then appealed to the emperor, who instructed John to judge their dispute with Theophilus and summoned the latter to the capital. Theophilus was naturally infuriated and in 403 arrived with a bevy of Egyptian bishops, determined to humble John. He found no difficulty in rallying John's enemies and collecting a number of charges against him. He then not only refused to submit to the jurisdiction of the council which John had summoned, but convened a council of his own at the Oak, a suburb of Constantinople, and arraigned John before it. Arcadius was persuaded by Eudoxia to take Theophilus' side and decreed John's banishment. Riots ensued, Eudoxia changed her mind and John was recalled, but he again quarrelled with the empress and was exiled in 404 to Armenia, where he died in 407. Theophilus won this round, but the power of Constantinople was if anything enhanced. Popular sympathy was on John's side and his name was soon restored to the diptychs and his body brought back to the capital.

In 425 Nestorius, another Syrian priest, was appointed to the see of Constantinople by Theodosius II. He was a bigoted and intolerant man who urged the emperor to persecute heretics, but his own theological views were suspect. He sharply distinguished the human and divine natures of Christ, declaring that Jesus was a man clothed with the godhead as with a garment, and that Mary could therefore not be called the mother of God. Cyril, Theophilus' successor as bishop of Alexandria, determined to crush him. He wrote to Pope Caelestine and persuaded him to condemn Nestorius, and meanwhile himself formulated Twelve Anathemas against his doctrine. Nestorius determined to strike first and persuaded the emperor to summon a general council at Ephesus on 7 June 431. When Nestorius arrived with his supporters he found himself in a minority, for Cyril had with him fifty or more Egyptian bishops, Memnon of Ephesus had rallied the bishops of Asiana against him, and Juvenal of Jerusalem brought fifteen Palestinian bishops to support Cyril. John of Antioch, who was on Nestorius' side, was delayed on his journey with his group of bishops. Cyril defied the imperial commissioner who had been appointed to preside and convened the council before John's arrival and condemned Nestorius. When John at last arrived he, with his own and Nestorius' followers, reversed this decision, condemning Cyril and Memnon. Theodosius II impartially accepted both decisions and decreed the deposition of Nestorius and of Cyril and Memnon. Cyril, however, by rousing agitation among the monks of the capital and by lavish bribery of the ministers and eunuchs of the palace, eventually got his way. He and Memnon were rehabilitated and Nestorius was relegated to his monastery at Antioch and later deported to the Great Oasis in Egypt. After long negotiations the breach between Cyril and John of Antioch was healed, John condemning Nestorius' views, Cyril dropping the Twelve Anathemas.

Among the ardent admirers of the Twelve Anathemas was Eutyches, an aged and respected abbot of Constantinople, who developed from them the Monophysite doctrine that Christ had one nature only, his

85

humanity being absorbed in his divinity. In 448 he was formally charged with heresy before Flavian, bishop of Constantinople, and was condemned by a small council. He appealed to Rome and Flavian sent Pope Leo all the documents in the case. Leo supported Flavian's decision, setting out his own doctrinal position in a document known as the Tome of Leo. Chrysaphius the eunuch and Nomus the master of the offices, however, persuaded the emperor to convoke another ecumenical council at Ephesus to reconsider the case. Dioscorus, Cyril's successor, was in the chair, supported by two imperial commissioners. Most of the 130 bishops were Egyptians or their Palestinian allies. The verdict of the council was inevitably to vindicate Eutyches and to condemn Flavian and set aside Pope Leo's judgment (August 449).

Three successive bishops of Alexandria had thus humbled the bishops of Constantinople. In the first contest no other issue can be discerned. It would however be wrong to dismiss the other two struggles as mere power politics. The bishops of Alexandria believed that they were the repositories of the true faith and that this faith was threatened by the heretical bishops of Constantinople.

VIII

The Revival of the East and the Fall of the West

On 28 July 450 Theodosius II died, leaving no son and having nominated no successor. Four weeks later, on 25 August, the senate elected Marcian, an obscure retired tribune, who had once been aide-de-camp (*domesticus*) of Aspar, the *magister militum praesentalis*. The virgin Pulcheria consented to go through a form of marriage with him,

BIBLIOGRAPHY. John Malalas and John of Antioch tell us something about affairs in the west, and Procopius gives an account of the usurpation of Odoacer and the reign of Theoderic in Italy in the first book of his *Gothic Wars*. The same ground is covered by the second Anonymus Valesianus (usually printed with Ammianus). The panegyrics of Sidonius Apollinaris on Avitus, Majorian and Anthemius contain much historical information.

For the Vandal kingdom there is C. Courtois, *Les Vandales et l'Afrique* (Paris, 1955). The principal primary sources are Procopius, *Vandal Wars*, Book 1, and Victor Vitensis. For the internal history of the Ostrogothic kingdom the principal authorities are Cassiodorus, *Variae*, Ennodius' *Life of Epiphanius* and his panegyric on Theoderic, and Theoderic's Edict. For the internal affairs of the Visigothic kingdom the chief source is the *Leges Visigothorum* and the *Breviarium* of Alaric; for the Burgundian kingdom the *Lex Gundobada* and the *Lex Romana Burgundionum*. For the Franks there is no significant earlier source than Gregory of Tours.

For the history of the east there survive only fragments of Priscus (down to 474). Candidus the Isaurian (457–91) and Malchus of Philadelphia (474–80). For the rest we are reduced to the unreliable later narratives of John Malalas and John of Antioch. There is however a very interesting local Chronicle of Joshua the Stylite (W. Wright, Cambridge, 1882), which covers events in Mesopotamia between 494 and 506. The biography of Daniel the Stylite (N. Baynes and E. F. Dawes, *Three Byzantine Saints*, Oxford, Blackwell, 1948) who stood on a pillar near Constantinople from 460 to 494, contains much important historical information. For ecclesiastical history there is Evagrius, and a Syriac summary of the Monophysite Chronicle of Zacharias of Mitylene (F. J. Hamilton and E. W. Brooks, London, 1899), who covered the years 450–91.

The Acts of the Council of Chalcedon are printed in full, together with much previous and subsequent correspondence and acts of minor councils in E. Schwartz, *Acta Conciliorum Oecumenicorum*.

thus endowing him with the hereditary prestige of the Theodosian house.

What had happened was that the group of senators which were opposed to Chrysaphius and Nomus, disliking both their ecclesiastical and their secular policy, had triumphed. Nomus fell from power, Chrysaphius was executed, and Marcian reversed their policies. The subsidies to Attila were strongly disliked by the senate, which Chrysaphius had forced to pay special levies. Marcian boldly refused to pay them. Luckily for him, and for the Illyrican and Thracian provinces, Attila was busy in the west and died before he could take vengeance, and Marcian was able to profit from the fall of the Hunnic empire to settle a number of barbarian tribes, including the Ostrogoths, as federates in the deserted frontier zone. Freed from the financial burden of the Hunnic subsidy, Marcian was able to gratify the senate by abolishing the *follis*. He also virtually abolished the other main charge on the senatorial order, the praetorian games, by reducing the number of praetors to three, making their games voluntary and limiting the choice to *illustres* resident in the capital.

In church affairs he decided to reopen the case of Eutyches. Pope Leo had naturally been infuriated by the second Council of Ephesus and demanded another council, to be held under his own presidency in Italy. Marcian persuaded him to abandon this idea and to send legates to an ecumenical council to be held in the east. Leo consented on condition that his Tome was accepted as a final doctrinal definition. The council was held from 8 October to 31 October 451 at Chalcedon, not at Nicaea as originally planned, in order to enable the emperor to intervene personally in its debates. Its deliberations were guided by a commission of ten ministers and twenty-seven senators. The acts of the second Council of Ephesus were duly annulled; Dioscorus and the Egyptian bishops who stood by him were condemned; the other bishops who had voted the wrong way at Ephesus were allowed to submit and were pardoned. The drafting of a creed caused some difficulty, for most of the bishops disliked Leo's Tome as much as Eutyches' doctrines, but the imperial commissioners firmly told them that they must choose between Leo and Dioscorus and thus compelled them to sign a creed which incorporated the doctrine of Leo's Tome.

The council also made two changes in the ecclesiastical hierarchy. Hitherto the patriarch of Alexandria—to use the term which henceforth becomes technical for the suprametropolitical sees—had possessed absolute control over the diocese of Egypt and the patriarch of Antioch had possessed a looser primacy over Oriens. Constantinople had a primacy of honour but no officially recognized area of authority. The council confirmed a compromise between Maximus of Antioch and Juvenal of Jerusalem, who had long been intriguing to make himself an independent patriarch with authority over the southern half of Oriens. He was accorded patriarchal rank but his sphere of authority was limited to the three provinces of Palestine. Secondly the council gave the bishop of Constantinople patriarchal control over the dioceses of Thrace, Asiana and Pontica. This change was bitterly opposed by Pope Leo, jealous and fearful of the rising power of the new Rome, but the bishops affected raised no objection and he was obliged in the end to acquiesce in it.

In the west Valentinian III murdered his patrician Aetius on 21 September 454 and on 15 March 455 was himself murdered by two of Aetius' retainers. Both assassinations were promoted by the great Roman noble Petronius Maximus, who was acclaimed emperor two days later. His reign was brief and disastrous. The Vandal king Gaiseric seized the opportunity to occupy the rest of Africa and Sardinia, and descended upon Rome itself and sacked it. Maximus was killed on 2 June. The Gallic nobility, supported by Theoderic, king of the Visigoths, took advantage of the confusion in Italy to elect one of themselves, Eparchius Avitus, as emperor, and he soon entered Rome. His reign was also brief and disastrous. There was famine in the city and Avitus withdrew to Gaul. On his return he was forced to resign by Ricimer, a Suevian officer, on 17 October 456.

Marcian died on 26 January 457 and on 7 February the senate elected another obscure army officer, Leo, tribune of the Mattiarii, who had once been agent of Aspar's estates. It is said that the senate offered the throne to Aspar himself despite his barbarian birth and Arian faith, but that he refused. Leo was immediately approached by Ricimer, who wanted to be appointed patrician and to secure the appointment of an emperor of his choice in the west. Leo acceded to the first request, making Ricimer patrician and Majorian his second-in-command as *magister militum* on 17 February, but agreement apparently was not reached on the choice of an emperor of the west. Eventually Majorian was elected by the senate and proclaimed by the armies without Leo's approval, on 28 December 457.

Neither emperor proved as docile as their respective emperor-makers would have desired. Majorian enacted a number of useful administrative reforms and reasserted Roman authority in Gaul and

Spain against the rebellious encroachments of the federate barbarians. A projected expedition against the Vandals, however, failed, and on his return to Italy Majorian was arrested by Ricimer and killed (2 August 461).

In the east the struggle went the other way. Leo was in a very weak position, since Marcian had appointed Aspar's son, Ardaburius, *magister militum per Orientem*, and in Thrace there was a large body of Ostrogothic troops engaged by Marcian under the command of Theoderic Strabo, who was allied by marriage to Aspar. In 466 Leo was able to strengthen his position. An Isaurian officer named Tarasicodissa produced evidence that Ardaburius was intriguing with the Persians, and Leo was thus able to replace him by a more reliable barbarian, Jordanes, a Vandal. Tarasicodissa, who took the more civilized name of Zeno after a distinguished Isaurian general of the previous generation, was appointed *magister militum* of Thrace and given Ariadne, the emperor's daughter, in marriage. Having thus fortified his position, Leo defied Aspar, embarking on an ambitious western policy. Ricimer was hard pressed by the Vandals and was willing to make concessions to Leo in return for naval and military support. He ultimately agreed to accept an emperor of Leo's choice, Anthemius, a distinguished Roman general, grandson of the Anthemius who had ruled the east in the reigns of Arcadius and Theodosius II. Anthemius marched west with a substantial army and a large sum of money and was proclaimed Augustus at Rome on 12 August 467. At the same time a powerful fleet sailed west under the command of Basiliscus, the brother of Leo's empress Verina.

The attack on the Vandals proved a complete fiasco, largely owing to Basiliscus' incompetence, and resulted in the loss of Sicily to the empire. At the same time the Thracian troops mutinied against Zeno, who was, as an Isaurian, very unpopular, and he had to be withdrawn. Nevertheless Leo persisted in his policy. Zeno was appointed consul for 469 and *magister militum per Orientem*, where his Isaurian origin was an asset. Aspar became alarmed. Ariadne had given birth to a son, who was named Leo, and he feared that the little Leo would succeed on his grandfather's death and that his father Zeno would hold the reins of power. He accordingly demanded that Leo should give his other daughter to Patricius, his second son, and nominate him Caesar. Leo was not strong enough to resist, and complied, but in 471 he treacherously murdered Aspar and his eldest son, Ardaburius: Patricius was deposed but allowed to live. Leo had to face a rebellion of Aspar's *domesticus*, Ostrys, and of the Gothic federates under Theoderic Strabo, but the former was defeated by the excubitors, the newly-formed Isaurian bodyguard, and the latter ultimately (473) made submission on condition of being appointed *magister militum praesentalis*, being recognized king of his body of Ostrogoths, and receiving a subsidy of 2,000 pounds of gold a year to feed and pay them.

In the west after the Vandal fiasco Ricimer and Anthemius soon fell out, the former calling Anthemius an excitable Galatian, the latter Ricimer a fur-clad barbarian. There was an open breach and eventually civil war, in which Anthemius was killed (11 July 472). A senator named Olybrius was proclaimed Augustus, but both he and his creator Ricimer died in the same year. The Burgundian king Gundobad, who succeeded Ricimer as patrician, created Glycerius, the *comes domesticorum*, emperor on 3 March 473, but Leo gave his support to Julius Nepos, the *magister militum* of Dalmatia, who marched on Rome, defeated Glycerius, and was proclaimed Augustus on 24 June 474.

Leo had died on 18 January of the same year and was succeeded by his grandson, who promptly appointed his father Zeno as his colleague and shortly died. Zeno's position was very weak. He enjoyed no hereditary prestige save as the husband of Ariadne, Leo's daughter; as an Isaurian he was generally unpopular; and the treasury was empty. As a result his reign was punctuated by revolts and it was only by adroit and unscrupulous diplomacy that he managed to survive for seventeen years. Shortly after his accession he was forced to flee from Constantinople by a conspiracy in which the dowager empress Verina, her brother Basiliscus, Theoderic Strabo and an Isaurian general named Illus all combined. Basiliscus was proclaimed emperor but he reigned only eighteen months (January 474–August 475), having alienated Theoderic and Illus and caused riots in the city by an encyclical reversing the verdict of Chalcedon. Illus changed sides, joining forces with Zeno, but Theoderic Strabo continued in rebellion, and Zeno tried to create a counter-irritant by taking into his service the main body of the Ostrogoths, settled by Marcian in Pannonia, and making their king Theoderic the Amal *magister praesentalis*. A great pincer movement was planned in which a large Roman army and the Ostrogoths of Theoderic the Amal were to close on Strabo, but the Roman troops failed to arrive and the two Theoderics decided to join forces. Eventually Zeno succeeded in detaching Strabo by the offer of generous terms, including reappointment to the mastership of the soldiers and an ample subsidy. The other Theoderic marched off and ravaged Macedonia.

In the west Nepos was in 475 expelled by Orestes, his patrician, who nominated his own son Romulus as Augustus. But in the following year there was a mutiny of the east German federates, who by now formed the bulk of the Roman army in Italy. They demanded a third of the land, like the settled federates in Gaul, and when Orestes rejected their demands elected Odoacer, a Scirian officer, as their king (23 August 476), ejected Orestes and deposed Romulus. Odoacer, like Ricimer, wished to be officially appointed patrician but, taught no doubt by Ricimer's experiences, he thought it wiser not to have an emperor on the spot. He accordingly got the senate to send an embassy to Zeno asking him to grant the patriciate to Odoacer and to entrust the administration of Italy to him. Zeno's rule, they declared, was sufficient for both parts of the empire. As Nepos was still alive and *de iure* emperor, Zeno's reply was in the negative, and there is no evidence that he changed his mind later when in 480 Nepos was killed and Odoacer occupied Dalmatia. Odoacer was not given the patriciate and continued to rule as king, tolerated by the emperor but not recognized.

The Roman empire thus ceased to exist in the west, having been parcelled out into a number of barbarian kingdoms. The Vandals ruled the African diocese, together with Sardinia, Corsica and Sicily. Sicily was ceded later to Odoacer for an annual tribute. Odoacer ruled Italy and Dalmatia and what remained of Raetia and Noricum. He evacuated Noricum in 458, but acquired Sicily. In Gaul the Visigoths, who had already extended their rule to the Loire and to the Saône and the Rhône, now occupied the territory between the Durance, the Alps and the sea. North of the Durance the Burgundians held all the country east of the Saône and the Rhône. North of the Loire were the independent Armoricans, now reinforced with Britons, and on the lower Rhine were the Franks. Between them an enclave of Roman territory survived in Belgica II, ruled by Syagrius, son of Aegidius, the *magister militum per Gallias*. It was conquered in 486 by Clovis, king of the Franks. In Spain the Visigoths had on Majorian's death established their rule throughout the country, except in the north-west, where the Sueves and the native Vascones still maintained their independence.

In 479 Marcian, son-in-law of the exiled dowager empress Verina, rebelled against Zeno but was quickly crushed. Next year Illus, who had been appointed *magister militum per Orientem*, combined forces with Verina, who proclaimed a senator named Leontius emperor. To crush the rebellion Zeno had to use his German federates in Asia Minor, but he prudently retained Theoderic at Constantinople. Illus was defeated and the Isaurians deserted him, but Theoderic, aggrieved at his treatment, rebelled and began ravaging Thrace. In 488 however he accepted a commission from Zeno to expel Odoacer from Italy and marched off west with his tribesmen. Zeno had at last freed himself from rebels and barbarians and enjoyed peace for three years, dying on 9 April 491.

Zeno succeeded to an empty treasury, and with the constant subsidies he had to pay to the two Theoderics and to the Isaurians he was always short of money. In view of his weak position he was afraid to increase taxation; his first praetorian prefect resigned rather than take this step. Sebastianus, who became prefect in 476, solved the difficulty by the systematic sale of offices. Since the early fourth century the great men of the court had made large sums by recommending candidates for offices to the emperor for a consideration (*suffragium*). Sebastianus now in effect made *suffragium* an imperial monopoly. Normally the treasury and Sebastianus himself secured the *suffragia*. Sometimes the right to nominate to a given office in perpetuity was sold for a capital sum.

The eastern churches had ever since Chalcedon been rent with violent dissensions. The monks of Palestine, when Juvenal returned from the council having changed sides, arose in rebellion and elected a rival patriarch. It required two years of fighting before Juvenal was restored to Jerusalem. In Egypt Proterius, the patriarch appointed by the council to succeed Dioscorus, could only be installed with the aid of imperial troops, and was lynched on Marcian's death. Leo, after some delay, finally expelled his Monophysite successor, Timothy 'the Cat', by armed force in 460 and substituted a Chalcedonian, Timothy 'the White Hat'. Basiliscus tried to win support for his cause by issuing an encyclical condemning Chalcedon. It was enthusiastically welcomed in Egypt and Ephesus and elsewhere but provoked riots in Constantinople, and before he was deposed Basiliscus thought it wise to reverse it by an anti-encyclical. Zeno seems to have favoured the Monophysites by conviction but attempted a compromise. By the Edict of Union (Henotikon) he affirmed his adherence to the Creeds of Nicaea and Constantinople, accepted the Twelve Anathemas of Cyril, condemned the doctrine of Nestorius and Eutyches and anathematized whoever believed otherwise or had done so at Chalcedon or elsewhere.

The Henotikon failed to satisfy the extreme Monophysites, particularly the Egyptians, who demanded a more explicit condemnation of Chalcedon, or the extreme Chalcedonians, but it appears to have pleased many moderates and the leaders of both parties signed it. Pope

Felix III, however, refused to accept it since it ignored the Tome of Leo, and implicitly condemned it; and he excommunicated Acacius, the patriarch of Constantinople, for signing it.

When Zeno died the choice of a successor once again devolved on the senate, which referred the matter to the empress Ariadne, who selected an elderly silentiary, Anastasius, and married him. Longinus, Zeno's brother, who had expected to succeed, raised a tumult in the capital and gained the support of the Isaurians, but Anastasius promptly arrested and exiled him. He fought the Isaurians to a finish: their final subjection took seven years. Henceforth the Isaurians formed crack regiments in the imperial army, but exercised no political influence, and forfeited the annual subsidy which Zeno had given to them. Anastasius had also to face Bulgar invasions in Thrace and in 502 a Persian war. He mustered very large forces for this war and after indecisive fighting a truce of seven years was signed in 506. It was not formally renewed in 513 but peace prevailed, despite the fact that Anastasius, contrary to the terms of the peace, built a great fortress-city, Dara, opposite to the Persian stronghold, Nisibis.

Anastasius was a convinced Monophysite and the patriarch Euphemius, who strongly objected to his election on this score, insisted on his signing a statement that he would respect the decrees of Chalcedon. Anastasius yielded but Euphemius continued to agitate and intrigue against the Henotikon; in 495 the emperor secured his condemnation as a Nestorian. He was succeeded by Macedonius, who was likewise a Chalcedonian. In 511 Anastasius decided to take a stronger line against the Chalcedonians, whose strength was growing, and he charged Macedonius before the consistory with perjury, since he had (despite signing the Henotikon) propagated Nestorian doctrines. The consistory and senate condemned the patriarch and he was exiled. His deposition was subsequently ratified by an episcopal council, and he was replaced by Timothy, a strong Monophysite. Next year the Chalcedonian patriarch of Antioch was deposed and replaced by the saintly and erudite Monophysite theologian Severus.

The Chalcedonian cause was taken up by Vitalian, the *comes foederatorum* in Thrace, who rallied to his cause not only the barbarian but the regular troops of the diocese and the local peasantry. Militarily Anastasius was very unsuccessful against Vitalian and he was obliged to promise to appoint Vitalian *magister militum* of Thrace and to hold a general council on the faith at which the pope should preside. Since Pope Hormisdas insisted as a preliminary condition that the emperor and all the eastern bishops should assent to the acts of Chalcedon and the Tome of Leo, negotiations broke down and Vitalian marched on Constantinople. This time he was decisively defeated and the rebellion collapsed.

Anastasius' great achievement was the rehabilitation of the finances of the empire. This result was achieved by careful and methodical reforms designed to prevent peculation and waste. His major reform was to reorganize the land tax so that the greater part of it was paid in gold and only so much levied in kind as was required for the troops' rations, and the supply of Constantinople, Alexandria and Antioch. Any additional supplies were obtained by compulsory purchase (*coemptio*) from the landowners, the price being set off against the gold tax due from them, or if it exceeded the tax, paid in gold. *Coemptio* was allowed only by the emperor's personal decision, except in Thrace, where the yield of taxation was so low and the number of troops so large that it was the regular practice. He also reformed the machinery of collection by the appointment of a *vindex* for each city, who took charge of the curial collectors. As the result of his economies, he was able to grant generous remission of taxes to provinces stricken by war and famine, to execute a great programme of public works including the fortress city of Dara and the Long Wall of Thrace, which formed the outer defence of Constantinople; and also to abolish in 498 the hated *chrysargyron*, which caused such distress to the urban poor. He also began the abolition of the *capitatio*, which was the heaviest burden on the peasantry. Despite these remissions, he left a reserve of 320,000 pounds of gold in the treasury when he died in 518.

Anastasius normally appointed barristers to the praetorian prefecture, but his two chief financial advisers were clerks of the prefecture whom he promoted to be prefects, Polycarp and Marinus the Syrian. The latter was responsible for the institution of the *vindices*. Another clerk of the prefecture, John the Paphlagonian, was made *comes sacrarum largitionum* and carried through a major reform of the copper currency. Since Arcadius' day, the mints had issued nothing between *solidi*, *semisses* and *tremisses* in gold and tiny copper pieces (*nummi*), of which many thousand went to the *solidus*. The lack of decent small change must have caused great inconvenience to the public, and the large new copper coins called *folles*, or *terunciani*, equivalent to forty *nummi* (with lower denominations at 20, 10 and 5), were welcomed by the public as well as being profitable to the treasury.

In the west the barbarian kings took over what remained of the

Roman administrative machinery, improvising for themselves central governments based on their Germanic households, and substituting for the Roman army their tribal levies. In the Vandal kingdom, which corresponded roughly with the diocese of Africa, we hear of a chief minister, the *praepositus regni*, who was a Vandal, but had under him Roman civil servants, doubtless the old officials of the vicar. Under him there continued to be provincial governors, including the proconsul of Africa.

In the Visigothic kingdom also, which comprised most of the dioceses of Spain and the Seven Provinces, the provincial system survived; the governors still had their assessors and *officia*, and were paid in *annonae* and *cellaria*. The cities still had their *defensores* and *tabularii*, elected by the citizens, but in each there was also a Gothic commandant, the *comes civitatis*. The old taxes, including the *chrysargyron* and the customs, survived, and the land tax was still assessed by the *tabularii* of the cities and collected by curial *susceptores*. The old imperial, now royal, estates (*domus fiscales* or *dominicae*) were managed by a *comes patrimonii* and were as of old leased to *conductores* under the supervision of *actores*.

We know very little of the Frankish kingdom at this date. Under Clovis the province of Belgica Secunda is mentioned, but later the provincial system disappears except in the little area in the extreme south-east which the Franks took over from the Ostrogothic kingdom; here a *rector provinciae* or *praefectus* still survived. Elsewhere the *civitas* under its *comes civitatis* became the basic administrative unit, though several cities were sometimes temporarily grouped under a *dux*. Here too the land tax, based on the old registers, was maintained. In the little Burgundian kingdom, which at its greatest extent comprised only fragments of two or three provinces, no trace of the provincial administration survived. The unit of government was the *civitas*, or its subdivision, the *pagus*, in each of which there were two *comites*, one Roman and the other Burgundian.

The situation was very different in Italy, where Odoacer and after him Theoderic took over intact not only the provincial and diocesan administration, but the central government which had administered the whole western empire, and Rome and the Roman senate. Like Odoacer Theoderic tried to secure official recognition of his position from the emperor, but he too apparently failed to reach agreement with Zeno or with Anastasius, and in 493, having killed Odoacer and occupied Ravenna, he had himself proclaimed king by the Ostrogoths 'without waiting for the command of the new emperor'; as he had long been king of the Ostrogoths, this acclamation presumably asserted his king-ship of Italy.

Though the emperors appointed neither Odoacer nor Theoderic as official regents, they gave them *de facto* recognition and maintained diplomatic relations with them, until they saw an opportunity of over-throwing them. On their side Odoacer and the Ostrogothic kings did their best to conciliate the Roman aristocracy, treating the senate with the utmost courtesy and deference, maintaining the whole administra-tive hierarchy almost unaltered, and appointing Romans to nearly all the civilian posts. There were still a prefect of the city and a praetorian prefect of Italy, and Theoderic even revived the praetorian prefecture of Gaul, when he annexed the former Visigothic dominions east of the Rhône. Under the prefect of the city the old departmental officers con-tinued to maintain the aqueducts, the drains and the public buildings and to organize the distribution of food to the population, while the quaestors and praetors continued to give their games. Under the praetorian prefects the vicars of the city and of Italy, and the provincial governors, administered justice to the Roman population according to the established laws, which Theoderic pledged himself to maintain unaltered, and collected the old imperial taxes, the land tax with the supplementary charge of $2\frac{1}{2}$ *solidi* per *iugum* which Majorian had added to cover the fees of the officials, the *chrysargyron*, the *siliquaticum*, which Valentinian III had instituted, and the customs.

The old offices of the *comitatus* were also preserved. The quaestors continued to draft royal constitutions; the master of the offices to organize the postal services, command the *agentes in rebus*, and control royal audiences; the *comes sacrarum largitionum* to control the mint and the group of taxes assigned to his care; the *comes rei privatae* to manage the old imperial lands.

By appointing Romans to all these offices Odoacer and the Ostro-gothic kings were enabled to bestow upon them the coveted ranks of *clarissimus*, *spectabilis* and *illustris*, and they likewise granted honorary codicils conferring these ranks. They continued to create patricians, and even nominated ordinary consuls. These were not officially recognized in the east, but the nominees, by a gentleman's agreement, normally received codicils from the emperor also, and thus achieved a place on the imperial *fasti*.

The military offices on the other hand were generally reserved for Goths. Odoacer appointed *magistri militum*, but Theoderic suppressed this title, preferring to call the generals of his expeditionary forces *comites* or *duces*; under his successor Athalaric the title of *patricius praesentalis* was revived. There were also *duces* or *comites* in the frontier provinces, Raetia, Pannonia, Dalmatia and Savia, and in some Italian provinces *duces provinciarum*, charged with the suppression of brigandage and violent crimes. Some cities had *comites civitatis*, who commanded the Gothic garrisons, and there were also in areas where Goths were settled on the land *comites Gothorum per singulas civitates*, whose primary function was judicial, to settle cases between Goths, and, with the aid of a Roman assessor, cases between Goths and Romans.

What remained of the Roman army was disbanded; the by now ornamental corps of the *scholares* and of the *domestici* were pensioned off and the *comitiva domesticorum* became a sinecure office, used to confer honorary illustrious rank. The army was formed by levies of Ostrogothic warriors, who were settled on the land and annually summoned from their homes to parade before the king and receive their donative; when mobilized for active service they received rations, and they were provided with arms from the old imperial arms factories.

Odoacer created and Theoderic maintained a new financial office, that of the *vice dominus* or *comes patrimonii*, usually a Goth, who supplied the funds needed for the king's personal expenditure, including the donatives he gave to his Gothic warriors, and managed a group of estates whose rents were earmarked for that purpose. He also received the taxes of Sicily and Dalmatia, which Odoacer apparently regarded as personal possessions, and under Theoderic those of Spain, when he took over the administration of the Visigothic kingdom. Theoderic seems to have taken over the *officium* of the *magistri militum* and used its members, the *comitiaci*, as his personal messengers and agents. He also maintained a corps of Gothic retainers, called *saiones*, for similar purposes.

One problem which the German kings had in common was the settlement of their tribesmen on the land. In the Frankish kingdom there was no great difficulty, for the bulk of the Franks seem to have remained in their old homes along the Rhine and in the Low Countries, and the kings possessed ample state lands, inherited from the empire or acquired by confiscation, with which to reward such of their nobles as migrated to the newly conquered territories. The Vandal king Gaiseric, having acquired Africa by conquest, had no scruples in using his rights as conqueror to expropriate Román landlords on a large scale. The land which he thus acquired in the proconsular province he distributed in tax-free allotments, the *sortes Vandalorum*, to his tribesmen; estates in the other provinces he kept for himself or granted to members of his family.

The allotment of land to the Visigoths and Burgundians was originally made under Roman auspices, when the two tribes were settled as federates, in Aquitania and Savoy respectively. The allotment was based on the rules of the imperial billeting system (officially known as *metata*, colloquially as *hospitalitas*), whereby a soldier was assigned one-third of the premises of his host. This rule was extended to the host's land, and the grant was made perpetual, and passed to the original grantee's heirs. He was not, however, supposed to alienate it, and if he did so, the Roman landlord had a right of preemption. It was only the cultivated land which was divided, the woodland and waste being held in common, unless one party enclosed a portion, in which case the other might enclose an equal area. The barbarian's share was later increased both in the Visigothic and Burgundian kingdoms to two-thirds.

The federates in Italy demanded a similar allotment of one-third of the land from Orestes, the patrician, and Odoacer when he became king carried it through. When Theoderic conquered Italy he massacred Odoacer's federates and assigned their third of the land to his Ostrogoths. In Italy the settlement was more equitable in that landlords who did not have to surrender a third of their land to a barbarian paid an equivalent tax (*tertiae*, or a third of the rent) to the crown, which retained the right to assign a third to a barbarian if need arose. In the Visigothic kingdom the barbarian allotments appear to have been tax-free, in the Ostrogothic they paid the regular land tax.

These vast measures of expropriation seem to have provoked remarkably little outcry. None at least has survived in our sources, which on the contrary give high praise to Theoderic's praetorian prefect Liberius, who carried out the allotment in Italy.

> It gives us pleasure to refer to the way in which in the assignment of the thirds he united both the possessions and the hearts of Goths and Romans. For though men usually quarrel when they are neighbours, the sharing of estates seems in this case to have produced harmony. . . . By the division of the soil the hearts of the owners have been united, the friendship of the peoples has grown by their losses, and at the cost of the land a protector has been acquired, so that the security of the estate is wholly preserved.[1]

[1] Cassiodorus, *Variae*, II. 16.

The provinces and dioceses of the empire according to the *Notitia Dignitatus* (*c.* A.D. 400)

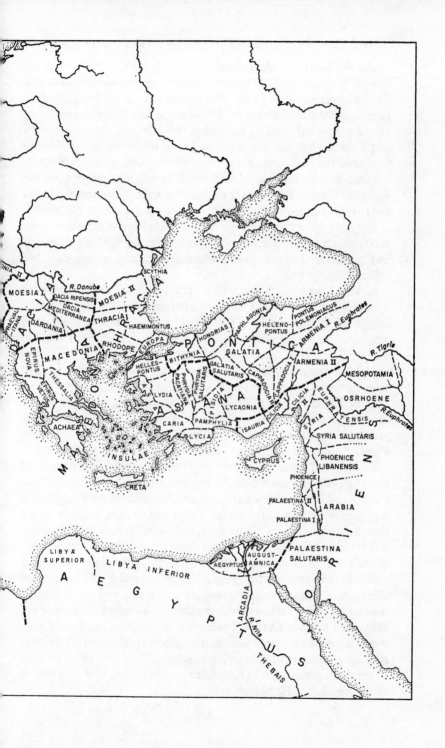

The barbarian kingdoms combined the characteristic vices of the Roman empire and of barbarism. Though many of them meant well, the kings were as powerless as the emperors to control corruption and extortion in the administration; the old abuses of bribery and mounting official perquisites went on unchecked. To these old abuses were now added the lawless violence of the barbarian tribesmen and of Romans who aped their manners. King Theoderic the Ostrogoth undoubtedly admired Roman civilization, and never ceased inculcating upon his barbarian subjects the virtue of *civilitas*, the spirit of law and order. But even he had solemnly to instruct his Gothic warriors not to plunder the countryside when they came up to Ravenna to receive their donatives, and regularly remitted the taxes of provinces through which his armies had passed, in compensation for the depredations which they had suffered.

He found it necessary, moreover, to grant protection (*tuitio*), enforced by the presence of a royal *saio*, to petitioners who declared that their lives were endangered by the lawless violence of their enemies, and moreover to extract from such petitioners an oath that they would not employ their *saio* for their own unlawful purposes; we know of one case in which a *saio* nearly killed the Roman with whose protection he had been entrusted. Such were conditions under so firm and enlightened a ruler as Theoderic, under whom Italy is said to have enjoyed a golden age of peace and prosperity. The pages of Gregory of Tours teem with gruesome stories of lawless brutality, which, after two centuries of Frankish rule, were accepted as normal incidents of life.

Gaiseric and his son Hunneric were fanatical Arians, and persecuted their Catholic subjects ruthlessly. Hunneric rounded up 4,966 Catholic bishops and clergy and relegated them to the southern deserts, entrusting them to the care of the savage Moorish tribesmen, and later exiled the bishops to Corsica, where they were employed on forced labour, felling timber for the fleet. A later Vandal king, Thrasamund, again closed the churches and deported the bishops to Sardinia, where they remained for over twenty years. The Burgundian, Visigothic and Ostrogothic kings, though Arians, were tolerant, and on the whole maintained friendly relations with the Catholic hierarchy; Theoderic was even asked to settle a disputed election to the papacy. The Franks, who were converted from paganism to the Catholic faith under Clovis, had no religious quarrel with their Roman subjects; but they were shameless in granting church lands to their followers and enforcing the election of their favourites to fat bishoprics.

IX

Justinian

On Anastasius' death, there was again a vacancy of the throne, and after some obscure intrigues, the senate elected Justin the *comes excubitorum.* Justin was of peasant origin, having risen from the ranks. He was still uncultured and, it was alleged, illiterate, using a stencil to sign papers. He came from a village near Naissus, and was thus Latin-speaking and a Chalcedonian by upbringing. He promptly reversed Anastasius' ecclesiastical policy, deposing Severus of Antioch and the other Monophysite bishops except Timothy of Alexandria, and renewing communion with the pope. Justin had no sons, but several nephews to whom he had given a good education. The ablest of them was Petrus Sabbatius, whom he had adopted and who therefore took the name of Justinianus. Justinian immediately came to the front, being appointed *comes domesticorum* and then *magister militum praesentalis,* and was generally regarded as being the virtual ruler under his uncle's nominal sovereignty. When in 527 Justin fell seriously ill, he crowned Justinian as his colleague (4 April). Two months later (1 August) he died and Justinian succeeded.

BIBLIOGRAPHY. For the reign of Justin I there is a detailed study in A. A. Vasiliev, *Justin the First, An Introduction to the Epoch of Justinian* (Cambridge, Mass., 1950). For the reign of Justinian the most important works are C. Diehl, *Justinien et la civilisation Byzantine au VIe siècle* (Paris, 1901), and the massive work of B. Rubin, *Das Zeitalter Iustinians,* of which the first volume only has appeared (Berlin, 1960).

The principal narrative sources are Procopius' *Wars,* continued by Agathias and Menander Protector. In his *Secret History* Procopius makes a malignant analysis of Justinian's reign. His *Aedificia* gives an elaborate account of Justinian's building activity. Malalas' popular history is also useful, as being contemporary. The Johannid of Corippus contains a diffuse poetic record of the exploits of John, Master of the Soldiers in Africa from 546 to 548. Evagrius records the history of the church from the Chalcedonian point of view, John of Ephesus from the Monophysite. The most important documentary sources are the Novels of Justinian, and the Acts of the Second Council of Constantinople.

Justinian was evidently a dominating personality. He chose able ministers of strong character and commanded their unfailing loyalty. He was himself of no mean ability and a most conscientious administrator, working long hours and giving infinite attention to detail. His fault was, perhaps, that he took too much upon himself. He was strongly religious and a theologian of some distinction. He set himself ambitious objectives. He wished to cleanse the administration of corruption and inefficiency, to reform the law and purify the courts of justice. He regarded it as of high importance to unite the churches in orthodox doctrine. Above all, it was his ambition to restore the territorial integrity of the empire, recovering the western provinces, and Rome itself, from the heretical barbarians who had overrun them. These ambitions formed one integrated plan. By achieving doctrinal unity and abolishing injustice and oppression, he hoped to win God's favour in his campaigns against the barbarians. By eliminating corruption and extortion, he hoped to make the empire more able to bear the financial burdens which his wars imposed. The conquest of the barbarians would enable him to stamp out heresy, in particular Arianism, in the west, and thus confer God's favour upon the empire.

Before his accession, Justinian had fallen in love with an actress named Theodora and, defying social prejudice, had married her. Theodora was much hated and has been much maligned, but there can be no doubt that she was a devoted and faithful wife to Justinian until her death in 548. She was an able and strong-minded woman, a generous benefactor of her friends and vindictive towards her enemies. Justinian at a critical moment of his reign, the Nika rebellion, was inspired by her to take courage, and in one of his laws openly acknowledges his debt to her advice and encouragement. It is often stated that she dominated Justinian, but the evidence does not bear this out. She was strongly opposed to her husband on the religious issue, being an ardent Monophysite, but she went no further than giving comfort and support to the persecuted members of the sect. Justinian's ecclesiastical policy was unaffected by her views. She bitterly hated Justinian's great praetorian prefect John the Cappadocian, but Justinian kept him in office for ten years and only was induced to disgrace him finally by a trick.

Justinian was supported by a galaxy of able ministers, whom he himself picked out and promoted often from quite humble origins. He entrusted his legal forms to Tribonian, an outstanding lawyer whom he appointed quaestor. In his dealings with foreign powers, he used Peter the patrician, a clever diplomatist whom he employed as his master of the offices. He promoted John the Cappadocian from a clerkship in the office of the *magister militum*—he no doubt came to appreciate John's abilities when he held that office under Justin—to praetorian prefect of the East. John carried through great administrative reforms and proved himself a very able if ruthless financier. Belisarius, the brilliant general whom he employed against the Persians, the Vandals and the Ostrogoths, started his career as one of Justinian's military retainers. In his wars he also employed his cousin Germanus, an able general, and one of his eunuchs, Narses, who proved himself an outstanding commander.

Early in the reign (January 532) Justinian was faced by a serious rebellion. The trouble began as one of the usual circus riots, but on this occasion the two circus parties, the Blues and the Greens, united under the slogan of *Nika* (conquer) to storm the urban prefect's house and rescue their partisans. The popular movement seems to have been exploited by a discontented faction among the aristocracy, who inspired the crowd to demand the dismissal of John the Cappadocian and Tribonian and, when Justinian weakly yielded to these demands, to proclaim Hypatius, a nephew of Anastasius, as emperor. There were few troops in the city and their loyalty was dubious. Justinian meditated flight, but Theodora inspired him to stand his ground with a handful of loyal troops. Belisarius and Mundus, the *magistri* of the East and of Illyricum, who happened to be at Constantinople, massacred the crowd in the hippodrome and quelled the revolt.

War with Persia had already broken out under Justin. Justinian had no ambitions in this quarter, but merely wished to maintain the *status quo*. In 532, after some rather indecisive operations, he signed an Eternal Peace with Chosroes, the new Persian king. By this treaty, he agreed to pay the Persian king 11,000 pounds of gold in final settlement of the latter's claims to a subsidy towards the defence of the Caucasus.

Justinian now had his hands free for his designs in the west. The Vandal kingdom was the most aggressive and most hated of all the barbarian kingdoms. The Vandals had built up considerable naval power and practised organized piracy. They were, moreover, rabid Arians and ruthlessly persecuted their Catholic Roman subjects. King Gaiseric (428-77) had launched the persecution and his son Hunneric (477-84) carried it on. Gunthamund (484-96) had allowed it to lapse, but Thrasamund (496-523) had renewed it, deporting the Catholic bishops to Sardinia. Under Hilderic, the persecution had been relaxed and relations with Constantinople had improved, but in 530 Hilderic was deposed by Gelimer. Justinian seized this opportunity to protest against the deposition of a friendly king and proposed to intervene militarily. His design was opposed by all his generals, who remembered too well the disasters which had overwhelmed previous expeditions against the Vandals, and by John the praetorian prefect, who recalled the ruinous financial loss caused by Leo's campaign. Justinian nevertheless persisted and the expedition proved a brilliant success. Belisarius sailed for Africa with only about 20,000 men, effected an unopposed landing, was welcomed by the Roman population, and in a single battle crushed the Vandals. The survivors were shipped to Constantinople and enrolled in five regiments of Justininiani Vandali who served on the eastern front. Africa was organized as a separate praetorian prefecture comprising the six African provinces together with Sardinia (534).

Justinian's next ambition was the recovery of Italy. Here Theoderic had, on his death in 526, been succeeded by his ten-year-old grandson, Athalaric, under the guardianship of his mother, Amalasuntha, Theoderic's daughter, who carried on her father's pro-Roman policy and gave Athalaric a liberal education. The Goths chafed under her rule and insisted that Athalaric be brought up in German fashion with a group of young Gothic nobles; under their influence the young prince took to drink and died in 534. Amalasuntha, hoping to fortify her position, married her cousin Theodahad, a weak character who she thought would submit to her will. But he promptly imprisoned and then killed her (535). This gave Justinian his opportunity. He protested vigorously and occupied Sicily and Illyricum, at the same time secretly offering terms to Theodahad. Theodahad hesitated, but eventually refused, and Belisarius marched north with his little force of about 10,000 men, captured Naples, the only city which resisted him, and entered Rome without opposition (536). The Ostrogoths deposed Theodahad and elected as king in his place Vitigis, a cautious but competent commander. He laid siege to Rome in February 537, but Belisarius held out until, in the winter of 537–38, reinforcements of about 6,500 men arrived. The Goths raised the siege and Belisarius pressed on northwards, occupying Liguria, where Milan revolted from the Goths, and seizing Rimini. The tide of war now changed and the Goths were able to recapture Milan, slaughtering its male inhabitants and selling off the women and children as slaves. Belisarius, however, soon regained the initiative and the Goths agreed to withdraw beyond the Po and surrender the rest of Italy. Justinian was satisfied with these terms. A mutiny had broken out among the Roman troops in Africa and the Moors had rebelled. The situation was restored by Justinian's cousin Germanus, but there was a yet more serious threat in the east, where the Persian king Chosroes was chafing against the Eternal Peace, which tied his hands while Justinian made fresh conquests in the west. Belisarius, however, was not satisfied with a partial victory. By an adroit and not very scrupulous manœuvre, he got possession of Ravenna, of the royal treasure and of the person of Vitigis himself. The Gothic war seemed to be finished and Belisarius sailed for Constantinople (540).

In the meanwhile, Justinian had been busy with legal and administrative reforms. On 13 February 528 he appointed a commission to compile a single code of all valid imperial constitutions. The first edition of the Justinian Code, which superseded the Gregorian, Hermogenian and Theodosian Codes, was published on 7 April 529. The emperor next, on 15 December 530, appointed a second commission to codify the works of the classical jurists. This work took three years to complete, the Digest being published on 16 December 533. During these years, many reforms of the law were enacted and the Code was revised. The second and final edition was issued on 16 November 534. An official textbook of Roman law for the use of students, the Institutes, was also published on 21 November 533.

The most important of the administrative reforms was the suppression of the *suffragia* (535). The system, Justinian rightly thought, lay at the root of the corruption and extortion which prevailed in the provinces, since provincial governors, having bought their offices for exorbitant sums, had to recoup themselves. At a considerable expense to the treasury, Justinian bought out those who had received the right of nominating to various posts and receiving the *suffragia* therefrom and undertook to refrain from exacting *suffragia* himself. All those appointed to governorships had to swear a solemn oath that they had neither given nor promised to give anything for their posts. Justinian also drafted a standard series of instructions (*mandata*) for governors, and strengthened the *defensores civitatis* in the hopes that they would defend their cities from illegal exactions. He furthermore carried out an extensive reorganization of the provincial system. The vicariates and the corresponding offices of *comes Orientis* and *praefectus Augustalis* had, it would seem, by this time ceased to fulfil any very useful function. The vicariates were all abolished, though the titles of *comes Orientis* and *praefectus Augustalis* were retained for the governors of Syria I and Egypt I. In Asia Minor the vicariates of Asiana and Pontica were combined with the governorships of Phrygia Pacatiana and Galatia I; two pairs of provinces were amalgamated; and in two other provinces the military and civil commands were united, while in Cappadocia the post of governor was combined with that of the *comes domorum*, the manager of the imperial estates of the province. The new governors were given both military and civil powers, were granted the superior rank of *spectabilis*, and were accorded superior powers of jurisdiction, judging all cases up to the value of 750 *solidi*, and in some cases receiving appeals from an adjacent province. The two existing provinces of Armenia I and II, together with Great Armenia and the satrapies, were reorganized as four provinces. In Oriens also changes were made, but here the military commands were kept separate from the civil governorships and several governors were upgraded to *spectabilis* so that they could stand up to the *duces*. The difference in treatment was because in Syria the *duces* had a real military duty to resist the Persians, whereas in Asia Minor the military powers of the governors were required only for suppressing brigandage. In Egypt, military and civil powers were combined as in Asia Minor, for there also the problem was civil disorders.

In Constantinople Justinian strengthened the office of the chief of police, the *praefectus vigilum*, renaming him the *praetor plebis*, and created a new office of *quaesitor* to deal with the crowds of visitors and immigrants who thronged to the city. He also created a new office of *quaestor exercitus* to facilitate the supply of the lower Danube armies. Thrace was too exhausted to support these armies and the *quaestor* was assigned, in addition to Scythia and Moesia I where the armies were stationed, the prosperous maritime provinces of Caria, Cyprus and the Islands, whence supplies could be shipped to the Danube.

Since the success of his armies depended on God's favour, Justinian was zealous in reforming the church. Many laws were issued to ensure that simony was suppressed and that worthy bishops and clergy were elected, and that they led seemly lives. Other laws regulated the election of abbots and abbesses and the discipline of monasteries and nunneries. In 529 a purge of the aristocracy was held and many who were convicted of the secret practice of pagan rites were punished. All pagans were ordered to receive Christian instruction and to be baptized; the alternative was exile and the confiscation of their property. The penal laws against the Manichees and Montanists were reinforced and increasing disabilities were inflicted on the Jews and Samaritans. With the Monophysites Justinian attempted conciliatory methods. As a result of a conference between six Chalcedonians and six moderate Monophysites, a formula was reached which the emperor promulgated in 533 and for which he obtained the approval of Pope John II in 534. It made no mention of the one or two natures of Christ, but enunciated that Christ 'who was incarnate and made man and crucified is one of the Holy and Consubstantial Trinity'. Neither the extreme Chalcedonians nor the extreme Monophysites would accept this formula, and in 536 Agapetus, who succeeded John II as pope, visited Constantinople and apparently convinced Justinian that it was unorthodox. At any rate, Anthemius, the patriarch of Constantinople who had been one of the principal promoters of the Edict of 533, was deposed and a persecution of the Monophysites was launched.

Directly Belisarius left Ravenna in 540, the Goths resumed the struggle, electing a new king, Ildebad, and on his death shortly afterwards, Eraric. Soon after Eraric was deposed as a traitor and the Goths elected the great leader who was to carry on the war for over ten years, Totila. Totila swiftly gained the initiative from the Roman generals who had succeeded Belisarius and was soon in occupation of most of southern Italy. In 544 Belisarius returned, but with only 4,000 men to reinforce the depleted army, and Totila continued to make progress, recapturing Rome in 546. In 550 he even invaded Sicily.

In 540, the same year that the Ostrogoths rallied and resumed the struggle, Chosroes broke the Eternal Peace, making a sudden inroad into Syria, where he captured many cities including Antioch itself and withdrew with an immense quantity of booty and prisoners. Next year he attacked Lazica in the Caucasus and captured its principal fortress, Petra. After this he was less successful, and in 545 signed a truce for five years in return for a payment of 5,000 pounds of gold. This truce did not apply to Lazica, where Chosroes refused to restore his conquests. The Romans eventually recaptured Petra in 551, and in the same year the truce was renewed. It still did not apply to Lazica, but in 557, when it was renewed again, Lazica was included, and in 561 a fifty-years' peace was signed. Chosroes abandoned his conquests and his claim to Lazica; Justinian undertook to pay him a subsidy of 30,000 *solidi* a year, nominally for the defence of the Caucasus against the northern barbarians. The payment for the first seven years was made in advance and in the eighth year the next three years' payment was to be made in advance.

Totila's success at last aroused Justinian to the seriousness of the situation in Italy. He assigned the Italian command to his cousin Germanus, who, with money drawn from the treasury and from his own ample private estate, rapidly collected a considerable army in Thrace. He died, however, before he could lead this army into Italy, and the command was given to Narses, one of the imperial eunuchs who had already shown remarkable military talents. Narses insisted on receiving enough money to pay up the long arrears due to the Italian regiments, raised yet more troops and enrolled larger forces of federate Lombards and Heruls. At Busta Gallorum, Narses inflicted a decisive defeat on the Goths, in which Totila was killed (spring, 552) and a few months later he defeated them again under Totila's successor Teias at Mons Lactarius (October 552). It remained to drive the Franks out of northern Italy, which they had invaded nominally to assist the Goths, and to reduce the remaining Gothic garrisons. In 554 Justinian was able to issue the Pragmatic Sanction which regulated the government of the recovered provinces of Italy. One interesting innovation was that provincial governors were to be nominated by the bishops and notables of their provinces. In the same year that Narses was completing the conquest of Italy, Justinian, taking advantage of a civil war in Spain, conquered the southern parts of that country including Nova Carthago, Malaca and Corduba.

In the latter part of his reign, Justinian's efforts at reform lost some of their momentum, but his laws prove that he continued to work for the wellbeing of the provincials and the good order of the church. His interest was more and more devoted to theology, and in particular to the problem of reconciling the Chalcedonians and the Monophysites. One of the stumbling-blocks which impeded conciliation was the fact that the Council of Chalcedon had rehabilitated Theodore of Mopsuestia, Theodoret of Cyrrhus and Ibas of Edessa, whom the Monophysites regarded as tainted with Nestorianism. Justinian came to the conclusion that their charges were in part true, and in 553–4 issued an edict in three chapters condemning certain works of Ibas and Theodoret and pronouncing Theodore a heretic. The eastern patriarchs were induced to subscribe to this edict but Pope Vigilius refused, and in the west in general the edict was badly received. Justinian had Vigilius conveyed to Constantinople in 547 and extracted from him a judgment, *Iudicatum*, approving the edict of the three chapters. Alarmed by the storm of protest in the west, Vigilius later retracted. Justinian then, in 553, summoned an ecumenical council at Constantinople, which duly confirmed the edict. Vigilius refused to attend but was ultimately bullied into submission. Justinian's efforts proved vain; the Monophysites were not appeased by this minor concession, and a schism was created in the west, where most of the churches refused for several decades to accept the verdict of the Council of Constantinople. The breach between the Chalcedonians and the Monophysites had now become permanent. James Baradaeus, a Monophysite monk, secretly consecrated bishop of Edessa in 542, spent the rest of his life building up an underground hierarchy of Monophysite patriarchs, bishops and clergy, and by the time that he died in 572 the Monophysites were a well-organized separate church.

Undeterred by his failure, Justinian went on searching for a formula, and towards the end of his life convinced himself of the truth of the extreme form of Monophysitism, Aphthartodocetism, the doctrine that the body of Christ was incorruptible and impassible. In 564 he issued an edict, declaring the Aphthartodocete doctrine orthodox and ordering the patriarchs to subscribe. They all refused, but the impending struggle was averted by the death of the emperor.

The reconquest of the western provinces did not strengthen the empire, and strained—perhaps overstrained—its resources. Though the initial victory in Africa in 536 was swift and complete, mutinies among the Roman troops and rebellions of the Moors produced constant disturbances until 548, and the country suffered severely. In Italy, again, the initial success of Belisarius was striking and the conquest seemed complete by 540, but another twelve years hard fighting was required before the country was fully subdued, and in the process it was reduced to desolation. In both these cases Justinian made the mistake of not following up Belisarius' initial success. He sent few reinforcements and, what was worse, insufficient money, expecting the new provinces to pay for themselves. The result was that the pay of the troops in Italy and Africa fell into arrear and that their morale declined even if they did not actually mutiny or desert. The emperor was unlucky in being faced in the east by an exceptionally resolute and aggressive enemy in the Persian king, Chosroes. He had either to maintain large bodies of troops on the eastern front to keep Chosroes in check, or to buy peace from him with heavy subsidies. He also had to cope with constant invasions of the Bulgars and Sclavenes in Illyricum and Thrace. But it was not so much from lack of resources as from a failure to appreciate the situation that the western armies were starved of men and money. It was possible in 551 to raise a large army for Narses and to provide him with enough money to pay off all arrears. If this had been done ten years earlier, Italy would not have been ruined before it was finally annexed.

The empire under Justinian

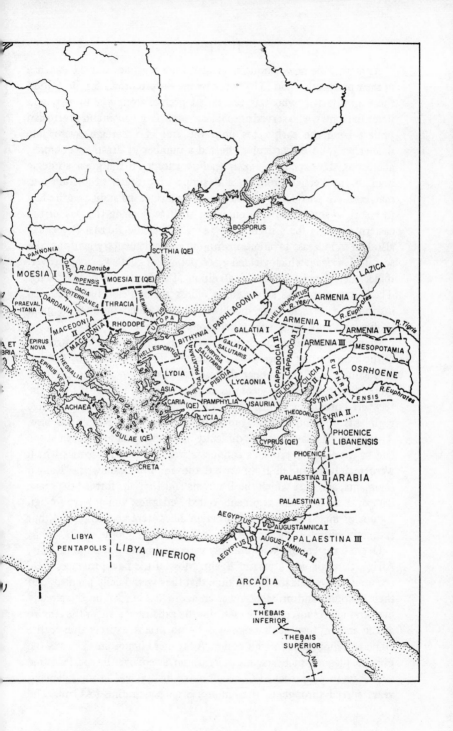

As it was, the new conquests yielded little revenue. and the expense of their pacification had to be borne by the eastern provinces. Both John the Cappadocian, who was praetorian prefect from 531 to 541, and Peter Barsymes, who served as *comes sacrarum largitionum* and praetorian prefect from the early 540s until the end of the reign, were able financiers. John in particular effected a number of drastic economies, abolishing the expensive *cursus publicus* except on the great strategic road to the Persian frontier, and suppressing much peculation and malversation, particularly in the army, by a rigorous audit; but he had to resort to some unwise economies, such as docking the pay of the eastern *limitanei* for a number of years during the Eternal Peace. He also had to increase taxation, instituting a supplementary land tax, the so-called *aerikon*, which yielded 3,000 pounds of gold a year. Moreover, under the financial strain the abolition of *suffragia* did not last long. The government was soon selling offices again. Peter Barsymes also instituted a *de facto* state monopoly of silk, which brought in great profits, and apparently sold other monopolies freely.

In manpower the conquest of the west was not so costly. The strength of the army had, of course, to be increased. The field army, by the end of Justinian's reign, numbered close on 150,000, nearly 50 per cent more than the eastern *comitatus* in the early fifth century. But the recovered provinces furnished recruits: Africa yielded not only the five regiments of Vandal horse, but units of Moors and Numidians also. There seems to have been no difficulty in raising volunteers, even at the end of the reign. Justinian's conquests were effected by armies which were mainly recruited from within the empire. Besides the Roman regiments, amongst which the Isaurians and Illyrians formed the crack troops, there were also regiments called Federates, which were foreign legions of mixed barbarians. Barbarian allies were also employed, but sparingly except in the final campaign against the Goths.

Overall, the empire was probably weakened by the addition of Italy, Africa, Sardinia and a part of Spain. Most of the new provinces were economically exhausted by the time that they were finally pacified, and their conquest and protection was an additional burden on the already overstrained resources of the east. But the exhausted state of the empire at the end of Justinian's reign was by no means entirely due to the emperor's ambitious foreign policy. A far more important fact was the bubonic plague which, starting at Pelusium, swept over Egypt, Palestine and Syria in 542, reached Constantinople in 543, and in the following years spread throughout the empire, even penetrating to Gaul. The initial onset was followed by many recurrences: particularly serious outbreaks are recorded in Constantinople in 558 and in Italy and Gaul in 570–71, and in Constantinople again in 573–74. We have no figures of the mortality, but we hear that in many places the land lay uncultivated for lack of men.

X

The Successors of Justinian

Justinian died on 14 November 565 without having nominated a successor. The most distinguished of the surviving members of his family was Germanus' son Justin, *magister militum* of Illyricum, but another Justin, a nephew, who had for many years been *cura palatii*, was on the spot and secured his own election. Germanus' son was transferred to Alexandria and then executed.

Justin II appears to have been a megalomaniac. He held, at any rate, a very inflated view of the power and might of the empire and of his own dignity as emperor. It was beneath his dignity, he felt, to pay subsidies to barbarians, a Roman emperor should command and impose his will by arms; and when embassies came from Persia and from the Avars, he treated them with studied discourtesy. His reign opened with a series of disasters. In 569–71 Africa was troubled by a Moorish rebellion. In 571–72 the Visigoths recovered much of the Roman province including Corduba. Worst of all, in 565 the Lombards, led by their king Alboin, migrated from their previous home in Illyricum and invaded Italy, swiftly overrunning Venetia, Aemilia and Liguria. Despite these disasters, Justin in 572 deliberately provoked a war with Persia, refusing to pay the annual subsidy stipulated in the treaty, and taking under his protection the Armenians, who had rebelled and asked for

BIBLIOGRAPHY. The history of this period is covered by the *Cambridge Medieval History*, II, ix. In P. Goubert, *Byzance avant l'Islam*, there is a detailed study of the Persian wars and negotiations (Tome I, *Byzance et l'Orient*, Paris, 1951) and of relations with the Franks (Tome II, *Byzance et l'Occident*, Paris, 1955).

The main primary sources are the fragments of Menander Protector, the summary of Theophanes of Byzantium, and the introduction of John of Epiphaneia. For the reign of Maurice there is a full narrative by Theophylact Simocatta. Events in the west are recorded by Paulus Diaconus, and the letters of Pope Gregory the Great provide a fund of information on Italy in the late sixth century.

Roman aid. This rash action was followed by further disasters in 573. Chosroes invaded Syria, sacked Apamea and captured the great frontier-fortress of Dara.

The shock of this news upset Justin's precarious mental balance and he became insane. The empress Sophia took advantage of a lucid interval to get him to nominate Tiberius, the *comes excubitorum*, as Caesar; and Tiberius, taking the additional name of Constantine, governed the empire in Justin's name until the latter's death in 578, when he succeeded as Augustus. Tiberius' immediate aim was to secure a breathing-space. He agreed to pay the Avars an annual subsidy of 80,000 *solidi*, and thereby kept them quiet for a few years. In 580, however, they seized Sirmium, and in 582 Tiberius had to yield to them. In Italy too he preferred bribery to military action. The Lombards, on Alboin's death, had not elected a king to succeed him, but split up into thirty odd groups led by *duces*. They continued to press southwards, and one *dux* established himself at Spoletium, another at Beneventum. Tiberius was, however, able by subsidies to induce some *duces* to take service under the empire and fight their colleagues.

In the east Tiberius only wished to restore Roman strength and prestige sufficiently to extract a fair peace from the Persians. But even for this modest end he needed a temporary truce to give him time to build up his forces. He eventually achieved a three-year truce (for which he paid 30,000 *solidi* a year) in Mesopotamia, but not in Armenia. He succeeded in recruiting a large army and in 578 appointed Maurice, an able Cappadocian officer, as *magister militum* of the East. Maurice won some successes and Tiberius was now able to negotiate a truce, and offered generous terms to Chosroes, the restitution of Armenia, Iberia, and Arzanene, which the Romans had conquered, in return for Dara, which Chosroes had captured. The treaty was all but signed, when in 579 Chosroes died and his successor, Hormisdas, fearing to lose face by making any concession to Rome, broke off negotiations. The war dragged on until Tiberius died on 14 August 582, having named Maurice as Augustus.

At home, as in foreign affairs, Tiberius reversed his predecessor's policy. Justin, after an attempt at reconciling the Monophysites by an Edict of Union, in 571 launched a persecution. Tiberius relaxed the persecution and let the Monophysites be. Justin had been careful, even parsimonious, in his finance. He had, it is true, abandoned *suffragia* at the beginning of his reign, extending to the whole empire the scheme initiated by Justinian in Italy, whereby the bishops and notables of the provinces chose provincial governors. He soon, however, revived *suffragia* and he imposed a duty on wine and made the holders of bread tickets at Constantinople pay for them. By these measures and by cutting off subsidies he seems to have accumulated a considerable balance. Tiberius was, on the other hand, lavish. Not only did he again renounce *suffragia* and annul Justin's new taxes in 574: on his accession as Augustus in 578, he remitted one year's taxation by reducing the tax by one-quarter for four years. He spent lavishly on subsidies to the barbarians and on building up his army. He seems to have left his successor with heavy commitments and an empty treasury.

Maurice continued to concentrate his strength on the Persian front and to hold off the barbarians in the west and in the Balkans by subsidies. He was tolerably successful in Italy, where he induced the Frankish king, Childebert, to invade northern Italy in 584, 585, 588 and 590. The Lombards reacted to the Frankish threat by once again electing a king, Authari. But not all the *duces* submitted to him and several took service under Rome. The Italian provinces had by this time been reduced to a number of enclaves surrounding Ravenna, Rome, Genoa, Naples and a few other towns, and communications between these areas were intermittent and insecure. Wars alternated with truces, and the country was reduced to a miserable condition. The Romans had some successes—Gregory the Great mentions the recovery of Auximum from the Lombards in 599—but on the whole barbarians continued to encroach; Gregory records the loss of Venafrum and of Croton. Moreover many of the cities in the Roman areas were abandoned by their inhabitants as a result of constant raids: the pope had to amalgamate the bishoprics of many deserted towns with those of their surviving neighbours. Only Sicily was spared invasion and still prospered.

In these circumstances the Roman government became increasingly military. At its head stood the *magister militum*, now styled the exarch, who resided at Ravenna. He was virtually a governor general, and the praetorian prefect of Italy played a very subordinate role. In the provinces there were still civil governors, but the *duces* and *magistri militum* of the military districts were far more important. Even the individual cities were governed by the tribunes or *comites* of their garrisons.

In Africa also the supreme control was vested in the exarch, and the praetorian prefect was subordinated to him. The enemy here was the Moorish tribes, who twice revolted in Maurice's reign. The towns were all fortified, even in the long peaceful areas of Proconsularis and

Byzacena, but conditions were by no means so unsettled as in Italy, and the country seems to have enjoyed some prosperity.

On the Danube Maurice secured some measure of peace by agreeing to raise the Avar subsidy from 80,000 to 500,000 *solidi* a year. On the eastern front, the war dragged on and Maurice found the financial strain more and more severe, until, in 588, he decided to cut the soldiers' pay by 25 per cent. The result was a mutiny, in which Priscus, the *magister militum*, was chased away and the soldiers elected Germanus, the *dux* of Phoenice, as their general. Under his command, however, they carried on the war with Persia, and eventually, by the good offices of Gregory, the patriarch of Antioch, they returned to their allegiance on condition that the pay cut was cancelled. Germanus was court-martialled and formally condemned to death, but was reprieved and rewarded for his services.

In 591 there was a dramatic reversal of fortune. Hormisdas was assassinated and his son, Chosroes, unable to hold his own against Varanes, the rebel satrap of Media, took refuge in Roman territory and flung himself on Maurice's mercy, offering to cede Martyropolis, Dara, Armenia and Arzanene, in return for Roman aid. Maurice provided him with an army and with this help Chosroes recovered his kingdom and fulfilled his side of the bargain.

Maurice was now able to transfer his troops to the Danubian front. From 592 to 602 a series of campaigns was fought against the Avars and the Slavenes. Maurice was still short of money and he made himself unpopular by ordering the army to winter north of the Danube and live on enemy territory in 593–94; and also by issuing arms and uniforms in kind instead of paying a cash arms and uniform allowance. In 601 Maurice once again ordered the army to winter north of the Danube and the result was a mutiny led by a non-commissioned officer named Phocas. The rebels offered the throne to Maurice's son, Theodosius, but he refused; and then to Theodosius' father-in-law, Germanus, who took sanctuary. Unable to offer any resistance, Maurice also took sanctuary, and Germanus then made a bid for the crown. The army decided that they would prefer Phocas and the senate obediently elected him on 23 November 602. Phocas proceeded to massacre Maurice and all his family.

The reign of Phocas, 602–10, was an unmitigated series of disasters. As a low-born pretender, he commanded no loyalty and there were many conspiracies against him, which he suppressed with savage brutality. The Avars promptly overran Thrace and Illyricum; Narses, the *magister militum* of the East, raised a rebellion; Chosroes, pretending to avenge his benefactor, invaded the empire and occupied Syria and Palestine and Cappadocia, and even penetrated to Chalcedon. The only part of the empire which remained intact was Africa, and it was Heraclius, son of the exarch of Africa, who, occupying Egypt by land and Constantinople by sea, overthrew Phocas and was proclaimed emperor in his stead. The first ten years of Heraclius' reign were as disastrous as those of Phocas. Chosroes captured Jerusalem and carried off the True Cross and invaded and occupied Egypt. Heraclius thought of returning to Africa, but was forced to remain in the capital by popular clamour. From 622 onwards, by a series of brilliant campaigns, he defeated the Persians, and in 629 the Persian king restored the True Cross to Jerusalem. But Heraclius' restoration of the empire was short-lived. In 634, the Arabs, inspired by the teaching of Mohammed, invaded Palestine, and in 636 won a decisive victory over the imperial forces at the battle of the Yarmuk. In 638 Jerusalem surrendered to the Arabs, and before Heraclius died in February 641 they had occupied Egypt.

XI

The Emperor and his Advisers

Both in theory and in practice the later empire was an absolute monarchy. The emperor personally made all appointments down to provincial governor and regimental commander. He made war and signed treaties; he levied or remitted taxes at will. He had the power of life and death over his subjects and was the supreme source of law. There were some ghosts of the past, when the emperor had been a republican magistrate who owed his power to his people. 'What the emperor decides has the force of law', wrote Ulpian[1] in the early third century, 'because in the royal law, which is passed about his sovereignty, the people confers upon him all its sovereignty and power'; and this dictum is preserved in Justinian's Digest and repeated in his Institutes. Since the people was deemed by one act to have made over to the emperor the plenitude of its power, and was incapable of recalling it, the doctrine did not have much practical importance except in a vacancy of the throne. From it, it was deduced that *senatus consulta*, decrees of the senate, had independent validity, 'for when the Roman people was so greatly increased that it was difficult for it to be convened in one place to enact a law, it was deemed proper that the senate should be consulted instead of the people'.[2] Ever since the first century A.D., however, the senate had never done more than register its assent to an imperial motion. It was also, no doubt, a survival of republican thinking that the emperor, though he was personally freed from the laws (*legibus solutus*) and could make new laws and alter the old at will, was expected to obey the law: as Ambrose[3] puts it, 'the emperor enacts laws which he is the first to keep'. He was in fact an absolute but not an arbitary monarch:

BIBLIOGRAPHY. There is no systematic account of this subject except Chapter XI of my *Later Roman Empire* (Oxford, 1964). For the relations of church and state see S. L. Greenslade, *Church and State from Constantine to Theodosius* (London, 1954).

[1] *Digest.* I, iv. I, proem.   [2] *Digest.* I, ii. 2 §9.   [3] *Epist.* 21 §9.

hence the distinction drawn by Gregory the Great:[1] 'This is the difference between barbarian kings and the Roman emperor, that barbarian kings are the lords of slaves, but the Roman emperor is the lord of free men.'

On the other hand, the emperor still retained many vestigial traces of the time when he had been a god. The earlier emperors had officially not been gods to Roman citizens, but only to the provincials. But when all the inhabitants of the Roman empire became Roman citizens, this distinction had become blurred. Some emperors of the third century had, like Aurelian, claimed outright to be 'lord and god' (*dominus et deus*). Others, like Diocletian, preferred to be *Iovius*, vice-gerent and representative of *Jupiter optimus maximus*. It is very difficult to discern what this claim to divinity really meant. The speakers of panegyrics make great play with it, sometimes openly addressing the emperor as a god, at other times alleging more subtly that the emperor enjoys some special communion with the gods. When the emperor became a Christian, he could no longer be a god, but he remained vice-gerent of God. Constantine was personally convinced that he was God's servant and that the highest divinity had, by his celestial will, entrusted the government of the world to him. Eusebius, in the panegyric which he delivered on the thirtieth anniversary of Constantine's accession, elaborates this idea, almost making Constantine a fourth member of the Trinity. Everything connected with the emperor—his palace, his treasury, his bedchamber—remained sacred, so much so that *sacra* became the ordinary Greek word for an imperial constitution: disobedience to the emperor was sacrilege. How much all this meant it is difficult to divine. Despite it, good Christians sometimes thought it their duty to defy the emperor, and rebels did not hesitate to lay hands on his sacred person.

The political theory of the later empire is not unnaturally very jejune. Absolute monarchy was the only conceivable form of government and required no justification. Philosophers and rhetoricians frequently addressed to the emperors orations on kingship, but these consist merely of a catalogue of the virtues which a good king must possess, and which the emperor addressed is deemed to possess in high degree. Most prominent among the royal virtues is philanthropy—love for his fellowmen.

The only constitutional problem was the relation of the emperor to the church. In their early days, the churches had been independent, self-governing societies which formed their own rules. On the other

[1] *Epist.* XI. 4, XIII. 34.

hand, in the pagan scheme of things, the emperor was deemed to be ultimately responsible for maintaining the *pax deorum*, that is of ensuring that the empire enjoyed the favour of the gods by seeing that their worship was duly performed and that the inhabitants of the empire kept certain moral rules.

When Constantine was converted, he assumed that it was still his duty to maintain the *pax Dei* by making the church offer to the highest divinity that united worship which he demanded. He believed that 'the highest divinity may perhaps be moved to wrath not only against the human race but also against myself, to whom he has by his celestial will committed the government of all earthly things',[1] if he allowed quarrels within the church, and held that he had no 'higher duty in virtue of my imperial office and policy than to dissipate errors and suppress rash indiscretions and so cause all to offer to Almighty God true religion, honest concord and due worship'.[2] It might have been expected that the churches would have rejected these claims, used as they were to independence. But in point of fact they welcomed and even invited imperial interference. The Donatists asked Constantine to settle their dispute with Caecilian and, condemned by two councils of bishops, appealed to him personally. Athanasius, condemned by the Council of Tyre, appealed against the verdict to Constantine himself. The only sign of misgiving is a canon of a council held at Antioch soon after Nicaea, which enacted that 'if any priest or deacon, condemned by his bishop, or any bishop condemned by a council, dares trouble the ears of the emperor when he ought to resort to a larger council of bishops, he is to receive no pardon or opportunity of defence and expect no hope of restitution'.[3] It was under this canon that Athanasius was later condemned by his enemies in the east. His supporters made light of the charge.

The emperor was thus generally accepted as the ultimate arbiter for ecclesiastical disputes. He was expected to take the advice of councils of bishops on points of doctrine, but he summoned the councils and presided over them in person or by deputy and confirmed and executed their verdicts. Most emperors accepted this position. Valentinian I was very exceptional in granting toleration to all sects and refusing to summon a council on the faith, declaring that 'it is not right that I as a layman should meddle in such things. The bishops whose business it is may meet and discuss them if they wish.'[4] Some emperors were more

---

[1] Optatus of Mileve, *App.* iii. [2] *ib.*, *App.* vii.
[3] H. G. Opitz, *Athanasius Werke*, III, 18. [4] Sozomen, *Hist. Eccl.* VI, 7.

passive in fulfilling their role: others more active. Some, like Theodosius I, Zeno and Justinian, took action without any prior consultation of the bishops, laying down the true faith by imperial edict and inviting the bishops to subscribe to their views. But this roused no public protest, except from those whose views did not coincide with the imperial will.

The doctrine of toleration and religious liberty was in fact preached only by the defeated parties in ecclesiastical conflicts. The Donatists had originally invoked Constantine's intervention. It was not until he had finally rejected their claims that they adopted the cry, 'What has the emperor to do with the church ?'.[1] Athanasius appealed to Constantine against an episcopal council. It was again only when Constantius II supported his opponents in the Arian controversy that he and his ally Hilary preached the doctrine of religious liberty and deplored imperial intervention in ecclesiastical disputes.

In 494 Pope Gelasius,[2] boldly rebuking Anastasius from Rome, where he enjoyed the protection of an Arian king, enunciated the famous doctrines of the Two Powers:

'There are, your Majesty, two things whereby this world is chiefly governed, the sacred authority of bishops and the imperial power. Of them, the burden of the priests is the greater, in that they must render account in the divine judgment for the kings of men also: for you know, most clement son, that though you preside over the human race in dignity, you submit your neck humbly to the leaders of things divine and seek from them the cause of your salvation. . . . You know that you ought to submit yourself in religious issues rather than take the lead, and that in these matters you depend on their judgment, and that you should not wish them to be subject to your will, for if in matters of public order the leaders of religion, recognizing that the government has been conferred on you by heavenly decree, themselves obey your laws, with what feelings ought and must not you obey those who have been allotted the role of presiding over the divine mysteries?

Most emperors would have demurred at this presentation of the case. They were, they would have argued, entrusted by God not only with the secular government of the world, but with its spiritual guardianship as well. They would have agreed that on technical points of theology, it was their duty to respect the opinion of the bishops, but they might

---

[1] Optatus of Mileve, III, 3.   [2] *Epist*. XII, 2.

have asked 'Which bishops?' Relations between the emperor and the church in fact only became difficult when the church spoke with two voices and the emperor did not know which voice to obey. Anastasius could have claimed that he was obeying the bishops of the east, who had all subscribed to the Henotikon, and it was the pope who was out of step.

The later Roman empire was generally ruled by a college of emperors, who were either all Augusti, equal save in seniority, or some Augusti and some Caesars of inferior rank. In fact, during the two centuries which elapsed from Diocletian's appointment of Maximian as Caesar of the west in 285 to the deposition of Romulus in 476, there were only about three years in all during which the empire was ruled by a single emperor. Constantine was the only Augustus from the defeat of Licinius in 324 till his death in 337, but during all this period parts of the empire were ruled by his sons as Caesars. Constantius II, again, was sole Augustus from the defeat of Magnentius in 353 to his own death in 361. But before starting on his campaign against Magnentius, he appointed Gallus Caesar in the east, and before he returned to the east he created Julian Caesar in the west. From Constantius II's death (3 November 361), Julian (*ob.* 26 June 363) and then Jovian (*ob.* 17 February 364) were sole emperors, but Valentinian after a month's sole rule created his brother Valens Augustus to rule the east. On Valens' death on 9 August 378 Gratian was *de facto* sole emperor for five months, till on 19 January 379 he nominated Theodosius emperor of the east, but during this period his younger brother Valentinian II was his nominal colleague. During the interregna between Avitus and Majorian, 27 October 456 to 28 November 457, and between Libius Severus and Anthemius, 19 November 466 to 25 March 467, Marcian and Leo were technically emperors of the whole empire.

It is clear that it was considered impossible for one emperor to cope with the problems of an empire which stretched from Britain to the Tigris. At least two emperors were required, one in the west and one in the east, if the barbarians were to be held on all fronts and usurpers not to arise in neglected sectors of the empire. In theory the emperors, whether Augusti or Caesars, formed a single college which jointly ruled the whole empire. All laws and official pronouncements by any emperor were issued in the name of all, and all letters to the emperor were addressed to the whole college. Even the praetorian prefects were officially a college, jointly administering the whole empire, and an edict of any praetorian prefect was headed by the names of all of them. In practice, the relations between the colleagues varied greatly. Diocletian was *de facto* the master of his team of four emperors, though technically Maximian was his constitutional equal. Constantius II kept a very tight rein on his Caesars, appointing their praetorian prefects and other ministers, and allowing them no control over the cash revenues of their administrative areas. Valentinian and Valens co-operated fairly closely in their administrative reforms, though they differed radically in their religious policy. Gratian gave military support to Valens and to Theodosius I, and after Gratian's death Theodosius was virtually sole ruler, exercising authority over both Valentinian II in the West and Arcadius in the East. But from 395 to 408 there was continual friction and at times a cold war between Honorius' and Arcadius' governments, and thereafter the western and eastern halves of the empire went very much their own ways. They were generally in friendly alliance and the eastern government several times helped the western, once against Alaric in 408, once against the usurper John in 425, twice against the Vandals in 431 and 467. But the emperors were far from being colleagues in a real sense. There was free trade and free migration between the two parts, and the currency of either was valid in both, but the law did not keep strictly in step, since constitutions issued by one emperor were generally promulgated in his part only. After the Theodosian Code was received in both parts in 438, it was officially enacted that a constitution issued by one emperor should not apply in the other's dominions unless he formally accepted and promulgated it.

The throne was never legally hereditary in the Roman empire. There was a school of thought, of which the last exponent was Diocletian, which held that the emperor should ignore the claims of birth and choose the best man available as his heir. Dynastic sentiment was, however, strong among the people, and particularly in the army, and from Constantine onwards the throne always passed to sons and other near relatives of the emperors, even if they were children. Despite the disadvantages of minorities this arrangement made for stability, for dynastic loyalty was built up. Even when the male heirs failed, the women of the imperial family could hand on the inherited goodwill of the dynasty to an outsider by marrying him. Thus Marcian's position was confirmed by his marriage to Pulcheria, the last survivor of the Theodosian house, and Anastasius' by his alliance to Ariadne, the daughter of Leo and the widow of Zeno.

Constitutionally an Augustus could create an emperor, either another Augustus, his equal, or a Caesar, his inferior colleague; and so long as any member of the imperial college survived, a second emperor could only be created with his consent. If no member of the imperial college survived, a new emperor was elected. The electors, according to the old constitutional theory from the principate, were the senate and people, but the people soon dropped out and were replaced by the army. From the fourth century, the effective electoral body was 'the palace' or 'the ministers', whose choice was formally confirmed by a vote of the senate and the acclamation of the army. Very often the emperor was *de facto* the nominee of some powerful emperor-maker. In the west Majorian, Libius Severus, and Olybrius were nominees of Ricimer, the patrician and commander-in-chief; in the east Marcian and Leo were the choice of Aspar, the *magister militum praesentalis*.

Emperors generally assured the succession of their sons or other persons of their choice by creating them emperor during their own lifetime. Diocletian worked out an elaborate and artificial scheme whereby the two Augusti were to abdicate simultaneously, having made their Caesars Augusti and nominated two new Caesars. This scheme, which ignored the claims of birth, broke down at once and Constantine, reverting to the hereditary principle, created his sons and a nephew Caesars as they came of age. Valentinian went further and nominated his son Gratian as Augustus in 367, when he was only eight years old. Theodosius did the same by his two sons, whom he made Augusti as children, and Arcadius made Theodosius II Augustus almost from his birth.

Usurpers normally began by getting themselves acclaimed by the army, or rather a part of the army. They might also, if they gained control of Rome or Constantinople, secure their election by the senate; but so long as there was another emperor, they could only legitimize their seizure of power by securing his recognition, and their first act was generally to announce their acclamation or election to the existing emperor and ask his approval.

When an emperor chose a colleague or successor, he normally selected a man with some administrative and military experience. Gratian's choice, Theodosius I, had been a successful *dux*. Leo's nominees for the western empire, Anthemius and Nepos, were both men of tried talent. Emperors who were put up by the great generals were, not unnaturally, often men of no distinction, who might be expected to be obedient figureheads. Marcian and Leo were mere tribunes and were chosen by Aspar because the former had been his aide-de-camp and the latter the manager of his estates. Arbogast selected Eugenius a *magister scrinii* and Castinus John the *primicerius* of the notaries, both holders of minor palatine dignities.

When there was a genuine election, it was rarely that a senior and experienced minister or general was chosen. Salutius, the praetorian prefect of the East, was offered the throne on Julian's death, but on his refusal a very junior officer, Jovian, the *primicerius* of the *protectores*, was elected. It would appear that mutual jealousies normally barred the election of any prominent men, and the rival factions compromised on a nonentity whom they thought that they could control. Pretenders and usurpers were on the whole as obscure a group. Magnentius was only commander of the Ioviani and Herculiani, and Theodore, who was alleged to have conspired against Valens, was the second senior notary.

Powerful generals usually preferred to remain the powers behind the throne, governing through puppet emperors, and did not aspire to the purple themselves. In some cases this may have been because, being German and Arians, they were unacceptable as emperors, but *magistri militum* of Roman birth and orthodox faith like Castinus or Orestes were equally reluctant to become emperors, while Aspar, who refused the purple for himself when it was offered to him by the senate, demanded that his son Patricius, who like himself was an Arian and a barbarian, should be made Caesar. It may be that the military commanders feared to lose touch with their troops, on whose loyalty their power rested, if they withdrew into the seclusion of the sacred palace, or that they preferred to exercise *de facto* control, unhampered by the many ceremonial duties with which the emperor was burdened.

The emperors had two official bodies of advisers, the senate and the consistory. The senate had even under the principate ceased to be an effective council of state. Under the later Roman empire the Roman senate could hardly be so, since its sessions were held at Rome, and from the middle of the third century the emperor rarely visited the city. The senate of Constantinople was, it would seem, more regularly consulted, but there was rarely a serious debate in either house.

After the battle of Adrianople, when Valens was dead and Gratian was inaccessible in the west, the senate of Constantinople authorized Julius, the *magister militum Orientis*, to massacre the Gothic troops recently enrolled in his army. In 408 and 409, when Rome was invested by Alaric and his Visigoths and Honorius was shut up in Ravenna, the Roman senate had to take the responsibility of negotiating the ransoming of the city, and later of proclaiming a rival emperor, Attalus, at Alaric's behest. But these were quite exceptional cases.

Normally the function of the senate was not to advise the emperor but to ratify his decisions and sometimes to strengthen his hand by sharing the odium of unpopular measures. Thus Stilicho put the issue of peace or war with Alaric to the Roman senate and made it vote for the heavy subsidy demanded for keeping the peace. Zeno put to the senate of Constantinople the question of the two Theoderics, eliciting from it the judgment that the treasury could not afford to pay both what they demanded, and thus making it share the responsibility for the war with the rejected claimant which was bound to follow. It could in the theory of the constitution legislate. Normally it merely registered imperial constitutions, but by an eastern law of 446 it was enacted that proposals should be discussed by the ministers of the palace and by the senate, severally and jointly, before being formally promulgated. The eastern senate sometimes also acted as a supreme court under the presidency of the emperor or his representative. The practice first appeared under Marcian and became regular under Justinian.

The consistory was a less ancient and venerable body than the senate, but its origins went back to the beginning of the principate. The emperor, like all magistrates, in making any decision took the advice of a council of assessors (*concilium*) chosen by himself. The *concilium principis* became the *consistorium* when its members no longer sat but stood in the emperor's presence. The membership of the consistory was fluctuating and depended on the choice of the emperor, but normally his chief ministers were summoned, as well as a number of unofficial members. The emperor's choice was not limited to senators and equestrian officials often took part in the sessions. In the reign of Constantius II the consistory was still a genuine council of state in which problems were debated and decisions reached. Ammianus gives a vivid picture of the agitated sessions of the consistory which discussed the measures to be taken to cope with the revolt of Silvanus. Gradually however the membership of the consistory expanded and its time came to be more and more occupied with formal business, the grant of codicils of office and rank, the distribution of largesse and donatives, the receipt of loyal addresses, and so forth. Its sessions had by the fifth century become as formal as those of the senate if not more so.

To replace it there seems to have developed an inner cabinet described as the palace (*palatium*) or the notables of the palace (*proceres palatii*). It appears to have consisted of the chief ministers and one or two additional members. There was however nothing like cabinet government. On most questions, it would seem, the emperor took action on the advice of the minister concerned with that department of government and it was only rarely that he consulted his ministers jointly. The emperor might also habitually consult advisers of his own choice who were not ministers. Datianus, patrician and consul under Constantius II, never held any office but appears to have been an influential counsellor of the emperor. He is said to have played a large part after his death in the election of Valentinian I. Marinus the Syrian was Anastasius' financial expert and the author of important fiscal reforms while he was only a clerk in the praetorian prefecture, several years before he became praetorian prefect.

The absence of any effective cabinet system is shown by the contradictory laws issued and annulled on the suggestion of different ministers. Thus a law issued in 440 on the suggestion of the praetorian prefect, giving him jurisdiction over soldiers and civil servants, was three months later annulled so far as soldiers were concerned and six months later restricted in its application to officials of the *magistri militum*. The last law was addressed to one of them and probably suggested by them. The lack of a cabinet is also demonstrated by what happened when the emperor was a minor or weak-minded or indolent. The government was not controlled by the senate or the consistory or by an inner cabinet of imperial ministers, but by individuals or cliques who secured the emperor's ear and could control his signature. Such powers behind the throne were often high ministers of state or generals, such as Anthemius, the praetorian prefect of the East in the last years of Arcadius and in the minority of Theodosius II, or Stilicho, the *magister militum praesentalis* in the first thirteen years of Honorius. But they might be palace eunuchs, who had no official part in the administration, like Eutropius for a brief period at the beginning of Arcadius' reign, or Chrysaphius in the last decade of Theodosius II. They might even be women of the imperial family. His mother Justina governed in the name of little Valentinian II; his elder sister Pulcheria and his wife Eudocia in that of Theodosius II; Galla Placidia in that of her son Valentinian III.

In the east the prestige of the imperial office stood very high; even when the throne was occupied by men of very feeble character like Arcadius' son Theodosius II the authority of the emperor was not overtly challenged and the empire was ruled in his name by those who could establish a personal ascendancy over him. Emperors like Marcian and Leo, who were obscure men of no particular ability and owed their elevation to the backing of the general Aspar, were able to assert themselves and take an independent line: Leo was ultimately able to rid himself of his too overbearing patron. Rebellions were very few in the east and were easily suppressed. Under Diocletian Domitius Domitianus was quickly subdued; under Valens Procopius gained very little support. Only Zeno, who was hated as an Isaurian, despised as an upstart, and, it would seem, was not a man of striking presence or ability as a statesman or as a soldier, was troubled by many rebellions, and even he won through in the end.

In the west the imperial office commanded less unquestioning obedience. Under Diocletian Carausius ruled Britain for nearly ten years in defiance of the tetrarchy, and after his death Constantine and Maxentius were proclaimed by their troops. Constans was overthrown by the usurper Magnentius, Gratian by Magnus Maximus, and Valentinian II was assassinated by his *magister militum*, Arbogast, and replaced by Eugenius. Honorius was troubled by a series of pretenders, Attalus, Constantine and his son Constans, and Jovinus, though he managed to survive them all. On his death the throne was bestowed on John by the *magister militum*, Castinus. After Valentinian III's death there followed a series of emperors who were many of them puppets of the great *magistri militum* Ricimer, Gundobad and Orestes.

This difference between east and west was partly due to the long and scarcely interrupted tradition of monarchy in the east. The Persians had been succeeded by the Hellenistic kings and after a brief and unhappy interlude of republican rule the eastern provinces had welcomed Augustus as a king. In the west, it seems, the same traditional sanctity did not surround the person of a legitimate emperor, and an ambitious or discontented general could more easily induce his army to proclaim him as emperor. Another reason for the greater stability of the monarchy in the east was that its emperors less often failed in their primary function of protecting their dominions against external enemies. Only the Balkan provinces were subject to barbarian inroads: the rest of the empire was normally secure. In the west on the other hand Illyricum, Gaul and Italy itself were vulnerable, and when an emperor like Honorius failed to protect his out-lying dominions it was natural that they should support a local rival like Constantine.

From the end of the fourth century the contrast between the two parts of the empire was accentuated by their different military organization. This again was partly due to strategic considerations, but more to the situation which followed the death of Theodosius the Great. When he died shortly after the defeat of the usurper Eugenius he left the western parts under the control of Stilicho, his favourite general, who was in command of the united armies of the empire, and commended to him the protection of his son, the boy-emperor Honorius. Stilicho took advantage of the youth of Honorius to enhance the power of his own office, making the *magister utriusque militiae praesentalis* commander-in-chief of the armies, with the *comites rei militaris* and *duces* under his disposition. He also got into his hands the issue of commissions to all officers and exercised administrative control over the *comites* and *duces*, appointing members of his own *officium* to hold the principal posts in their offices. Thereafter the *magister militum praesentalis* or, as he came to be called, the patrician, became the *de facto* ruler of the western empire. He commanded the loyalty of the armies and, sure of their support, could make and unmake emperors at will. The growth of the office was assisted by the weak characters of the two emperors who reigned for the sixty years which followed Theodosius' death, Honorius and Valentinian III. Stilicho ruled unchallenged for thirteen years. After his death there was a brief interlude of civilian rule, but Constantius soon asserted his supremacy and ultimately in the last year of his life became colleague of Honorius. Early in the reign of Valentinian III there were bitter struggles, and even open battles, for the office of patrician, until about 433 Aetius imposed himself upon the emperor and ruled the empire for over twenty years. On his and Valentinian III's death Ricimer quickly established himself as patrician, and henceforth any emperor who showed any signs of independence was promptly deposed. Ultimately Odoacer conceived the idea that the patrician might rule the west under the nominal sovereignty of the eastern emperor.

In the east the situation was very different. When Theodosius marched west against Eugenius he left the eastern parts under the nominal charge of his son Arcadius and under the actual control of Rufinus, the praetorian prefect. Rufinus was succeeded by Eutropius, the chief eunuch. These civilian heads of the government were naturally jealous of the generals and when the eastern armies returned from the west they were equally divided between five co-ordinate commanders, the two *magistri praesentales* and three *magistri* of Illyricum, Thrace and the East. The failure of the bungling Gainas to seize power confirmed the power of the civilian ministers and during the long reign of Theodosius II the empire was ruled by the praetorian prefect Anthemius, the master of the offices Helio, and finally the eunuch Chrysaphius, together with the master of the offices Nomus. After Theodosius II's death Aspar, who had been one of the two *magistri praesentales* for some twenty years, aspired to play the same part which the western patricians played. He appointed two successive emperors, Marcian and Leo, and even went so far as to compel Leo to nominate his son Patricius as Caesar; but when Leo challenged his supremacy it was the emperor who prevailed. Aspar never commanded more than two-fifths of the army, even when his son Ardaburius was his colleague as *magister militum* of the East, and Leo was able to depose Ardaburius on an accusation of treason and finally free himself of Aspar's domination by assassinating him. Thereafter no general challenged the authority of an eastern emperor. Vitalian, it is true, raised a rebellion against Anastasius, but he did not venture to claim the throne but contented himself with trying to dictate the emperor's ecclesiastical policy. Maurice's fall was not due to the ambition of a general but to the bitter discontent of the armies with the emperor's harsh discipline and his economies at their expense. It was a spontaneous military revolt which raised Phocas to the throne.

In the west, then, down to the end of the fourth century, and in the east for long after, any emperor of reasonable ability and strength of character was not only theoretically but actually absolute, and a weak emperor was controlled by intrigue and influence: his authority was never openly opposed. The absolutism of the emperors is demonstrated by the appointments they made to high offices of state. The type of men promoted varies strikingly from reign to reign. Constantius II, who was very susceptible to the influence of those who immediately surrounded him, appointed many of his notaries to high offices of state. Julian promoted cultured men of letters. Under Valentinian and Valens many of the high offices were occupied by fellow Pannonians, usually men of little education. One of Theodosius' praetorian prefects of the East was Rufinus, an Aquitanian, and another, Cynegius, a Spaniard.

The emperors were of course to some extent influenced by their entourage. In the west the ancient and wealthy senatorial aristocracy, which Diocletian had virtually excluded from high office, began under Constantine to make their influence felt, and increasingly established their claim to hold the great civilian offices, until by the middle years of the fifth century they had established a virtual monopoly: but they never had any share in the military commands, which were politically more important. In the east there was no entrenched hereditary aristocracy and the emperors had a much freer hand. A new aristocracy, it is true, gradually grew up from the descendants of the new men whom Constantius II had ennobled, and in the fifth century we often find sons and grandsons of Constantius' favourites holding the praetorian prefecture and the high military commands. But the promotion of commoners never ceased. Anastasius normally appointed barristers to the praetorian prefecture and occasionally civil servants. Nearly all of Justinian's famous ministers and generals were men of humble origins whom he himself had picked out for their ability.

The emperors could make drastic changes in religious policy without regard to public opinion. Constantine, though the vast majority of his subjects and almost all the aristocracy and the army were pagans, was able to despoil the temples of their treasures, confiscate their lands and finally prohibit sacrifice without a sign of overt opposition. Two generations later, when Christianity had under the patronage of Constantine and his sons made great progress, Julian was able to reopen the temples and re-endow them. Constantine, under the guidance of Hosius, imposed the homoousian doctrine on the reluctant eastern church at Nicaea. His son Constantius II made the western churches, despite their fanatical adhesion to the Nicene formula, vote at Ariminum for a semi-Arian creed. Theodosius I who, as a westerner, personally believed in the Nicene Creed, imposed it by imperial decree on the eastern churches and got his decision ratified by the Council of Constantinople in 381. Chrysaphius, the all-powerful eunuch of Theodosius II, who favoured the monophysite doctrine of Eutyches, had it confirmed by the ecumenical council at Ephesus in 449. Marcian and Pulcheria, who took the opposite view, imposed the Tome of Leo on the eastern churches two years later at Chalcedon.

In the secular affairs also the emperor's will, if he chose to enforce it, was paramount. Valentinian, who was a military man of peasant origin, favoured the army and endeavoured to protect the lower classes. He revised the official order of precedence to give high standing to *magistri militum* and *duces*, and instituted the *defensores plebis* to protect the humble. Anastasius' keen interest in finance is reflected by a whole series of laws and a number of notable reforms. A change of reign might often mean a reversal of foreign policy. Chrysaphius and Nomus in the latter years of Theodosius II had favoured paying subsidies to Attila, even though this meant extra levies on the wealthy. Marcian on his accession defied Attila. Justinian insisted on his ambitious policy of reconquering the west despite the unanimous opposition of his generals and ministers. Justin II abruptly reversed his uncle's policy of paying subsidies to the barbarians.

The government was then in a real sense the emperor or, if the emperor was a child or a weakling, the person or clique who for the time being controlled him. Like most governments, the imperial government did not often take the initiative and formulate a planned policy. In general the emperors were content to repel attacks on the empire or at most to conduct punitive wars against the barbarians. It was only exceptional emperors like Julian or Justinian that took the offensive. In domestic affairs too planned measures of reform were rare. Valentinian I took the initiative in instituting the *defensores plebis* and also in a short-lived attempt to transfer the duty of collecting the taxes and managing the public post from the decurions to *honorati* and retired officials. Anastasius also took the initiative in converting land tax to gold, in instituting the *vindices*, in abolishing the *chrysargyron*, and in reforming the copper currency. Justinian planned his great reform of the law and of the provincial administration.

In general, however, the imperial government was content to tackle problems as they arose, or rather as they were brought to its attention. Its policy was thus influenced by various groups who pressed their grievances or ambitions upon it. By reading between the lines of the Codes, one can to some extent evaluate the influence exercised by various groups.

Among the least influential were not unnaturally the peasantry, who had no means of voicing their grievances. There are occasional laws designed to protect the peasants from oppression by their landlords or by officials, but in general legislation is obviously inspired by landlords, in whose interests tenants were tied to their holdings. The series of laws against patronage is clearly designed to protect the revenue, and not the peasantry, who are as severely penalized for seeking patronage as are great men for imposing it. Urban craftsmen are given as little regard: most laws, such as those forbidding combinations, or those tying them to their trade, are dictated by the consumer interest. The guilds of Rome and Constantinople had more opportunity to voice their points of view through the prefect of the city, who was naturally interested in seeing that they functioned efficiently in order to prevent agitation or riots in the capital. But here again, though the ancient privileges of the guilds are often confirmed, the legislation is normally repressive. The guilds of shippers (*navicularii*) had more influence with the government. They not infrequently sent delegations to the court to urge their suits, and these delegations often obtained not only confirmations of their old privileges, but favourable rulings on such questions as the apportionment of loss in a case of shipwreck.

The landed interest in the provinces had a regular channel for presenting their grievances in the provincial assemblies. These were in origin federations of provincial cities, founded to conduct the worship of the emperor, but they had soon begun to represent the common interests of the cities, particularly by prosecuting corrupt governors. Although from Constantine the emperor was no longer a god, the provinces continued to elect annual high priests (*sacerdotes*) who gave splendid games. By the fourth century the provincial assemblies had come to consist of the members of the imperial aristocracy, the *honorati* resident in the provinces, and of the decurions of the cities, and thus represented the greater and medium landowners. They met annually, passed resolutions and appointed delegations to present them at the *comitatus*. From the laws issued to the provincial assemblies it would appear that the imperial government took their pleas seriously. Remissions of taxation were not infrequently granted at their request, and regulations were issued curbing the exactions of imperial officials and soldiers.

Despite the religiosity of the age the clergy exercised surprisingly little influence. Constantine in the ardour of his conversion gave them somewhat extravagant privileges; they were exempted from curial duties and bishops were empowered to pass judgment without appeal in any civil case if either party sought their jurisdiction. His pious son Constantius II also exempted them from the *capitatio* and the *chrysargyron*. The latter also enacted that bishops accused on criminal charges should be tried not by the ordinary courts but by a council of bishops, and in the west Honorius in 411 extended this privilege to the lower clergy. Even Constantius II, however, rebuffed a petition of the Council of Ariminum that the clergy should be exempted from the land tax, and quickly withdrew the immunity which he had granted to lands corporately owned by the churches. The immunity of the clergy from the *curia* was never formally annulled, but Constantine later in his reign forbade the ordination of decurions or their sons, or of persons financially qualified for curial duties, and subsequent emperors insisted on curial ordinands surrendering their property, or at least two-thirds of it. The fiscal privileges of the clergy were later curtailed. Immunity from the *capitatio* was limited to a fixed number of clergy for each church and any above this number had to pay. The exemption from the *chrysargyron* was confined to the humblest and poorest grade of the clergy, the *copiatae* or grave-diggers. Church lands were exempted from the supplementary charges on the land tax, the *extraordinaria* and *sordida munera*, but with a few special exceptions paid the ordinary land tax. The jurisdictional privileges of the clergy were also curtailed. After Julian's reign bishops never recovered their former power of acting as judges in the civil disputes of secular persons: they could only be appointed arbitrators by the consent of both parties. The right of the clergy to be judged by ecclesiastical courts in criminal cases was abolished by Valentinian III, but later revived. In the east bishops retained their privilege, but the clergy lost it. Justinian conceded that a layman who had a case against a cleric should first try to obtain satisfaction from his bishop, but insisted that he should retain his right to sue in the civil court if dissatisfied with the bishop's decision.

Among government servants the rank and file of the army were also surprisingly ineffective in pressing their claims. It is a significant fact that not only the pay but the quinquennial and accession donatives given to the troops remained static from the fourth century to the sixth. In the fourth century some immunities were granted to encourage recruitment and the privileges of veterans were guaranteed and the grants of money or land given to them were increased. But there is no further legislation on these questions after the fourth century, and it would seem that the grant of discharge bounties was abandoned. In general military legislation is designed to repress exactions by the troops and is evidently inspired by civilian complaints. The only bodies of troops which received privileges were the *protectores* and *domestici* and the *scholae*, who served immediately under the emperor's eye and could readily press their claims upon him.

Lawyers not unnaturally pressed their claims with success. Here again their privileges varied in proportion to their propinquity to the emperor. The bar of the praetorian prefect of the East received marked and ever-increasing favours. The bars of the urban prefect and the prefect of Illyricum lagged some stages behind and below them came the bars of the diocesan and provincial courts. Even the last were in some degree privileged.

Among civil servants there was a much greater contrast between the central and the provincial staff. The *cohortales* and *Caesariani*, the officials of the provincial governors and the diocesan *rationales*, were rigorously forbidden to aspire to any higher branch of the service and were more and more severely punished if they evaded the law; their meagre privileges were not enlarged after Diocletian's time. At the other end of the scale the officials in immediate attendance on the emperors, the *cubicularii* of the sacred bedchamber and the notaries and silentiaries who attended the consistory, received ever-increasing honours and privileges from the fourth century to the sixth, rising steadily in official rank, gaining more extensive fiscal immunities and privileges of jurisdiction. Below them the *agentes in rebus* and the clerks of the *sacra scrinia* fared well, and below them again the *palatini* of the *sacrae largitiones* and the *res privata*. The officials of the praetorian prefects and the *magistri militum*, whose work was more important, but who came less closely in contact with the emperor, were less honoured and privileged.

Finally, the men who filled the great offices of state inevitably favoured the interests of the class from which they were drawn. In the east, where they were recruited not only from the landowning aristocracy but also from lawyers and officials, their influence was less marked. Periodic attempts were made with varying success to curb the major abuses from which the governing class derived its wealth, *suffragium* in the appointment of provincial governors, *petitio* of state lands, and the grant of fiscal immunities to great landlords. In the west, where the great landowners of the senatorial aristocracy acquired a virtual monopoly over the high offices of state, little attempt was made to curb these abuses. Among the last fiscal measures of Valentinian III are a general remission of arrears of land tax granted at the petition of the senate, and the establishment of a new tax on trade, the *siliquaticum*. At this same period in the east wealthy landowners were being compelled to refund a part of the profits which they made from tax concessions, and senators were being charged with special levies to pay the subsidies to Attila.

XII

The Administration

Since the emperor was an absolute monarch, on whose signature every act of government depended, the central administrative offices had to be in constant attendance upon him wherever he might be. The capital of the empire was the emperor's residence for the time being, and in the fourth century, when the emperors were continually on the move, conducting wars and supervising the defence of the frontiers, the central government, the *comitatus*, was a migratory body. Constantius II and Valens spent much time at Antioch, the western emperors were often at Trier in Gaul or Sirmium in Pannonia; when in Italy they usually stayed at Milan, but rarely visited Rome. From the end of the fourth century, when the emperors ceased to conduct campaigns in person, the administration became more static. The western emperors normally resided at Ravenna and the eastern at Constantinople.

The *comitatus* was a very considerable body of people. It included in the first place the emperor's household, the eunuchs of the sacred bedchamber (*cubicularii*) and the subordinate domestic staff (*castresiani*). It also included the imperial guard (*scholae palatinae*), and the corps of officer cadets (*protectores et domestici*). The members of the consistory were also naturally in attendance and the ushers (*silentiarii*) and the secretariat (*notarii*) of the consistory. Then there were the principal ministers, the four *comites consistoriani*, the quaestor (*quaestor sacri palatii*), the master of the offices (*magister officiorum*) and the *comites*

BIBLIOGRAPHY. There is no systematic account of this subject except Chapter XII of my *Later Roman Empire* (Oxford, 1964). The principal documentary sources are the *Notitia Dignitatum* and Book I of the Theodosian Code and Book I, xxvi ff. of the Justinian Code, together with Cassiodorus' *Variae*. For a list of praetorian prefects see myself in *Journal of Roman Studies*, LIV (1964), for the prefects of the city of Rome, A. Chastagnol, *La préfecture urbaine à Rome sous le bas-empire* (Paris, 1960); for the *magistri militum*, Ensslin in *Klio*, XXIV (1931), 102–47, 467–502; for the proconsuls of Africa, A. C. Pallu de Lessert, *Fastes des provinces Africaines* (Paris, 1896).

sacrarum largitionum and *rei privatae* with their respective ministries. Below these ranked the *magistri scriniorum*, who controlled the departments of *memoria*, *epistulae* (and in the east *epistulae graecae*) and *libelli*.

The quaestor was the chief legal officer, who drafted laws, dealt with petitions and from the middle of the fifth century normally acted with the praetorian prefect as the judicial delegate of the emperor's personal jurisdiction. The office was a creation of Constantine and took over from the *magistri scriniorum* the more important part of their work, leaving them the routine secretarial duties. The senior notary (*primicerius notariorum*) with his assistant (*adiutor*) also had special secretarial duties, issuing codicils to all office-holders, and in the east commissions to most tribunes of regiments. The third notary dealt with *pragmaticae*, that is imperial constitutions which were not general laws but were issued to particular groups or individuals.

The master of the offices had a curiously mixed bunch of duties. He was the administrative controller of the secretariats (*sacra scrinia*) which served the *magistri scriniorum* and provided assistants for the quaestor. He had under him the corps of imperial couriers (*agentes in rebus*), who carried imperial despatches to the provinces: the more senior of these acted as inspectors of the post (*curiosi*), and the master of the offices thus exercised a supervisory control over the public postal service (*cursus publicus*). The master also exercised administrative and disciplinary control over the guard (*scholae*), and had under him the *officia dispositionum* and *admissionum*, which managed the emperor's timetable and regulated audiences with him, and the corps of interpreters who translated the speeches of foreign envoys. He thus had control over imperial audiences and in particular over foreign affairs. The master later, probably when Rufinus held the office under Theodosius I, took over the management of the state arms factories from the praetorian prefects, and later still in 441, when Nomus held the office, became inspector general of the frontier forces (*limitanei*) in the eastern parts.

The *comes sacrarum largitionum* controlled the mines of the precious metals, the mints and all revenue and expenditure in coin. He also managed the state weaving and dyeing factories and distributed uniforms to the army and the civil service. The *comes rei privatae* managed the vast accumulation of imperial lands, collecting their rents, selling or granting them on occasion, and collecting and incorporating in the crown property any estates which fell in by escheat or confiscation.

Among the military members of the *comitatus* the most important were the two *magistri militum praesentales* who commanded the mobile field force, *palatini*, at the immediate disposal of the emperor; the office was created by Constantine, the praetorian prefects having hitherto been commanders-in-chief. Next them ranked the *comes domesticorum* who commanded the corps of officer cadets; from the early fifth century the cadets were divided into infantry and cavalry, and there were correspondingly two *comites domesticorum peditum* and *equitum*. Next ranked the tribunes, later styled *comites*, of the several regiments of the *scholae*, with whom were classed the *comes stabuli*, who not only controlled the imperial stable but supplied remounts to all the army, and the *cura palatii*, who was in charge of the imperial quarters.

In attendance on the emperor there was also always one of the praetorian prefects. This office had by the fourth century undergone a strange transformation. Originally the prefect was commander of the praetorian guard. He early acquired important judicial functions as the emperor's principal delegate judge and became the emperor's chief of staff, sometimes commanding the armies in his stead; his adjutant general controlling the recruitment and discipline of the armed forces; and his quartermaster general providing rations for the troops and for the civil service. When during the inflation of the third century the money taxes and money paid diminished in importance, and the state came to rely on levies in kind and to pay soldiers and civil servants by rations in kind, the praetorian prefect became *de facto* the chief financial minister.

This was the praetorian prefect's position in Diocletian's time. He had become a kind of grand vizier with a finger in almost every branch of the administration; he ran the public post and the arms factories, organized the levies of men and materials for public works and exercised general supervision over the provincial governors, whom he could cashier if they were unsatisfactory. Constantine disbanded the praetorian guard and created the office of the *magistri militum* who took over the operational command of the armies and their discipline. The praetorian prefects thus became civilian officials with two main functions—judicial and financial. They remained the chief judges of appeal, hearing cases in the emperor's stead (*vice sacra iudicantes*), and no appeal lay from them to the emperor. They also later acted with the quaestor as the emperor's delegates for the emperor's personal jurisdiction. They continued to organize levies in kind and to distribute their rations to the troops and the civil servants. They also continued to levy recruits for the army and to run the post and public works and to supervise the provincial governors, and until the latter years of the fourth century supplied arms from the state arms factories.

The office was originally personal, each emperor, whether Augustus or Caesar, having his own prefect. Constantine created a regional prefect of Africa, but this office disappeared on his death. The three sons of Constantine each had their own prefect. On Constantine II's death, however, Constans still maintained a prefect in his brother's former dominions, the Gauls with Britain and Spain, and when the empire was reunited under Constantius II he still kept three praetorian prefects, the prefect of the Gauls, the prefect of the East, who managed his original dominions, and the prefect of Italy, Illyricum and Africa who managed Constans' original share of the empire; the large central praetorian prefecture was sometimes divided into two, Illyricum and Italy with Africa. From 395 there came to be four standing territorial prefectures, the Gauls and Italy under the western emperor and Illyricum and the East under the eastern emperor.

After the fall of the empire in the west the praetorian prefecture of Italy was maintained by Odoacer and the Ostrogothic kings; its area was confined to Italy. Theoderic even re-established a prefect of the Gauls for the tiny fragment of Gaul which he ruled, and the title survived in the Frankish kingdom when the Franks annexed Provence. After the reconquest of the Vandals, Justinian created a praetorian prefecture of Africa, which also included the former Vandal possessions of Sardinia and Corsica, and on defeating the Ostrogoths, revived the prefecture of Italy. He also withdrew five provinces, Moesia II and Scythia, Caria, Cyprus and the Islands, from the prefecture of the East, and placed them under a *quaestor exercitus*, who was in all but title a praetorian prefect, supplying the lower Danube armies from the taxation of his provinces, and hearing appeals from all his provinces.

The *magistri militum* underwent a similar evolution. Under Constantine there were two *magistri* only, one of infantry and the other of the cavalry, in immediate attendance on the emperor. Under his sons there came to be regional *magistri*, one for the Gauls (the Rhine front), one for Illyricum (the upper Danube), one for Thrace (the lower Danube) and one for the East (the Persian frontier), in addition to the two *magistri* in attendance on each member of the imperial college.

Under the Severi there had been about fifty provinces, mostly governed by senators, proconsuls or *legati Augusti*, commonly called *consulares*, a few by prefects or procurators of equestrian rank. From the reign of Gallienus senators were largely excluded from provincial governorships. Diocletian approximately doubled the number of provinces and eliminated all senators except the proconsuls of Africa and

Asia and the *correctores* of the Italian provinces which he created, and of Sicily and Achaia. All other governors were of equestrian rank and styled *praesides*. Constantine changed the *corrector* of Achaia into a proconsul and upgraded many *praesides* to *consulares*, thus readmitting senators on a large scale to provincial administration. Thereafter there was little substantial change. A few more provinces were subdivided, most of the *correctores* and many *praesides* were upgraded to *consulares* and finally at the end of the fourth century the remaining *praesides* were elevated to senatorial rank. Justinian created more proconsulships, revived the ancient republican title of praetor and coined that of moderator.

From Constantine's reign governors no longer, with a very few exceptions, held command of the troops in their provinces, until Justinian combined the military with the civil government in several provinces of Asia Minor and in Egypt, in order to enable the governors to deal more effectively with brigandage and other internal disorders. The governor was responsible for all other departments, finance, justice, public works and the postal system.

Diocletian grouped the small provinces which he had created into larger circumscriptions, the dioceses. There were originally thirteen of them, the Britains, the Gauls (north Gaul), Viennensis or the Five or Seven Provinces (south Gaul), the Spains (including Tingitania), Italy (the region north of the Apennines with the Alpine provinces), the Suburbicarian diocese (south Italy with Sardinia, Corsica and Sicily), Africa, Pannonia, Moesia and Thrace (the Balkan peninsula), Asiana and Pontica (Asia Minor), and Oriens (Syria, Mesopotamia, Palestine and Egypt). Constantine split Moesia into two, Dacia in the north and Macedonia, including Epirus, Greece and Crete, in the south. Valens divided Egypt with Libya from the rest of Oriens.

Each diocese was governed by a deputy praetorian prefect or vicar; in Oriens the governor bore the title of *comes Orientis* and in Egypt that of Augustal prefect. The vicars gradually sank in importance. In dioceses where a praetorian prefect resided there generally came to be no vicar; the prefect of the Gauls governed the diocese of the Gauls directly, the prefect of Italy Pannonia and the prefect of Illyricum Dacia. Only the praetorian prefect of the East had deputies in all his five dioceses, the vicars of Thrace, Asiana and Pontica, the *comes Orientis* and the Augustal prefect of Egypt. Anastasius seems to have abolished the vicar of Thrace and Justinian suppressed the other four, making them governors of the provinces where they resided—they had already combined the offices of vicar and governor. It would appear that the vicars and corresponding officers had become redundant. In financial matters the praetorian prefect no longer acted through the vicar, but dealt with the provincial governors direct; and appeals from the governor's court usually went to the praetorian prefect, from whom there was no appeal, rather than to the vicars, whose courts were corrupt and from whom there was a further appeal to the emperor. Justinian later found that the absence of any authority higher than the provincial governor made it difficult to control civil disorders, since brigands migrated from province to province, and he created some diocesan officers with military powers, such as the vicar of Pontica, to deal with this problem.

The military chain of command was simpler. The central field armies, *palatini*, were as we have seen, under the command of the *magistri militum praesentales*. The larger regional field armies, *comitatenses*, were under *magistri*, smaller groups under *comites rei militaris*. Thus in the early fifth century there was in the west a *magister equitum* in Gaul and *comites* in Africa, Tingitania, Illyricum, Spain and Britain. In the east there were *magistri* of Illyricum, Thrace and the East. This last command was divided by Justinian into Armenia, the northern sector, and the East, the southern. The frontier armies (*ripenses* and *limitanei*) were divided into sectors commanded by *duces*. Some *duces*, e.g. those of Egypt and Isauria, bore the title of *comes*, probably because their armies were stiffened with *comitatenses*.

The financial ministries also had their representatives in the provinces. For the *largitiones* there were in the west the *comites titulorum largitionalium* in Italy, Africa, Gaul and Illyricum and the *rationales summae* for each diocese or half diocese; in the east the *comites largitionum* of each diocese. For the *res privata* there were *rationales rei privatae* in each diocese or sometimes half diocese.

The official hierarchy of the Roman emperor was not so tidy as might appear from the *Notitia Dignitatum*. The emperor did not always communicate with *duces* through the *magistri militum* or with provincial governors through the prefects and vicars. A provincial governor might write direct to the emperor, and receive a direct reply, and the praetorian prefects came habitually to bypass the vicars. There was also much overlapping and conflict of jurisdiction between the civil, military and fiscal hierarchies despite their theoretical separation. Military officers were always tending to usurp the authority of their civilian opposite numbers. We find the emperor rebuking the *magister militum* of the East for arresting the *corrector* of Augustamnica, and reminding him that provincial governors were subject to the sole control of the praetorian prefects. Later we find the *magister militum per Orientem* giving orders to the consular of Cyprus and threatening him with a fine if he disobeys. The *rationales* of the *largitiones* and *res privata* fought a long battle with the provincial governors over fiscal suits.

There were a very large number of posts to fill, especially in the lower grades of the administration. From Diocletian's time there were over a hundred provinces; by the beginning of Justinian's reign the number of eastern provinces had risen to sixty-two. The *Notitia Dignitatum* records sixty-nine posts under the disposition of the *comes sacrarum largitionum* in the west and twenty-four under the *res privata*. There were fifteen minor offices under the disposal of the prefect of the city of Rome. In the early fifth century there were 400 tribunates to fill in the western army and some 500 in the eastern.

Offices were held as a rule for brief periods only. The prefects of the city of Rome between the accession of Diocletian and the death of Honorius averaged about one year each. The proconsuls of Africa also averaged about one year. The governors of Egypt between 328 and 373 held office for less than two years each, and if one exceptional term of seven years be omitted, the average drops to eighteen months. Later in the century the Augustal prefects of Egypt had a roughly annual tenure.

In the higher offices of state the movement was not at first so rapid. There were eleven men who held the praetorian prefecture of the East between 337 and 369, an average of three years, but in the fifth century the norm sank to eighteen months. The figures for the praetorian prefects of Italy are similar. Military offices were on the whole held for longer terms. The *duces* of Egypt in the fourth century held their command for three to five years, and so did the *magistri militum*.

Exceptions to this rule are rare and generally indicate that the minister or general concerned exercised some special political influence. Anthemius' ten-year tenure of the prefecture of the East was due to the fact that he was virtually regent of the eastern empire during the period. Helion's dozen years as master of the offices seem again to mark a virtual regency under the weak Theodosius II. The long tenures of Modestus and of John the Cappadocian show the ascendancy which these two ministers established over Valens and Justinian respectively. In the west again, when the *magister militum praesentalis* became the virtual ruler of the empire, several holders of this post, Stilicho, Constantius, Aetius and Ricimer, held office until they died. In the east also there was a similar tendency for the *magistri praesentales* to hold office for life in the fifth century.

The fundamental reason for the rapid turnover of official posts was, it would seem, that they were regarded by their holders and the emperors as prizes (*honores*, *dignitates*) rather than as administrative jobs (*administrationes*). The salaries which they carried were, it is true, not very attractive. Provincial governors and procurators had been highly paid under the principate, but the great inflation of the later third century had drastically reduced the real value of their salaries, and it would seem that in the fourth and fifth centuries offices of state were somewhat meagrely remunerated. We have no figures until the sixth century, when Justinian reveals that the salary of the Augustal prefect of Egypt was 50 *annonae* and 50 *capitus*, commuted for 400 *solidi*. The basic salary of the *dux* of Libya seems to have been the same, and in Pisidia and Lycaonia the combined salaries of the *praeses* and *dux* came to 800 *solidi*. This compared very poorly with the 100,000 sesterces (roughly equal to 1,750 *solidi*) earned by a junior procurator under the principate. Justinian greatly increased salaries, but the highest recorded figure which he paid, one hundred pounds gold to the praetorian prefect of Africa, was far below the million sesterces (over 240 pounds of gold), which the proconsul of Africa had received for a much less responsible office under the principate.

Ministers of state, provincial governors and military officers increased their official pay by a variety of perquisites, as will be seen, but even so the profits of offices remained on the whole a minor consideration. What gave value to office was the rank it conferred on its holder. For men of humble degree there were concrete privileges—for *curiales* for instance release from their hereditary status for themselves and sometimes also for their sons. If they rose into the senatorial order or into the highest grade of *illustres* they also enjoyed fiscal immunities, exemption from *extraordinaria* and *sordida munera*, and jurisdictional privileges, the right of being tried before the prefect of the city. But yet more important was the prestige which rank conferred. A senator had the right of *entrée* to a provincial governor and could sit beside him on the bench in his court. A mere decurion could, despite the law, be bullied and flogged, but a senator was exempt from such ill-treatment, and might if of superior grade defy the governor's lawful commands.

There was as a result an immense pressure of applicants for posts. A few great nobles, certain of receiving the patriciate or the ordinary consulship, might regard office as beneath them; but the great majority of the official aristocracy expected to hold a few posts to maintain or enhance their precedence. The wealthier decurions pressed to free themselves from their curial duties and the higher palatine officials sought to enhance their retiring rank.

It was in these circumstances considered grasping for a man to hold on to a post for a long while, thus keeping others out, or to hold a succession of posts of the same grade of precedence. Libanius[1] praised the sons of Constantine for changing their prefects frequently because 'if the business of office is laborious, they do not demand that the same person should be oppressed by a continual load, or if it involves happiness, they invite many to share that happiness'. Valentinian I is said to have executed a barrister for petitioning for a second province having already governed one, and a law of Honorius formally forbids applicants to seek a proconsulship, a vicariate or the office of consular or *praeses* twice. Each of these offices represented a grade of precedence and it was a legitimate ambition to aspire to hold each in turn once, but to hold two offices in one grade was grasping.

Officially the emperor appointed to all these posts, but it was obviously impossible even for two emperors to select the most deserving applicants, when they had every year to make appointments by the hundred from throngs of candidates who must have run to thousands. They naturally chose their chief ministers, the masters of the soldiers, the praetorian prefects and the *comites consistoriani*, but for lower appointments they had to rely on the recommendations of their ministers. We find that the praetorian prefects recommended candidates for provincial governorships, and it seems likely that the *magistri* put forward the names of *duces* and tribunes. If the empire had developed a regular system of recommendations, in which the ministers chose the men who were going to work under them, it might have worked more or less satisfactorily. But the system was not rationalized. Symmachus as prefect of the city of Rome had no voice in the appointment of the minor magistracies of the city, and was severely snubbed when he suggested that the emperors should exercise more care in their selection. We find Theodosius, the *magister militum*, recommending a lawyer for a provincial governorship and Maximinus the praetorian prefect getting his son promoted to be a *dux*. Like everything else in the empire appointments went by intrigue and by wire-pulling, and those who pulled the strings were those who were closest to the emperor and had his ear. Symmachus, who lived at Rome and had little contact

[1] Oration LIX, 164.

with the court, had no pull. Theodosius and Maximinus could intervene outside their official departments.

In bestowing an office the emperor thought not so much of whether the candidate would fulfil the duties of the post satisfactorily as of his general merits, as they were measured by the standards of the day, his birth, wealth, education and moral qualities. This statement is of course only partially true. The emperors tended to give a preference to lawyers in all civil posts, from provincial governor to praetorian prefect, because the duties of these posts were largely judicial. They chose tribunes, *duces, comites rei militaris* and *magistri militum* mainly for their courage, initiative and experience. They promoted rhetoricians to be *magistri scriniorum* and quaestors because these officers had to draft imperial constitutions, letters and rescripts. Some emperors in the interests of financial efficiency promoted revenue clerks of the prefecture to be praetorian prefects. In general, however, the imperial government paid little attention to special experience except in the army. Noble birth was a passport to office in most reigns, lesser posts were traditionally given to provincial notables whose main distinction was their wealth and ancestry. High regard was also had to literary distinction, and rhetoricians and poets were rewarded with administrative posts. Civil servants, whose administrative experience might have been valuable, were rarely promoted, and among them it was those whose duties brought them into personal contact with the emperor who were most favoured. Tribunes and notaries, silentiaries and *agentes in rebus* had a better chance of a provincial governorship than a clerk in the prefecture, and the imperial physicians were often honoured with administrative or financial posts.

The great men at court did not personally know many of the suitors who thronged their salons, but they were not averse from displaying their influence and thus enlarging their circle of patronage, particularly if it were made financially worth their while. Hence arose the system of *suffragia* which we find already flourishing in the time of Constantine and his sons, and which always revived, however often it was uprooted. Julian, as soon as he was proclaimed Augustus, announced that he would make appointments by merit, and to discourage *suffragia* enacted a curious law that a man who failed to get an appointment could not recover what he had paid to his patron. Evidently Julian hoped by making corrupt bargains unenforceable at law to discourage them. Theodosius I, on the other hand, enacted that a *sponsio* whereby land or money were promised for aid in gaining an office was a legal contract and could be enforced. According to Zosimus the sale of office was rampant under Theodosius I, the principal sellers being the influential palace eunuchs, and according to the same author and to Eunapius Rufinus, Eutropius and Pulcheria openly auctioned offices of state. This may well be pagan prejudice, but it is evident that by 439 the purchase of office had become a regular institution in the east. In that year a law was passed whereby all persons who became provincial governors were obliged to swear an oath that they had neither given nor promised any consideration for their office.

Hitherto, it would seem, the crown had not directly profited by the sale of offices; it was the favourites and ministers of the emperor who reaped the harvest. Under Zeno, who was perpetually in financial difficulties, the praetorian prefect Sebastianus (474-80) exploited the system of *suffragia* for the interests of the treasury. When offices were sold Sebastianus took his commission, but the crown got the bulk of the prices. The right to nominate to certain offices was also, it would seem, sometimes sold in perpetuity for a capital sum.

Not only did the system become more and more regular and spread from provincial governorships to vicariates and other posts of *spectabilis* grade, the prices paid continually rose in a vicious spiral. Since salaries were low those who bought offices had to recoup themselves by bribes, extortion and other illegal perquisites; and as such perquisites became hallowed by custom, the price of posts rose and increased extortion became necessary to make ends meet.

Suffragia seem to have been most rampant in civilian appointments of middle and lower grade. The great offices of state could not be bought and the grant of military commissions seems to have been relatively free from corruption. Flavius Abinnaeus, it is true, when appointed from the ranks to be prefect of the *Ala Praelectorum* at Dionysias, was informed by the *officium* of the *dux* that the post was already preempted by another claimant, but he petitioned successfully against being thus pushed aside by those who attained promotion not by merit but by *suffragium*. We hear of some other cases of civilians buying commissions in the *limitanei*, but commissions in the *comitatenses* and *palatini* seem to have been given on the whole by merit or seniority, and there is no suggestion that *duces* could purchase their posts.

In 535 Justinian, inspired by Theodora and supported by John the Cappadocian, made a vigorous attempt to eliminate *suffragia* root and branch. He was convinced that the oppression of the provincials was in large measure due to the system and that it not only caused grave injustice but weakened the finances of the empire; the provincials were unable to pay their regular taxes because they were fleeced by the governors. He accordingly not only imposed the most frightful oaths on vicars and governors, but at a considerable loss to the revenue abolished imperial *suffragia* and compensated those who had bought *suffragia* from Zeno. He also, to reduce the temptation to extortion, raised the salaries of many governors. According to Procopius this law was hardly issued before it became a dead letter. This extreme statement may be doubted, but it would seem that before the reconquest of Italy was completed, *suffragia* had come back, for the rule laid down in the pragmatic sanction of 554, whereby the notables and bishops of each province were authorized to nominate their own governor, was designed to eliminate the purchase of offices by outsiders. Justin II in 569 extended this rule to the whole empire, but this reform was very shortlived; in 574 Tiberius Constantine again suppressed *suffragia*; nevertheless they were still flourishing under Maurice.

The emperors strove to combat corruption in the provinces by ever-increasing centralization. The empire possessed an elaborate and expensive system of communications. For carrying his routine messages the emperor had at his disposal the corps of imperial messengers, the *agentes in rebus*, who numbered some 1,250 men in the fifth century in the eastern parts. For more confidential missions he could employ his notaries, silentiaries, *protectores*, *cubicularii* and *scribones*. The principal ministers, such as the praetorian prefects, and the *comites sacrarum largitionum*, had their own corps of messengers or *mittendarii*. Vicars and provincial governors employed their ordinary officials. All these were entitled to make use of the imperial post according to the importance of their offices. Provincial governors were given two annual warrants, one for use within the province, the other for communication with the emperor. Vicars had twelve warrants, *duces* normally five, *magistri militum* fifteen except for the master of the soldiers in the East who had twenty-five. The *comites sacrarum largitionum* and *rei privatae* could obtain warrants whenever they required them, the praetorian prefects issued them themselves.

The express post (*cursus velox*) was provided with major and minor posting stations (*mansiones* and *mutationes*) at intervals of about a dozen miles along all the major roads of the empire. In these stations relays of horses and mules were kept available. Messages could in an emergency be carried very fast. When a dispute arose over the papal elections in 418 Symmachus, prefect of the city, wrote to Honorius at Milan on

29 December, Honorius replied on 3 January and Symmachus, having taken action, wrote again on 8 January. More usually, however, a constitution given at Milan took three weeks or a month, sometimes six weeks, to reach Rome. One law signed in Milan on 11 April was read to the senate at Constantinople on 9 May, but this again was a record; a law issued by Constantine at Sardica took three months to reach Corduba. Journeys which involved a sea crossing might be greatly delayed. On one occasion a law issued at Sirmium on the Danube on 17 April was posted up at Carthage on 18 May, but usually constitutions dated in the summer or autumn at Milan or Paris did not reach Africa until the following spring.

Despite slow communications the emperors and the central ministries allowed little discretion to the diocesan and provincial authorities, and in some departments of government their centralizing policy was relatively successful. Diocletian had evidently intended that the provincial governors should each year draw up the detailed financial schedules and forward them to the vicars who after checking them would forward them through their *curae epistularum* to the praetorian prefect, in whose office there was a *cura epistularum* for each diocese. Actually as early as the middle of the fourth century there was in the office of the prefecture an official styled a *tractator* who checked the figures for each province, and every year a *canonicarius* was sent to each province to supervise the collection of the tax. The *comites sacrarum largitionum* and *rei privatae* were also originally intended to deal with the provincial governors through the diocesan *rationales*, but they too by the early fifth century were sending their own central officials as *canonicarii* to the provinces. The collection was slow and expensive since the *canonicarii* exacted an ample rake-off, but on the whole the land tax seems to have come in eventually. The government made periodical remissions of arrears, but these were made at long intervals and did not include recent arrears. Some wealthy landowners no doubt evaded payment by postponing it long enough, but the ordinary taxpayer had to pay in the end. The remissions of arrears were in fact intended to protect the humble taxpayer by preventing the officials from raking up dubious claims from the distant past.

Remissions of taxation, temporary or permanent, were rigorously centralized, but with less success. Despite the penalties with which the quaestor and his clerks were threatened, great landlords could generally get their estates assessed at below the standard rate. Petitions for crown lands were also too readily granted to influential applicants, and though surcharges to meet local deficits were strictly forbidden to the diocesan and provincial authorities from the reign of Constantius II onwards, such surcharges were made, and increased the burden on the humble tax-payers, who alone were bound to pay them.

The emperors, justifiably mistrusting the purity of the provincial and diocesan courts, encouraged appeals to the praetorian prefects and to themselves. This centralization of justice tended to defeat itself. The delays and expenses of the high courts were so great that humble litigants were denied effective redress. Justinian was very conscious of this abuse and endeavoured, by establishing intermediate courts of better quality, and by limiting the jurisdiction of the high courts to important cases, to relieve the congestion of the judicial system.

In other matters the imperial government seems to have been impotent to enforce its will. Despite the scores of penal laws against heretics, and later against pagans, heresies and paganism continued to flourish, or at least to subsist. It was difficult to check that such laws were rigorously enforced, and provincial governors, reluctant to antagonize local magnates, and often themselves sympathetic with the condemned sectaries, were not zealous to take strong action. Gratian[1] wrote angrily to Simplicius, vicar of the city, that a schismatic bishop of Puteoli, expelled from his see fifteen years ago, was still at large, 'relying, of course, on the inactivity of our governors, who pay more attention to private influence than to imperial commands, and, because they themselves neglect it, patiently allow the religion which we rightly venerate to suffer disturbance . . . the passive connivance of governors must stop, the supine inertia of officials must, I repeat, be brought to an end'. Two centuries after the official prohibition of all pagan cults by Theodosius I the pagan villagers of Sardinia were still practising their ancient rites, and paying the provincial governor a regular tax for his connivance; what was worse, when by Pope Gregory the Great's efforts they were baptized, the governor continued to exact his tax—he had paid so large a *suffragium* for his post, he explained, that he could not afford to forgo this customary perquisite.

The government's efforts to maintain the curial order were also very ineffectual. Though it was to the public interest that the city councils should be strong, it was to no one's private interest to enforce the law. The richest and most influential decurions desired promotion, and had powerful patrons to support them. Their colleagues on the council did not wish to offend the leading men of the city, who could be dangerous

[1] *Coll. Avell.* 13 §7.

enemies if crossed, and useful patrons if they succeeded in their ambition, and were in any case not reluctant to see them go and thus succeed to their influence in the council. The provincial governor was likewise reluctant to offend the leading decurions of the province and their patrons, whose influence could make or mar his career. Despite the threat of heavy fines the city councils connived at the escape of their leading members, and the governors turned a blind eye on the transaction.

When the task to be fulfilled was, like the collection of the revenue, quantitatively measurable, the government could make its agents perform their task, though it could not prevent them from making additional illegitimate extortions. Where it was not possible to keep a check on the results achieved, provincial governors could neglect their duties without much fear of detection, and, when it paid them to do so, commonly connived at breaches of the law.

Centralization in the end defeated itself. The clerks of the central ministries were by no means proof against corruption and would, for a consideration, draft and submit illegal petitions to their chiefs. The ministers of the *comitatus* themselves, even if they were incorruptible— and they were, it would appear, often susceptible to influence and bribes—found it difficult to keep a check on the vast mass of business which passed through their hands. The emperor himself, snowed under with papers, could not examine every document submitted to him. He regularly threatened with penalties the clerks who prepared illegal rescripts and sometimes the ministers who submitted them. But he openly admitted his impotence by declaring invalid in advance any special grants in contravention of the law, even if they bore his own signature.

XIII

Finance

The financial system of the later Roman empire was the product of a long historical evolution and had as a result a complicated structure. Under the early principate, the chief financial minister was the *a rationibus*, who controlled the currency, the mines and the mints and the taxes, and handled the main items of expenditure. Beside him stood the *procurator patrimonii* who managed the property of the emperor, whose revenue was largely spent on public purposes. The patrimony came to be regarded as crown property and no longer the personal estate of the emperor, and Septimius Severus founded a new department, the *res privata*, to control the latter, which he rapidly built up by extensive confiscations. Later the patrimony was merged in the *res privata* and the *magister rei privatae* became almost as important as the *rationalis rei summae* as the *a rationibus* was now called. Finally in the great inflation of the third century the yield of the old money taxes sank to a negligible sum and the office of *rationalis* declined in importance. The state came to rely on requisitions in kind to meet its principal needs, and to pay the army and the civil service largely in kind, food, uniforms, horses and arms. These requisitions and payments were made by the praetorian prefects, as quartermasters general of the army, acting through the provincial governors. The praetorian prefecture by the end of the third century became *de facto* the most important financial ministry. In the fourth century the resulting triple division had some rational justification. The *res privata* handled the rents from the state property and from them supplied the needs of the imperial household and money for imperial benefactions. The *res summa* or, as it was called from Con-

BIBLIOGRAPHY. There is no systematic account of the whole financial system except in Chapter XIII of my *Later Roman Empire* (Oxford, 1964). For the land and poll taxes see A. Déléage, *La capitation du bas-empire* (Macon, 1945). The principal documentary sources are Books XI and XIII. i of the Theodosian Code and Book X. i–xxx, XI. lxi ff. of the Justinian Code.

stantine's time, the *sacrae largitiones*, managed the currency and the revenue and expenditure in money. The praetorian prefecture handled revenue and expenditure in kind. From the end of the fourth century the requisitions and payments in kind were gradually commuted into gold and the special role of the praetorian prefecture disappeared. But the structure of the financial departments was now ossified and the prefecture continued to handle the bulk of the revenue and expenditure.

The lands owned by the *res privata* were by the fourth century very extensive. The patrimony had absorbed the properties of the wealthy families which had successively held the throne, and had been increased through three centuries by a continual flow of legacies and bequests. From an early date properties which strictly belonged to the public treasury of the Roman people had been diverted to the imperial patrimony. The estates of condemned felons (*bona damnatorum*) went to the *res privata* as also did *bona vacantia*, the estates of persons dying intestate without heirs, and *bona caduca*, properties which were left to unmarried or childless persons and which such heirs were debarred from accepting by the social laws of Augustus. The *res privata* seems also to have absorbed what remained of the old *ager publicus* of the Roman people, the territories of destroyed cities and the royal lands of annexed kingdoms. Constantine confiscated the land of the pagan gods and added them to the *res privata*, where they formed a separate schedule, the *fundi iuris templorum*, and Constantius II appropriated the lands owned by the cities, which became the *fundi iuris rei publicae*.

The estates of the crown, which included house property as well as agricultural land, were scattered over every province; after the confiscation of the temple and civic lands there can hardly have been a city of the empire which did not contain some parcels. In some areas there were great concentrations of imperial estates. In Cappadocia I the greater part of the province apart from Caesarea, the capital, seems to have consisted of *regiones* of imperial land, probably the old royal lands of the Cappadocian kingdom. In Africa and Byzacena we have some exact figures; the lands of the *res privata* in the early fifth century comprised 14,702 *centuriae* in the former province and 15,075 in the latter. The gross areas of the two provinces can be calculated at about 80,000 and 100,000 *centuriae*, so that the *res privata* owned 18·5 per cent and 15 per cent of the total land; and, since a great deal of the province was desert, a much higher proportion of the cultivable land. We possess only one other precise figure. At Cyrrhus in Syria 10,000 out of the total 62,000 *iuga* of the city's territory were imperial property; but this figure may not be typical, for Avidius Cassius, who raised a rebellion against Marcus Aurelius, was a citizen of Cyrrhus, and his confiscated estates may have been considerable.

To administer this vast and scattered complex of properties the *comes rei privatae*, as the head of the department was called from the time of Constantine, had a large diocesan and provincial staff. The higher officials were styled *rationales rei privatae* and each controlled a diocese, or half a diocese, or sometimes a large group of estates which had belonged to a single owner; the lands of Gildo, the rebel *magister militum* of Africa who was subdued in 398, were so extensive that they were placed under a *comes Gildoniaci patrimonii* who ranked above *rationales*. Below the *rationales* were the procurators, normally responsible for a province, and below them the *actores* who controlled groups of estates.

In Cappadocia the imperial estates seem to have been directly managed by the officials of the *res privata*, the thirteen *magistri* each responsible for a 'house', and under them procurators, *tractatores* and *exactores*, who collected the rents from the cultivators, the *coloni*. Elsewhere the *res privata* normally leased estates (*fundi*) or blocks to estates (*massae*) to contractors or head tenants (*conductores*), who subletted them to *coloni*. Originally it would seem the estates were let for a five-year term at rack rents, the lease being assigned by auction to the highest bidder. This system might seem to have been the most profitable to the crown, but there were disadvantages. Good tenants could not always be found on such terms and bad tenants were liable to leave the land in poor condition; moreover a heavy burden of administrative work was involved. Already by the fourth century it had become common to let the crown lands on what were called emphyteutic or perpetual leases. Emphyteutic leases were originally granted to persons who undertook to improve derelict land on condition of initial rebates of rent and thereafter a perpetual tenure at a fixed rent. A perpetual lease was granted for land in good condition and did not carry any rebate of rent or obligation of improvement. In the administration of the *res privata* the two terms seem to have become synonymous before the end of the fourth century, the word emphyteutic being more commonly used and in the eastern parts superseding perpetual altogether.

Emphyteutic or perpetual lessees should have enjoyed complete security of tenure so long as they paid their fixed rent punctually, but in practice their position was somewhat precarious. There was a great pressure of applicants for land, and such applicants were often prepared to offer higher rents. There were moreover many suitors for gifts of crown lands whom the emperor wished to oblige. In these circumstances *rationales* and procurators were quick to seize on any technical fault to resume lands for the crown, and often rode roughshod over the rights of leaseholders. So long as the lands remained on the lists of the *res privata* the tenants could not feel secure. To meet this difficulty the imperial government invented in the third quarter of the fourth century a new form of tenure, *ius privatum salvo canone*. Under this tenure the leaseholder acquired full ownership of the land, subject to a fixed annual rent charge. He was able to dispose of it freely and even to manumit the slaves upon it, which the leaseholder could not. If he failed to pay his rent he was not liable to expropriation like a leaseholder, but could only be proceeded against in the ordinary way for debt. And finally the land was removed from the register of imperial lands, and could not be given away to others over his head. Tenants were naturally willing to pay for the additional security of this tenure, and Valentinian I, who appears to have initiated the new tenure, sold much land on these terms. Theodosius II tried to compel all emphyteutic lessees to purchase their freeholds by instalments, but in 434 remitted arrears in the capital payments and allowed the lessees to become freeholders none the less.

By these processes nearly all the lands of the *res privata* seem to have come to be held on a perpetual tenure, whether by emphyteutic lessees or by owners subject to an annual rent charge. In Ostrogothic Italy Cassiodorus speaks of the *comes rei privatae* as being responsible only for lands held on perpetual tenures. The government was assured of a fixed annual revenue with the minimum of administrative trouble. The system was also satisfactory to the public, always hungry for land in which to invest their surplus money; for *ius privatum salvo canone* was little, if at all, inferior to freehold. Most holders of imperial land seem to have been men of wealth and station; Valentinian I speaks of *comites consistoriani* and senators. Small pieces of land, once civic or sacred, were generally let to decurions.

The rent of state lands was from Constantine's time payable in gold or occasionally silver. The payment might be made annually or in not more than three instalments at the tenant's option. Lessees paid the ordinary land tax but were immune from *extraordinaria* and *munera sordida*. They were excused the levy of recruits and if they paid commutation for recruits (*aurum tironicum*) were allowed to deduct the sum paid from their rent.

The *res privata* continued to receive accessions and it was one of the functions of the *comes rei privatae* to collect and incorporate them. Private persons still made gifts, bequests or legacies to the emperor; Constantine records several estates thus acquired among the lands which he gave to the Roman churches. It is probable, however, that as bequests to the church became more regular, bequests to the crown fell off. *Bona vacantia* also continued to accrue. The government, it is true, renounced its claim to certain categories; Constantine enacted that the estate of a *navicularius* (shipper) who died intestate without heirs should go to his guild and those of a decurion to his *curia*. Under a law of his son estates of soldiers went to their regiment and those of officials to their *officium*, and Theodosius allowed *fabricae* (arms factories) and churches to claim the *bona vacantia* of *fabricenses* and of the clergy. These were, however, on the whole small estates and the law still held for large private estates. Cases of *bona vacantia* seem to have been fairly common; the testamentary rules were rigid and complicated and wills could thus be often quashed, and in the disturbed days of the fifth century in the west much land must have lapsed to the crown by the sudden death or captivity of its owner.

Constantine, no doubt under pressure from the church, which held celibacy and continence in high esteem, revoked the clauses of the Augustan laws which confiscated estates left to unmarried or childless persons. Theodosius I, however, and later emperors created a new class of *caduca* by forbidding Manichees and other extreme heretics to inherit or to make wills.

Bona damnatorum had always been the most important accessions to the *res privata*. Here again the government charitably reduced its claims. Valentinian I allowed the children of condemned persons to claim their father's estates except in the case of treason. This generous rule was stiffened by Theodosius I; if a felon was deported he could retain one-sixth of his property and his near relatives a sixth or a third, the treasury taking a half or two-thirds. If he was executed his sons or grandsons could claim the whole, other relatives smaller proportions up to a half. In 426 the law was stiffened again, but up to half the property might be claimed by children or grandchildren. Treason was excepted in all these laws. This exception was important, for the major gains of the treasury were from the estates of wealthy senators accused truly or falsely of plotting against the emperor. For an increasing number of offences partial confiscation was made the penalty. Thus a landowner who knowingly allowed a heretical service or a pagan sacrifice to be held on his lands lost the estate on which the offence took place.

Whether the flow of gifts, bequests, *bona vacantia*, *bona caduca* and *bona damnatorum* decreased or increased it is impossible to say, but it is fairly clear that relatively few of these accessions were actually incorporated in the *res privata*. The government, except in the case of *bona damnatorum*, had no machinery for discovering when land had lapsed to the crown, and had to rely on private informers (*delatores*). Informers were supposed to pass their information to the *advocatus fisci* of the province, who pleaded the crown's claim before the courts; the informer received a reward when a claim was successful. It is plain, however, that most informers preferred to sell their information to private persons of influence, and that the latter passed it on to the government, at the same time petitioning for a grant of the lands if the crown's claim should be sustained. Normally it would appear that the government granted such requests, only insisting that the petitioners must not occupy the land forthwith but first prove the crown's case. Petitions were also frequently made and granted of *bona damnatorum*, This was obviously a dangerous practice, and according to Ammianus Constantius II's courtiers made a practice of playing on his fear of conspiracy to denounce wealthy men and petition for their estates. Theodosius I placed an absolute ban on petitions for *bona damnatorum*. but later emperors weakened; in 401 and again in 426 it was however enacted that two years must elapse after a condemnation before any petitions for the property could be made.

The government thus tended to give away its gains before it acquired them. From the time of Constantius II it recouped part of its loss by a special tax in gold and silver on grantees, and under Honorius and Theodosius II granted lands were occasionally subjected to special levies calculated according to the extent of the lands and varying according to the length of time that they had been enjoyed.

In 425 the government of the eastern parts made petitioners share their gains half and half with the treasury, and in 444 prohibited the petition of crown lands altogether. Henceforth the claims of the crown were to be judged by the praetorian prefects, and estates successfully claimed were to be equally divided between three treasuries of the *res privata*, the *largitiones* and the praetorian prefecture. If the law was observed one may suspect that informers, deprived of their profits, no longer reported state claims.

The government also sometimes sold state properties. In the east in 378 Valens ordered all house property which, owing to the negligence of the *rationales* and procurators, was in ruinous condition to be sold off for what it would fetch, and in 398 Honorius did the same in the west. In the difficult days of the early fifth century the government was selling lands at such a rate that the emperor had to call a halt 'to prevent our eternal house being stripped of all its property by sales'. Free grants were also made to suitors not only of new claims but of estates already incorporated in the *res privata*.

The funds of the *res privata* were not allocated to any specific public expenses. The emperor might use them to subsidize other treasuries and Valentinian III boasted that he frequently did so. But in principle they were reserved for the personal expenditure of the emperor. Leo and Zeno emphasized the personal character of the department by dividing it into two and allocating one half to the empress. The allocation of a major department to casual benefactions of the emperor may seem extravagant, but it must be remembered that the emperor was subject to a constant bombardment of petitions, and public opinion demanded that he should be liberal. Themistius in his panegyric on Valens finds some difficulty in praising that parsimonius emperor's backwardness in making grants; lavish grants, he laboriously explains, mean loss of revenue and therefore a higher rate of general taxation, and disappointed suitors ought to be grateful that they paid less tax on the lands which they already possessed. Not only were lavish grants of land part of the perquisites of all servants of the crown, from the highest ministers to the ordinary palatine civil servants; no one who interviewed the emperor went away without a gift of gold, great or small.

For the maintenance of the imperial household two groups of land were specially earmarked. In the west there was the *domus divina per Africam*, managed by a special *rationalis* under the disposition of the *comes rei privatae*. In the east there was the *domus divina per Cappadociam*, which passed in the late fourth or early fifth century from the jurisdiction of the *comes rei privatae* to that of the *praepositus sacri cubiculi*. Justinian merged the office of the *comes domorum*, who managed these estates, with that of the provincial governor, but the new proconsul of Cappadocia remained responsible to the *praepositus* for their revenues.

Under Justinian there were also a number of separate groups of estates, 'houses', administered by *curatores* of illustrious rank and thus co-ordinate with the *comes rei privatae*. The 'houses' were groups of properties formerly owned by a wealthy subject—the houses of Placidia, Marina, Hormisdas and Antiochus are known—which had lapsed one way or another to the crown and were maintained intact.

The *comes sacrarum largitionum*, as the *rationalis rei summae* was called from Constantine's day, controlled revenue and expenditure in coin, the currency with the mines and mints, and the collection and manufacture and distribution of uniforms to the troops and the civil service. He had under his disposition a considerable diocesan and provincial staff. In general charge of each diocese or half diocese were officials known in the west as *rationales summarum*, in the east as *comites largitionum*. In the west there were also superior officers known as *comites largitionalium titulorum* in charge of larger circumscriptions—Illyricum, Africa, Italy and Gaul. There were in the provinces depots or storehouses (*thesauri*), where gold and silver and clothing were stored pending local distribution or transmission to the *comitatus*. Twelve are recorded in the west in the dioceses of Illyricum, Italy, Gaul, the Seven Provinces and Britain (the omission of Africa and Spain is presumably accidental). No figures are available for the east. In the east there were also controllers of foreign trade, *comites commerciorum*, and one controller of the mines, the *comes metallorum per Illyricum*. In both parts there were procurators of state weaving and dyeing works.

The *largitiones* received such old taxes as had survived the inflation. Of these the most important were the customs. Duties were levied at $12\frac{1}{2}$ per cent (*octavae*) on the frontiers of the empire, and in the interior there were sundry inter-diocesan dues levied at much lower rates, 2 or $2\frac{1}{2}$ per cent. Constantine also took over the customs dues levied by the cities of the empire; they were probably managed by the *largitionales urbium singularum* who are mentioned in the fourth century. The customs were farmed, being allocated for a term of not less than three years to the highest bidder. As under the principate the collection of customs seems to have been compulsorily allocated when the bids were not high enough to satisfy the government; in some dioceses such as Egypt the task was allotted to the decurions of the cities.

Another old tax was the *aurum coronarium*, originally a free will gift of gold crowns made by the cities of the empire to the emperor on his accession and on other festal occasions, including his quinquennial celebrations. The levy remained voluntary in so far as the exact amount was not fixed. On Julian's accession, Libanius tells us, some cities offered as much as 1,000 or 2,000 *solidi*, but Julian fixed 70 *solidi* as a maximum. This tax was paid by the decurions. Similar to the *aurum coronarium* was the *aurum oblaticium* offered on the same occasions by the senate. Its amount too was not fixed; the Roman senate voted 1,600 pounds of gold to Valentinian II on his tenth anniversary.

Among the new taxes two were created by Constantine, the *follis* or *gleba senatoria* and the *chrysargyron* or *collatio lustralis*. The former was a tax levied on all senators at three rates of eight, four or two *folles*; the *follis* appears to have been rated at 125 *milliarenses* or about five *solidi* for this purpose. Modest though the tax was it created great grumbling among poorer senators and in 393 Theodosius I created a fourth class which paid only seven *solidi*. The tax was abolished in the east by Marcian.

The *collatio lustralis* was a levy of gold and silver payable on the same occasions as the *aurum coronarium*, that is every five or later four years, by all traders; in the fifth and sixth centuries it was collected in gold only. Traders were defined in the widest terms to include all who sold goods or services. Teachers and doctors were expressly exempt, but moneylenders and even prostitutes were liable. Landowners and peasants who sold their own produce were also exempt, and Valentinian I gave special immunity to rural craftsmen, but urban craftsmen who sold their own products were liable; painters were expressly excused in 374. Other specially exempt classes were veterans and the poorest clergy, but this exemption applied only to those with a modest capital of ten or fifteen *solidi*. The tax was assessed on the person of the trader and his family and slaves, animals and the tools of his trade. It seems a reasonable tax since the urban population was otherwise untaxed but by universal consent it was highly oppressive and caused great distress. This was no doubt partly due to its irregular incidence; the ordinary improvident taxpayer did not save up beforehand and when the tax fell due was driven to desperate expedients, such as selling his children as slaves. Some craftsmen, however, formed provident societies to save up for the tax and in 399 a law was issued making this practice general in the eastern parts. It does not, however, seem to have improved the situation and complaints of the misery caused by the tax are as bitter in the fifth as in the fourth centuries. The *chrysargyron* was particularly offensive to Christian sentiment in that it gave implicit recognition to prostitution. It was finally abolished in 498 by Anastasius in the eastern parts. It continued to exist in the west in the Ostrogothic and the Visigothic kingdoms.

The yield of the tax was, it would appear, meagre. Edessa, an important commercial town, paid 140 pounds of gold every four years or about 2,500 *solidi* a year, while two Egyptian cities of comparable size paid over 55,000 *solidi* in land tax. These figures suggest that the *chrysargyron* yielded in the neighbourhood of 5 per cent of the land tax. The misery that it caused suggests that the tradesmen and crafts-men who paid it were a poverty-stricken class.

The *largitiones* also received the *aurum tironicum*, the commutation that was paid instead of recruits in some years in some provinces. In the east from 429, when the Jewish patriarchate died out, it annexed the contributions which the synagogues had hitherto paid to the patriarchs. In the west it probably received a tax of one-twenty-fourth on sales, the *siliquaticum*, instituted in 444 by Valentinian III. It also received most fines until the reign of Justinian, who diverted them to the *res privata*. The *largitiones* also received a gold tax on land which was levied on the same basis as the *annona*, or levies in kind. This tax may be a survival of the older money tribute of the principate, but it is more probably descended from the special levies of gold and silver made upon land-owners by the emperors of the tetrarchy. Its amount was small; in an Egyptian document of the sixth century it comes to about an eighth of the *annona* and in a contemporary Italian document the *tituli largitio-nales* amount to about one-fourteenth of the *canon praefectorum*.

Finally the *largitiones* supplied uniforms to the army and the civil service. A proportion of the garments required were woven and dyed in state factories which will be described in a later chapter, but a large proportion, as much as five-sixths, it would seem, in the fifth century, were obtained by a levy in kind, assessed like the *annona* on land and the agricultural population. In Diocletian's time garments were compulsorily purchased at the prices officially laid down in the edict on prices, and in the diocese of Oriens they were still in the fourth century paid for in gold; but as the provinces concerned paid a special gold levy to cover the purchase money they did not gain by this privilege. A law of 377 gives a full schedule of assessments for the eastern parts. In Thrace one garment was levied on every twenty *iuga* or *capita*, except in the frontier provinces of Moesia and Scythia, which enjoyed a lower rate, one for every thirty *iuga* or *capita*. In Asiana and Pontica the rate was the same as in Moesia and Scythia. In Oriens and Egypt one garment was levied on thirty *iuga*, *capita* not being taken into account. Since many lesser landowners and villages were assessed well under twenty *iuga* they were liable for fractions of garments only; we possess a number of Egyptian schedules setting out fractional assessments of garments. In practice such assessments were commuted, and curial collectors of uniforms bought the clothing required with the money thus obtained. By the end of the fourth century both the issue and collection of garments was mostly commuted; the state factories supplied the garments required by recruits and private soldiers, receiving one-sixth of the gold tax which was substituted for the clothing levy. The other five-sixths of the tax was expended on clothing allowances to the troops.

With so large a diocesan staff the *sacrae largitiones* might have been expected to assess and collect its own taxes. It did not do so in fact. The *follis* and the *aurum oblaticium* were managed by the *censuales*, who kept the register of senators and their property. The assessments of the *collatio lustralis* were maintained by the praetorian prefecture, and the tax levied by special collectors elected by the guilds of merchants in each city. The customs were farmed under the supervision of the vicars and provincial governors. The *aurum tironicum*, the gold taxes on land and the clothing levies were assessed and collected in the same way as the *annona* by the provincial governors and the city councils. From 382 every provincial governor had to appoint a special accountant (*numerarius* or *tabularius*) and collector general (*susceptor*) in his office for the *largitionales tituli*. The praetorian prefects were expected to include the *largitionales tituli* in their indiction. The *comes sacrarum largitionum* annually sent one of his *palatini* as *canonicarius* to each province to supervise and accelerate the collection of his taxes by the provincial *officium*.

Apart from clothing the only regular outgoings for which the *sacrae largitiones* was responsible were the money pay, so long as it subsisted, of the civil service and the troops, and the accession and quinquennial donatives. It was also expected to supply gold and silver for all purposes, and in the eastern parts controlled the factories of *barbaricarii* which produced ornamental parade arms and armour with decoration in the precious metals; in the east these factories were transferred in the latter part of the fourth century to the administration of the master of the offices.

The *sacrae largitiones* was responsible for the currency. There were in the fourth century about a dozen mints in the empire. The *Notitia Dignitatum* gives Treviri, Lugdunum and Arelate in Gaul, Aquileia and Rome in Italy, and Siscia in Pannonia. Earlier mints at London and Carthage had by this time been suppressed. In the east there were besides Constantinople, Thessalonica in Macedonia, Heraclea in Thrace, Cyzicus in Asiana, Nicomedia in Pontica, Antioch in Oriens and Alexandria in Egypt. The mints were managed by procurators and the *monetarii* who staffed them were, as under the principate, public slaves. They had by the early fourth century become a hereditary caste some of whose members were rich and ambitious enough to acquire equestrian rank.

Each mint had to produce an annual quota of coins. The charcoal required was supplied as a *sordidum munus* by the neighbouring land-owners. The metal for the bronze coins must have been furnished by the copper levy (*collatio aeraria*), which was imposed on metalliferous lands. Nothing is known of silver production. Gold-mining areas were partly in private possession, in which case the owners paid a gold levy (*collatio auraria*), partly state owned; gold was also washed from some rivers. The gold miners and workers were a hereditary caste who had to produce a certain quota for the state and to sell the rest of their product to the treasury for payment in the copper currency.

The production of gold and silver does not, however, seem to have been large, and most of the metal for new issues was obtained by melting down the coins received in taxation. The practice had apparently always been normal: otherwise it is impossible to account for the large number of new issues. It was made compulsory for gold by Valentinian I, who ordered that all *solidi* received in tax were to be melted down and sent up to the *comitatus* in bar. The primary object was to ensure that lightweight and adulterated coins were not accepted, but the practice ensured that *solidi* maintained their proper weight and quality as they did for many centuries. Valentinian also concentrated all minting of gold at the *comitatus*, in order presumably to keep a close supervision on the *monetarii*, who were according to contemporary complaints liable to strike lightweight coins; one petitioner suggested that the only remedy for this abuse was to put the mints on desert islands where the *monetarii* would be completely cut off from contact with the public.

The history of the currency in the later Roman empire is highly obscure, as the laws and literary authorities have little to say about coinage and we have very little except the coins themselves to go upon. When Diocletian came to the throne the principal coin was the *nummus* initiated by Aurelian, which was tariffed at five *denarii*; it was a small copper piece washed with silver. There was also a smaller denomination tariffed, it would seem, at two *denarii*; there were no silver coins and the issues of gold were irregular and sparse, being made only to provide donatives on festal occasions. Diocletian evidently attempted to establish a stable coinage in gold, silver and copper. He issued gold coins at sixty to the pound and silver coins like the old *denarii* at ninety-six to the pound. As silver was priced at five gold coins to the pound, twenty-four silver coins must have gone to one of gold. Diocletian also issued large silver-washed copper coins marked like the Aurelianic *nummi* XX.I. but of double the weight and apparently, like them, tariffed at five *denarii*, and small copper coins probably tariffed at two *denarii*. The new coinage was thus an attempt at deflation, the Aurelianic coins being halved in value, and Diocletian no doubt hoped to reduce and stabilize prices. He did not, however, command sufficient supplies of bullion to make large issues of gold and silver. The precious metals had during the inflation disappeared into hoards and silver was in particularly short supply, as much was used in plating the debased copper coins. Diocletian and his colleagues made efforts to extract the gold and silver from hoards by making levies of bullion on land and compulsory purchases of gold from the cities, but they were only partially successful and were compelled to meet their expenditure by making large issues of copper *nummi*. The inflation therefore progressed, and the gold and silver coins soon came to be worth more than their face value. In 302 Diocletian attempted to check the inflationary movement by an edict in which he fixed maximum prices for all goods and maximum wages for all workers, enacting the death penalty for any breach of the law. In this edict prices were fixed in *denarii communes*, that is in the copper currency, and gold and silver whether in bar or coin were valued in *denarii*, all attempt at a unified currency being abandoned. The only result of the edict was that goods disappeared from the market. It soon became a dead letter and inflation resumed its course. The currency had to be debased yet further, the copper coins being reduced in weight and retariffed at larger numbers of *denarii*.

Constantine initiated a new gold coin, the *solidus*, struck at seventy-two to the pound. Towards the end of his reign, by confiscating the temple treasures, he acquired large stocks of bullion, and was able to issue *solidi* and silver coins in profusion. Silver was officially priced at four *solidi* to the pound and the silver coins struck at ninety-six to the pound, and now called *milliarenses*, thus still went at twenty-four to one of gold. There was henceforth no change in the gold currency, which was issued in *solidi*, half *solidi* (*semisses*) and *tremisses*, which at first weighed $1\frac{1}{2}$ scruples (three-eighths of a *solidus*), but from the reign of Theodosius I $1\frac{1}{3}$ scruples (a third of a *solidus*). The silver coinage was less successful. The relative value of silver and gold seems to have fluctuated considerably in the fourth century and the government twice reduced the weight of the silver coins. After the time of Theodosius I the issue of silver was virtually abandoned, only a few pieces being struck for special purposes, such as donatives.

Constantine not only confiscated the temple treasures. He instituted new taxes in gold and silver, like the *follis* and the *chrysargyron*, and collected the rents of imperial lands in gold and silver, thus extracting more precious metals from hoards. As a result the empire acquired a stable and steadily more voluminous gold currency. The inflation of the copper currency continued unchecked, however, and despite several attempts at reform rapidly gathered momentum. We know from the Egyptian papyri that in 324 about 4,500 *denarii* went to the *solidus*. By Constantine's death in 337 the figure was about 275,000 and in the latter part of Constantius II's reign it had reached about 4,600,000. A later papyrus states 'the *solidus* now stands at 2,020 myriads of *denarii*; it has gone down'.[1]

The *denarii* in which the Egyptians reckoned prices were of course notional units of account; there had long ceased to be any coins as small as the *denarius*, and the little copper pieces which circulated must have been tariffed at increasingly large numbers of *denarii*. Elsewhere in the empire people ceased to reckon in *denarii* and sometimes called the copper pieces *denarii*. From the end of the fourth century copper was only issued in tiny coins weighing 1 scruple, $\frac{1}{288}$ of a pound; these pieces went at about 7,000 to the *solidus*.

The reasons for this curious development are obscure. The government collected all money taxes and dues in gold and silver, from the fifth century in gold alone. Outgoings were also mainly in gold and silver, later in gold alone. It apparently, however, during the fourth century, still paid their annual *stipendium* to the troops in *denarii*, and therefore had to mint fresh copper coins every year. The copper coinage was thus regularly inflated. The government seems moreover to have bought in *solidi* from the public through the money-changers; we know at any rate that in Egypt the officials who handled the money taxes were called gold-buyers, and that the guild of money-changers (*collectarii*) at Rome was charged with the duty of buying *solidi* from the public, being supplied with copper coins from the *arca vinaria*. The state both kept its accounts and stored its reserves in gold, and was indifferent to the condition of the ordinary currency which its subjects used. If it exploited it to increase its stock of gold, the policy was probably not deliberate. The ancients thought that the value of a coin depended on the amount of metal in it, and were unaware that, if the number of

[1] *Ec. Hist. Rev.* v (1953), pp. 307–9.

coins increased and the goods on the market remained the same, prices would rise. Diocletian and his successors thought that, if they continued to issue coins of the same weight, they ought to have the same value, and attributed the constant rise in prices to the insatiable avarice of merchants.

It must have been very inconvenient to have no coins intermediate between a *tremissis* and tiny copper pieces of which over 2,000 went to the *tremissis*, and even more inconvenient that the exchange rate between *nummi* and *solidi* fluctuated according to the state of the market day by day. The first attempt to remedy this state of affairs was made by the Roman senate under Odoacer, which started an issue of large copper pieces marked XL and worth forty *nummi*. At about the same time the Vandals issued similar large copper coins labelled NXLII. Smaller denominations marked XX, X, and V in Italy and XXI in Africa were also issued. The Italian coins were apparently based on an exchange rate of 7,200 *nummi* to the *solidus*, so that 180 of the largest copper coins went to a *solidus*. The African coins were perhaps calculated at an exchange rate of 7,500, and would yield the same relation of the copper to the gold coins as in Italy.

In 498 Anastasius carried through a similar reform in the east, issuing coins marked XL, XX, X, and V (in Greek M, K, I, and E). In the first issue the largest denomination, which was commonly called a *follis*, was struck at thirty-six to the pound, and hence also known as a third of an ounce piece (*teruncianus*). These coins apparently proved a failure, for the next issue was made double the weight. These coins were later slightly reduced from eighteen to twenty to the pound. The exchange rate of the *solidus* was at first apparently 180, later 210. Justinian in 539 increased the weight of the *follis* and restored the rate of 180.

Silver coins were also revived in the Ostrogothic and Vandal kingdoms; they too were marked with their value in *nummi*. Justinian continued the Italian silver coinage, but did not attempt to reintroduce silver in the east.

The new copper coinage was popular and the government found no difficulty in selling it for *solidi*. At the same time it brought in great profits to the treasury, for it required 25 pounds of copper to mint 7,200 *nummi* and less than 10 pounds to produce 210 *folles*.

It was Diocletian who first systematized and regularized the irregular levies in kind (*indictiones extraordinariae*) on which the government had come to depend during the middle years of the third century for its major needs—the rations (*annonae*) of the troops and the civil service, the fodder (*capitus*) for their horses, foodstuffs for feeding the populace of Rome, materials and labour for public works, the animals for the postal service and the fodder to feed them, the raw materials for arms and the rations for the armourers who made them. The requisitions were henceforth consolidated into an annual indiction levied at more or less uniform rates and based on a more or less uniform assessment of agricultural land (*iugatio*). From Constantine's time the assessment of the agricultural population (*capitatio*), on which a money poll tax had been levied in Diocletian's day, was added to the *iugatio*, and the total units of land and people used as a basis for the indiction.

Though the indictions were thus regularized, they remained variable. Unlike the *comes rei privatae*, who had merely to collect the fixed rents of the state property, and the *comes sacrarum largitionum*, who levied certain taxes at a fixed rate, the praetorian prefects had each year to calculate the estimated needs of the government in the districts which they administered for wheat, barley, meat, wine, oil, timber and labourers, to divide the totals by the number of *iuga* and *capita* at which their districts were assessed, and then to work out the amount of the levy on each unit of assessment. The figures were circulated in advance of the beginning of the fiscal year or indiction (1 September) to vicars and provincial governors, and by them to the cities. The *tabularii* of the cities then drew up demand notes to the individual taxpayers on the basis of their assessment. The levies were from Valentinian I's time collected in three instalments, no doubt to avoid over-loading the transport system and the capacity of the imperial store-houses. Even when later the levies were commuted into gold they were still paid in three instalments; this was for the benefit of the taxpayers, who were not obliged to dispose of all their surplus crops at once, directly after the harvest, thus getting low prices, but could spread out their sales over the year.

The task of the praetorian prefects was thus much more complicated than that of the other financial ministers. They had each year to obtain returns from the *duces* and *magistri militum* of the ration strength of the troops under their command, to estimate the requirements in craftsmen, labourers and materials for projected public works, and to work out the needs of the *cursus publicus* for replacements of animals and fodder: the exact amounts of the various kinds of foodstuffs needed also had to be calculated. Allowance had moreover to be made for probable arrears in collection. If these estimates were too high, perishable foodstuffs would go to waste; if they were too low, supplementary indictions would be needed and these were unpopular and regarded with disapproval by the emperors. Constantius II, Julian, Valens and Gratian all enacted that the prefects must accurately assess the entire annual needs of the state for all purposes, and refused their prefects, still more the vicars and provincial governors, authority to order superindictions; all supplementary demands had, like the indictions themselves, to be signed by the emperor himself.

To cope with all these calculations the prefect had a large body of financial clerks. In the praetorian prefecture in the East, there was a department (*scrinium*), headed by a *numerarius*, for each diocese, and also *scrinia* for public works, for arms, and for the city of Constantinople. Each *numerarius* had an assistant and an accountant, and under him there were *tractatores*, who handled the accounts of each province. There was also a *cura epistolarum* for each diocese, who handled financial correspondence with his opposite number, the *cura epistolarum* of the vicar. The vicars also had their *numerarii*, and the provincial governors had two *numerarii* each, one of whom dealt with the prefect's accounts and the other with those of the *largitiones*. Each year the prefecture sent down to each province an official (*canonicarius*) to supervise and check the collection of the tax and if necessary a second official (*compulsor*) to round up arrears. The provincial office had to make returns every four months (*quadrimenstrui breves*) of the amount of tax collected and the amount outstanding and the sums spent locally and those to be remitted to the prefecture.

The taxes were normally collected by *susceptores* appointed annually by the city councils, arrears were levied by *compulsores* drawn from the provincial office. Separate boards of *susceptores* were appointed for the various levies, wheat, wine, meat, labourers and so forth. They had not only to collect the quota from the landowners or from the villages of peasant proprietors, who appointed village collectors, but to transport and deliver it to the state storehouses. If they failed to collect the full amount they had to make up the deficit out of their own property, and, if this was inadequate to cover the loss, the city council as a whole was responsible, and a levy was made on all its members in proportion to their wealth. These amateur curial collectors were not, it would seem, very efficient, and at various times the government tried to appoint imperial officials to keep them up to the mark, or even to substitute officials for them. Diocletian appears to have appointed a collector-general (*exactor civitatis*) for each city, but this official came later to be elected by the council. The reason appears from an Egyptian document in which the city council disputes the liability for arrears which had accrued under the *exactor* Taurinus. The government was apparently claiming that they should be made good by a levy on the councillors, but they cited an imperial constitution and two edicts of the prefects, whereby no one was to undertake a curial office without being nominated by the council, and deficits of curial officers were to be made good by a levy on the council. If Taurinus had been nominated by the council, they admitted the lawfulness of a levy, but if he had, contrary to the imperial constitution, been appointed without their consent, they disclaimed responsibility and demanded that he be removed from office.

Valentinian and Valens attempted to replace curial electors by ex-officials or *honorati* nominated by the provincial office, on the grounds that such persons would be more effective. This attempted reform was, however, shortlived. The provincial offices found great difficulty in imposing the service on the persons liable, who were skilled at evading it, and eventually the emperors had to go back to curial collectors, consoling themselves with the reflection that if they did default then the council had to make up the loss.

In 384 it was enacted that in Pontica the collection should be divided into three parts. The curial *susceptores* were to collect only from their fellow decurions, the provincial office from the great landlords who were senators or *honorati*, and the *defensor civitatis* from the poor. The intention seems to have been to protect the humbler classes from the extortion of the decurions, and at the same time to relieve the decurions of the difficult task of extracting taxes from their social superiors. The experiment does not seem to have been a success and is not heard of again. In 396 it was again enacted in the east that the taxes of senators should be collected by the provincial office, but next year it was reported that half the tax due from senators was still unpaid and the experiment was abandoned.

Anastasius, on the suggestion of his financial adviser, Marinus, instituted the system of *vindices*. These were imperial nominees, appointed one for each city to organize the tax collection. Those who offered the highest returns are said to have been appointed. The result of the reform was, its critics admitted, that the revenue was substantially increased, but they alleged that the councils were thereby ruined. From this it would appear that the curial tax collectors normally did not lose by their activities. The decurions still, it would seem, actually collected the taxes and remained liable for arrears under the new system, but were kept under control by the *vindex*.

Normally local expenses were a first charge on the provincial revenues—the salary of the governor and his assessor, the pay of his *officium*, the cost of the postal service, and the rations of the local troops if any. The frontier provinces, however, which were heavily garrisoned, could not support the whole charge for their troops, and special arrangements had to be made for the offices of the *comitatus* and for the regiments of the field army, which were concentrated in or around the capitals or in regional centres such as Trier or Antioch. The static frontier garrisons of *limitanei* were supplied by a system, which appears to date from before Diocletian's time, known as *primipili pastus*. The *princeps*, the centurion who was chief clerk of the *officium*, retired each year and was promoted *primipilus*. As such he had to convey supplies from the province to a frontier army and consign them to the *dux*. Such a system was not adapted for the regiments of the field army or for the offices of the court, which were mobile. They were issued with warrants (*delegatoriae*), entitling them to draw specified amounts of supplies from the revenues of named provinces which had a surplus. They sent an agent styled an *opinator* to collect the supplies, which the provincial *officium* had to deliver within a year.

In the fourth century the indiction certainly varied from year to year, and usually in an upward direction. Julian, as Caesar in Gaul, by economizing in his expenses, and by careful collection, was able to reduce the rate from 25 to 7 *solidi* per *caput*. According to Themistius, during the forty years preceding 364 the indiction had been gradually increased to double the figure prevailing in 324; then the careful and parsimonious Valens had stabilized the amount for three years and in the fourth reduced it. By the fifth century, however, the indiction seems to have been stabilized at a customary figure, and any additions were reckoned superindictions. This practice was inequitable since privileged categories of taxpayers, such as the churches and lessees of imperial lands and *illustres*, were exempt from superindictions, and it was forbidden in 416 by Honorius, who ordered the existing superindiction to be consolidated with the regular indiction. It would appear, however, that this was an exceptional measure, and the tax normally became fixed. Emperors both in the east and the west not infrequently gave relief to provinces which had suffered from barbarian invasions by reducing their taxes to a stated fraction of the normal total; thus in 413 Honorius permitted the Suburbicarian provinces to pay one-fifth only of their regular tax, and Theodosius II scaled down the taxes of Achaia to a third and those of the other provinces of the Macedonian diocese to a half. Valentinian III, reducing the tax of Numidia and Mauretania Sitifensis to one-eighth, stated the precise sums which would henceforth be annually paid.

As the gold coinage became more abundant, payments and levies in kind were gradually commuted to *solidi*. The process began in the third quarter of the fourth century, when Valens enacted that the *limitanei* should receive rations in kind for nine months of the year and money for the remaining three. The horses levied for the army were also commuted for a gold payment as early as 367. Commutation of *annonae* and *capitus* was gradually extended, and by the early fifth century was applied to the *comitatenses* as well as to the *limitanei* in the west; in 429 we find *opinatores* collecting not foodstuffs but gold from the provinces. In the east the *comitatenses* still continued to draw rations in kind, but those of the *limitanei* were commuted. The *annonae* of palatine officials were converted into *solidi* in 423, and those office-holders of the rank of *spectabilis* and *clarissimus* in 439. Levies in kind were similarly commuted. In the early fifth century in the east the tax was still assessed in kind, and the commutation was calculated by a five years' average of prices. It was still a rare concession; in the latter part of Theodosius II's reign out of 62,000 *iuga* at which the territory of Cyrrhus was assessed only 10,000 paid in gold. It was Anastasius who made commutation of the land tax the regular rule, and he maintained levies in kind to feed Constantinople, Alexandria and Antioch, and to supply rations to most of the field army. When the taxes levied in kind did not produce enough foodstuffs, these were compulsorily purchased from the taxpayers, the price being set off against their gold tax, or, if it exceeded their liability, paid in *solidi*. This procedure (*coemptio*) was, however, allowed only in exceptional circumstances by the emperor's express permission, except in the diocese of Thrace, where the poverty of the provinces and the large number of troops made *coemptio* regularly necessary. In the west the commutation of levies in kind was universal by the early fifth century; the taxes on Numidia and Mauretania Sitifensis were already reckoned entirely in gold before the Vandal invasion, and Majorian assumes in his laws that the land tax in Italy was paid in *solidi*. Supplies needed for the troops were regularly obtained by *coemptio*. The conscription of labour for the public works was also abandoned and labourers hired for cash wages.

While we have a good deal of detailed, if rather obscure, information about the intricate mechanism of the fiscal system, we are ill-informed on more general financial questions. The system seems to have been tolerably efficient; on the whole the government succeeded in collecting the revenue which it demanded. We hear of occasional large-scale peculation; in 450 the province of Sardinia was excluded from a general remission of arrears because its taxes from the previous year had mysteriously failed to reach the treasury, but this was under the inefficient administration of Valentinian III's last years. There were, of course, arrears, as in any fiscal system however efficient, and some of these eventually had to be written off as bad debts in periodical remissions. Julian refused to grant such remissions on the ground that they favoured the rich, who managed to postpone payment, and did not help the poor, who were compelled to pay on the nail. His criticism may have been justified for his own period, but in the fifth and sixth centuries general remissions were only given at long intervals, and usually excluded arrears of the immediately preceding five to eight years. Only very adroit or influential persons can have postponed payment for so long as this, and the main object of the remission seems to have been to clear the books of the manifestly bad debts, and to prevent ingenious officials from raking up alleged claims from many years past, for which the taxpayers had lost their receipts. This was one of the many forms of extortion practised by officials, and in another effort to combat it Marcian enacted that a taxpayer who could produce receipts for three consecutive years was to be deemed to have satisfied all previous demands.

The expenses of collection were borne by the taxpayer, who was expected to pay supplementary fees of many kinds to all those concerned in collecting the taxes. Some of these fees were justified as compensation for deterioration of the goods collected in storage or transit, or for the acceptance of worn or lightweight *solidi*; others appear to have been outright tips or payments for the receipt. The amount of these supplementary payments varied very greatly according to the strictness and efficiency of the central government. Under the careful rule of Anastasius they were limited to one carat, one-twenty-fourth of a *solidus*, for each *iugum*, which had to be divided between the curial collectors, the provincial office and the central offices of the praetorian prefecture and the *largitiones*. Under the inefficient rule of Valentinian III they had been consolidated at two *solidi* per *iugum*, and Majorian, finding that many additional exactions had been added since, added another half *solidus* to the consolidated fees in compensation for their abolition. The officials of the praetorian prefecture received the lion's share of these fees, thirteen *siliquae* out of each *solidus*; those of the *largitiones* got one *siliqua* for their small share in the land tax, the exactor got two; the curial collectors and the provincial officials who did all the hard work had only eight between them. It would appear that the contemporary rate of tax was seven *solidi* per *iugum*, so that the perquisites of the officials added 35 per cent to the tax burden in the last days of the western empire. By contrast the fees from the east were a sixtieth of what they were in the west.

Besides these recognized fees, there was much illicit extortion. Valentinian III draws a lurid picture of the *canonicarii* producing 'alarming demands for numerous different taxes', putting out 'a smoke-screen of minute calculations involved in impenetrable obscurity', and demanding 'receipts for a long series of past years, receipts which the plain man confident that he owes nothing does not bother to preserve'.

The *canonicarii* of the praetorian prefecture and the *largitiones* were the worst offenders. They were high officials who could terrorize the local collectors and the taxpayers alike. They could be sued for their misdeeds only in the distant and expensive court of the praetorian prefect or the *comes sacrarum largitionum*, and finally, not being natives of the province, they had no reason to conciliate local opinion. The curial *susceptores* and the *compulsores* of the provincial office were of relatively humble status, and could be sued in the provincial court. They were, moreover, natives of the area, and had to live with the people whose taxes they collected. As a result they were less extortionate—at any rate towards the upper and middle classes—than the *canonicarii*. It was for this reason that provincial assemblies frequently petitioned the government that *canonicarii* be abolished, and the government from time to time acceded to such requests, and consistently forbade the *canonicarii* to take any part in the collection of the taxes or arrears, and to confine themselves with supervising and stimulating the activity of the provincial officials.

Another favourite device of the tax collectors was to give the taxpayer a receipt in return for a bond, naturally charging high interest, for the sum owed, and then to postpone payment to the state until the arrears were wiped out by a general indulgence; later emperors from Marcian onwards expressly exclude from their edicts of indulgence arrears for which collectors had thus made themselves responsible.

The assessment of the land tax had from the beginning varied considerably in accuracy and fairness in different parts of the empire. In

Syria, the fiscal units of land, the *iuga*, were carefully calculated so as to be of equal value, account being taken of differences both of its use and of its quality. In Asiana and Egypt the assessment was less careful, no account being taken of the quality of the land. In Africa the unit was an area of land, the *centuria* of 200 *iugera*, and in southern Italy similarly the *millena* of 12½ *iugera* was the unit. This was both inequitable and inefficient; the owner of rough pasture paid the same rate as the owner of vineyards and olive-yards, and as a result a rate of tax which was low for the latter was ruinous for the former. There were also quite irrational customary variations in the assessment of *capita*; males only were counted in Egypt, both sexes in Oriens, while in Pontica a woman counted for half as much as a man. The assimilation of *capita* to *iuga* was also arbitrary and inequitable; it meant that a poor peasant with a large family might pay more than a neighbour who had more land but fewer children. The emperors who cared for the welfare of the peasantry remitted or reduced the *capitatio*. Valentinian I abolished it in the provinces of Illyricum, which had suffered severely from the barbarians, and Theodosius I did the same for the Thracian diocese, and ruled that in Pontica four women and two-and-a-half men should count as a *caput* instead of two and one as hitherto. Anastasius having relieved the urban poor of the *collatio lustralis* was in process of abolishing the *capitatio* of the peasantry when he died.

If the assessment was to remain accurate and equitable it ought to have been revised at regular intervals. Changes of land ownership were regularly recorded, but the evidence suggests that the laborious task of reassessing the land and the numbers of the population was neglected. Revisions seem only to have been made occasionally on the request of a diocese, province or city, or even of individual large owners, whereupon the government appointed a special *censitor* or *peraequator* for the area concerned. When a reassessment was made, the government's object was to avoid an overall loss, and the *censitor* or *peraequator*, as the latter title suggests, was expected to set off reductions of assessment on one farm by increases on others.

Elsewhere the census remained unrevised for many years. Thus in Egypt the original census of Sabinus made in 298–302 was still quoted as valid in 348, and a census made by John in 524 was cited in 565. The government must have lost by its negligence, for those who had improved their land or acquired more agricultural labourers naturally did not request reassessments, while those whose lands had deteriorated or whose *coloni* had fallen in number did. Not only was the valuation of land maintained at the same figure over many decades, but the *capitatio* was also left unchanged whether the population had actually risen or sunk. It is evident from the laws on the exemption of recruits that many landlords had more *coloni* than the number registered on their farms, and their assessment of *capitatio* was only reduced if they could not make up the theoretical total from persons qualified but not entered on the register. On the other hand, landlords whose *coloni* had run away could not claim a reduction in their assessment; it was their business to recover the runaways and it was only by special request that the figures of the *capitatio* were revised if the number had fallen for other reasons.

Apart from negligence, the assessment was often unfair. It was frequently complained that the *tabularii* of the cities, in order to win the favour of great landlords, under-assessed the estates of the *principales* and over-assessed those of the lesser decurions and peasantry. *Peraequatores* were similarly susceptible to social pressure or to bribes, and as a precaution against undue lenience to the rich, Theodosius II and Anastasius enacted that a *peraequatio* should not be allowed for an individual landowner, but only for a city or a province as a whole. An eastern law of 430 suggests that many great landowners had secured an unduly favourable reassessment of their estates during the previous thirty-five years. If the rebate was 400 *iuga* or *capita* or less, half was allowed to stand, but if it exceeded that amount all except 200 *iuga* or *capita* were cancelled. Landlords who had received remissions on this scale must have had very extensive estates.

The taxation of the empire was with very few exceptions not progressive. There was a special surtax on land, the *follis*, which fell upon senators, but it was a very small tax, and it was abolished by Marcian in the east. *Honorati*, those who received grants of rank or titular offices, were during the fourth and early fifth centuries liable to special levies of horses or recruits, but these levies appear to have been abandoned in the course of the fifth century. Senators had also to contribute to the *aurum oblaticium* and decurions to the *aurum coronarium*, and the former had the expense of their praetorian games and the latter their curial *munera* to perform. Apart from these special levies, all landowners from the wealthiest senator to the poorest peasant paid the same rate of tax. The land tax was, in fact, regressive, since senators and tenants of imperial land, who were generally wealthy, were excused extraordinary levies in excess of the regular indiction. In practice, moreover, as we have seen, the lands of the great landlords and of the leading decurions were often under-assessed or granted special rebates and it was easier for the rich to postpone payment for long periods and thus profit from the general indulgences of arrears.

A very large proportion of the burden of taxation fell on agriculture, landlords and the peasantry. The *iugatio* fell exclusively on agricultural land, not even on gardens or house property, and the *capitatio*, except in Africa and a few other western provinces, was assessed on the agricultural population only. The land tax assessed on the *iugatio* and *capitatio* covered, it would seem, the greater part of the expenditure; it was the praetorian prefects, who controlled the land tax only, who had to provide for the rations and fodder of the army and the civil service and for the post and public works, and the levies of clothing were assessed on the *iugatio* and *capitatio*, and so also was the recruit tax and the levy of horses. The *res privata* depended on the rents of the imperial estates. Of the taxes of the *largitiones* the *follis* was a surtax assessed on land, and the *aurum oblaticium* and *coronarium* were levies on landowners. The only direct tax on trade and industry was the *collatio lustralis*, which, as we have seen, seems to have yielded about five per cent of the amount yielded by the land tax. The customs fell on all consumers alike and do not seem to have contributed much to the budget. While the burden thrown on agriculture was severe, the apportionment of the tax load was probably reasonable, for the economy of the Roman empire was predominantly agricultural, and the great bulk of the national income was derived from the land. The attempt to tax trade and industry yielded little revenue and at the same time inflicted great hardship.

Figures are so sparse that it is impossible to make any estimate of the total revenue and expenditure of the empire which is not pure guesswork, and there are very few figures for individual provinces. Egypt in the sixth century yielded eight million *artabae* of wheat for the feeding of Constantinople, which was worth 800,000 *solidi*, and a few scattered figures suggest the diocese yielded about as much again in gold, say 1,500,000 *solidi* in all. Numidia before the Vandal invasion paid 78,200 *solidi* and Mauretania Sitifensis 41,600. Of the other African provinces Tripolitania and Mauretania Caesariensis are unlikely to have paid more than Mauretania Sitifensis, bringing up the total to about 200,000. Even if the addition of the two richest provinces, Proconsularis and Byzacena, doubled this figure, the grand total would come to only about 400,000 *solidi*, less than a third of what Egypt contributed.

The only hint of a global figure is Procopius' statement in the *Secret History* that in the nine years of Justin's reign 4,000 *centenaria* of gold came into the treasury. This implies that the annual income of the eastern empire was about 3,200,000 *solidi* in gold. Procopius probably did not take revenue in kind into account, and as we have seen Egypt paid as much again in kind as in gold, and the dioceses of Dacia, Macedonia and Thrace must have paid largely in kind, having large armies to feed and being very poor. Egypt would then have paid rather under a quarter of the gold revenue and Oriens, Pontica and Asiana rather over a quarter each; the three last dioceses would also have paid substantial sums in kind to feed the praesental armies and those of the East and of Armenia. The figures correspond roughly with what we are told about the wealth of the several dioceses, for Egypt was undoubtedly the richest and seems to have paid nearly double the amount of tax. In the west, Africa was generally esteemed one of the richest dioceses, yet paid only one-third of what Egypt did. This suggests that the western empire was very much poorer than the eastern.

For the rate of taxation we have three figures only. In southern Italy the tax under Valentinian III was 7 *solidi* per *millena*, that is nearly half a *solidus* per *iugerum*; to this must be added 2 *solidi* of fees, bringing the total up to nearly three-quarters of a *solidus* per *iugerum*. In Numidia the tax was at this period, after having been reduced to one-eighth, 20 *siliquae* per *centuria*. This implies a normal rate of 7 *solidi*, to which once again must be added 2 *solidi* for fees. It would appear that the western government levied the same rate of tax on the fiscal unit whatever its size. The rate per *iugerum* works out at only about one-twentieth of a *solidus*. The contrast with Italy is startling, but the average productivity of land in Africa was very much lower than in Italy, much being arid pasture too dry to have a crop.

In Egypt we have the complete tax register of the city of Antaeopolis under Justinian, giving the total area, 51,655 *arurae*, nearly all arable, and the total tax in corn, 61,674 *artabae*, and in money, including fees, 10,322 *solidi*. The rate per *arura* works out about 1·2 *artabae* of wheat and 0·2 *solidi*. If the wheat is commuted into gold the rate is 0·32 *solidi*, equivalent to 0·3 *solidi* per *iugerum*. Egyptian land was thus taxed at about two-fifths of the Italian rate but at six times the African rate. Egyptian land was undoubtedly on average the best and the rate of tax on Italian land seems crushing.

Some estimate of the weight of taxation can be worked out. Good average land in Egypt produced, it would seem, something like 10 *artabae* per *arura*. The total tax of Antaeopolis reckoned in wheat comes to 3·2 *artabae* or approximately a third of the total crop. This is a very high rate compared with the tithe levied on land under the republic. The Italian rate is equivalent to more than two-thirds of the crop, presuming the yield of Italian land was as high as that of the Egyptian. The interpretation of the figures is somewhat dubious, but they go some way to confirm the complaint of contemporaries that in the fifth and sixth centuries the load of taxation had become crushing. The effects of this enormous burden on agriculture will be discussed in a later chapter.

XIV

Justice

The stately fabric of Roman law as we know it is the product of Justinian's codification, and before that date the structure was somewhat ramshackle. The law was uncertain on a number of points, the authorities being divided, but above all it was obscure, being derived from a vast array of scattered sources. The sources of law, as recognized by the courts, fell into two main groups, the works of the classical jurisconsults, who wrote from the reign of Augustus down to the Severan period, and imperial constitutions. The work of the jurists was immensely voluminous: those which Justinian's commissioners read and excerpted amounted to three million lines, or twenty times the length of the Digest. Many of them were moreover very rare, existing only in a few law libraries. Yet all were authoritative, and a learned barrister could baffle the judge by producing an opinion from a manual unknown and inaccessible to the judge. For the unlearned judges of the fourth and fifth centuries this proved so embarrassing that in 426 Valentinian III issued the famous law of citations, whereby he gave primary authority to five leading jurisconsults, Papinian, Paulus, Ulpian, Modestinus and Gaius, and enacted that where they differed the majority should carry the day, and if there was a tie Papinian was to have the casting vote. This was a crude rule but it had at least the merit that a diligent lawyer could say what the law was on most disputed issues. The opinions of jurists had to yield to subsequent imperial constitutions. The term 'constitution' covered a wide range of

BIBLIOGRAPHY. The best account of the development of Roman law is H. F. Jolowicz, *Historical Introduction to the Study of Roman Law*² (Cambridge, 1952). For the composition of the Theodosian Code see *Cod. Theod.* I. i. 5, Theod. II, *Nov.* i, and *God. Theod. Gesta Senatus*. For the Justinian Code and the Digest, the constitutions '*Haec*', '*Summa*', '*Deo auctore*', '*Tanta*', '*Omnem*' and '*Corda*', printed before the Code and Digest. For the whole subject see Chapter XIV of my *Later Roman Empire* (Oxford, 1964). The rules of judicial procedure are set out in Cod. Just. II and III.

pronouncements. There were in the first place *decreta* or actual judgments made by the emperor on a specific case which was tried before him. Then there were rescripts, which fell into two classes. Some were answers made to the enquiries (*relationes*, *consultationes*) of judges who, being uncertain of the law in a case which they were trying, asked for an imperial ruling on the issue. Others were answers to private citizens, who, before initiating litigation, asked the emperor how the law stood in their case; this practice was very common in the third and early fourth centuries, and hundreds of such rescripts are preserved in the Justinian Code. Both *decreta* and rescripts, however, later fell out of favour as a source of law. Too often the judgment or opinion of the imperial court or chancery in particular cases was warped by the undue influence of powerful litigants or petitioners. In 398 rescripts were denied authority and in 426 the same rule was applied to *decreta*. Justinian, however, arguing that it was absurd to query the judgment of the emperor, the sole font of law, restored the authority of both as sources of law.

There remained imperial edicts issued to the population at large, with which may be classed the *senatusconsulta* (which were virtually imperial edicts read to the senate), edicts of the praetorian prefects, who could interpret but not change the law, and other general laws (*leges generales*), as opposed to *pragmaticae*, constitutions issued to particular provinces, cities or corporations. The distinction between the last two categories was not in practice very clear, as most laws were issued to high officers of state, with instructions to promulgate them, and some of the laws were of general application, others referred to the particular area or department under the jurisdiction of the recipient. In practice, a fair number of *pragmaticae* issued to provincial assemblies, cities or to the guilds of shippers or of the city of Rome, were accepted by the courts as generally valid and were in due course incorporated in the Codes. Further confusion was introduced by the fact that while a constitution issued by any emperor was in theory issued by the imperial college and valid throughout the empire, laws were in fact normally promulgated only in the area governed by the emperor who issued them. A cunning lawyer could thus confront the court by producing an imperial constitution from another part of the empire. In Honorius' reign the Jews of Calabria claimed immunity from curial duties under 'some law which has been issued in the eastern parts', and Honorius, much annoyed by this chicanery, had to abrogate 'the same law—if there be such a law—which is manifestly harmful to my parts'.[1]

[1] *Cod. Theod.* XII. i. 158.

The causes which prompted the imperial government to enact changes in the body of private law are summarized by Valentinian III in an oration to the senate delivered in 426, and his analysis is borne out by a study of the preambles of the novels. A law might be issued on the spontaneous initiative of the emperor—or of his legal advisers: it was no doubt Constantine himself who, in deference to Christian sentiment, revoked those parts of the Augustan laws which penalized celibates, legislated against bastards and stiffened the law of divorce. More often the existence of some anomaly or contradiction, or an issue on which the existing law was contrary to contemporary standards of equity, was brought to the emperor's attention by a suit tried before him in the first instance or on appeal, or referred to him by a judge, or again by the petition of a subject. Thus Marcian was moved to abrogate a law of Valentinian I, annulling bequests by women to clerics, by a case which he personally tried in the senate, and to reinterpret a law of Constantine forbidding marriage between senators and women of lower degree, by a case referred to him by his praetorian prefect. It was two petitions of the *vir spectabilis* Leonius and the *femina illustris* Pelagia which moved Valentinian III to issue two constitutions modifying testamentary law, and a petition from two moneylenders of Constantinople which produced Justinian's novel on maritime loans. Sometimes also the provincial bars brought to the emperor's notice knotty points which they could not solve: we know of three questions put by the bar of the praetorian prefect of Illyricum, and one raised by that of the governor of Palestine.

Edicts and general laws were posted in the principal cities of the empire, or rather of the dominions of the emperor who issued them, and remained on view for a limited period—perhaps a month. *Pragmaticae* were communicated to the bodies to whom they were issued, and rescripts to the judges or individuals who elicited them; rescripts were also posted at the place at which they were issued. *Decreta* were not, it would seem, officially published, but could become known from the record of the case issued to the successful litigant, and rescripts were also recited in court and thus preserved in the court record. Legal enactments thus became known to lawyers and the public as they were made, but no permanent central record of imperial legislation was maintained. This seems incredible, but the fact is plain from a study of the Theodosian Code, whose compilers, it is evident, had to search the archives of provincial offices and even to draw on the collections of private lawyers to obtain copies of imperial constitutions.

This lack of any official collection of imperial constitutions was to some extent remedied in the reign of Diocletian by the private enterprise of two lawyers, Gregorius and Hermogenian. Gregorius made a collection of constitutions from Hadrian to 291, arranging them by subject matter according to the traditional scheme of the legal commentaries in books and titles, and chronologically within each title. Hermogenian published a supplementary collection of laws issued between 291 and 295. His book was arranged in titles only, but it must have been of considerable size—we know of the 120th law of the 69th title. Though unofficial and no doubt incomplete, the Gregorian and Hermogenian Codes were so useful that they were soon recognized by the courts as authoritative and exhaustive records of all legislation up to 295.

Imperial constitutions continued to be issued thick and fast, and some were apparently added to the Hermogenian Code, from which a few laws of Valentinian I are cited. But the vast majority remained hidden in the archives of provincial offices, in records of legal proceedings, or in the private collections of lawyers. At length, in 429, the eastern government, probably moved by the praetorian prefect Antiochus, who had earlier in his career been quaestor, decided that 'the mass of imperial constitutions, which, sunk in a thick fog, has by a bank of obscurity cut off knowledge of itself from human minds',[1] must be codified. A commission was appointed under the presidency of Antiochus, to collect all extant general laws from 312. The commission was authorized to cut out the preambles and other superfluous matter and to arrange the laws according to the traditional scheme in books and titles, cutting up composite laws where necessary. It was instructed to publish all laws, whether still valid or obsolete; the chronological sequence would show which laws were still valid, and therefore only dated laws were to be included.

The first commission seems to have made little progress, for in 435 a second commission was appointed under the same Antiochus, and in 438 they published the Theodosian Code, which was promulgated in both east and west. It was enacted that henceforth western laws should not be applicable in the east unless officially transmitted to the eastern government and promulgated by it, and similarly in the west with eastern laws. Under these arrangements some thirty-five laws of Theodosius II were promulgated in the west in 447, and later five laws of Marcian. No western laws were received in the east.

[1] Theod. II, *Nov.* i. 1.

The next attempts at codification were made by the barbarian kings in the west. The most ambitious was the Breviarium of Alaric II, king of the Visigoths, which was issued in 506. It comprised a few laws selected from the Gregorian and Hermogenian codes and a much larger selection from the Theodosian and from the novels issued since its publication by both the western and eastern governments. Large numbers of laws irrelevant to the Visigothic kingdom, particularly those concerning the central administration, were omitted, and while the full text of the laws included was given, a brief interpretation in simple language was added to each. The juristic literature was very drastically pruned; only Gaius' *Institutes* and a summary version of Paul's *Sententiae* were kept, with one chapter from Papinian's *Responsa*. King Gundobad of the Burgundians produced the *Lex Romana Burgundionum* and King Theoderic of the Ostrogoths his Edict. But these were mere handbooks, containing 166 and 154 laws respectively.

In the east the codification of the law was left to a later date, but it was carried out much more scientifically. As soon as he came to the throne, Justinian appointed a commission to prepare a single code of imperial constitutions, which should comprise all laws still valid from the Gregorian, Hermogenian and Theodosian codes and subsequent novels. The editors were empowered to omit all obsolete laws and to revise those which they retained to bring them up to date. The first Justinian Code was published on 7 April 529. A second commission was appointed on 15 December 530 to carry out the much more laborious and complex task of codifying the juristic literature. At the same time a number of obsolete institutions were abolished and the major outstanding questions on which the authorities conflicted were settled. The commission, working with amazing speed, produced the Digest in exactly three years. It was promulgated on 16 December 533. The considerable number of legal changes suggested by the production of the Digest had already made the Code out of date, and a second edition, which we possess, was issued on 16 November 534.

Tribonian, Justinian's quaestor, who sat on the first Code commission and presided over the commissions which produced the Digest and the second edition of the Code, probably inspired the whole operation. He succeeded in six years in reducing the vast bulk of Roman legal literature to two manageable volumes. This in itself was a great boon to lawyers and to the public. But he did more. He clarified the law and settled a number of problems which had remained unsolved for centuries, and he cut out great quantities of dead wood, by abolishing a number of legal distinctions which went back to the principate and even to the republic, and had long ceased to have any meaning.

Justinian did not abandon legal reform after the great work of codification was completed. He issued a large number of 'novels', of which 180 are preserved, between 534 and his death in 565. Many of these were administrative enactments, others made changes in the private law, and some were codifying statutes consolidating the law on subjects such as marriage and divorce. The ultimate result might have been the supersession of the Code and the Digest by one code of Roman law, but this final step was never taken.

When Diocletian came to the throne, the empire was ill supplied with courts of justice. The municipal courts, never important, had faded away, and the normal court of first instance was that of the provincial governor. A few governors had judicial assistants, the prefect of Egypt had his *iuridicus* and the proconsuls of Africa and Asia two and three legates respectively, but most were single-handed. Diocletian substantially improved the situation by doubling the number of provinces. Appeals all went to the emperor or his praetorian prefect; here again Diocletian improved things by creating four emperors and four prefects; he also granted appellate jurisdiction to a few important provincial governors; the governor of Syria received appeals from all the diocese of Oriens.

The first radical improvement in the situation was the institution of the *defensor civitatis*. The office first appears in the diocese of Oriens under Licinius. It was extended to the whole of the empire by Valentinian and Valens. The *defensor* had a minor jurisdiction, subject to an appeal to the provincial governor, in civil cases; the limit, which is undefined in the Theodosian Code, is stated in that of Justinian to be fifty *solidi*. It was raised by Justinian to 300 *solidi*. The *defensor* also acquired a petty criminal jurisdiction, and arrested and sent up to the governor those accused of major crimes. His court was intended to provide cheap and speedy justice to the poor and seems to have been successful in so doing.

Constantine also empowered bishops to decide civil cases at the instance of either party. This power was later abolished, probably by Julian, and was never revived in its full form. Bishops could, however, still decide cases submitted to them by the agreement of both parties, and their courts, being cheap and expeditious, were popular; Augustine and others complained of the amount of time they had to devote to their judicial duties. They were not always uncorrupt—Silvanus, bishop of

Alexandria Troas, found that his clergy, to whom he delegated his jurisdiction, were taking bribes, and in future appointed carefully selected laymen as judges. Some bishops employed barristers as legal assessors.

Constantine also greatly increased the number of appeal courts, giving appellate jurisdiction not only to the praetorian prefect and the prefect of the city of Rome, but to proconsuls and vicars. Only the praetorian prefects, however, had final jurisdiction—and even against their judgments a *supplicatio* could later be made to the emperor; from the other appellate judges (*vice sacra iudicantes*) a further appeal lay to the emperor himself. The territorial limits within which the appellate judges exercised their jurisdiction often overlapped. An appeal could, for instance, be made from a provincial governor's court either to the praetorian prefect direct or to the vicar and in some cases to the prefect of Rome or Constantinople or to a proconsul.

The emperors had a justifiably low opinion of the learning and integrity of the lower courts and gave very wide latitude to appeals. Only in a very few cases could a judge refuse an appeal—criminals convicted on confession or by manifest proofs and fiscal debtors. An appeal was also barred on a preliminary issue before the whole case had been heard and judgment given. The result was that vast numbers of appeals, often on trivial issues, flowed into the praetorian prefects and the emperor, and the central courts were congested with a mass of business with which they could not cope.

Justinian endeavoured to cope with this problem. He abolished the vicariates and with them their courts, which had apparently owing to their corruption been little used, but he created a number of provincial governorships of high official grade (*spectabiles*) and with increased salaries. These governors had final jurisdiction in all cases up to 500 *solidi*, later raised to 720, and some of them took appeals from neighbouring provinces. The reform was curiously incomplete, in that there remained some provinces from which there was no appeal except to the praetorian prefect or the emperor, but it did something to relieve the pressure on the overburdened central courts.

The system of courts described above dealt with the ordinary run of cases between private citizens, whether civil or criminal. There were also a large number of special courts, which dealt either with cases of a particular type, usually administrative, or where one of the parties, usually the defendant, belonged to a particular group or class. Most of these courts had their origins in two principles long rooted in Roman ideas: that a magistrate had an administrative jurisdiction in cases arising out of his departmental duties, and a disciplinary jurisdiction over his subordinates, whether clerks or soldiers. The special jurisdictions tended to expand in the fourth century at the expense of the ordinary courts, and there arose many conflicts of jurisdiction. The ordinary rule of venue in Roman law was that the plaintiff, or accuser, in both civil and criminal cases, had to sue the defendant, or the accused, in the court of the area in which the latter was domiciled; there were some exceptions, notably that in criminal cases the accuser could prosecute in the court of the area in which the alleged crime was committed. Under the special jurisdictions certain types of case had to come before departmental courts, and certain categories of privileged persons could claim to be tried before special judges.

The most important groups of departmental courts were those of the *largitiones* and the *res privata*. Not only the *comites* of the two financial departments but the *rationales* in the dioceses had their own courts which tried various kinds of fiscal cases. The boundaries between the jurisdiction of these and the ordinary courts were ill-defined and fluctuating. Appeals from the *rationales*, for instance, at first went to the ordinary appellate judges, but later to the *comes sacrarum largitionum* and *rei privatae*. Claims that property had lapsed to the crown or had been usurped from it could be tried before provincial governors, but might be instituted before the *comes rei privatae* and delegated by him to his *rationales*. The *res privata* also claimed jurisdiction over cases in which its tenants and lower officials, procurators and *actores*, were the defendants; the former claim was generally accepted, the latter denied. The other administrative courts were of minor importance. The *praefecti annonae* had jurisdiction in such matters as claims to bread rations at Rome and Constantinople, disputed membership of the bakers' guilds, or claims of shippers for loss of corn by shipwreck. The prefect of the city at Constantinople had an exclusive jurisdiction on building regulations.

The disciplinary jurisdiction of magistrates over their subordinates expanded steadily from the fourth century onwards until it embraced all cases, civil or criminal, in which civil servants or soldiers were defendants, and sometimes even those in which they were the accusers also. The government's policy towards this tendency was uncertain; sometimes in the interests of the ordinary citizen it curbed special jurisdictions, at other times it confirmed them, on the ground that soldiers and civil servants ought not to be interrupted in the performance of their functions by having to attend an outside and distant court. Military commanders and heads of departments naturally fought for their special jurisdictions, which enhanced their authority and were profitable to them in fees and bribes, and soldiers and civil servants preferred the jurisdiction which was likely to be biased in their favour. Even their prosecutors often preferred to use the military courts, since they found that the ordinary courts were powerless to execute judgment against a soldier or even to serve a summons on him. There was even a tendency, which the government had frequently to denounce, for civilians to bring actions against civilians in the military courts, whose drastic procedure was more efficacious than that of the civil courts.

It is difficult to trace the growth of these special jurisdictions, which developed by gradual usurpation, alternately checked and confirmed by imperial constitutions. The right of soldiers to be tried by their commanders when sued on civil issues is affirmed in a surviving law in 413, but the practice had already been condemned in 355. From the early fifth century at any rate this jurisdiction was regular. The *limitanei* appeared before their *duces*, and appeals at first ran to the *magistri militum*, later to the master of the offices, as inspector-general of the frontier armies. *Comitatenses* normally appeared before the *magistri militum*, but Anastasius ruled that men belonging to units attached to frontier armies should be subject to the *dux* of the area.

Palatine civil servants came generally under the head of their department, *privatiani* under the *comes rei privatae*, *largitionales* under the *comes sacrarum largitionum*, *domestici* under the *comes domesticorum*, and most of the others under the master of the offices, who was the judge not only of the civil servants under his administrative control but also of the eunuchs of the bedchamber, silentiaries and *castrensiani*. Officials of the praetorian prefects and *magistri militum* came under their respective chiefs. This rule caused no difficulty so long as the central officials were residing at headquarters, but when they went out on missions to the provinces it was highly oppressive to their civilian victims, who could only obtain redress by bringing an expensive action in the distant capital.

Several attempts were made to bring officials of the central ministries under the jurisdiction of provincial governors when on mission, but they and their chiefs always secured the abrogation of such laws. An even more unjustifiable abuse was that there were many sinecure members of the central ministries, who lived in the provinces on permanent leave and used their privileged status to defy the ordinary courts; they were for this reason much in demand as agents of estates. In 440 Cyrus and Florentius, praetorian prefects of the East, made a great attack on this abuse, which among other things impeded the collection of the revenue, and achieved some partial success in curbing it.

Another privileged class were senators, who were deemed, wherever they might live, to be domiciled at Rome or Constantinople, and therefore claimed the jurisdiction of the prefects of the two capitals. Constantine restricted this privilege, enacting that if accused of crime they must submit to the jurisdiction of the provincial governor. Later emperors made the verdicts of provincial governors in such circumstances subject to review by the emperor or the urban or praetorian prefects, and in the fifth century Theodosius II and Zeno gave special privileges in criminal proceedings to *illustres*. In the civil courts the privileges of provincial senators were abolished in 376.

The clergy also from time to time enjoyed certain jurisdictional privileges. In 355 Constantius enacted that bishops accused of criminal charges should be tried before a council of bishops, with an appeal to the imperial appellate courts. In 413 Honorius extended this privilege to all the clergy. The privilege of the clergy was revoked in the west by Valentinian III in 452, but was apparently restored by a later emperor, for it prevailed in the Visigothic and Ostrogothic kingdoms. In the east it would seem that only bishops were privileged to be tried before their peers on criminal charges, until Justinian placed monks and nuns under the exclusive jurisdiction of bishops.

Several cases which came before Symmachus as prefect of the city illustrate the way in which conflicts of jurisdiction could be exploited by influential litigants. In one a *protector*, Marcianus, had obtained the conditional grant of the estate of a lady named Aggarea, which he claimed to have lapsed to the crown, as she died without natural heirs and her will was invalid. He brought the case before the *rationalis* of Rome, who, six years after Aggarea's death, quashed the will. The heir under the will appealed to Symmachus, to whom, as prefect of the city, appeals from the *rationalis* should normally have gone. But Marcianus claimed that the *rationalis* had been acting as delegate of the *comes rei privatae* and the appeal therefore ought to go to him. Symmachus could only refer the issue to the emperor. In another an Apulian landowner, named Marcellus, had sued one Venantius before the provincial governor for evicting him from his estate. Venantius appealed to the vicar of the city on a preliminary issue, but the vicar properly rejected the appeal and the provincial governor convicted him. Venantius then appealed to Bassus, prefect of the city, who had concurrent appellate jurisdiction with the vicar of the city. Although the time limit for the appeal had run out, Bassus accepted the case, but it came up before Symmachus, who succeeded Bassus, and he very properly rejected it. Venantius still had another string to his bow; on the ground that he was an imperial *strator* he claimed the jurisdiction of the master of the offices, and Symmachus had to allow him to be taken away to the *comitatus* under the escort of an *agens in rebus*.

The conflicts of jurisdiction would have been complicated enough if the government and the courts had kept to the rules, but confusion was increased by their laxity in granting special exceptions. In theory it was the right of humble litigants to claim the jurisdiction of a higher court if they suspected that a powerful adversary would intimidate the provincial governor. More often rich and influential litigants obtained rescripts summoning their opponents to a distant and expensive court. In this way highly placed civilian claimants dragged soldiers from the provincial armies to the capital, and civilians haled other civilians before the military courts.

Justice was extremely slow. Justinian, 'to prevent lawsuits being almost immortal and exceeding the term of human life',[1] ruled that in courts of first instance judgment must be given within three years in civil cases and two in criminal. Appeals were supposed to be heard after an interval of six months, but could be adjourned for two further periods of three months; Justinian ruled that the trial must be concluded within a year, unless the appellant could prove that the delay was due to the judge, in which case he was given another year. These rules applied to the appellate courts of the vicars and praetorian prefects. In the imperial high court the procedure was different. Originally appeals to the emperor were tried *more consultationum*, that is to say the lower court sent up its record to the emperor and the litigants were not allowed to appear. Owing to the interminable delays that ensued, Theodosius I in 386 allowed litigants to come to the capital after a year had elapsed. In the sixth century appellants had two years within which to introduce their appeals. There was no time limit for the trial of a case in the consistory.

Attempts were made to speed the course of justice but without much success. The reason was partly the slowness of communication. When Justinian[2] ruled that appeals must be brought to court within two years, many appellants complained that 'they had not been able to sail from

[1] *Cod. Just.* III. i. 13.   [2] *Nov.* xlix, proem.

the provinces because of contrary winds and could not come by land because they were too poor or lived on islands'. Another reason for delay was the congestion of the courts and the fact that the judges were not full time, but had heavy administrative duties. Provincial governors were too busy collecting taxes to have much time for justice, and the praetorian prefects and the emperor himself were even more heavily occupied.

Justice was also expensive. Apart from lawyers' fees and bribes to judges, and in the case of appeals long journeys and long stays in distant towns, court fees (*sportulae*) were considerable. They were in origin tips demanded by the officials of the court for issuing and serving summonses, for introducing the case into court, for providing a transcript, and for executing judgment. Constantine endeavoured to prohibit them altogether. 'Let the rapacious hands of officials forthwith refrain,' he wrote in 331, 'let them refrain, I repeat, for if they do not after this warning they will be cut off by the sword.'[1] A generation later *sportulae* were officially regulated; we have the schedule of prices laid down by the consular of Numidia under Julian. Despite the periodic attempts to curb them, they tended always to increase. Exact figures are unfortunately not available, but it would appear that in the sixth century even privileged categories of persons, like higher civil servants and the clergy, who paid reduced tariffs, had to spend at least three *solidi* whenever they were defendants or plaintiffs in the courts of first instance; and three *solidi* was a year's income for a poor man. In the high courts fees were very much higher. In the praetorian prefecture one process, a *postulatio simplex*, cost thirty-seven *solidi*.

Proceedings before the *defensor* or bishop were much cheaper. Governors were also instructed to hear petty actions *sine scriptis*, without the formal record, which accounted for much of the cost, and even to give free justice to the poor; but few apparently did so. We know of a governor of Osrhoene who put up a box outside his office, in which the public could drop their petitions, and sat every Friday in the church administering justice free. This was an event which deserved record in a local chronicle.

The Romans had never believed in a professional judiciary. The administration of justice was the function of magistrates, who normally had other functions, and, even if they were judges only, were not chosen for legal learning. In the later empire this tradition was maintained, with the result that in the military courts the judges were army officers and

[1] *Cod. Theod.* I. xvi. 7.

might be illiterate barbarians. In the civilian courts the position was rather 'better, since the government often appointed barristers to be provincial governors, vicars and praetorian prefects. But even among these there were nobles or wealthy men without legal learning.

The ignorance of the judges was relieved by the institution of legal assessors. Every magistrate had one, and important magistrates more than one. They were appointed by the magistrate whom they were to serve, and received modest salaries from public funds, about 10 per cent of what their principal received. Barristers were always chosen for these posts. It was the normal ambition of a rising barrister to serve two or three terms as an assessor, after which he might well hope for a provincial governorship. Barristers were also often appointed as *defensores*. Zeno instituted and Justinian revived a panel of twelve professional judges (*iudices pedanei*) at Constantinople, from which illustrious ministers could choose their delegate judges. Eight of those whom Justinian appointed were barristers.

Judges are normally expected to be not only learned in the law but also uncorrupt and independent, susceptible neither to bribes nor to intimidation. The emperors freely admitted that their judges, those of the lower courts at any rate, were none of these things. This was due in part to the system of *suffragia*, whereby provincial governors, and even vicars, had to buy their posts at high prices and expected to recoup themselves mainly by the sale of justice. It was also due to the low rank in the official hierarchy of provincial governors, and the relatively low rank of vicars, to their short tenure of office and their uncertainty of promotion. In these circumstances judges were fearful of offending litigants of high rank, who could make or mar their future career, and be dangerous enemies if they retired into private life. This, of course, applied also to assessors. Augustine[1] records the admiring astonishment caused by the fairness of his friend Alypius as assessor to the *comes largitionum Italicianarum*.

There was at that time a very powerful senator by whose favour many were obliged and by fear of whom many were terrorized. He wanted, as powerful men do, to be allowed to do something or other which the laws forbade. Alypius resisted him. He was offered a bribe but laughed it to scorn. He was subjected to threats, but he spurned them. Everyone marvelled at the unusual spirit with which he neither desired as a friend nor feared as an enemy so great a man, who was

[1] *Confessions*, VI. 16.

notorious for the countless means which he possessed for conferring benefits or doing injuries. The judge himself, whose adviser he was, though he himself did not wish to give way, did not openly stand up to the senator, but, thrusting the onus upon Alypius, declared that he would not permit him to yield; and in fact if he had done so Alypius would have left him.

Standards were low not only among judges but among the general public also. Men of influence felt themselves free to exercise pressure not only on their own behalf but for their friends and dependants. They are in a number of laws forbidden to lobby judges, calling upon them in the afternoon, or to sit on the bench beside them, as they were entitled to do, if they belonged to the official aristocracy, when cases in which they were interested came up. In the correspondence of such men as Basil, bishop of Caesarea, and Libanius there are many letters written to judges on behalf of their friends, whose cases are *sub judice*. Libanius usually prefaces his appeals with a disclaimer that he does not wish to deflect the course of justice, but he makes his plea none the less. Men of less probity than Basil or Libanius were doubtless less scrupulous.

The high courts of the praetorian prefects and the emperors were, to judge by the volume of appeals that flowed into them, held in better esteem. The emperor, by a tradition which went back to Augustus, was expected to exercise personal jurisdiction, and we find emperors down to Justinian hearing and delivering judgment. The burden, however, was too much for one man to bear, and in 440 Theodosius II enacted that appeals from the intermediate judges of appeal, the proconsuls and vicars, should come before the praetorian prefect of the East and the quaestor sitting together. This still left appeals from the illustrious judges and *supplicationes* against the judgments of the praetorian prefects to the emperor himself. The emperors and, it would seem, their delegates sat in consistory to hear cases: any member of the consistory might attend, but in judicial sessions the legal ministers, the *magistri scriniorum* and the legal *comites consistoriani*, who were usually retired barristers of the high court of the praetorian prefecture, no doubt played a more prominent role. In the east the emperor sometimes sat with the senate, and Justinian made this a standing order.

If civil justice was often corrupt, criminal justice was normally inefficient and brutal, especially for the lower orders, the *humiliores*. Though the cities had their nightwatchmen, and the *riparii* and the eirenarchs who maintained order in the countryside had their constables,

there was no police in the modern sense to detect and investigate crime,
It was left to the injured parties, or to private informers, to bring
persons suspected of crime before the courts; informers were encouraged
by rewards for successful prosecutions and discouraged by penalties for
abandoning a case, or failing to secure a conviction. Once arrested the
accused might languish for months in prison, starving if he had no
friends or relations to feed him, waiting till the provincial governor had
leisure to hear his case. Libanius records how a number of villagers
accused on suspicion of the murder of a landowner waited seven months
before their case came up: it was then adjourned and five of the accused
had died in prison when Libanius wrote, and the case was still unsettled.
Some attempts were made to remedy these abuses. Honorius ordered
that the governor should hold a parade of prisoners every Sunday,
receive their complaints and allot rations to those who were destitute.
They were also to be taken under escort to the baths. Justinian limited
the period for which prisoners could be held for trial to six months, or
in some cases a year, and made provision for bail.

When the case ultimately came up for trial very little attempt was
made to sift evidence; judges were indeed forbidden by Constantine to
pass a death sentence unless the witnesses were unanimous or the
prisoner confessed. In these circumstances judges were tempted to make
free use of torture, when the witnesses or the prisoner were *humiliores*,
to extract concordant evidence, or best of all a confession. Jerome tells
a terrible story of a man and woman who were accused of adultery. The
man confessed under torture. Encouraged by this partial success the
judge tortured the woman until she died.

The legal profession was always regarded as in some sense a public
service (*militia*) and even officially recognized by Leo as such in 469.
It was rigidly controlled by the government. All barristers had to enrol
themselves in a particular court and remained in it for life; a young man
therefore had a difficult choice, when he embarked on his career, between
a safe but undistinguished life at a provincial bar, or the risk of failure
in the high courts. Constantine fixed a maximum number of barristers
for each bar, but this rule was later abolished. Theodosius I appears to
have introduced a rule both in the eastern and western parts limiting a
barrister's career to twenty years. This rule was abolished in the east by
Theodosius II in 439 and his law was received in the west in 448. Six
years later, however, Valentinian III, in deference to the protests of the
younger members of the bar, who saw their prospects of advancement
blocked by aged seniors, revoked Theodosius II's law. In the east the

problem was solved by reintroducing a *numerus clausus* for each bar and ruling that the senior barrister of each should become *advocatus fisci*, or government counsel, and retire after one or two years' service, thus making way for the next senior. The pressure of numbers was naturally heaviest in the superior courts, and in the praetorian prefecture of the East a maximum of 150 barristers had already been fixed by 439. Lesser bars were limited in their turn; the bar of the Augustal prefect of Egypt was reduced in 468 to fifty and that of the provincial governor of Syria Secunda in 518 to thirty.

There was no qualification for being called to the bar. Aspiring barristers naturally took the course in rhetoric which was the normal form of higher education, but according to Libanius they were not in his young days expected to know any law; if they wanted a legal opinion they went to a jurisconsult. In Libanius' later years, however, in the last decades of the fourth century, things were changing, and he complains that young men instead of learning rhetoric went off to Berytus or even to Rome to learn law. In 460 Leo ordained that postulants for the bar of the praetorian prefecture of the East must produce certificates of proficiency from the professors of law under whom they had studied; there was a regular four years' course at Berytus and at Constantinople, the two chief centres of legal studies. This requirement was soon extended to the inferior bars, down to those of the provinces. The increased learning of the bar is demonstrated by the composition of the commissions which drew up the Theodosian Code in 429–38 and the Digest in 530–33. The former consisted of seven law officers of the crown, one *comes consistorianus* and one practising barrister; the latter of two law officers, four academic lawyers and eleven barristers.

In the fifth century barristers advanced strictly by seniority to the post of *advocatus fisci*. An aspirant first enrolled himself as a supernumerary and waited until a vacancy occurred on the establishment. He then advanced year by year; if he did not practise he could be disbarred, but he was forbidden to purchase seniority by exchanging places with an impecunious senior. In the sixth century the legal profession tended to become hereditary. Barristers could nominate their sons for places on the establishment, but outsiders had to buy vacancies from outgoing seniors.

Fees were regulated. We possess the schedule for the consular of Numidia in the mid-fourth century and the figures are very modest, the highest being 15 *modii* of wheat, equivalent to about half a *solidus*, for an urgent case. Fees were of course higher in the superior courts and

tended to increase as time went on. There was a legal maximum of
100 *solidi*, but it was evaded by bargains for payment in slaves and cattle
and land. The major profits of a lawyer's career, however, accrued in
his last year as *advocatus fisci*, when he received a substantial salary—
600 *solidi* in the court of the urban prefecture. *Advocati fisci* also received
codicils of official rank, varying from *illustris* in the court of the praetorian prefect of the East to *clarissimus* in that of the proconsul of Asia,
and sundry privileges and perquisites.

Much lower in the social scale stood the notaries (*tabelliones*) who
drew up wills, conveyances, leases and all kinds of contracts. They were
normally commoners, and if a humble decurion practised as a notary
he forfeited his immunity from torture. We know them best from the
deeds they drew, which became increasingly lengthy and replete with
legal jargon; no doubt they wished to impress their clients by their legal
learning—and they were paid by the line. At the capital they were
registered with the *magister census* and in the provinces probably with
the governor. They appear to have learned their trade by apprenticeship.
They existed not only in towns but in the larger villages.

When Priscus of Panium went as an ambassador to Attila's camp, he
met a Greek prisoner who had elected to live among the Huns. Priscus
was shocked, but the Greek justified his conduct by an indictment of the
Roman empire. One of his theses was the burden of taxation, the other
the state of Roman justice:

> The laws are not the same for all. If a rich man breaks the law he can
> avoid the penalty for his wrongdoing. But if it is a poor man who
> does not know how to pull strings, he suffers the penalty of the law—
> unless he departs this life before the trial, while proceedings drag on
> interminably and vast expenses are incurred. That is the most
> monstrous thing of all, to have to pay for justice. An injured party
> cannot get a hearing unless he pays money to the judge and to his
> officials.[1]

Priscus endeavoured to rebut this attack. He admitted that justice was
slow, but declared that hasty judgments were often wrong and it was
better to spend a long time to obtain a just verdict, than to allow an
unjust judgment. He also admitted that court fees were high, but justified them on the ground that the courts now executed judgments and
no longer as in the classical period left claimants to recover their own
damages. That there was one law for the rich and another for the poor

[1] *Frag. Hist. Graec.* IV, pp. 86–8.

he vehemently denied. A wealthy wrongdoer might evade the law but so might a poor one. Priscus is not very convincing. In the criminal law there was a legal distinction between the lower classes, the *humiliores*, and the *honestiores*—an ill-defined category including decurions, civil servants and soldiers, and the official aristocracy. The former were liable to torture while the latter were exempt. *Humiliores* were, moreover, subject to severer penalties for crimes, hard labour in the mines and quarries or execution, while the severest penalty for *honestiores* was *deportatio*, forced residence on a remote island or oasis and loss of property.

In civil actions some classes suffered legal disabilities; freedmen could not sue their patrons nor could tied tenants (*coloni adscripticii*) sue their landlords except for excessive rents. But the major disadvantage of the humble citizen in a dispute with a wealthy neighbour was that justice was so slow and expensive. The fees, even in the provincial court, were high and in the supreme courts prohibitive. The lower judges were generally corrupt and weak, and his opponent could bribe or intimidate them. If he won the first round his opponent could wear him out by lengthy and expensive appeal proceedings, or, if he belonged to a privileged category, by claiming the jurisdiction of a distant court.

XV

The Civil Service

All forms of the service of the state were known as *militia*, but there was a sharp distinction between the higher posts, the *dignitates*, *honores* or *administrationes*, and *militia officialis*, the subordinate jobs of the clerks, accountants, orderlies and messengers. A *dignitas* was conferred by a codicil signed by the emperor himself and was held during the emperor's pleasure, usually for a brief term of a year or two; only in very exceptional cases did a man hold a *dignitas* for as much as five or ten years. An ambitious man might hold a series of *dignitates* increasing in importance and rank, but he rarely held more than half a dozen posts in a lifetime and often fewer, quite often one or two only, and his term of office was not necessarily or usually continuous. A *militia* on the other hand was conferred by a simple administrative document, a *probatoria*, issued from the imperial secretariat, and was held continuously until retirement, often for twenty or thirty years.

Under the principate the civil service had been sharply divided into two major branches, soldiers seconded from their regiments for clerical duties, and slaves and freedmen of the emperor. The former staffed the offices of the praetorian and urban prefects and the provincial governors and was mainly occupied with judicial business; from the latter were

BIBLIOGRAPHY. For the offices of the *sacrum cubiculum* and for those under the disposition of the *magister officiorum* there are two useful monographs, J. E. Dunlap, *The Office of the Grand Chamberlain in the Later Roman and Byzantine Empires*, and A. E. R. Boak, *The Master of the Offices in the Later Roman and Byzantine Empires* (New York and London, 1924). For the praetorian prefecture, E. Stein, *Untersuchungen über das officium der Prätorianerpräfectur seit Diokletian* (Vienna, 1922) is basic. On the urban prefecture of Rome there is W. G. Sinnagan, *The Officium of the Urban Prefecture during the Later Roman Empire* (Rome, 1957).

The main primary sources are *Cod. Theod.* VI and *Cod. Just.* XII. xvi ff., the *Notitia Dignitatum*, and John Lydus, *de Magistratibus*.

See also Chapter XVI of my *Later Roman Empire*.

drawn the household staff of the emperor and his central secretariats and accountancy departments, and the financial staffs of his procurators in the provinces. Procurators also had military clerks to assist them in their judicial functions. The military clerks soon became a separate profession, retaining only nominal links with their regiments; the slaves and freedmen became a hereditary class, son succeeding father.

Diocletian greatly increased the military side of the civil service by enlarging the praetorian prefecture, multiplying the provinces and instituting vicars whose offices were modelled on those of the provincial governors. The new military commanders, the *duces* and later the *magistri militum* and *comites rei militaris*, were given similar staffs. The slave and freedmen service gradually faded out or was assimilated with the military type. The process is obscure. The clerks of the diocesan *rationales*, who succeeded the provincial procurators, were still in the later empire known as *Caesariani*, a term which had denoted imperial slaves and freedmen, but they do not seem to have differed in status from other civil servants. The financial clerks of the provincial governors were still known by the freedman title of *tabularii*, but they held military rank, though they were looked down on by the old judicial clerks. In the central government the eunuchs of the sacred bedchamber were still bought as slaves and acquired freedom on entering imperial service. In the other offices many of the old titles and grades appropriate to slaves and freedmen survived; the chief and second clerks of the secretariats were still termed *proximi* and *melloproximi* and the domestic staff of the palace, the *castrensiani*, and the mass of the lower clerks in the financial ministries, were graded in three *formae*—a classification alien to the military offices and probably servile by origin. Constantine seems to have militarized these offices by granting specific privileges to their personnel.

From this time all civil servants were officially soldiers. They wore military uniform, they received rations and, if graded as troopers, fodder; these issues in kind were not regularly commuted for gold until 423. In most offices they held the old non-commissioned ranks of the army, *beneficiarii*, *speculatores*, *commentarienses*, *corniculari*, and the chief clerk (*princeps*) was a centurion, who still carried his baton on ceremonial occasions. They were still entered on the rolls of fictive regiments; the clerks of the praetorian prefecture belonged to Legio I Adiutrix. Nevertheless the *militia officialis* was quite separate from the *militia armata* of the army.

There were naturally great differences of status within the civil service. The palatine ministries ranked highest; among them there were sharp contrasts between the imperial notaries, who from the late fourth century ranked as senators, and the *lampadarii* who looked after the lights. Officials of the praetorian prefecture were in general superior to those of vicars, and those of vicars ranked above the *cohortales*, who served the provincial governors. But within each of these offices there was a great gulf between the *exceptores*, or official stenographers, who could rise to be *cornicularius* or even *princeps*, and the *scriniarii*, or accountants, who could rise to *numerarius*, on the one hand, and the ushers, messengers and the like who spent their whole career in these subclerical grades.

The *cubicularii*, or eunuchs of the sacred bedchamber, were a very peculiar group. Since castration was forbidden within the empire they were all by origin imported slaves; most of them came from the Persian empire or from Caucasian lands—in Justinian's time the main source of supply was the tribe of the Abasgi on the east coast of the Black Sea. The organization of the sacred bedchamber varied from time to time. In the fourth century there was only one bedchamber, shared by the emperor and the empress, and this continued to be the case in the west in the fifth century. In the east the empress acquired a separate bedchamber; the empress also had ladies-in-waiting, *cubiculariae*, like the eunuchs of servile origin. The head of the bedchamber was styled the *praepositus sacri cubiculi* and was chosen by the emperor or empress and served during his or her pleasure, sometimes for a long term. Next in precedence was the senior eunuch, *primicerius*, and the *castrensis*, who looked after the domestic staff. These posts were held by seniority. There were also the *sacellarius*, or keeper of the privy purse, the *comes sacrae vestis*, who had charge of the wardrobe, the *spatharius*, or commander of the eunuch bodyguard, and the *comes domorum*, who had charge of the imperial estates which supported the sacred bedchamber.

Despite their servile origin, their close and intimate contact with the emperor gave the eunuchs great power and influence, and wealth naturally followed. Since the emperor lived in seclusion, only emerging in public on official occasions, they controlled all intimate audiences with him. Ambrose, sent by Valentinian II on a diplomatic mission to Magnus Maximus, was refused entrance to the bedchamber by the chief eunuch, and he had to content himself with a formal public reception in consistory. Aspirants to office had to persuade or bribe the eunuchs in order to interview the emperor, and by the sixth century there was an authorized scale of fees which those who obtained codicils of office paid to the principal eunuchs. In the reign of a weak emperor a eunuch might become virtual ruler of the empire. For many years Constantius II was dominated by his *praepositus*, Eusebius. Eutropius, the *praepositus* of Arcadius, was in complete control for a short period. In the latter years of Theodosius II, Chrysaphius, the *spatharius*, shared the government with Nomus, master of the offices. The power of the eunuchs was reflected in their official rank. The *praepositus* was an *illustris* by the end of the fourth century and was in 422 put on a par with the praetorian prefects and the *magistri militum*. The *primicerius* and the *castrensis* were *spectabiles*. Their power was also reflected in their immense wealth. Theodore, who retired prematurely from the rank of *castrensis* in Justinian's reign, spent his fortune, which amounted to 1,500 or 2,000 pounds of gold, on charity and was thus reduced to poverty. Justinian solaced him with a pension of 1,000 *solidi* a year.

Eunuchs were much hated by the aristocracy, who attributed to them every vice, but especially avarice. Ammianus apologizes for praising the only virtuous eunuch of whom he knew. 'The incident suggests that I should say a few words about this Eutherius, which will perhaps not be believed; for if Numa Pompilius or Socrates said any good thing about a eunuch and swore to it on oath, they would be accused of straying from the truth.'[1] The only eunuch who is in general well spoken of, though he is accused of avarice and meanness, is Narses, for many years Justinian's *sacellarius* and *praepositus*. He is unique in having been given command of great armies and proved himself a very able general.

The domestic staff of the palace, the *castrensiani*, were not eunuchs. The service was much sought after and their number was swelled by large numbers of supernumeraries who waited for a place on the establishment. The posts seem to have become sinecures by the sixth century and were bought by the wealthy bankers and merchants of Constantinople, both for the prestige which they carried, and as investments, for they were well paid.

A much more select and distinguished group of the palace staff were the thirty silentiaries with their three decurions, who served as ushers. They received high official rank; by the early fifth century the decurions retired as *spectabiles*, and by the sixth all silentiaries became *illustres*. The corps was by this time quite aristocratic, including among others an ex-king of the Lazi, and posts were obtained by purchase.

Among the public offices of the *comitatus* pride of place was taken by the corps of notaries, who kept the minutes of the consistory. They first

[1] Ammianus Marcellinus, XVI. vii. 4.

appear in the early fourth century and were originally quite humble persons, mere stenographers. But being admitted to the secrets of the consistory and being in close contact with the emperor, they rapidly rose to influence and power. Constantius II employed them on confidential missions and promoted them to be ministers, quaestors, *comites sacrarum largitionum* and even praetorian prefects, and bestowed upon some the supreme honour of the ordinary consulate. Libanius was deeply indignant and cited a number of examples of men who were sons of sausage-sellers, bath attendants, or simple working men, and rose to the highest offices of state, including four praetorian prefects. In these circumstances men of higher standing were attracted to join the corps, and in the second half of the fourth century sons of praetorian prefects, Procopius, a relative of the emperor Julian, and Theodore, of ancient and wealthy Gallic family, served as notaries. The rank of notaries was also rapidly upgraded and in 381 senior members of the corps, who ranked as tribunes, were equated with vicars and thus *spectabiles*, and juniors who ranked as *domestici* with consulars and thus *clarissimi*. In the early fifth century we find Roman nobles of the bluest blood starting their official career as notaries and the poet Claudian was enrolled in the corps. By the middle of the fifth century notaries had ceased to keep the minutes, and this lowly task was left to the members of the *agentes in rebus*, who served *a secretis*. Posts were by the sixth century obtained by purchase. The corps was grossly inflated by sinecurists, and had according to Libanius, who is probably speaking of the eastern parts only, risen to 520. But only a few of these were in active attendance in the palace; the number would appear to have been thirty in the west in the early fifth century.

The senior notary, *primicerius notariorum*, had the important function of keeping the *laterculum maius* or *notitia* of all the dignities and administrations, both civil and military, and issuing the codicils to holders of offices, receiving from them a rich harvest of fees. In the east, and probably in the west before Stilicho's day, he also issued commissions to all regimental commanders except those of the cohorts and *alae*. The second notary probably acted as his assistant, the third looked after the issue of *pragmaticae*. They were served by clerks drawn from the *agentes in rebus* and *memoriales*.

Next in dignity came the three imperial secretariats, *sacra scrinia*, which served the *magistri memoriae, epistolarum* and *libellorum*; in the east there was a separate *scrinium epistolarum Graecarum* which drafted letters written in Greek and translated Latin constitutions into Greek.

The *scrinium memoriae* drafted rescripts to private citizens and the *scrinium epistolarum* rescripts to judges and replies to delegations of provincial assemblies and cities, the *scrinium libellorum* prepared cases for the imperial high court. All three dealt also with miscellaneous petitions and issued *probatoriae* or certificates of enlistment to civil servants and soldiers. They also received sundry returns and reports ranging from the annual returns of ration strengths from the *magistri militum* to progress reports on the students attending the university at Rome.

The *scrinia* were small bodies; Leo fixed the establishment at 62 *memoriales*, 34 *epistolares* and 34 *libellenses*. They served not only the *magistri scriniorum* but the quaestor, who was allowed to have twelve clerks from the *scrinium memoriae* and seven from each of the other two *scrinia*. They assisted him in his duties of dealing with petitions and drafted imperial constitutions. He also in the east had charge of the *laterculum minus*, from which commissions were issued to the commanders of *alae* and cohorts; his senior assistant, who managed this business, was accordingly called the *laterculensis*.

Promotion was by seniority in each *scrinium*, the clerks rising one place every three years, later two, and finally one year, until they became *melloproximi* and finally *proximi*. In 444 Theodosius laid down rules for the purchase of posts. The retiring *proximus* each year sold the vacancy which arose from his resignation for the fixed sum of 250 *solidi* to the senior supernumerary clerk, or, if he could not afford it, to the next senior. Vacancies which arose by death were similarly sold, the price going to the heirs of the deceased clerk. In addition entrants had to pay 15 or 20 *solidi* to the establishment officer of their *scrinium*. Places among the quaestor's assistants were also sold; Justinian fixed the price at 100 *solidi* for all except the senior assistant of each *scrinium*, who could charge the market price.

Since they drafted the imperial pronouncements, the members of the *sacra scrinia* had to be men of some education and in particular to know Latin, which was a rare accomplishment in the east. They seem often to have been the sons of decurions or civil servants. The sons of *proximi* had a special claim to enter their father's *scrinium*. In the late fourth century retired clerks enjoyed high official status, *proximi* ranking with vicars and all clerks of twenty years' service with consulars. Rather inferior to the *sacra scrinia* were the *scrinium dispositionum*, which probably arranged the emperor's movements and timetable, and the *officium admissionum*, which regulated audiences.

Next came the *agentes in rebus* or imperial couriers. They were a much more numerous body; in the east their establishment was fixed at 1,174 in 430 and at 1,248 by Leo. They were graded as troopers and held the same N.C.O. ranks as in an ordinary cavalry regiment. Their primary duty was to carry government despatches to the provinces, and after serving in this capacity for some years they rose to be inspectors, *curiosi*, of the post, one or two to each province, checking the warrants of those who made use of it. After this they returned to the court to serve as assistant, *adiutor*, and deputy-assistants, *subadiuvae*, of the master of the offices; in this capacity some acted as central controllers of the arms factories. Finally, by a system inaugurated by Constantius II, on leaving the corps they went out to be chief clerks, *principes*, for a year in the offices of vicars and corresponding officers, proconsuls and the urban and praetorian prefects: they also provided *principes* for the *duces* of the eastern frontier, but not elsewhere. The primary object of the system was no doubt to exercise a check on the doings of the outlying magistrates, for the *principes* had to countersign all the official orders. But the system also provided an ample retirement bounty for *agentes in rebus*, for the *princeps* received a fee for every signature. *Agentes in rebus* also received high official status, when they had completed their *principatus*, those who had served in the lower offices acquiring the rank of consulars and later vicars, those who served in the prefectures that of proconsuls. Promotion was however rather slow and many failed to persevere to the end: in the early fifth century they were allowed to retire after twenty, later twenty-five, years' service, with the rank of honorary *principes*.

The career of an *agens in rebus* was lucrative, especially in its later stages. Even as an ordinary courier he was entitled to accept tips from the provincials, later limited by law, for announcing the names of the consuls and the imperial anniversaries and victories. As *curiosus* he received an inspection fee of one *solidus* per vehicle and finally as *princeps* fees for signatures. The career evidently attracted *curiales* and the lower ranks of the civil service and their sons. The *agentes in rebus* were used as a kind of secret service by Constantius II, the *curiosi* being charged to report suspected conspiracies to the government, and some achieved a sinister reputation as spies and informers. But this seems to have been a temporary phenomenon.

We are exceptionally well informed about the office of the *largitiones*, as we possess not only the summary description of it in the *Notitia Dignitatum*, but a full list of the establishment as laid down by Theodosius I in 384; it was still in force in the sixth century. The total number was 446, divided into eighteen departments or *scrinia*. The senior clerks held equestrian rank, being graded as *perfectissimi*, *ducenarii*, *centenarii* and *epistolares*. The great majority, 312 out of 446, were divided into three *formae*, probably in origin servile grades. The senior *scrinium* was that of the *exceptores* or stenographers. There were also *scrinia* of accountants and of couriers, and for gold and silver bullion, for the gold and silver and copper coinage, for the imperial wardrobe, for taxes and for 'the regiments'—this perhaps calculated the figure for donatives. There were in addition groups of artificers, the moneyers of the gold coinage and goldsmiths and silversmiths. It is curious that there were no *scrinia* to control the imperial weaving and dyeing factories, the responsibility for which was shared between the *scrinia* of the stenographers and the accountants and the taxes. This may be because the factories were an innovation to which the organization of the central office never fully adjusted itself.

We know much less about the office of the *res privata*. Its establishment was fixed at 300 in the west in 399, and it was divided into five *scrinia*, the stenographers, rents, receipts, grants and benefactions. Promotion in both offices was by seniority in each *scrinium*, transfer being forbidden; the senior clerk of each *scrinium* retired after three, later reduced to two and finally to one year. The *largitionales* and *privatiani* seem to have been humbler and less well off than the other officials hitherto mentioned. It was not until the early fifth century that the retiring senior clerks of the *scrinia* were awarded senatorial rank as consulars, and in 428 they renounced it as being too expensive for their modest means.

Minor palatine offices included the interpreters, who translated for foreign envoys, the *cursores* (runners), the *decani* and *cancellarii* (doorkeepers), the *lampadarii*, who trimmed the lamps, and the *mensores* or billeting officers. These last must have had a Herculean task when the *comitatus* was on the move and had to stop at small cities and posting stations en route. Even at Constantinople they had no sinecure, for there seems always to have been a shortage of accommodation, and only persons of the most exalted rank enjoyed immunity from billeting.

Outside the *comitatus* the most important offices were those of the praetorian prefects. We know a good deal about the praetorian prefecture of the East, thanks to John Lydus, who served in it for forty years and left an elaborate if rather confused description of it. We also possess the establishment list of the new praetorian prefecture of Africa which Justinian established. Here alone do we have any figures: the total was 396, divided into 98 on the judicial side, 130 on the financial, and 168 in the subclerical grades. In the other prefectures the numbers were probably much higher, since they were responsible for much larger areas and also contained much dead wood, which Justinian cut out in the new prefecture. It is only in Africa too that we know the salary grades. The great majority of the clerks, 280 out of 396, received one ration allowance and one fodder allowance, commuted for 9 *solidi*. Fifty-two received $11\frac{1}{2}$ *solidi* and the others, mostly heads of departments, 14, 16 or 23. The four heads of the chief financial *scrinia* got 46 *solidi*. This was, however, only basic pay, and supplemented by fees. John Lydus made as much as 1,000 *solidi* in this way in his first year, but he was exceptional in that he enjoyed the patronage of the prefect, who happened in that year to be a fellow-townsman of his. But normally the assistants of the principal officers could count on 1,000 *solidi* a year and senior clerks on the judicial side on about double that sum.

We know very little about the subclerical grades, the ushers, messengers, warders, torturers, etc., except their titles. On the judicial side after the *princeps*, who was an *agens in rebus*, the principal clerks were in order of seniority, the *cornicularius*, who dealt with civil cases, the *adiutor*, who nominated clerks to serve summonses and execute judgments, the *commentariensis*, who handled criminal cases, and the *ab actis*, who kept the judicial records. Next came the *curae epistolarum*, one for each diocese, who conducted the financial correspondence with the vicars, and the *regendarius*, who issued postal warrants. Each of these principal officers, except the *princeps*, chose three assistants (*adiutores*) and they in turn chose their secretaries (*chartularii*) from the pool of stenographers (*exceptores*).

On the financial side the organization was similar: at the top were the *numerarii*, one for each diocese, and also for the departments of arms and of public works and of the treasury. They had under them assistants and secretaries chosen from the pool of accountants (*scriniarii*) and also *tractatores*, who managed the accounts of each province. They annually sent out *canonicarii* to oversee the collection of the taxes in each province, and, if necessary, *compulsores* to extract arrears and, as occasion demanded, auditors (*discussores*) to check the accounts of public works and of regiments of the army.

All posts in the prefecture were annual and promotion was by seniority. After serving as a supernumerary a judicial clerk became an established *exceptor*, eligible to be chosen as a *chartularius*, and after nine years he became eligible as an *adiutor*. He might serve several times in different departments in these capacities. At length he rose to be *regendarius* and moved step by step to *cornicularius*. *Scrinarii* similarly would serve first as *chartularii*—they were allowed to hold four such appointments at intervals of not less than a year—and then as *adiutores*— a maximum of four appointments with an interval of not less than two years between them—before rising to be *numerarius*.

The retiring senior clerks received handsome bonuses; in the prefecture in Italy the *cornicularius* got 700 *solidi*. They also by the end of the sixth century were accorded the rank of praetorian tribunes.

The offices of the urban prefects and vicars and proconsuls were similarly organized, but smaller. Vicars in general had offices of 300; the *comes Orientis* was exceptional in having 600 clerks. The proconsul of Africa had an office of 400. Below these again were the offices of ordinary provincial governors, which numbered 100. The provincial officials were known as *cohortales* and were peculiar in that they were a hereditary class and were forbidden, they or their sons, to migrate to higher offices. This rule, established by Constantine, was reiterated with ever-increasing severity down to the sixth century. It was evidently often evaded or ignored. Their pay was miserable—two *officia* are known to have received 407½ *solidi* and others only 360. This is an average of 4 or 3½ *solidi* per man, and their fees were on a much smaller scale than those of the central ministries.

The offices of the *magistri militum, comites rei militaris* and *duces* were organized on a similar pattern, but normally lacked a *cornicularius*, since their chief had originally possessed no civil jurisdictions. In the western parts, by a system probably introduced by Stilicho, the chief clerk (*princeps*) and *commentariensis* on the judicial side and the two *numerarii* on the financial were in nearly all inferior offices men sent from headquarters, being drawn from the offices of the *magistri praesentales*. The offices of *magistri* in the east seem to have numbered 300, those of *duces* only forty. In the office of the *dux* of Libya pay was calculated at one ration allowance and one fodder allowance per man, commuted at the odd sum of 387½ *solidi* for the whole office, which could distribute the total among its members as it wished. In the African ducal offices Justinian made more liberal arrangements, allocating salaries ranging from 11½ to 33 *solidi* and totalling 622½.

There were many more minor offices. The *rationales* of the finance ministries had their *Caesariani* and the diocesan treasuries were staffed by *thesaurenses*. The minor magistrates of Rome and Constantinople had their *officia*; the *praetor plebis*, or chief of police, in the latter city had twenty soldiers and thirty clerks at his disposal. The ordinary cities also had their civil servants, the most important of whom were the *tabularii*, who maintained the register of assessments and calculated the taxes due from each resident.

The civil service of the later Roman empire had all the typical vices of a developed bureaucracy. It was highly conservative, clinging to old forms and excessively addicted to red tape. John Lydus, a century after the change, was still indignant with Cyrus, the praetorian prefect in 439–41, who had abolished the use of Latin, which none of the clerks knew, in the official proceedings of the prefecture, and lovingly quotes the obsolete *formulae*. The service was riven with interdepartmental feuds. We can trace in the Codes battles between the various departments for the fees which all business brought to those who conducted it. John was particularly bitter against the office of the *magister officiorum*, which had intruded one of its own men into the senior post of the prefecture two centuries earlier, and within the prefecture was indignant at the growing power of the financial side, which had usurped business from the judicial side.

The numbers of the higher offices at any rate always tended to swell. The government periodically ordered purges and fixed establishments, but as soon as the number of established clerks was fixed, supernumeraries accumulated. The structure of the service was also very rigid. Transfers from one ministry to another, even one *scrinium* to another, were generally prohibited, and promotion was almost always by strict seniority. In most offices promotion was also very slow, and the seniors who held the top posts were often so infirm that they were authorized to perform their duties by deputy. To give them a flying start, some provident parents enrolled their children at birth. Libanius wrote on behalf of the sons of Marcellus, whom their father had entered for some office as soon as they were weaned; they had now been summoned to take up their duties, but their education, he urged, was not completed. By a law of 394 it was ordered that henceforth infants and children should begin to acquire seniority only when they commenced their duties.

There were many sinecure posts whose duties were nominal or non-existent; John Lydus complains that the *curae epistolarum* had virtually nothing to do as the financial staff had absorbed their work. Absenteeism was common in the superior offices and was very mildly penalized; by a law of 379 *agentes in rebus*, clerks of the *sacra scrinia* and *palatini* of the two financial offices lost five years' seniority for being absent without leave for six months, ten years for a year's absence, forty years for four years; only if they stayed away more than four years were they cashiered. We are told of a pious clerk in the praetorian prefecture of the East who decided to become a monk; he appointed a deputy to do his work and continued to draw his emoluments, which he spent on charity.

The service was also undoubtedly corrupt and rapacious: this was excusable in that the basic salaries were low, and in the junior grades quite inadequate, and the clerks had to make them up by demanding tips (*sportulae*). These were, to a large extent, standardized as fees, but they always tended to increase. These fees, as we have seen, made justice very expensive, particularly in the superior courts, and added substantially to the burden of taxation. Here again the major profits went to the central ministries. But besides the regular fees there were bribes— the clerks of the *sacra scrinia* are constantly denounced for corruptly drafting illegal petitions—and extortion, particularly by the *canonicarii* of the central finance ministries.

. The civil service does not seem to have attracted men of ambition or enterprise. It offered a safe career, in which dismissal was impossible, save for the grossest neglect of duty, but a dull one, in which promotion was by seniority with very little regard to ability or diligence. Apart from the early notaries, very few civil servants rose to eminence. In the fourth century two financial clerks in the offices of the *magistri militum*, Leo and Remigius, rose to be masters of the offices, and in the sixth century another, John the Cappadocian, became the praetorian prefect of the East. Under Anastasius two financial clerks of the prefecture, Polycarp and Marinus, became prefects and another, John the Paphlagonian, *comes sacrarum largitionum*. A silentiary, Anastasius, became emperor. These are the only cases of which we know.

Despite its many faults and failings, the Roman civil service adequately performed an essential function in the government of the empire. Civil servants, being professionals, were far more experienced in administrative technique than the majority of the ministers whom they served, who were for the most part amateurs. They were on the whole, moreover, less corrupt and rapacious. Unlike their chiefs, who had to make their pile in a brief term of office, they had a lifetime in which to accumulate their fortunes. The *cohortales*, moreover, were natives of the province in which they served, had many ties with the provincials and did not wish to make themselves too unpopular. The central government relied to a considerable extent on the *officia* to keep the provincial governors in order. In many laws not only was the governor threatened with a fine if he flouted or failed to execute the law, but an equal fine was imposed on the *officium* if it did not resist the governor or remind him of his duties.

Above all the civil service kept the essential routine of government going. It maintained and revised the assessment lists and computed the annual rate of taxation, supervised and stimulated its collection. It kept count of the numbers of the army, annually computed public expenditure and audited the accounts of the spending authorities. It saw to it that the armies on all the many fronts were duly fed, clothed, armed, paid and supplied with remounts and recruits. It kept the machinery of justice going, serving summonses and orders of the court on litigants, keeping the record of proceedings and executing judgments.

In view of its many and various tasks, the numbers of the imperial civil service even in the fifth and sixth centuries, when it had greatly swollen, were by modern standards very low. There are many gaps in our knowledge, but sufficient figures survive to make a rough estimate. We need not take into account supernumeraries, who received no salary, and if they were not merely on a waiting list for vacancies on the establishment, worked as deputies of the senior clerks and were paid by them or subsisted on fees. Counting established clerks only and excluding the purely domestic staff of the palace, each *comitatus* numbered about 2,500, that is, there were some 5,000 men in all in the central ministries when there were two emperors. The four praetorian prefects had perhaps 1,000 each and the urban prefects 1,000 between them. In the military offices there were 2,400 serving the 8 *magistri*, 1,000 under the 25 *duces*, and perhaps 1,000 men under the *comites rei militaris*. Proconsuls, vicars and equivalent officers accounted for 5,400 clerks, and 113 provincial governors between them had 11,300. No figures are known for the staffs of the *rationales* and other minor officers of the finance departments, but they cannot have added appreciably to the total. The grand total of civil servants was therefore not greatly excess of 30,000, and certainly well under 40,000, not a vast number to administer an empire which stretched from Hadrian's wall to beyond the Euphrates.

XVI

The Army

The army of the principate had been a professional, long-service force. The men served for twenty-five years, or longer if they attained non-commissioned rank, and were for the most part recruited voluntarily. Service tended to be hereditary, as most of the soldiers followed in their fathers' profession, and recruitment was very largely confined to the frontier areas where the bulk of the army was stationed. Apart from the praetorian guard, the army had consisted of thirty-odd legions of 6,000 men, infantry with a small cavalry element, and a much larger number of auxiliary units, infantry cohorts and cavalry *alae*, numbering generally 500, sometimes 1,000 men. The original distinction between the legions and the auxiliaries, that the former were Roman citizens, the latter provincials, ceased to exist in A.D. 212, when all free inhabitants of the empire became citizens, but the cohorts and *alae* continued to be inferior and less privileged units. The whole army was static, being

BIBLIOGRAPHY. The standard work on the later Roman army is R. Grosse, *Römische militargeschichte von Gallienus bis zum Beginn der byzantinischen Themenverfassung* (Berlin, 1920). On the early development of the army the latest is D. van Berchem, *L'armée de Dioclétien et la réforme constantinienne* (Paris, 1952). For the sixth-century army there is a useful article by A. Muller, 'das Heer Justinians', *Phililogus*, LXXI (1912), 101–38, and for Egypt, J. Maspéro, *Organisation militaire de l'Egypte byzantine* (Paris, 1912).

See also Chapter XVII of my *Later Roman Empire* (Oxford, 1964). For the later *foederati* see Maspéro, *Byz. Zeitschrift*, XXI (1912).

The main primary sources are Vegetius, *de re militari, Cod. Theod.* VII, *Cod. Just.* XII. xxvi–xlvii, the army lists in the *Notitia Dignitatum, The Abinnaeus Archive; papers of a Roman Officer in the reign of Constantius II*, H. I. Bell, V. Martin, E. G. Turner, D. van Berchem (Oxford, 1962); *Veröffentlichungen aus der Papyrussammlungen der K. Hof- und Staatsbibliothek zu München; Byzantinische Papyri* (A. Heisenberg and L. Wenger, Leipzig and Berlin, 1914), and *P. Lond.* V. 1719–37, the family papers of a group of sixth- and seventh-century *limitanei* at Aswan; and *Excavations at Nessana, conducted* H. D. Colt jr. vol. III, *Non-literary Papyri* (C. J. Kraemer, jr., Princeton, N.J., 1958), papers of soldiers from a fort in southern Palestine.

distributed (except for the praetorians) in permanent camps or forts all round the frontiers. When a particular sector of the front needed reinforcement, detachments, normally 1,000 strong, were temporarily withdrawn from the legions elsewhere, which together with cohorts and *alae* withdrawn from the other provinces, formed a temporary expeditionary force.

To meet the increased barbarian attacks of the middle of the third century, Gallienus considerably strengthened the cavalry, creating units, called vexillations, which ranked with the legions; many of them were new and mainly drawn from the Moors and Dalmatians, and the old legionary cavalry, the *promoti*, were given independent status. Out of these units and legionary detachments of infantry Gallienus formed a more or less permanent field force which he could use for dealing with emergencies.

Diocletian seems to have been conservative in his strategy. His main achievement was to strengthen the frontier, both by building forts and roads, and by greatly increasing the garrison. The extent of the increase is difficult to gauge, but it would appear that he doubled the number of legions and he also considerably increased the number of vexillations, cohorts and *alae*. According to John Lydus the army under Diocletian numbered 435,266. John, who was an antiquary, may have discovered this figure, whose precision demands respect, in some old file of the praetorian prefecture: it probably refers to the latter part of the reign. But Diocletian seems to have reduced the field army or *comitatus*. Many units of *promoti*, Moorish and Dalmatian cavalry, are found stationed on the eastern frontier, and very few regiments are attested as belonging to Diocletian's *comitatus*, among the cavalry regiments the Promoti and Comites, among the infantry the Lanciarii and Ioviani and Herculiani. When a large expeditionary force was required it was assembled from detachments from the frontiers as under the principate.

To supply recruits for his great army voluntary enlistment no longer sufficed and Diocletian not only made hereditary service compulsory but instituted an annual regular conscription from all the provinces. He also enrolled barbarians from beyond the frontiers in new cohorts and *alae*.

Constantine was the great innovator who created the army of the later Roman empire. He greatly expanded the *comitatus*, partly at the expense of the frontier armies, by withdrawing more legionary detachments from them, partly by creating more vexillations of cavalry and new infantry units called *auxilia*. The new *comitatus* seems to have been formed in Gaul for the war with Maxentius, and the new vexillations and *auxilia* were mostly drawn from the eastern Gallic provinces and from west German tribes beyond the Rhine. Constantine is said to have used a quarter of his total forces in his war against Maxentius; at this time according to Zosimus, a not very reliable guide, his total forces amounted to 98,000, while Maxentius' came to 188,000. Constantine no doubt later increased the *comitatus* when he became emperor of all the west and finally of the whole empire, but perhaps not to so large a proportion of his total forces.

From his reign soldiers of the field army, *comitatenses*, were given higher privileges than the frontier troops, now distinguished as *ripenses* or *limitanei*, and received recruits of better quality. The frontier forces, though thus reduced to second-class troops, were however not neglected and on the Danube frontier in particular Constantine seems to have carried out a thorough reorganization, strengthening the garrison with *auxilia* of infantry and cavalry *cunei equitum*, which largely replaced the old cohorts and *alae* on this front.

Constantine also remodelled the system of command. In Diocletian's time the praetorian prefects had been, under the emperors, in supreme command of the army, sometimes taking operatior al command of field armies, and controlling the frontier forces through their vicars. The frontier armies were sometimes commanded in the old style by the governor of the province, but in some cases sector commanders, *duces*, were instituted; they normally controlled the troops of several provinces. Constantine seems to have appointed *duces* all around the frontiers; henceforth it was only exceptionally and temporarily that the posts of civil governor and military commander were combined. He also created two new offices, the *magister peditum* and the *magister equitum*, to command the infantry and cavalry of the *comitatus*.

After Constantine's death his sons divided up the *comitatus* and each had his two *magistri*. They soon carried the division of the *comitatus* further. Owing to the slowness of communications it was difficult to cope with the frequent emergencies which arose both on the lower Danube and the eastern frontier with a force stationed halfway between them, and in the west similarly one force could not deal with simultaneous troubles on the Rhine and on the upper and middle Danube. Regional groups of the *comitatus* were accordingly formed as local reserves for the main sectors of the frontier in Gaul, Illyricum, Thrace and the East, commanded by *comites rei militaris* or *magistri equitum*. The central groups of the *comitatus*, now distinguished as *palatini*, remained under the command of the *magistri peditum* and *equitum praesentales*. Smaller groups of *comitatenses* were also sometimes assigned temporarily or permanently to outlying provinces such as Africa or Britain, being commanded by *comites*.

Beyond the frontier the Roman government had always tried to create an outer protective screen by making treaties with the neighbouring barbarian chieftains, whereby they undertook to refrain from raiding the provinces themselves and provided forces to protect it. In return they received protection against their neighbours and often a subsidy. In some areas the chieftains came to value imperial recognition and took pride in the titles and royal insignia conferred upon them. On the desert frontier of Syria, Arabia and Palestine a regular system was built up, whereby the Roman government appointed paramount chiefs or phylarchs over the Saracen tribes adjacent to each province. In Africa the system was developed yet further, Roman prefects being substituted for native chiefs over the nearer and more settled tribes. Barbarian tribes thus allied to the empire (*foederati*) might be called upon to supply contingents for distant operations. Thus we find Mavia, a Saracen queen, sending a force of Bedouin from the Syrian desert to defend Constantinople against the Goths in 378.

Such barbarian contingents were harmless and useful so long as they were sparingly used and went back to their homes beyond the frontier when the campaign was over. The situation was entirely changed when Theodosius I, after long and indecisive warfare with the Goths whom Valens had received into the empire in 376, gave the entire tribe of the Visigoths lands in Thrace, allowing them to remain a federate people under their own king. The Visigoths were ultimately settled in Aquitania under the same conditions, and various other barbarian groups which had forced their way into the empire, such as the Burgundians and the Alans, were given similar terms. Such federate bands were highly unreliable, since their chiefs naturally exploited their position to blackmail the government and to win larger and better territories and increased subsidies for their tribesmen. The Roman government was impelled to use them since they were there, and would, if left idle, be even more dangerous to the internal peace of the empire.

In the western part of the empire, the Roman government in the fifth century tended to make increasing use of federates of one kind or another and to allow the Roman army to run down. This was partly due to the very heavy losses which the western armies underwent in the civil wars in which successive usurpers, Maximus, Eugenius, Constantine and John were crushed, and in the great barbarian invasions of Italy by Alaric and Radagaesus, and of Gaul by the Vandals, Alans, Sueves and Burgundians. It can be deduced from the *Notitia Dignitatum* that over half, perhaps two-thirds, of the field army was destroyed in these struggles. The *comitatus* was nominally brought up to strength, but only by transferring to it many regiments of *limitanei*, and thus stripping the frontier bare, particularly in Gaul.

The federate troops were of various types. There were the contingents of the tribes settled within the empire, like the Visigoths, the Burgundians and the Franks. Aetius made extensive use of contingents of Huns, supplied by the Hunnic kings, with whom he had personal ties, having served as a hostage at their court in his youth. There were also more casual groups which rallied round some notable warrior, like Sarus the Visigoth, who put them at the disposal of the Roman government. These smaller groups were more reliable since they were much more dependent on their paymaster, and were sometimes embodied into the Roman army as *auxilia*, changing their names but not their nature.

It is impossible to trace the decline and ultimate disappearance of the Roman army in the west. In the relevant chapters of the *Notitia Dignitatum*, which was probably kept up to date down to the end of Honorius' reign, it still makes quite an impressive show. In the army of Italy there are forty-four regiments, in that of Gaul fifty-eight; smaller groups of the *comitatus* are stationed under *comites* in Illyricum (22), Spain (16), Africa (36) and Britain (5). The total is about 110,000 men. Appearances are, however, deceptive. The army of Africa consists almost entirely of *limitanei*, upgraded to *comitatenses*, and in the other armies many units are *limitanei*, in Gaul at least twenty-six out of the fifty-eight. The *limitanei* appear to be strong along the upper Danube (117 units) and in Britain (46 units); elsewhere, in Africa, Gaul and Spain, only fifty-two units are recorded in all and twenty of these ought to have been deleted, having been transferred to the *comitatus*. The nominal grand total of *limitanei* is about 130,000 men, but one may wonder how much of this existed only on paper.

The British army ceased to belong to the Roman forces some time in the latter part of Valentinian III's reign; the African was presumably disbanded when the Vandals conquered the whole of Africa on Valentinian's death in 455; the Spanish was presumably disbanded when the Visigothic kings took over Spain on Majorian's death in 457. The army of Gaul was cut off not long after; it apparently continued to maintain itself in Belgica until Clovis defeated and killed its last commander,

Syagrius, in 486. The army of Illyricum presumably lasted until the death of Julius Nepos, who reigned in Dalmatia till 480. The army of Italy, which was all that remained at the disposal of the last emperors of the west, seems to have dwindled from lack of funds and of recruits. In the final crises we hear of nothing but federates in Italy. Eugippius in his life of Severinus, who lived in Noricum between about 450 and 482, describes the gradual run-down of the *limitanei* on the upper Danube. 'While the Roman empire still stood, soldiers were maintained with public pay in many of the towns for the defence of the frontier, but when that custom lapsed the military units were abolished together with the frontier.'[1] He mentions a regiment which was still stationed at Favianae in Severinus' day, and tells how the last surviving unit at Batava drew their last instalment of pay and were disbanded.

In the east the Roman army in the reign of Arcadius consisted of some 100,000 *comitatenses*, divided into five equal groups, two under the *praesentales*, and one each in Illyricum, Thrace and the East. The *limitanei* numbered about 250,000, of whom about 65,000 were on the Danube and the rest on the eastern frontier, including Egypt. After the defeat of Gainas and his rebellious Goths in 400, federates seem to have been sparingly used until after the fall of the Hunnic empire, when Marcian settled a number of barbarian tribes, including the Ostrogoths, in the desolated area south of the Danube. The Ostrogoths were the only large and compact tribal group in the east and caused grave trouble to Leo and Zeno, until eventually they were persuaded to march west and occupy Italy.

Otherwise the eastern government seems to have employed only small mixed bands of barbarians, and the term *foederati* had come by Justinian's reign to mean standing 'foreign legions' of mixed barbarians, supplied and maintained by the government. Justinian also occasionally made use of federates in the old sense, now called 'allies', contingents supplied by tribes like the Lombards, Heruls and Gepids, who lived outside the limits of the empire. The armies of Justinian contained another element, the *bucellarii* of the generals. Even in the fifth century some of the great *magistri militum*, Stilicho and Aetius in the west and Aspar in the east, are recorded to have kept considerable bodyguards. In the sixth century the *bucellarii* were given official recognition, swearing the military oath to the emperor as well as to their employer, and sometimes ran to very large numbers; Belisarius had as many as 7,000, divided into units under their own officers. They were recruited from

[1] Eugippius, *Vita S. Severini*, 20.

Romans and barbarians indifferently and were used on campaign just like regular troops.

As we have no army list like the *Notitia Dignitatum* for the sixth century, it is difficult to estimate the size of the army and its constituent elements. According to Agathias the army at the end of Justinian's reign in Italy, Africa and the Danubian and Eastern fronts numbered barely 150,000 men. It is fairly certain that he excluded from his count the *limitanei*, who continued to guard the Danube and the eastern frontier. Justinian seems to have increased the eastern field army by about 50 per cent from the figure of 100,000 at which it stood a century and a half before. Part of the increase was supplied by the new style *foederati*, part by new regular regiments which he raised, some from barbarians, like the Justiniani Vandali formed from the remnants of the Vandals or the Perso-Justiniani and the Felices Perso-Armenii, recruited from prisoners and deserters from the Persian empire, others, like the Numidae Justiniani, from Roman citizens, including those of the reconquered western provinces.

Constantine disbanded the praetorian guard in 312, but it is probable that even before that date Diocletian had created a new guard, the *scholae*, consisting of cavalry regiments, each 500 strong. There were originally at least two regiments, the Scutarii and the Gentiles, of which the latter to judge by its name was recruited from barbarians. Other regiments appear at the end of the fourth century, including the Armaturae, and by the time of the *Notitia* there were five regiments in the west and seven in the east. From Ammianus' references to the *scholae* they seem by his day to have consisted almost exclusively of barbarians, mostly Franks and Alamans, and were crack fighting troops; but later, when the emperors ceased to take the field themselves, they became ornamental parade ground troops. In the west they were eventually pensioned off by King Theoderic. In the east places in the *scholae* were bought by the sixth century. Justin I profited from this situation by enrolling four extra regiments, which Justinian disbanded without compensation. Justinian also exploited the unmilitary character of the *scholae* by ordering them to the front on several occasions, and graciously consenting that they might stay at home if they forfeited several years' pay.

To protect the palace Leo instituted a new guard, the excubitors. It was a small corps, only 300 strong, and recruited from Roman citizens. Its commander, the *comes excubitorum*, became very important; several, including Justin I, Tiberius Constantine and Maurice, became emperors. Its officers, who were called *scribones*, were often used for special missions; one of them arrested Pope Vigilius and carried him to Constantinople.

The army was recruited both from Roman citizens and from barbarians. Slaves were normally excluded; we know in fact of only two emergencies, the revolt of Gildo in 397 and the invasion of Radagaesus in 406, in which slaves were called to the colours. Freedmen were also excluded and so were those who followed degraded occupations, such as innkeepers and cooks. From the fifth century *coloni adscripticii* were (in the interests of their landlords) declared ineligible, and sons of provincial officials and of decurions, who were bound to their fathers' occupations, were not accepted for military service. Volunteers were always acceptable, but in the fourth and fifth centuries do not seem to have formed a significant proportion of the intake. Sons of soldiers and veterans were from Diocletian's reign legally obliged to serve; the rule applied to all grades of the service, *comitatenses* and *limitanei*, and even to officers' sons, it would seem, but it was not systematically enforced. Periodically the government would conduct a round-up; those who were too old or otherwise unfit were enrolled in their city councils, the remainder allocated to the *comitatenses* or *limitanei* according to their physique. Persons who had received honorary codicils of rank were during the early fifth century periodically ordered to furnish one, two or three recruits according to their rank, but these levies were often commuted.

The main source of recruits in the fourth century was the regular conscription instituted by Diocletian. The levy was annual and affected all the provinces, but it was sometimes commuted for gold. It was based on the same schedule as the land tax, the combined *iugatio* and *capitatio*, and thus fell only on the rural population. The obligation fell on landlords, who were required to produce the number of recruits for which they were assessed from amongst their tenants. They naturally, as Vegetius remarks, fobbed off on the government their worst men, and often, by paying bounties, persuaded tramps or other undesirables to fill up their quota. As the assessment for a recruit was large, there were many small landowners who were liable for only a fraction of a man and these were grouped in consortia (*capitula* or *temones*). Valens laid down careful rules for equalizing the burden between the members of a consortium. A recruit was valued at 30 *solidi* plus 6 *solidi* for uniform and expenses, and the partners each paid a sum proportionate to his assessment into a pool. They took it in turn to provide the actual recruit and the member who did so received the 36 *solidi* (including his own contribution) and paid the recruit his 6 *solidi*. Similarly in villages of peasant proprietors the villagers subscribed 30 *solidi*, which went to the man who served.

Recruits received immunity from the *capitatio* and, if enrolled in the *comitatenses*, after five years' service also gained immunity for their wives, fathers and mothers. A landlord was also entitled to deduct the *capitatio* of a recruit from his assessment if his departure reduced the number of his tenants below his registered figure. Despite these privileges, conscription was very unpopular, it would seem, both among landlords and the peasantry. The former greatly preferred to pay commutation at the rate of 25 or 30 *solidi* per man, rather than actually furnish a recruit. The latter were closely guarded while in transit to their units, but despite these precautions deserted in large numbers on the way. Not a few even cut off their thumbs to make themselves ineligible. It is difficult to tell how general these phenomena were. According to Ammianus the Gauls never cut off their thumbs like the Italians, and it seems likely that in the frontier provinces, such as Gaul, Illyricum and Thrace, where military service was traditional, there was little difficulty in obtaining recruits. In the interior provinces, on the other hand, where there was no such tradition, and where service in the army meant lifelong exile in some distant areas, the conscription caused terror. There is evidence from Egypt that service in the *comitatenses*, though privileges were higher and prospects of promotion greater, was more unpopular than local service in the *limitanei*.

The Code of Justinian contains no laws on conscription or on the obligation on the sons of soldiers and veterans to serve. The conclusion seems inevitable that recruiting was by this time entirely voluntary, and this conclusion is borne out by what little positive evidence there is. When reinforcements were required for the Italian wars, Belisarius, Germanus and Narses conducted recruiting campaigns in Thrace and Illyricum, attracting recruits by liberal bounties. Another favourite recruiting ground, it would seem, was eastern Asia Minor, whence came the crack Isaurian and Armenian regiments. It was from these areas that the field forces were recruited. Service in the *limitanei* was by this time, it would seem, hereditary, but a privilege rather than a burden; a recruit had to prove that he was of military family. For the many regiments of *comitatenses* which had become static garrison troops, recruitment seems to have been local; in Egypt at any rate many of the men have Egyptian names and, when their origin is specified, they come from the city where their regiment is stationed.

The great majority of barbarian recruits were probably volunteers; though they were more adventurous, they sometimes stipulated that they should not have to serve in distant parts of the empire. The Roman government also often enrolled prisoners of war, and sometimes demanded a regular quota of recruits from allied tribes. It also bred barbarians for the army within the empire. Barbarian prisoners of war or refugees were allotted lands and settled in small groups under Roman prefects as *laeti*, with a special obligation of furnishing recruits to the army. The *Notitia* gives a list, which is certainly incomplete, of over thirty such settlements, mostly of Sarmatians, Franks and Sueves, scattered through most of the provinces of Gaul and Italy. The institution goes back to Diocletian and was still functioning in the last days of the western empire.

It is impossible to gauge what proportion of the regular forces was barbarian and what Roman. The proportion varied at different periods and in different branches of the service. On the whole barbarians were considered better fighting material and were enrolled in the highest ranking regiments. In the fourth century, as we have seen, the imperial guard of the *scholae* consisted predominantly of Franks and Alamans, and of the *auxilia palatina* and *vexillationes palatinae*, which were the crack regiments of the field army, many bear barbarian names. On the other hand very few units of *limitanei* have barbarian names, and these are old formations dating back to Diocletian.

Synesius, in a loyal address delivered to Arcadius in 399, vehemently denounced the lavish use of Gothic troops, and advocated their expulsion and the formation of a purely citizen army. At that time Theodosius I, in his desperate efforts to fill the gaps caused by the battle of Adrianople, had recently flooded the army with barbarians, and the revolt of Gainas had just demonstrated the danger of employing large masses of Goths. But Synesius himself changed his mind later, and gave lavish praise to the barbarian regiment of Unnigardae, who alone gave effective defence to his native province of Cyrenaica against its nomad invaders. Ammianus, who was an experienced officer, never suggests that German soldiers were unreliable: he records a few cases where deserters or men on leave betrayed military secrets to their tribesmen, but evidently attaches no importance to these incidents. There is in fact no evidence that Germans recruited into regular units, subject to Roman discipline, and commanded by regular officers, whether these were Roman or German by origin, were unreliable. It was the federates, tribal groups under their own chieftains, who could not be trusted.

Under Diocletian and Constantine the troops received pay, and annual donatives on the birthdays and accession anniversaries of the emperors. These payments were in copper *denarii* and depreciated in value very greatly during the fourth century. They appear to have still been paid under Julian and Valentinian and Valens, but had disappeared by the sixth century. The accession donative, on the other hand, which was paid in gold and silver, retained its value and survived. It remained at the same figure, 5 *solidi* and 1 pound of silver, equivalent in all to 9 *solidi*; these figures are recorded from Julian to Tiberius Constantine. The quinquennial donative stood at 5 *solidi* in the sixth century: this was also no doubt a traditional figure.

Pay and donatives were issued by the *sacrae largitiones*, and the same department supplied uniforms, some manufactured in the state weaving mills which it controlled, the bulk, it would seem, obtained by levies. The uniform seems to have consisted of a shirt, tunic and cloak, but we do not know how often garments were replaced. Boots were also supplied; one law alludes to state boot factories in 344, but they do not appear in the *Notitia*, and boots were normally, it may be presumed, obtained by levy. Issues of uniform were by the end of the fourth century beginning to be commuted into gold, and by the sixth century the practice was apparently general. Maurice made himself very unpopular by going back to issues in kind. Arms were issued from state factories, controlled in the fourth century by the praetorian prefects, later by the masters of the offices. Arms had also by the sixth century been commuted, until Maurice revived issues in kind.

Horses were supplied to troops by the *comes stabuli*, who either obtained them from the imperial stud farms or levied them from the provincials. Here commutation began early. The provincials paid sums varying from 15 to 20 *solidi* per horse, but the soldiers received only 7 *solidi* to buy their remounts. The difference between these sums was partly absorbed by a fee of 2 *solidi* to the *comes stabuli* and 1 *solidus* to the *strator*, who checked the quality of the horse; the rest presumably went to the treasury.

Finally rations were supplied by the praetorian prefecture, acting through the vicars and provincial governors, under whose direction the curial collectors conveyed the foodstuffs to the public storehouses and issued them daily against warrants to the actuaries or quartermasters of the regiments. These rules applied to the static regiments of the *limitanei*. The regiments of the *comitatenses*, when scattered in winter quarters or at their peacetime stations, obtained their supplies in bulk from the office of a designated province, sending an *opinator* to collect them. When a field force was assembled, the praetorian prefect of the area himself took charge of collecting supplies in the fourth century. In the fifth and sixth century it was more usual to appoint a special praetorian prefect *ad hoc* for the expedition.

The ration consisted of bread, meat, wine and oil; on active service biscuit was partially substituted for bread, sour wine for ordinary wine, and salt pork for fresh meat. Various ration scales are recorded in the Egyptian papyri and some are very liberal—3 pounds of bread, 2 pounds of meat, 2 pints of wine and one-eighth of a pint of oil per day.

Rations also came to be commuted. As early as 365 Valens enacted that the *limitanei* should receive their rations in kind for nine months only and for three months in money, and by the early fifth century all rations of the *limitanei* had been commuted. In the west the rations of the *comitatenses* were also commuted by the early fifth century, but in the east they continued to draw them in kind unless detached from their units for special duties. This at any rate was the rule, but from actual accounts from Egypt it would appear that levies assessed in kind for the static units of *comitatenses* were actually collected in gold.

The *limitanei* lived in permanent forts, which are depicted in the pages of the *Notitia Dignitatum*, and many of which survive almost intact in Syria and north Africa. The *comitatenses*, who had no fixed stations, lived in billets. Officially they were allowed one-third of the house and the householder was not obliged to provide more than the bare rooms. Actually soldiers constantly exacted bedding and wood and oil for heating and lighting and sometimes supper. Officers were also prone to demand baths, a concession officially allowed only to *magistri militum*. There were regimental surgeons to attend to the men's health, and from the fifth century at any rate regimental chaplains for their spiritual welfare.

Soldiers were allowed to marry and during some periods received rations for their sons. Valentinian I abolished this privilege in the west in 372, and Theodosius I seems to have done the same in the east, but here family allowances were soon revived. Allusions to them have been deleted in Justinian's Code, and presumably they had ceased to be paid by then.

Soldiers were usually promoted by seniority, though notable acts of courage were taken into account. In the old units inherited from the principate, the old N.C.O. grades of decurion and centurion were still preserved, but in the new types of formation, the *vexillationes* and *auxilia,* there was a new set of ranks—*circitor, biarchus, centenarius, ducenarius, senator* and *primicerius.* N.C.O.s were paid multiple rations, ranging from two *annonae* for a *circitor* to five for the *primicerius.*

The period of service in order to achieve an honourable discharge was twenty years, but for the full privileges of a veteran twenty-four years were required. These periods were minima, and those who achieved N.C.O. rank often stayed on for as much as forty-eight years. Veterans enjoyed various fiscal privileges, such as immunity from the poll tax for themselves and their wives, and, if they went into trade, exemption from the *collatio lustralis.* In the fourth century they also received allotments of land (with oxen and seed corn) or, if they preferred, a cash bounty. There is no allusion to these in Justinian's code, but by this time the senior men, up to 5 per cent of the strength of the unit, were entitled to remain in the service, however infirm, until they died. This rule must have not only slowed up promotion unduly, but considerably reduced the effective strength of the army, and Justinian revoked it; but he does not seem to have made any financial provision for the infirm seniors whom he discharged.

It was always possible for a common soldier to obtain commissioned rank. The first step was to be enrolled in the corps of officer cadets (*protectores*). The history of the *protectores* is obscure, but it is reasonably certain that under Diocletian they formed a corps attached to the emperor. In the early fourth century a distinction was made between *protectores domestici,* who were commanded by the *comes domesticorum,* and ordinary *protectores,* who appear to have been under the *magistri militum.* The *domestici* were apparently divided into four battalions or *scholae,* the senior and junior infantry and cavalry, and from the end of the fourth or the beginning of the fifth century the infantry and cavalry were commanded by separate *comites domesticorum, peditum* and *equitum.* Both *domestici* and *protectores* received their rank in consistory, by personally 'adoring the sacred purple'; the emperor's verbal command '*adorato protector*' or '*adorato protector domesticus*' sufficed and no document was issued until Justinian's day. They were employed for staff duties at headquarters, and for miscellaneous missions in the provinces, rounding up sons of veterans, marching squads of recruits to their units, arresting important persons and escorting them to court. The *domestici,* despite their name, did not all serve in the *comitatus,* some of them being regularly seconded to the *magistri militum.* After a few years' service, they were given commissions as regimental commanders.

The rank of *protector* seems in the early fourth century to have been in principle reserved for deserving soldiers, and we know of several who were so promoted, some after long service in the ranks. In the middle years of the century, however, we find the youthful sons of high military officers serving in the corps, probably without previous experience, and officials and decurions and other civilians also made their way into it. In 364 Valentinian I drew a distinction between those who entered the corps after long service and those who 'adored the sacred purple by the interest or favour of the great', making the latter pay fees amounting to 50 *solidi*, but cutting down the fees of the former to 5 or 10 *solidi*. By the same law, however, he allowed the sons and relatives of *domestici* to be enrolled as children and to receive rations at home until of age to take up their duties. By the end of the century the corps contained many absentee members 'who have never applied themselves to our service, or, seconded to certain offices, executed public orders', and by the early fifth century both the *domestici* and the *protectores* seem to have become ornamental bodies whose members served for life, gradually rising by seniority until they became *decemprimi* and eventually *primicerii* of their respective corps: these ranks now carried senatorial status. In the west they were eventually pensioned off by King Theoderic: in the east they still survived as ornamental sinecure regiments. Places were purchased, and for very high sums; it was a privilege for the *advocati fisci* of the praetorian prefecture of the East that they were allowed to buy two places for anyone they pleased for 2,000 *solidi* each. Justinian ordered the *domestici* and *protectores* to the front, like the *scholares*, and let them off active service on condition that they surrendered their pay for a term of years.

Of the tribunes, prefects and *praepositi*, who commanded the regiments, some at any rate in the fourth century were commissioned from the *protectores*. We know of Valerius Thiumpus, who after service in the ranks and five years as *protector* became prefect of a legion, and of Flavius Memorius, who served twenty-eight years in the ranks and six years in the *protectores domestici* before becoming prefect of the Lanciarii Seniores. But civilians were often, it would seem, given commissions. In the fifth century soldiers were sometimes promoted to officers—an instance is the future emperor Marcian—but we do not know how common the practice was. *Duces* seem usually to have been experienced officers of many years' service, though we know of a few sons of great men, like the future emperor Theodosius, who were appointed young. *Duces* rarely received any further promotion; they were no doubt normally too old. The usual avenue to the supreme command was in the fourth century tribune of the *scholae*, *comes rei militaris*, or *comes domesticorum*, *magister militum*. We know of half a dozen *comites* or *magistri* who rose all the way from the ranks, but such advancement must have been rare.

A high proportion of officers and generals were during the fourth and fifth centuries barbarians, mostly Germans, though a Sarmatian and several Persians are known. These barbarian officers became completely assimilated; none are known to have returned to their native people, and several founded families which served the empire for generations. Some, like Stilicho the Vandal, were *de facto* rulers of the empire under feeble emperors, others like the Frank, Arbogast, the Alan Aspar and the Sueve Ricimer, ruled through puppet emperors whom they appointed. Some, like Aspar, even aspired to put their sons on the throne. But in this they were no different from ambitious Roman generals, and they all served the empire to the best of their ability.

Officers, like N.C.O.s, were paid in rations and fodder. We do not know the rates of pay except for *duces*, who received 50 *annonae* and 50 *capitus*. They naturally found it inconvenient to receive all their emoluments in foodstuffs, and as early as the reign of Constantine were compelling the curial *susceptores* to pay them in money instead. By the early fifth century their allowances were officially commuted.

Salaries on such a scale might seem adequate, but they were much lower than those of the principate, and officers regularly supplemented them by intercepting part of the emoluments due to their men, and some of these forms of peculation, originally condemned as abuses, became established perquisites, hallowed by custom and confirmed by law. Tribunes became entitled to *stellatura*, or one week's rations per annum from all their men. The *limitanei* had one month's rations deducted and distributed between the *dux* of the province and the commanders of the regiments. Some more unscrupulous officers peculated their soldiers' uniforms, boots, arms and horses, but such abuses were never officially sanctioned. A more common device was to sell prolonged or even indefinite leave to soldiers, and to keep dead men on the books, drawing their pay and allowances. This last practice was pernicious in that it both reduced the real strength of the army and blocked promotion—it was naturally the seniors, who were drawing multiple rations, whom it was most profitable to keep on the list when they died—but it was eventually, it would seem, given official sanction. Perquisites thus accumulated and came greatly to exceed the official salary: the *dux* of Libya in the sixth century drew 50 *annonae* and 50 *capitus*, commuted to 400 *solidi*, in pay, and 90 *annonae* and 120 *capitus*, commuted for 1,005¼ *solidi*, from other sources.

If soldiers had always received all that was legally due to them, they would have been very well off, far better clothed and enjoying a far more ample and varied diet than the peasantry from whom they were drawn. In practice, conditions varied very greatly in different grades of the service and even in different regiments. The *scholares*, serving under the emperor's eye, could readily voice their grievances to him, and came to enjoy a luxurious standard of living and a very lax discipline. The *limitanei*, living in desolate provinces on the frontier, were very much at the mercy of their officers, and were often grossly exploited by them. In general soldiers were, it would seem, a fairly prosperous class. They not uncommonly owned slaves, who were relatively cheap and plentiful on the frontier; N.C.O.s seem normally to have had slave batmen, and Martin when serving as a private in the *scholae* was considered very ascetic for contenting himself with only one slave. Many soldiers, moreover, owned some land. Sons of veterans inherited their fathers' allotments in due course, and a fair number of conscripts were sons of peasant proprietors. By the fifth century the *limitanei* in the eastern provinces had acquired the prescriptive right to cultivate allotments in the territories attached to their forts.

On the other hand it would appear from a law of Anastasius that soldiers were not uncommonly in debt to their actuaries before pay day came round; and it is not likely that under so careful and provident a financier as Anastasius this was due to the pay being in arrears. Under Justinian the pay of the armies in Africa and Italy fell into serious arrears and mutinies and desertions resulted; but this seems to have been exceptional, and due to Justinian's excessive optimism about the revenue which would accrue from the newly conquered provinces of the west.

Discipline also varied very greatly in different branches of the service. In the *limitanei* it was scandalously lax by the fifth and sixth centuries, and the same was true of the units of *comitatenses* which had become static garrisons. Leo had to inform Aspar that 'the soldiers who are armed and fed by the state ought to be occupied in the public interest only, and not in agriculture and cattle-farming or in trade'. There are many other allusions to soldiers serving as land agents and the papyri show one leasing a bakery. Moschus in his *Spiritual Meadow* highly praises a soldier of Alexandria, who used to pray and weave baskets from dawn until the ninth hour, and then (at 3 p.m.) put on his uniform and go on parade. This he did for eight years without exciting any adverse comment from his officers. From Syene, the southern border fort of Egypt, we have a set of family papers of Flavius Patermuthis, who with engaging frankness describes himself on legal documents as 'soldier of the regiment of Elephantine, by profession a boatman'. The papers contain one military document, the enrolment certificate of one member of the family; the rest are all sales and purchases of boats and houses and litigation and legal settlements over the family estate.

Vegetius in his manual on the art of war paints a gloomy picture of the degeneracy of the army, but he was an antiquarian, whose standard was the ideal, and not the real, imperial army of the principate. The fighting regiments of the field army, even if they did not, according to Leo's instructions, 'prepare themselves for war by daily arms drill', must have been adequately trained by their regimental drill sergeants, the *campidoctores*. At any rate small Roman forces, if competently led, could defeat immensely larger barbarian hordes, as Stilicho proved at the battles of Pollentia, Verona and Faesulae, and Belisarius in his conquest of the Vandals and Ostrogoths.

It may seem strange at first sight, in view of the large numbers of troops which the empire maintained, that it could assemble such small forces for a given campaign. The largest expeditionary force recorded, that of Julian on his Persian campaign, numbered 65,000 men. Rather earlier Julian as Caesar had only 13,000 men in Gaul, while Constantius II's *magister militum* Barbatio, supporting him further south, had 25,000. Stilicho managed to muster 30 regiments, perhaps 20,000 men, to fight Radagaesus: Anastasius assembled 52,000 for the Persian war in 503, and Procopius declares that this was the largest concentration of troops ever made on the eastern front.

Belisarius conquered Africa with 15,000 regular troops (and 1,000 allies and his *bucellarii*), and occupied Sicily and south Italy and Rome with an even smaller force, 7,000 regulars (with 500 allies and his *bucellarii* again).

It is of course true that many of the soldiers on the army list either did not exist, or were engaged in civil avocations, but those that remained had an immense task to perform. The empire had hundreds of miles of frontier to protect against persistent raiding. Of the 350,000 men which the eastern empire maintained in the early fifth century, 250,000 were *limitanei*, who patrolled the lower Danube and the long eastern front from the Black Sea to the Gulf of Aqaba, and the Nile valley and the desert of Libya. In the west the proportion was not so high, 140,000 out of 250,000, but this was because many of the *limitanei* had been drafted into the field army. The frontier troops were for the most part of very poor quality, but they fulfilled an essential role in policing the boundaries of the empire, and the eastern government appreciated their value, making a vigorous attempt in 443 to bring them up to strength, restore their military efficiency, and prevent their pay and allowances being peculated by their officers. Justinian thought *limitanei* so useful that he gave detailed instructions for their reconstitution in Africa after the reconquest.

An increasing number of the field army regiments also came to be tied down to garrison duty in the fifth and sixth centuries. In areas like Thrace and Illyricum, where barbarian hordes constantly broke through the frontier defences, they were needed to garrison the cities of the interior, and in Asia Minor they were required to suppress the brigandage of the Isaurians. But the imperial government may be criticized for dispersing its forces to excess, and using too many for internal security, though it must be remembered that it possessed no police to enforce law and order.

Finally, of that part of the field army which remained mobile most had to be distributed in regional groups, committed to the defence of each of the major fronts. Communications being so slow, it would have been very risky to withdraw any large proportion of the troops in Illyricum or Thrace to fight on the eastern frontier, or to move the field army of Gaul to meet an invasion of Italy. Only the praesental armies in northern Italy and round Constantinople formed fully mobile reserves. Anastasius' great force of 52,000 men must have comprised the greater part of both the pracsental armies and of the army of the east, which numbered about 20,000 each.

XVII

The two Capitals

Rome was already a declining city when Diocletian came to the throne. It had never been a commercial or industrial town; its merchants, shopkeepers and craftsmen served only the local population. It had owed its importance to the fact that it was the administrative capital of the empire, and now it was no more important as a centre of government than Carthage or Arles. Yet it remained a huge city down to the fall of the empire in the west and indeed still under the Ostrogothic kingdom. There were still in the mid-fifth century, and it would seem even in the sixth, 120,000 persons who received the free ration of bread and pork, and as these were probably for the most part heads of families, the free plebeian population, including women and children, must have numbered four or five times that total. To these must be added a modest number of officials, lawyers, doctors and professors, and a more considerable body of clergy, the students at the university, the senatorial aristocracy, and finally the slaves who served the upper and middle classes. The total may well have exceeded two-thirds of a million inhabitants.

The survival of Rome as a great city was mainly due to three factors. In the first place it was still the main focus of the immensely wealthy families of the old senatorial aristocracy, who, though they spent much

BIBLIOGRAPHY. A good recent book on Rome in the later empire is A. Chastagnel, *La Préfecture urbaine à Rome sous le bas-empire* (Paris, 1960), which deals with all aspects of the administration. There is no parallel work on Constantinople.

The *Notitia Urbis Constantinopolitanae* is printed in Seeck's *Notitia dignitatum*, pp. 229–43. The *Notitia Regionum Urbis XIV* and the closely parallel document, the *Curiosum Urbis Regionum XIV*, are published by H. Jordan in *Topographie der Stadt Rom in Alterthum*, II, 551–74, and by A. Nordh in *Libellus de regionibus urbis Romae*, *Acta Inst. Rom. Regni Sueciae*, III (1949), 73–106. The principal laws about Rome and Constantinople are in *Cod. Theod.* XIV, *Cod. Just.* XI. xiii–xxiv. There is also a very interesting exchange of letters between the Prefect of the City and the emperor in *Collectio Avellana*, 14 ff.

of their time in their country villas, passed part of the year in Rome and maintained vast town houses, staffed with hundreds of slaves, and provided custom for a host of craftsmen, shopkeepers and importers of luxury goods. The great families, moreover, made Rome a centre of fashionable life and attracted to it many more recently ennobled senators. In the second place, not only did the Roman church possess huge and ever-growing endowments and support a large body of wealthy clergy; the widening spiritual authority of the popes drew to the city a steady stream of petitioners, while the shrines of SS. Peter and Paul and numerous other martyrs attracted flocks of pilgrims. Thirdly, Rome was the greatest educational centre of the west, both for literary studies and more particularly for law, and drew ambitious and wealthy students not only from all the western provinces but even, during the fourth century at any rate, from the east.

Constantinople, on the other hand, was a growing city. Constantine gave it a flying start by granting fiscal privileges to the wealthy settlers who built houses in his city, and establishing a free bread distribution for 80,000 persons. The growth of the city can be gauged from the building of new aqueducts by Valens, Theodosius I and Justinian, and by the doubling of the city's area in 413, when a new wall was built on the landward side about a mile further west than Constantine's. In Justinian's reign the annual governmental shipment of corn from Egypt amounted to 8,000,000 *artabae*, enough to feed 600,000 persons, and this supply was supplemented by a corn-buying fund, which was used to finance additional purchases, and no doubt by private imports.

Despite its favourable position, Constantinople does not seem at this time to have been a great commercial centre. As at Rome, its merchants were mainly importers who supplied the local market, and we hear of only one Constantinopolitan clothier who exported his wares to Africa and the west. Constantinople had its university, established in 425, but as an educational centre it was rivalled by Athens in literature and philosophy, by Alexandria in literature and science and medicine, and by Berytus in law. The see of Constantinople grew in wealth and its clergy in numbers; Justinian tried to reduce the staff of the Great Church (which comprised two other churches besides S. Sophia) to 525. It also grew in importance, establishing a jurisdiction over the three dioceses of Thrace, Asia and Pontica, which was officially confirmed in 451 by the Council of Chalcedon. But in the ecclesiastical field Constantinople was rivalled by Alexandria and Antioch, not to speak of Jerusalem and Thessalonica.

The prosperity of Constantinople was primarily due to its being both the administrative and the social capital of the eastern empire. There must have been about 6,000 civil servants in the palatine ministries, the praetorian prefecture of the East and the offices of the two *magistri militum praesentales*. The city was the seat of the imperial court and of the senate, whose most important and richest members normally resided in it. As the judicial centre of the empire it was thronged with litigants from all the provinces, and it attracted thousands of immigrants who hoped to make their fortunes in the service of the emperor or of the great men who surrounded him. Such was the congestion of the city that Justinian instituted a special magistrate, the *quaesitor*, whose function it was to control immigration, making sure that those who had come on business returned when their business was done and deporting to their provinces those who had no business and no visible means of support. He also put able-bodied residents to work on the public buildings, in the bakeries or in one of the guilds, and licensed the aged and infirm to beg.

The different social structure of the two capitals is reflected in their housing statistics. At Rome there were in the early fourth century over 40,000 *insulae*, or tenements in blocks of flats, which were for the most part inhabited by the poorer classes, and under 1,800 *domus*, or separate houses occupied by upper-class families. In Constantinople we do not know the number of *insulae*, but there were 4,388 *domus*, corresponding to a much larger middle class of civil servants, barristers and professional men. Moreover, some of these did not live in houses; we happen to know that Anthemius of Tralles, the architect of S. Sophia, lived in a flat and that one of his neighbours was a prosperous barrister.

Rome had from the beginning of the principate been directly administered by the imperial government. In supreme control was the prefect of the city, a magistrate of the highest rank, equal to the praetorian prefects and the *magistri militum*, and usually chosen from the most aristocratic families. Under his general direction, but appointed by the emperor, were a number of departmental officers, the prefects of the corn supply and of the fire brigade, the curators of the aqueducts, of the drains, of the public buildings, of the statues, the tribune of the cattle market, the *comes* of the port, and sundry others. We know less of the administration of Constantinople but it appears to have been closely modelled on that of Rome. From 359 Constantinople had its own prefect of the city and we hear of prefects of the corn supply and of the fire brigade.

In two respects Rome was less well governed in the later empire than under the principate. The three urban cohorts, which had formed the city police force, had melted away, and to enforce law and order the prefect of the city had only his officials and a body of nightwatchmen (*vicomagistri*), forty-eight for each of the fourteen regions; in Constantinople the situation was even worse, with only five *vicomagistri* for each region. The result was that in any serious disturbance the prefects of the capitals were helpless, as many accounts of bread riots, fights of the circus factions and bloodily contested papal elections amply demonstrate. In the second place, though there was a prefect of the fire brigade (*praefectus vigilum*), the old seven cohorts of *vigiles* no longer existed, and amateur firefighters were provided by the guilds of the city. The same system applied in Constantinople, where the number of firefighters was 560.

The aqueducts were maintained by a staff of public slaves and supplied water not only to the baths, the ornamental fountains and to numerous public fountains (there were 1,352 in Rome) from which the humbler citizens drew their water, but also, under imperial licence, to private houses. The largest houses, which had superior sets of baths, might be granted a two-inch or even a three-inch pipe; medium-sized houses with baths could have a one-and-a-half-inch pipe; smaller houses were limited to a pipe of half-an-inch diameter.

In both capitals there was a daily free distribution of bread to those inhabitants who held bread tickets. The amount of the ration was fixed at Rome by Valentinian I to six half-pound loaves, and the number of recipients was, it would appear, 120,000; at Constantinople the original issue in 332 was to 80,000 persons, but this was later increased. The bread was distributed at 'steps' (*gradus*), of which there were 117 at Constantinople. Any free inhabitant, apart from soldiers and officials, was apparently eligible for a ticket, and Valens enacted that *tesserae* should be surrendered and reallocated on the death or departure from the city of the beneficiary. This law, however, seems to have soon become a dead letter, and tickets were in practice hereditary and saleable; by the sixth century many had been given or bequeathed to churches. There were also bread rations allocated to those who built houses, payable in perpetuity to the occupiers of these houses so long as they maintained them in good condition.

The government not only supplied this free ration, but imported sufficient corn to feed the entire population. The grain was mostly obtained by taxation in kind, levied in Africa for Rome and in Egypt for

Constantinople: deficiencies were made up by compulsory purchases in other provinces. The grain was milled into flour and baked into bread by the guild of bakers; the mills were worked by donkeys at Rome until the end of the fourth century, when the water power of the aqueducts began to be used for the purpose. In Constantinople there were twenty public bakeries, which produced the bread for the free issue, and 120 private bakeries, which produced bread for sale. In Rome the arrangements were more complicated and are somewhat obscure. The number of private bakers is unknown, but there were 274 public bakeries, which were considerable establishments manned by slaves or convicts. They must have baked much more bread than was required for the free issue (*panes gradiles*) and perhaps also produced the *panes fiscales* or *Ostienses*, which were sold at a fixed low price.

Even under the principate the baker's trade had not been very popular and Trajan had endeavoured to attract freedmen and others to it by the grant of privileges. By the fourth century membership of the bakers' guild was compulsory on anyone who acquired a baker's property by inheritance or gift or purchase, or by marrying a baker's daughter. Bakers were forbidden to alienate their property, even that which they received from outside sources. There were also estates, which had presumably belonged to extinct bakers' families, assigned to the several public bakeries. From the income of these estates and their own property, the bakers subsidized their business.

In Rome, but not so far as we know in Constantinople, there were also free distributions of oil, made through 2,300 shops, and of pork. The latter was issued only during five months of the year, and the ration was 5 pounds per month. The guild of pork butchers was responsible for levying the pigs from the provinces of Campania, Lucania and Samnium, driving them to Rome and there slaughtering them and distributing the meat. The process caused endless difficulties. During the journey to Rome the pigs lost weight, and the pork butchers claimed and obtained a rebate of 15 per cent, later 20 per cent, on this score. If they preferred to take money instead of pigs, the price at which pigs were commuted in the south was lower than that at which they could buy pigs near Rome, and they suffered a loss that way. Eventually the whole supply was put on a cash basis, the pork butchers receiving 14,700 *solidi* from the revenues of the provinces concerned and buying for this sum 3,628,000 pounds of pork, which (allowing for wastage) would supply the ration.

Wine was not provided free, but at Rome was sold at 25 per cent below the market price; it was supplied by a levy in kind on the Suburbicarian provinces.

Both capitals were equipped with huge public baths, eleven at Rome and nine at Constantinople: there were also 830 private baths at Rome and 153 in the sister city. The public baths at Rome were financed by making the lessees of the salt pans, a profitable contract, undertake their management. They were supplied with wood for fuel by a levy on designated cities and the transport of the wood was imposed on the guild of the river boatmen.

There were many other guilds at Rome, which in return for certain privileges and immunities rendered service to the public either gratis or for a modest payment. The bread supply required not only the bakers but the tally clerks (*mensores*), who checked the cargoes of corn which arrived at the port of Rome, the stevedores (*saccarii*), who unloaded it from the ships, the bargees (*caudicarii*), who carried it up the Tiber, and the carters (*catabolenses*), who distributed it to the bakeries. Besides the pork butchers there were beef and mutton butchers. For public works there were the masons and carpenters and to supply lime, which was obtained from designated estates in Campania and Tuscia, the lime burners and the lime carters. Certain guilds also, as we have seen, provided nightwatchmen and firefighters.

Valentinian I instituted a public health service for Rome. There were twelve public doctors, one for each of twelve of the fourteen regions, who were instructed to treat poor patients gratis: they were also allowed to have private patients, who might pay them a retaining fee, but were forbidden to charge for their services.

Public entertainments were provided on a lavish scale for both capitals, occasionally by the emperor, more regularly by the senators, who were obliged to give games when they held the ancient republican magistracies, the quaestorship (at Rome only), the praetorship and the ordinary consulate. The games comprised chariot races, mimes, wild beast hunts and, in fourth-century Rome, gladiatorial combats; these last were probably never given at Constantinople, since Constantine prohibited them in 326, but continued at Rome until they were abolished by Honorius. At Rome the members of the ancient senatorial families, with their vast wealth and old traditions of conspicuous expenditure, set a very high standard, which was embarrassing for their humbler colleagues. Symmachus spent 2,000 pounds of gold on his son's praetorian games, and Petronius Maximus 4,000 on his own. To judge by Symmachus' correspondence they also took infinite pains to put on a show worthy of the family traditions. He sent agents to Spain to buy the best racehorses that its famous stables could provide; he secured antelopes from Africa, bears from Dalmatia, crocodiles from Egypt and hounds from Ireland; he got the emperor to give him some Saxon prisoners to fight as gladiators—but they committed suicide, to his great annoyance: he hired mimes from the east, it would seem—we possess a frantic letter to the prefect of the city, begging him to send an official to round up his troupe, which had last been reported in Sicily. In Constantinople the new aristoctacy was neither so rich nor so public-spirited, and the games were less splendid. Even an ordinary consul's games cost only 2,000 pounds of gold, and of this sum a substantial part was provided by a treasury grant. Nevertheless the consul provided seven days of entertainment, including two days of chariot races, a wild beast hunt, boxing matches and a display of mime.

XVIII

The Cities

The Roman empire consisted, with a few insignificant exceptions, of cities, that is self-governing communities occupying a territory and almost always possessing an urban centre. Geographically the empire was a mosaic of city territories. All Roman citizens, that is all indigenous free inhabitants of the empire, belonged to some city. Local citizenship went not by residence, or place of birth, but by descent, or in the case of freedmen by their patron's registration. A man was a citizen of Syracuse or Antioch because his father (or patron) was a Syracusan or Antiochene, and he remained a citizen of Syracuse or Antioch even if he—and his father before him—had established a permanent domicile in Carthage. At Carthage he was a resident alien (*incola*), and, while he became subject to obligations to the city of his domicile, the city of his origin always retained its claims upon his services.

Besides the cities there were some communities of humbler status, villages and rural cantons, but they were a tiny minority. In the eastern parts, for which we possess tolerably full and accurate statistics, there were over 900 cities, ten rural cantons in the backward mountainous centre of Asia Minor, and about thirty villages, or village groups, mostly in Arabia and the adjacent provinces. In Gaul, the only area of the west for which we have statistics, there were 114 cities and eight *castra*,

BIBLIOGRAPHY. In this chapter I rely largely on my own two books, *The Cities of the Eastern Roman Provinces* (Oxford, 1937) and *The Greek City from Alexander to Justinian* (Oxford, 1940). I have also derived much profit from P. Petit, *Libanius et la vie municipale à Antioche au IVe siècle après J. C.* (Paris, 1955). There are no comparable studies for the West.

The laws on the cities are mostly in *Cod. Theod.* XII, *Cod. Just.* X. xxxi ff. Other important documentary sources include the Album of Thamugadi; the text (CIL viii. 2403 + 17824, partly reproduced in *ILS* 6122) has been greatly improved by L. Leschi in *Révue des Etudes Anciennes* L (1948), 71 ff.; the minutes of the council at Oxyrhyncus (*P. Oxy.* 2110) and the foundation charters of Orcistus and Tymandus (H. Dessau, *Inscr. Lat. Sel.* 6090, 6091).

237

towns of more recent origin. The villages, and probably the cantons and *castra*, were self-governing communities, but they had a simpler structure than the cities. They had no councils, but a mass meeting of the villagers elected the magistrates and passed by-laws on local affairs.

There were also in the eastern parts (we have no information for the west) a certain number of areas known as *regiones*, *tractus* and *saltus*, or estates. They were apparently blocks of imperial land directly administered by the *res privata*. They numbered between forty and fifty in all; some half-dozen were converted into cities during the fourth, fifth and sixth centuries. Most of the *regiones* were concentrated in the interior of Bithynia, in central Cappadocia and in eastern Palestine, and were probably remnants of the royal lands of the old Bithynian, Cappadocian and Herodian kingdoms.

The cities varied enormously in the size of the town, the extent of the territory and their economic and social structure. Alexandria, which was the third city of the empire after the two capitals, and had a population of about a third of a million, was peculiar, and probably unique, in possessing no rural territory. Its wealth was derived from its position as an administrative, ecclesiastical and educational centre and from trade and industry. It was the seat of the Augustal prefect, the *dux*, the *rationalis* and the *magister rei privatae* of Egypt, with their officials and lawyers, and its bishop occupied one of the wealthiest sees of the empire and exercised absolute control over all the churches of Egypt, the Thebaid and Libya. Its university attracted students from as far afield as Asia Minor. Its docks handled the annual shipment of 8,000,000 *artabae* of wheat to Constantinople. It possessed important industries, manufacturing fine linen, glass, silver plate, perfumes and spices made up from oriental imports, and having a virtual monopoly of papyrus. Its merchants controlled the sea-borne trade with South Arabia, the Persian Gulf and India in incense, spices, and perfumes, jewels and silk, and made regular voyages to Gaul and Spain.

In the west Carthage occupied a rather similar position. It was the administrative capital of the African diocese, and its bishop held sway over all the African churches. It possessed a university of some repute. It was a major port, handling shipment of the Roman corn supply, and also of the olive oil which Africa exported to Italy and Gaul. It was probably also the chief centre of the manufacture of the cheap woollens called Africans.

Many of the major cities of the empire seem to have owed their greatness to being administrative centres. Trier was an important town in the late third and fourth century, when it was the seat of the praetorian prefecture of the Gauls, and an emperor often resided there; its population was swelled by the workers of two state arms factories, a state woollen mill and a mint. Later it declined when the praetorian prefecture moved to Arles at the beginning of the fifth century, and Arles, which also had an arms factory and a mint, became a great city. Ravenna sprang into sudden importance when in the early fifth century it became the residence of the western emperors. Antioch too flourished mainly because it was the seat of the *comes Orientis* and the *magister militum* of the East, and was the ecclesiastical capital of the diocese of Oriens. It also had two state arms factories and apparently manufactured the cheap linen clothing known as Antiochenes.

There were a number of other towns whose industries were important. In the east Tarsus, Laodicea in Syria, Byblus and Scythopolis produced highly priced linen clothing, while Berytus and Tyre were centres of the silk industry. In the west Amiens and Bourges manufactured high-class woollens. Other cities like Aquileia or Ephesus were important ports. Athens owed its modest prosperity almost entirely to its famous university, and Jerusalem flourished greatly on the pilgrim traffic.

The vast majority of cities, however, were simply the governmental and social centres of their territories. In them lived the wealthier of the local landowners, who formed the city council, the bishop with his clergy, the *defensor* with perhaps a few barristers. They also served as market towns for their neighbourhoods, buying the produce of the peasants and selling them such manufactured goods as the village craftsmen could not produce. Economically their range of influence was limited, and when cities governed extensive territories, the villages in the outlying areas had their own local industries and fairs.

The density of cities varied very greatly in different parts of the empire. In the two dioceses of Gaul, from the Pyrenees to the Rhine, there were 122 cities (including the eight *castra*) and in Britain there were only twenty-eight; they had extensive territories, but were for the most part small towns. In the African diocese, on the other hand, there were round about 650 cities, the vast majority little country towns with quite small territories. In the northern Balkans, the dioceses of Dacia and Thrace, there were only seventy-five cities, mostly along the Danube and in the area adjacent to Constantinople. In the much smaller area of the Macedonian diocese, which included Greece and Crete, there were about 170. In Asia Minor there was a similar contrast between Asiana, the west and south, which had about 330 cities, and

Pontica, the north and east, which was divided into only about seventy, most of which ruled very extensive territories. In Oriens some cities like Antioch, Apamea and Cyrrhus ruled territories forty miles across, while in Arabia the cities were only four or five miles apart.

Despite their very diverse origins, the cities of the empire had during three centuries or more of Roman rule acquired a basic uniformity of political structure. In the west, where large numbers of cities had been converted into colonies or *municipia* of Roman or Latin status before the Constitutio Antoniniana, the standard Roman pattern, with two *duoviri* as supreme magistrates, two aediles to look after the market, the streets, the drains and other municipal services, and two quaestors or treasurers, and a council of 100 decurions, was very common. In the east, where most of the cities had preserved their Greek constitutions, there was a greater diversity; the magistrates' functions were often differently allocated and their titles various, and the council was normally much larger—600 was the standard figure in Syria.

Beneath this superficial diversity, however, there was a basic uniformity. The Roman government had never favoured democracy, and had everywhere enacted that magistrates and councillors must be chosen on a property qualification, and that the council must be a permanent body, whose members sat for life, unless they forfeited their places by bankruptcy or for serious offences. The popular assembly played a very small role. In cities of the Roman model its sole function was to elect the annual magistrates, who became members of the council, and to affirm by acclamation grants of honours made by the council. In the east also the assembly, though it elected magistrates and passed decrees, lost all initiative, since motions had to receive the prior sanction of the council.

During the second and early third centuries, the system of civic government underwent a gradual but profound revolution. Magistracies and membership of the council had always been expensive. In the west it was normal to exact regular fees from those who were elected, and in the east it became customary for them to make a donation to the city. The cities, moreover, had meagre revenues, and magistrates were expected to contribute to the expenses of their departments. In the prosperous days of the early principate there was great emulation between cities to improve their amenities, in particular to adorn themselves with more splendid buildings and to celebrate more magnificent games, and there was strong rivalry between the local notables to win popular favour and thus secure election to office by contributing liberally to new projects. The final result was that so high a standard of expenditure was set for magistrates and councillors that only the wealth-iest citizens could compete, and they began to regard office as a burden and to evade it. It thus came to be difficult to find sufficient candidates for office and the whole system of local government threatened to break down.

To the imperial government it was essential that the city governments should continue to function, for not only did they provide all the amenities of urban life, they also did much of the basic work of the imperial administration. It was officers elected by the city councils that collected the tribute, levied recruits when conscription was enforced, built the roads and maintained the posting stations, and organized com-pulsory purchases of supplies for the army. The imperial government tried to curb civic expenditure, but without much effect, and eventually enforced the rule that qualified candidates duly nominated were obliged to hold office. This meant in effect that the council nominated the magistrates and filled vacancies in its own number. It also meant that the council became *de iure* what it had long been *de facto*, a mainly hereditary body, filled by members of the richest families in the city, occasionally supplemented by men of recently acquired wealth. This situation seems to have become fairly general by the early third century.

The cities gradually acquired a number of new magistrates in addi-tion to their original group. In the early second century the imperial government in its efforts to enforce economy began to appoint special commissioners (*curatores civitatis*) to reorganize the internal finances of individual cities. These *curatores* became regular and universal, and eventually came to be elected by the city councils. They still received imperial letters of appointment in Constantine's reign, but by the sixth century this formality had been dropped in the east; it still survived in the Ostrogothic kingdom.

Diocletian appears to have appointed an *exactor civitatis* for each city to organize the collection of the imperial revenue. This office underwent a similar evolution to that of *curator*, becoming elective in the latter part of the fourth century. There was here a special reason; the council was corporately responsible for the financial default of magistrates elected by itself but not for imperial nominees. Diocletian seems also to have instituted *praepositi pagorum*, who controlled the several rural districts (*pagi*) into which the city territories were divided. Valentinian and Valens made universal the *defensor civitatis* to protect the poor and pro-vide them with inexpensive justice. The *defensores* were originally nominated by the praetorian prefects and still in the sixth century received their official letters of appointment from them (in Ostrogothic Italy from the crown) but were by a law of 387 elected by the city council.

By the early fourth century the popular assembly had virtually ceased to exist. In the little cities of Africa the people still in Constantine's reign formally elected the council's nominees, and acclaimed honorific decrees, and we possess the minutes of an assembly of an Egyptian city held under the tetrarchy. The proceedings consist for the most part of loyal acclamation to the emperors, the provincial governor and the *rationalis*, but the people also vociferously demand the appointment to some office of the chairman of the city council, irregularly it would seem, since the matter is referred back to the council. Regular meetings of the assembly later lapsed, but the provincial governor would occasionally read imperial communications to the people assembled in the theatre for the games, and transact other public business before them. On such occasions acclamations were regularly shouted, and grievances could be similarly voiced: minutes of the proceedings were recorded and forwarded to the emperors. Constantine regarded such demonstrations as useful evidence for the conduct of his governors, but Libanius frequently warns *comites Orientis* and consulars of Syria not to be swayed by them, since they were not spontaneous expressions of public opinion but engineered by the professional cheerleaders of the theatre.

Such demonstrations might culminate in riots. We have in the popular chronicles many descriptions of riots, most in Rome and Constantinople but some in other large cities such as Antioch and Alexandria. One, at Antioch in 387, was provoked by the announcement of a special tax levy, several by bread shortages, more by religious controversies, but most by the rivalries of the circus factions.

The council was the effective governing body of the city. One of its principal tasks was to elect the magistrates and the numerous officers required by the imperial government to collect and deliver the levies of clothing and foodstuffs, exact money taxes, levy recruits from the landowners and villages, manage the post stations, mines and imperial estates. Elections were normally held once a year, on or before 1 March, three months before the magistrates entered on office; this allowed time for appeals to be heard and supplementary elections held if the nominees appealed successfully. A quorum of two-thirds was required for the election meeting. There was rarely, if ever, a contest, and the difficulty was to persuade or bully nominees into accepting office. We possess the

full minutes of a council meeting held in Oxyrhynchus in 370,[1] and an
extract will give some idea of the proceedings:

> After the acclamations, Theon, son of Ammonius, decurion, acting
> through his son Macrobius, came forward and made the following
> statement. 'You know, fellow decurions, that I am on the list due to
> come into force and am among the twenty-four persons ordained by
> his excellency Tatian (the prefect of Egypt) for the posts of *praepositus
> pagi* and *conductor*; the president has, perhaps by inadvertence,
> appointed me to the supervision of military woollen clothing for the
> 14th indiction, and this though I am providing horses for the games.
> For this reason I claim before you that the ordinances ought not to be
> infringed.' Ptolemianus, former curator, said: 'The ordinances laid
> down by his excellency Tatian with the concurrence of the whole
> council must remain undisturbed, so that the twenty-four do not
> serve any other charge whatever, but stick to the heaviest charges, not
> only in this presidency, but under future presidents, and if anyone
> wishes to serve another charge, he does not do so on the responsibility
> of the council. Macrobius ought not to be troubled.'

Nine other speeches follow all to the same effect and the president
bows to the unanimous protest of his colleagues:

> Your collective and individual pronouncements are duly recorded in
> the minutes: Macrobius will not be troubled about the supervision of
> military woollen clothing for the 14th indiction.

Only ten decurions participate in this debate, and it is probable that
they were the *principales*, or *decemprimi*, who formed an inner committee
of the council. By a law of 415 they were to be elected by the council and
to serve fifteen years before they were allowed to retire.

The qualifications for membership of the council were free birth
(freedmen were still debarred in Justinian's code), origin or domicile in
the city, and property. The amount of the property qualification must
have varied widely in different cities: there were far richer men in Carthage or Antioch than in the little cities of Africa or Arabia, and a
decurion had to shoulder far greater expenses in a big town than in a
small. A constitution of Constantius II, enacting that no one who
owned over 25 *iugera* of land should be exempted, must have laid down a
minimum for some tiny Arabian city, which was no more than a glorified
village—it was issued in response to a question from the *comes Orientis*;

[1] *Pap. Oxy.* 2110.

for 25 *iugera* (15 acres) is no more than a peasant's holding. A constitution of Valentinian III, which allows any citizen or resident whose
property exceeds 300 *solidi* in value to be enrolled, was of more general
application. The property almost invariably took the form of land. This
was partly because land was the only safe security, but more because
land was the most important form of wealth, and not many merchants
were financially qualified to serve except in a few cities such as Alexandria. Elsewhere merchants and manufacturers, whose wealth lay in
slaves, were only exceptionally enrolled.

Under the principate certain categories of persons had been excused
from holding office in their cities. These comprised senators, who were
deemed to be domiciled at Rome; persons engaged on the service of the
state, which included equestrian officials, and by extension all members
of the equestrian order, civil servants and soldiers; veterans; doctors and
professors; shippers engaged in the state service; tax farmers and lessees
of state lands. Constantine added the Christian clergy.

Decurions and their sons, and others who feared to be enrolled, made
persistent efforts to exploit one or other of these channels of escape
according to their wealth and station, and the government strove as
persistently to curb their exodus. The humblest decurions joined the
army or the provincial offices, those of middle status got themselves
enrolled as *protectores*, got commissions in the army, or secured posts in
the palatine ministries or in the praetorian prefectures. Diocletian forbade military service to decurions and Constantine and Constantius II
debarred them from the civil service. These rules were often repeated
but laxly enforced. Little effort was made to verify the antecedents of
applicants, but periodical purges of the army and the civil service were
held; in these purges decurions who had already served varying terms,
five, ten, fifteen, twenty, twenty-five or thirty years, were allowed to
remain.

The church attracted so many decurions that Constantius had to
limit the number of the clergy and to rule that no person of curial
family or property qualification should be ordained; 'for the rich ought
to undertake the responsibilities of this world, the poor be supported by
the wealth of the churches'. His sons introduced a more equitable rule
whereby curial ordinands had to surrender their property to their sons
or other relations, who would replace them on the council, or to the
council itself; they were allowed to retain a third if they had no sons.
Later emperors relaxed or reinforced this rule and frequently condoned
its breach in the past. Justinian enacted a severer rule that the son of a

decurion might be ordained only if before reaching man's estate he had entered a monstery and had been a monk for fifteen years.

The cream of the curial order sought to evade their duties by entry into the equestrian order, the *comitiva* and the senate. Here the imperial government rarely imposed any absolute ban, for it needed men of education and standing to fill the offices of state, and such men were chiefly to be found in the curial order. Down to the middle of the fourth century most offices carried equestrian rank or the *comitiva*, and the main battle raged over these. Since neither rank was hereditary, the problem was in principle simple. The government insisted that applicants for office must hold their civic magistracies first, and that only actual tenure of an office gave immunity and not titular offices or honorary codicils of rank, which were often obtained by corrupt means.

From the time of Constantine, and more rapidly from that of his sons, an increasing number of posts came to carry senatorial rank, and the senate of Rome and the new senate of Constantinople expanded from hundreds to thousands. Many, probably the great majority, of the new senators were ambitious decurions, and the loss to the cities was all the more serious because senatorial rank was hereditary. The situation had evidently become serious by 361, when Constantius II expelled all senators of curial origin from the senate and forbade their admission for the future. Valens and Valentinian relaxed this rule, which would have debarred many candidates from the service of the state. A decurion might be admitted to the senate, and thereby earn immunity from the *curia*, provided that he had filled a post carrying senatorial rank, and not merely secured honorary codicils, and provided that he left a son in his native city to be a decurion, leaving him a reasonable share of his property. A new rule was, moreover, laid down, that not all sons of a senator, but only those born after his admission, inherited his rank.

In the west this appears to have remained the law. In the east Theodosius I in 386 enacted a stricter rule whereby senators of curial origin remained with all their descendants liable to their civic charges. This rule proved difficult to enforce, as decurions, claiming that their senatorial expenses exhausted their resources, failed to fulfil their curial duties, and from time to time decurions were accordingly forbidden to enter the senate. These laws, however, were not enforced, and in 436 the eastern government compromised. Decurions who became *clarissimi* or *spectabiles* had to perform their civic duties in person and those who became honorary *illustres* might perform them by deputy; those who received illustrious offices were released together with their children born after their promotion. Zeno tightened the rule, granting immunity only to those who held the highest illustrious offices, the praetorian prefecture, the urban prefecture and the mastership of the soldiers.

Decurions also disappeared from the city councils if they lost their property. This might happen in various ways. Some of the humbler sort found their civic charges too heavy for them, and went bankrupt; but this seems to have been a rare event. Others sold their property and with the proceeds bought an office; Libanius tells of one who sold his ancestral estates, but later bought them back and as much again from the profits of his offices. Others were intimidated into selling by powerful neighbours, either members of the imperial aristocracy or their own richer colleagues, the *principales*. It was mainly to check the last abuse that the government in 386 enacted that no decurion might sell his real estate without the authorization of the provincial governor, and should have to prove reasonable cause, such as repayment of debts. Some decurions refrained from marriage, and thus enabled themselves to leave their property to relatives or friends or patrons immune from curial duties; for bastards could not inherit. The imperial government endeavoured to combat this abuse in two ways, by enacting that the city council could claim a quarter of any curial estate left to an outsider, and by enabling a decurion to legitimize a bastard son and bequeath his property to him provided that he enrolled him on the council. These two measures were later consolidated and tightened up. Under Justinian a decurion was obliged to leave at least three-quarters of his estate either to his legitimate sons or to his bastards (provided that they became decurions), or to his sons-in-law (on the same provision), or to a fellow decurion, or in the last resort to the council corporately. Later Justinian simplified the position by allowing decurions to bequeath their estates to anyone, provided that the heir took up testator's curial duties. Curial duties thus ultimately became a servitude on certain lands.

Outsiders were of course from time to time enrolled on the city councils to fill up vacancies. The laws of Diocletian and Constantine regard this as normal, forbidding not only decurions and their sons but financially qualified commoners to join the army or the civil service or to take holy orders. Later laws, however, confine their prohibitions to hereditary decurions and suggest that elections of outsiders were rare. A number of fourth-century laws enacted that sons of veterans, if they did not join the army, should be enrolled in their local council—their fathers' allotments would presumably qualify them. Cashiered officials were also sometimes enrolled by provincial governors, and by a law of

410 unfrocked clergy, if of sufficient means. There were also a number of general laws ordering the councils to elect all qualified commoners, by Julian in 362, by Theodosius I in 393, for the east; by Honorius in 415 and by Valentinian III in 439 for the west. These laws rather suggest that by the beginning of the fifth century at any rate the cities were scraping the bottom of the barrel, and that nearly all landowners either were already decurions or belonged to the immune classes. There were no doubt a few humble social climbers who sought to raise their status by getting on to a city council—we hear of a slave of the Roman church who at the end of Justinian's reign illegally became a decurion—but they must have been rare.

Continuous losses, particularly of the richer decurions, and meagre accessions, resulted in the situation which Justinian described in 536; 'if one counts the city councils of our empire one will find them very small, some well off neither in numbers nor in wealth, some perhaps with a few men but none with any wealth'.[1] The result was that the councils lost their initiative in civic affairs, and that the provincial governors tended more and more to usurp their functions, particularly in the sphere of public works. The council ceased to be representative of the local landed gentry, who had mostly become immune, and the imperial government recognized the new situation. The decline was probably more marked in the west, where Honorius in 409 enacted that the *defensor civitatis* should be elected by the bishop and clergy and the landowners, besides the decurions. In the east the change came a century later under Anastasius, who also enacted that the city corn buyer and apparently the *curator* should be elected by the bishop, clergy and landowners; the decurions are not mentioned in these laws. He further-more appointed an imperial commissioner, a *vindex*, for each city to control the collection of the taxes, and also it would seem civic finance.

The councils seem after this date to have ceased to function in the east. John Lydus,[2] who was born in 490, wrote in the 550s: 'I myself remember that this custom (the wearing of the toga) used to prevail in the provinces too when the councils used to administer the cities'; and Evagrius, writing at the end of the sixth century, states that 'in the old days the notables were enrolled on the registers of the cities, and each city had a council like a kind of senate'. In the west the city councils continued to hold at least formal sessions down to the early seventh century or even later. One of their functions was to prove wills, register conveyances of land, and confirm the appointment of guardians. We

[1] Justinian, *Novel* 38, proem.   [2] *de Magistratibus*, I. 28.

possess contemporary records of their proceedings, which a few *principales* attended, under the presidency of the two chief magistrates.

The revenues of the cities were derived from three main sources, the rents of land and house property which had been given or bequeathed to them, sundry minor tolls, such as market dues and the *octroi* levied at the city gates, or customs at the port if any, and the contributions of the magistrates and decurions; it was also possible to levy a local rate for special purposes. The civic taxes were apparently confiscated by Constantine and the civic lands by Constantius II. Both were restored by Julian and again confiscated by Valentinian and Valens, who however later gave back one-third to the cities. In 401 urban sites and buildings, including temples, were restored to the cities, and they gradually acquired new endowments from bequests and from the estates of decurions who died intestate without heirs, or absconded without trace, or took holy orders; they also after 428 received a quarter of any curial estate left to an outsider and after 535 three-quarters of such estates. Some cities had by the sixth century built up from legacies capital funds, which they lent at interest.

The amount of the revenue deriving from rents and taxes varied greatly from city to city. A great port like Alexandria drew a considerable income from customs, while inland towns cannot have got much from their *octroi*. Some cities owned large estates, others very little. The burden thrown on the decurions thus differed from place to place. The confiscations by the imperial government initially paralysed the cities, so that they could not even make essential repairs to their walls and public buildings, and threw a heavy burden on the decurions. Gradually, however, as endowments were again accumulated and expenditure was cut down, the situation improved, and by Justinian's time most outgoings seem to have been covered by rents, interest on accumulated capital, and what survived of the civic taxes.

The services which cities provided for their inhabitants also varied greatly. Even under the principate a tiny city like Panopeus in the mountains of northern Greece possessed 'no municipal offices, no gymnasium, no theatre, no market, no water laid on to a fountain', while Antioch in the fourth century boasted of its eighteen public baths and its street lighting.

Most if not all cities had a police force of sorts. In the east (where alone we have adequate information) there were nightwatchmen for the towns under the commander of the night watch; we possess a list of the sixty men who served in Oxyrhynchus in 295 with their beats. For the countryside there were the guardians of the peace (eirenarchs or in Egypt *riparii*) with their constables, who were armed with truncheons. The men were conscripted from the humbler classes, serving for a year, but were paid.

Any city of any pretensions maintained paved streets; the principal streets had wide sidewalks, often sheltered by colonnades. In Antioch and in some other great cities the streets were lit at night, the shop-keepers being compelled to maintain lamps in front of their premises. Most cities also maintained a drainage system and a public water supply, often carried by aqueducts from distant springs. All respectable cities had their public baths: the fuel for heating them was a heavy charge on the civic revenues, or on the pockets of the decurions put in charge of them.

The city councils were responsible for controlling prices, and in particular for ensuring an adequate supply of bread at a reasonable price. A few very great cities, Alexandria, Antioch and Carthage, enjoyed like the two capitals a free distribution of bread, but the number of ticketholders seems to have been more limited; in the case of Alexandria the corn was provided by a grant, initiated by Diocletian, from the imperial corn revenues. In general the city councils had no such resources. If there was a shortage and the price of bread rose, their first step was to fix a moderate price and to flog the bakers if they overcharged. If this failed—on one occasion the bakers of Antioch decamped *en masse* into the mountains—they raised a fund and elected a public corn buyer to import corn; some cities maintained standing corn funds.

One of the heaviest items in the cities' expenditure was the production of games—chariot races, mimes and wild beast hunts. They were regular and magnificent in the larger cities, and were celebrated even in modest towns—we hear of a wild beast hunt, an expensive form of entertainment, at the modest Syrian city of Beroea. Games were sometimes endowed and occasionally subsidized by the imperial government, but the main burden fell on the decurions. Their production was one of the heaviest, but the least unpopular, of the curial charges. The large cities also maintained salaried doctors and professors of rhetoric and literature.

The greatest burden on the civic budgets was public works. They had to repair their walls, which had often been neglected in the peaceful days of the principate, but were now necessary even in the interior of the empire; they often had to rebuild them on a smaller scale, since the old circuits were extravagantly large and impossible to man. The cities were in general too lavishly equipped with magnificent public buildings erected in the palmy days of the principate, and their maintenance was an exacting burden. Temples, it is true, could be abandoned and used as quarries, but some effort had to be made to maintain aqueducts, baths, theatres, and the street colonnades. The labour for public works was supplied by *corvées* of the townsmen, and much of the material by demolishing derelict buildings, especially temples, but some materials had to be bought, and some skilled craftsmen, such as mosaicists and painters, had to be paid. Many cities failed to cope with the task. When Theodosius II visited Heraclea in 443, the citizens petitioned him for imperial aid in repairing 'both their walls and their aqueduct, and also their other public buildings which had been long neglected', and many emperors, notably Anastasius and Justinian, spent large sums in restoring ruined cities.

In the western provinces there are signs that the cities were sinking into economic decline by the end of the fourth century. From 395 onwards a series of laws were issued to the praetorian prefects of Italy and Gaul, enacting that members of the city guilds, together with their children, should be brought back to the cities which they had abandoned. Some had taken orders or joined the army or the civil service, but the majority had migrated to the country and taken up agricultural work. The decline was probably mainly confined to the smaller towns—great cities like Arles or Milan seem still to have been prosperous—and may be attributed to social change. In the principate and still in the fourth century there was in each city a substantial group of well-to-do decurions who resided (and were obliged by law to reside) in town, and provided a market for the local shopkeepers and craftsmen. Gradually the richest became senators, and migrated to the great cities or to their country villas, and only a rump of impoverished decurions was left, together with the bishop and his clergy, to give employment in the town.

In the east no such laws were issued and the archaeological evidence suggests that the cities were still fairly prosperous in the sixth century. The reason probably was that landed property was more evenly distributed in the eastern provinces, and that there was thus a larger class of medium landowners; and that the habit of urban life was more deeply rooted, so that even when they had attained immunity from curial service, these medium landlords continued to live in their towns.

The picture of urban life in the codes and the majority of the literary sources is rather depressing. The *principales* oppressed the lesser decurions, forcing them to sell their lands and allocating the most unpleasant tasks to them, while they pocketed the perquisites, assigning to themselves the leases of the civic estates. The other decurions oppressed the urban workers and peasantry. 'What cities are there', Salvian rhetorically asked, 'in which the *curiales* are not so many tyrants?' [1] 'It would not be right', Justinian declared, 'for a *cohortalis* or a *curialis*, bred in harsh exactions and the sins that are likely to ensue therefrom, at one moment to carry out the cruellest acts and the next to be ordained a priest and preach about loving kindness and contempt for wealth.' [2] At the same time they allowed the magnificent buildings with which their predecessors had adorned their cities to fall into squalid disrepair. The spirit of local patriotism which had been so vigorous under the principate seems to have died, and the local gentry thought only of how to evade their traditional responsibilities.

This picture is unduly gloomy. The letters of Libanius show that the wealthy decurions of Antioch still in the late fourth century spent lavishly on producing games, and Ambrose had to argue that such ostentatious expenditure had no moral value. Even in the fifth century there were members of the imperial aristocracy who were willing to hold expensive magistracies in their native cities, provided that such generosity did not involve their becoming decurions—and their sons after them—and thus liable to all the tedious tasks which the state imposed on the city councils.

[1] Salvian, *de Gubernatione Dei*, v. 18 or 27.   [2] *Cod. Just.* I. iii, 52 §1.

XIX

The Church

Long before Constantine was converted the Christian churches had evolved their basic organization. At the head of each community, or church, was a bishop, whose powers were autocratic. He chose and ordained the priests and deacons who assisted him; he admitted new members to the community by baptism and expelled by excommunication those who broke its rules; he gave letters of introduction to members of his flock who migrated elsewhere; and he had absolute control over finance. Bishops were elected by their clergy and the general body of the faithful, but had to be consecrated by another bishop, or preferably by several neighbouring bishops. They ruled for life, unless the neighbouring bishops condemned and deposed them for serious offences.

The area ruled by a bishop was normally a city (with its territory); it was not only the governmental but the natural social unit in most cases. There may have been a time when bishops ruled groups of cities, but by the early fourth century this practice was rare. By ancient custom the bishop of Alexandria included under his care the little neighbouring city of Mareotes, which was actually a rural district with no town. By ancient custom also the bishop of Tomi ruled all the fifteen cities of Scythia, and in Europa the bishops of the principal cities each ruled two or three smaller neighbours. It would appear that in Spain it was normal for a bishop to govern several municipalities. On the other hand towns or villages within a city territory sometimes acquired the right to have their own bishop; such village bishoprics were common in Cyprus and in Cyrenaica. Units of government which were not cities, the *regiones*, *saltus* and *tractus*, and the independent villages, often had their own

BIBLIOGRAPHY. The best account of the institutions of the early church is still Joseph Bingham, *The antiquities of the Christian Church* (London, 1726). See also Chapter XXII of my *Later Roman Empire* (Oxford, 1964).

The principal primary sources are the letters of the popes, the canons and acts of the councils, *Cod. Theod.* XVI and *Cod. Just.* I. i–xiii.

252

bishops, but were sometimes attached to a neighbouring city; the *regiones* of Bithynia were under Nicaea, and those of Cappadocia under Caesarea.

Bishoprics tended to become more numerous as time went on. This was often due to the growth of new centres of population, which acquired bishops, but more often to sectarian rivalries; in Africa Catholics and Donatists staked their claims by appointing rival bishops not only to every little African city, but to many large estates as well. On the whole bishoprics tended to conform more closely to cities; the Council of Chalcedon ruled that when the emperors founded a new city, the church must found a new bishopric for it, and Zeno enacted that every city—with a few named exceptions—must have its own bishop. This rule was not exactly enforced, and there remained bishoprics which were not cities.

Bishoprics varied very greatly in size from Rome and Constantinople, with populations approaching three-quarters of a million to villages with a thousand or so inhabitants. There was a rule laid down by the Council of Nicaea, and on the whole strictly observed, that a bishop once consecrated must never migrate to another see. This prohibition of promotion had unfortunate results. An able man like Gregory of Nazianzus, who accepted a small see, was inhibited from using his talents in a wider field, and the great sees, which came to control wide areas, had to be filled from men with no episcopal experience.

The larger bishoprics had already by the beginning of the fourth century begun to develop a parochial organization. At Alexandria there were before the council of Nicaea a number of city churches, each with its own permanent priest, and soon after Nicaea we hear of village churches in Mareotes, each again with its priest. The parochial churches fell into two classes. Some, usually in the town, technically known in the west as *tituli*, were closely affiliated to the bishop's church, being served by the same group of clergy, the *canonici* or *cardinales* who served the cathedral, and being financed from central funds. Others, known as *dioceses* or *parochiae*, were independent, supported by their own endowments and served by their own clergy: most rural churches fell into this category. As time went on the towns acquired more churches—by the sixth century a modest provincial city like Gerasa had ten—and most villages and many large estates had their own churches, the latter usually built and endowed by the landlord.

The churches had from the beginning devoted much of their resources to charity, and from the fourth century onwards established

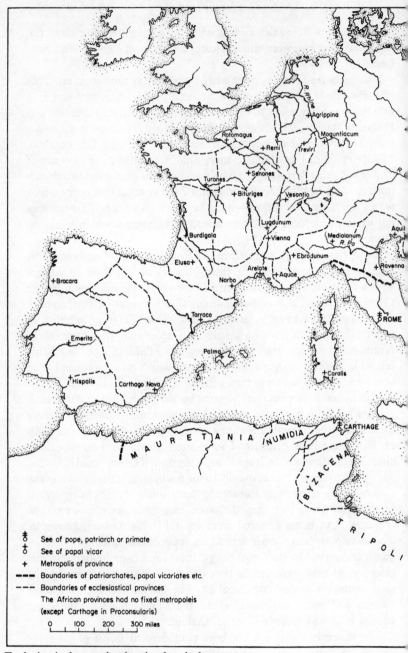

Ecclesiastical organization in the sixth century

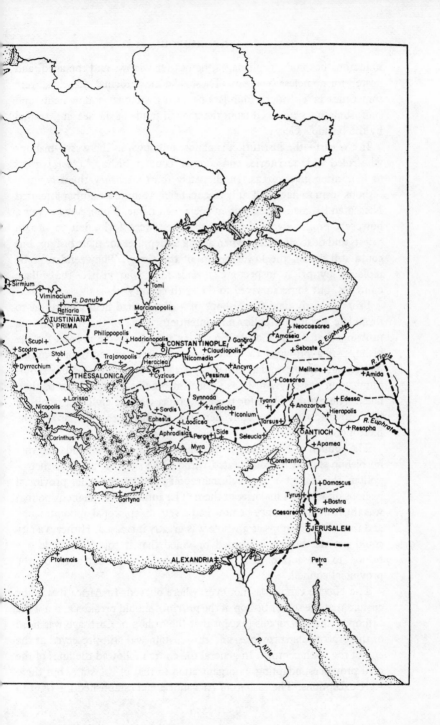

numerous hospitals, orphanages, homes for widows and the aged, and hostels for homeless strangers. These, like the parochial churches, were sometimes independent foundations with their own endowments and staff, sometimes financed from the general funds of the see and staffed by the bishop's clergy.

In the east—the institution is almost unknown in the west—bishops who ruled wide territories consecrated 'country bishops' (*chorepiscopi*) to look after given areas. In the early fourth century these country bishops seem to have had full episcopal rights; quite a number attended Nicaea and signed its canons in their own name. Their powers were, however, progressively diminished. They were forbidden to ordain priests and deacons except when acting as deputies for their bishop, but could still ordain the lower orders of the clergy. They tended to be replaced by priest inspectors (*periodeutae*), who visited the village churches, but some survived to the sixth century.

From an early date the bishops of a district had held congresses to formulate a common policy on contentious issues of the day, and it is probable that before Constantine's day it had become normal for the bishops of a province to meet twice a year to review more routine matters and in particular to hear appeals against sentences of excommunication passed by bishops against members of their clergy or their flock. The natural place for these meetings was the civil metropolis of the province, and the convener was normally the bishop of the metropolis.

The council of Nicaea made this custom a rule, and also enacted that no bishop should be consecrated without the agreement of the metropolitan, the bishop of the civil metropolis, and of the other provincial bishops or at least a majority of them. The authority of the metropolitan was thus enhanced, since he now had a veto on episcopal appointments, and that of the bishops as a whole was greatly increased. Hitherto a city could get the bishop it wanted provided that it could persuade one bishop to consecrate him; now their choice was controlled by the provincial council.

The Nicene canon was not everywhere obeyed. In Africa it was the custom that the senior bishop of the province should preside, and not the bishop of the metropolis (except that the bishop of Carthage was head of the proconsular province) and this custom was still preserved at the end of the sixth century. In general the church followed the lines of the civil provinces, adapting its organization to that of the state, but there were exceptions. The bishop of Alexandria had established his right to consecrate all bishops in the old province of Egypt, and he retained it even when it was divided into several provinces by Diocletian; similarly the bishop of Rome had by custom the right of consecrating all bishops in Italy south of the Apennines and in Sicily, and continued to do so, ignoring the new provinces. Elsewhere two important cities sometimes disputed the primacy of a province, and ultimately partitioned it. Thus Arles in the late fourth century resented subordination to the lesser city of Vienne, which was the civil metropolis, and eventually Pope Leo compromised the dispute by dividing the province. Similarly Pamphylia was divided between Side, the real metropolis, and Perge, which also had the title of metropolis in the civil sphere. Efforts by other honorary metropoleis, Berytus and Nicaea, to carve out ecclesiastical provinces for themselves were not successful.

The growth of any organization higher than the province was slow and irregular. The Council of Nicaea recognized certain old established primacies. It reaffirmed the ancient custom whereby the bishop of Alexandria ruled the cities of Egypt and Pentapolis; the inclusion of Pentapolis, which had always been a separate province, was not perhaps very ancient, for Pentapolis continued to have its own metropolitan, who, however, could consecrate his provincial bishops only by licence of the bishop of Alexandria. The council also confirmed the jurisdiction of Rome over the Suburbicarian provinces and in general terms the primacy of Antioch in the diocese of Oriens. The rule of the bishop of Antioch was indirect, for all the provinces had their metropolitans who consecrated their provincial bishops, but the bishop of Antioch consecrated the metropolitans. This at any rate was the later rule, but how old it was it is hard to say. In the early fifth century the bishop of Antioch was still trying to assert his right to consecrate the metropolitan of Cyprus, but the bishops of that province stoutly maintained that by ancient custom they consecrated him themselves, and at the Council of Ephesus in 431 they won their point.

In the west the bishop of Carthage had long enjoyed a vaguely defined but very real primacy in all the African provinces, summoning councils of bishops from the whole area. Here there was no question of consecrating metropolitans, as there were none, the chairmanship of the provincial councils going by seniority. In the east the bishop of Ephesus had some kind of primacy over the diocese of Asiana, but it does not seem to have carried any definite rights.

Elsewhere there was no organization above the province. The bishops of Rome had indeed long claimed, as successors of Peter, the prince of the apostles, the right to dictate on matters of doctrine to all the churches, and to receive and judge appeals from them. The popes were generally accorded a primacy of honour throughout the empire, but more, it would seem, as bishops of the capital than as Peter's successors; eastern bishops sometimes pointed out that Peter had been bishop of Antioch before he went to Rome. But there was no general acknowledgment of the pope's claim to decide on doctrinal issues and to take appeals. Defeated bishops, like Athanasius and Marcellus, naturally appealed to the pope against local councils, but the councils as naturally refused to accept the popes' verdicts. The Council of Sardica in 342-3 passed two canons conferring appellate jurisdiction on the bishop of Rome, and in 378 Gratian, in response to a Roman council, ordered his praetorian prefects, vicars and governors to enforce papal jurisdiction. The imperial constitution did not affect the east and became a dead letter in the west—it was not included in the Theodosian Code—and the canons of Sardica were not received in the east and were forgotten in the west. Pope Zosimus (417-18), thinking that they were canons of Nicaea, tried to act on them in Africa, but the African bishops successfully proved that they were not Nicene and refused obedience.

The council of Constantinople in 381 did not advance matters, merely enacting that the bishops of each (civil) diocese ought to manage their own affairs and not interfere in other dioceses, but leaving it uncertain what see was to take the lead, except in Egypt and Oriens. It also gave Constantinople, the new Rome, a vague honorary primacy, second only to the old Rome.

The churches had from an early date relied on councils of bishops to settle controversial issues, but here again no rules were worked out as to their convocation or jurisdiction above the provincial level, except that the greater sees had acquired the prescriptive right of convening councils from wider areas, Rome from Italy, Carthage from all the African provinces, Antioch from Syria in the widest sense, including Cilicia, Mesopotamia and Palestine, and Alexandria from Egypt. The rulings of these councils were generally accepted as binding on the areas concerned, but any attempt to convene councils representative of a larger area depended on the prestige and initiative of the convening bishop, and their decisions were normally disputed.

The lack of any kind of system is strikingly demonstrated by the conflict between Theophilus of Alexandria and John of Constantinople. Each was preferring charges against the other, and Theophilus summoned John before a council of thirty-six Egyptian bishops whom he had brought with him to Constantinople, while John summoned Theophilus before a council of forty bishops, including seven metropolitans, which he had convoked. John claimed that his council should have greater authority, as being more numerous and more distinguished, but Theophilus won the day by getting the emperor's support for his council.

Constantine was the first to summon a general council of the whole church, and he established the precedent that only an emperor could do so. This was inevitable, as only he had the authority to convene all bishops and to enforce their decrees. Constantine and his successors also frequently called smaller councils to settle disputes, selecting the bishops who were to attend, laying down the agenda, and often appointing a lay commissioner to preside. These councils rarely achieved their object, as the parties who were condemned declared that they were packed against them.

Pope Siricius (385–99), anxious no doubt lest the dioceses of Dacia and Macedonia, recently transferred to the eastern emperor, should slip out of his sphere of influence into that of the New Rome, appointed the bishop of Thessalonica his vicar, and authorized him to consecrate all metropolitans in the area and to control and confirm all episcopal elections. The popes certainly possessed no such powers in Illyricum, and there is no evidence that the bishops of Thessalonica had hitherto enjoyed any canonical authority, though they no doubt held some vague primacy in the area; but the new arrangement suited both parties, and the other metropolitans submitted quietly. The vicariate of Thessalonica became a standing institution, and kept Illyricum in the papal sphere; Theodosius II in 421 ordered that in accordance with 'antiquity and the ancient canons of the church' the bishop of Constantinople, 'which rejoices in the prerogatives of the old Rome', should judge all ecclesiastical disputes in Illyricum, but yielded to the protests of Honorius.

Pope Zosimus tried to establish a similar vicariate for Arles over the three provinces of Viennensis and the two Narbonenses. Here, however, the three metropolitans stoutly resisted the claims of the upstart city of Arles, and Pope Leo formally abandoned the experiment. Henceforth the popes occasionally appointed prominent metropolitans in Gaul and Spain as their vicars, but these posts were apparently personal and carried very modest powers, to report abuses and quarrels and issue letters of introduction to clerics who wished to visit Rome.

Nevertheless papal influence spread in the west. The popes made no further claims to control episcopal elections, directly or indirectly, but the metropolitans of northern Italy, Gaul and Spain not infrequently submitted their problems to their judgment, and the popes in response laid down the law on matters of doctrine and discipline. Only the African church under the leadership of Carthage jealously maintained its independence, until its power was broken by the Vandal invasion and persecutions.

In the east the rise of the New Rome was more spectacular. The see of Constantinople had neither apostolic foundation nor ancient custom on its side, and enjoyed no canonical rights except the primacy conferred by the council of 381. It had moreover a powerful and jealous rival in Alexandria, whose bishops had long been used to dictate to the east on doctrine. But Constantinople was the capital, and conferred on its bishop not only immense prestige but practical advantages. He could readily obtain imperial constitutions to back his claims, and from the many bishops who flocked to the capital to press their interests on the imperial government, he formed a more or less permanent 'visiting council' of changing membership, which could give him canonical sanction.

The churches of Thrace and Asia Minor came gradually to look to Constantinople for guidance and to submit their disputes to its bishop. The earliest instance of which we know is the accusation brought against Antoninus, bishop of Ephesus, by one of his bishops before John Chrysostom (398–404). After some hesitation John submitted the case to a visiting council, and sent down a commission of three bishops to investigate. Later, when Antoninus died, the bishops of Asia asked John to intervene, and he personally visited Ephesus, cleared up the scandals of the province and had a new bishop elected. Later we find John and his successors consecrating bishops to important cities like Nicaea, Philippopolis, Cyzicus and Caesarea of Cappadocia, sometimes on the request of the cities concerned, sometimes against their will by imperial authority.

The bishops of Alexandria viewed the growing prestige of Constantinople with jealous eyes and three times challenged and humbled their rivals. Theophilus' attack on John Chrysostom seems to have been motivated simply by power politics, and though it was successful eventually increased the prestige of Constantinople, since John enjoyed wide popular support and was after his death revered as a martyr, Cyril's attack on Nestorius was mainly a doctrinal controversy, and so was Dioscorus' attack on Flavian. Both won the day; it is perhaps significant that both councils in 431 and 449 were held at Ephesus, whose bishops strongly supported the Alexandrian interest, no doubt resentful at Constantinople's interference in Asiana. Dioscorus' attack was a boomerang, for in 451 Marcian decided to hold another council at Chalcedon to reverse the verdict of the second Council of Ephesus, and Dioscorus was deposed, and so also were the two rival bishops of Ephesus, where there had been a disputed election. There was thus no opposition, except for the papal delegates, who protested in vain at the advancement of the New Rome, when a canon was proposed giving the bishop of Constantinople the right of consecrating all metropolitans in the dioceses of Thrace, Asiana and Pontica.

The council also effected a compromise between Maximus, bishop of Antioch, and Juvenal, bishop of Jerusalem, who had been claiming extravagant powers for the mother church of Christendom; Juvenal received the three provinces of Palestine in settlement of his claims. The four eastern patriarchates, as they were henceforth called, were thus established, Constantinople, Alexandria, Antioch and Jerusalem. The only subsequent change in the structure of the church was effected by Justinian, who detached the diocese of Dacia (with the province of Macedonia II) from the vicariate of Illyricum and put it under the bishop of Justiniana Prima, his birthplace, which he had made into a city. Justinian ignored the rights of both the bishop of Thessalonica and the pope, but later acknowledged the latter by making the bishop of Justiniana Prima a papal vicar.

The churches had originally depended on the freewill offerings of their members (*oblationes*) for their financial support, and such offerings, often also called first fruits, continued to be an important source of revenue. Tithes, despite good biblical precedent, were not demanded. Some exceptionally pious persons gave a tithe of their income to the poor, but never to the church. A tithe for the church was first demanded in Merovingian Gaul by the second council of Macon in 585. Offerings were generally, it would seem, genuinely voluntary. Anastasius forbade the practice whereby some bishops, with their rural bishops and priest inspectors, used the threat of excommunication to compel the peasantry to pay them.

Before the great persecution of Diocletian some churches had also acquired, by what legal title is obscure, lands and house property from which they drew rents. Constantine expressly legalized bequests to the church, and himself set a magnificent example by giving to the churches of Rome estates whose rentals amounted to well over 400 pounds of gold per annum. Wealthy Christians, a growing class, followed suit, and so did the middle and lower classes, and it seems to have become a universal custom to leave something to the church in every will. We possess from the archives of Ravenna a large number of bequests, great and small, from wealthy landowners and merchants and from common soldiers and humble craftsmen. Even Flavius Pousi, a messenger in the provincial *officium* of Arcadia, who owned only his house, furniture and clothes, left half his house to the church, though he left a widow and another female dependent. Church lands were liable to the regular taxes, but exempt from superindictions and *sordida munera*. The churches also received regular subsidies in kind from Constantine's reign. They were abolished by Julian but restored by Jovian, who, however, reduced them to one-third of the original amount. They continued to be paid in the sixth century.

The wealth of the churches undoubtedly grew enormously, but we have few figures to measure its growth. John Chrysostom declared that the church of Antioch enjoyed in his day an income equal to that of one of the wealthier citizens, but not of the very richest. Augustine says that as bishop of Hippo he was twenty times as rich as his father, a poor decurion of the little African town of Tagaste. In the time of Pope Felix (528–30) the revenue of the see of Ravenna amounted to 12,000 *solidi* in rents alone, not counting offerings. John the Almoner, who became bishop of Alexandria in 611, found 8,000 pounds of gold in the episcopal treasury. Justinian, in fixing a sliding scale of consecration fees divided bishoprics into seven classes; the five patriarchates, those whose income exceeded 30 pounds of gold, those between 30 and 10 pounds, 10 and 5 pounds, 5 and 3 pounds, 3 or 2 pounds and under 2 pounds; the last were regarded as very poor and paid no consecration fees. These figures probably represent bishops' stipends; if so, they should be multiplied by three or four to obtain the revenue of the sees. They certainly do not include offerings or the endowments of independent parishes and charitable institutions.

A rough index to the growth of the wealth of the church is afforded by the rise of simony and other corrupt practices. There had always been isolated cases of simony, and the motive was not always pecuniary gain, but ambition or the desire to evade curial duties or military service. The first wholesale denunciation of simony comes from a Roman council probably held under Pope Siricius (385–99). The abuse was condemned in 451 at Chalcedon and by a council held at Arles at about the same date. The first imperial law on the subject followed in 469. A number of gratuities became hallowed by custom and were regulated and sanctioned. Bishops in the sixth century paid substantial fees to their consecrators, and the lower clergy might surrender up to a year's income to the bishop who ordained them, but were forbidden to pay gratuities (*insinuativa*) to their future colleagues when promoted.

Another growing abuse was the alienation of church lands. This was partly a by-product of simony, candidates for bishoprics, notably for the papacy, promising church property to their supporters if elected. It was also due to the natural desire of bishops to provide for their families and oblige their friends, and to the insatiable land hunger of the rich, who bullied bishops into surrendering to them perpetual leases on favourable terms. There was also some confusion between the property of a bishop, especially what he acquired during his episcopate, and the property of his church. Ultimately the severe rule prevailed that anything given or left to a bishop, except by his near relations, after his consecration was deemed to belong to his church.

The first imperial law against the alienation of church property was issued by Leo in 470. It applied only to the church of Constantinople and banned all sales, gifts or exchanges. It however allowed the church to cede the usufruct of an estate for a term of years, or for life, provided that the grantee on returning it added another estate of equal value. Anastasius extended the law to the whole patriarchate of Constantinople, but relaxed it by allowing sales or mortgages to pay debts, execute urgent repairs, or buy more valuable land. Justinian extended the ban on alienation to the whole empire, and also regulated long leases, which were not to exceed twenty years or three lives. He originally revoked Anastasius' concessions, but later had to allow the sale of land to pay debts, especially arrears of tax. He also allowed perpetual leases, provided that the rent was reasonable. In the west there was no imperial legislation, but councils enacted rules that bishops might not alienate land without the leave of the metropolitan or provincial council.

The early churches had apparently divided offerings between the bishop and the clergy and other needs in fixed proportions. In the west this dividend system was maintained and applied to all revenue. There were different systems of division. According to the Roman rule, which the popes enforced in the Suburbicarian diocese and advocated elsewhere, one quarter went to the bishop, one quarter was divided between the clergy according to their grade, a third quarter went to the upkeep and lighting of the building, and the last quarter to charity. In Spain there were three shares only, charity being omitted. In Gaul the bishop controlled all the revenue from endowments, and shared the offerings half and half with his clergy.

These rules applied to the cathedral and its *tituli*, with the *canonici* or *cardinales* who served them. Parish churches were separately endowed; from the end of the fifth century the popes forbade bishops within their jurisdiction to consecrate new churches without satisfying themselves that they were provided with sufficient endowments to maintain the lights and the fabric and to pay their clergy, and councils laid down the same rule for Gaul and Spain in 541 and 572. In the west the bishop retained an overriding control over the endowments of parishes and charitable institutions, and could annex some of their lands to the central fund, provided that he left enough to pay their clergy and maintain their buildings. Bishops also claimed a third of the parochial offerings, but were supposed to spend them on the repair of the church. They also at their annual visitation exacted a fee from each parish (*cathedraticum*), which was not supposed to exceed two *solidi*.

In the east the dividend principle was apparently maintained for offerings, but fixed stipends were paid to the bishop and the different grades of clergy out of the revenue from endowments; founders of parochial churches generally, it would seem, laid down a fixed establishment of clergy. This system caused grave financial embarrassment to the greater churches, especially Antioch and Constantinople, in the times of Anastasius and Justinian, as powerful persons, who could not be refused, asked for their numerous protégés to be given places among the cathedral clergy; the salary bill mounted and the churches got into debt. Under the western system, on the other hand, more clergy meant a lower dividend for each. As in the west parochial churches had to be separately endowed—the rule was enforced by Justinian—but the bishop under imperial legislation had no control over their endowments or those of independent charitable institutions.

Monasteries were originally unendowed. In *laurae*, where the monks lived in separate cells, and met only for divine worship on Sundays, they practised crafts, especially basket weaving, and sold their products, or hired themselves out as labourers in the harvest and vintage, often making enough to keep themselves for the rest of the year on their very abstemious diet. In *coenobia*, where the monks ate and worked in common, they not only cultivated the garden, but worked in teams on various crafts such as shoemaking and pottery, and the superior or his agents marketed their products. Houses of the Pachomian order, which Pachomius instituted in Egypt in the early fourth century, made a considerable surplus, which they devoted to charity. Monasteries, how-ever, inevitably attracted not only offerings but endowments, and by the time the movement reached the west in the fifth century, it was customary for founders to give them lands, which were cultivated by tenants or slaves. John Cassian complains that monks in the west were as a result relatively few, and were idle and ill-disciplined; but by his time most monasteries in the east also had become rich and idle. Monastic endowments were managed by their abbots and were no concern of the bishop. The bishop, however, had disciplinary control over the monks, whether clerics or laymen, and also appointed special controllers or inspectors to look after them. A few western monasteries were given special immunity from episcopal control.

So many clergy were ordained when Constantine freed them from curial duties that a few years later he enacted that no one should be appointed except to fill a vacancy caused by death. This law naturally soon lapsed. The only later attempt to curb numbers was the canon of Chalcedon that the clergy should be ordained only to specific posts. Numbers increased enormously through the centuries. In the year of the Great Persecution the church of Cirta, the capital of Numidia, had besides the bishop only three priests, two deacons, four subdeacons and seven readers. In the middle of the fifth century the church of Edessa, a town of comparable size, had seventy-five clergy, and in the early sixth century Ravenna had sixty and Apamea of Syria about eighty. These figures refer only to the cathedral clergy. Edessa had apparently about 200 altogether, and Carthage under the early Vandal kings 500 or more. These figures again do not include the country clergy; Cyrrhus, which had a large territory, forty miles across either way, had 800 rural parishes, each of which must have had at least one priest or deacon.

The great churches were of course more lavishly staffed. Rome even in the third century had 46 priests, 7 deacons, 7 subdeacons, 42 acolytes and 52 exorcists, readers and doorkeepers. Justinian tried to reduce the establishment of the great church of Constantinople to 60 priests, 100 deacons, 90 subdeacons, 110 readers, 25 singers and 100 doorkeepers, besides 40 deaconesses—525 persons in all.

In addition to these there were others who counted as clerics, though not in orders, such as the grave-diggers (*fossores*) and funeral attendants (*decani, copiatae*) and the male nurses in the hospitals (*parabalani*). The Alexandrian church had 600 *parabalani* in the fifth century, and at Constantinople there were 950 *decani*, who, under a scheme initiated by

Constantine and reformed by Justinian, provided free funerals for all unless the relatives liked to pay a supplementary fee for a superior display.

In the greater churches many of the clergy were engaged on administrative duties. In the east each bishop had a financial manager (*oeconomus*), usually a senior priest; this practice was made mandatory by the Council of Chalcedon to avoid the bishops being involved in financial scandals, but the office was rare in the west. There were also the wardens and treasurers of the orphanages, hospitals and so forth, sacrists, keepers of the archives, and groups of notaries to keep the records, and of *defensores*, whose duties were legal and disciplinary: we find them arresting clerical offenders. In the east notaries and *defensores* took orders, advancing from readers to priests. At Rome they were laymen, or held minor orders only, resigning their posts if they were promoted to the subdiaconate. They were extensively used as managers (*rectores*) of the several patrimonies or groups of church lands, and often continued to do this work when they became subdeacons and deacons.

The higher clergy, bishops and priests and deacons, were all paid. The lower orders, subdeacons, readers, acolytes (only in the west), singers, exorcists and doorkeepers, were paid in great churches like Rome and Constantinople, but in many cities were part time, working for their living. Funeral attendants were also part time; at Constantinople the *decani* were supplied by 950 shops or workshops, which enjoyed fiscal immunities in return for the service.

By a rule laid down at Nicaea and often repeated, clergy were not allowed to migrate from the see to which they had originally been ordained without their bishop's permission. The popes from the early fifth century tried to insist that ordinands must start from the bottom and pass through the orders in due succession, serving four or five years as readers, subdeacons and deacons; but the rule was frequently ignored and laymen ordained deacons or priests. Laymen also were still not infrequently consecrated bishops in the sixth century. Small children were often given minor orders, but were not allowed to be ordained subdeacons until they were twenty; the minimum ages for deacon and priest were thirty and thirty-five. On the other hand quite a number of men took orders at an advanced age, having retired from the civil service, or after long practice at the bar. Of fifteen aged priests and deacons at Mopsuestia in 550, six had received their first orders at under ten, and five between thirty and forty, four between fifteen and twenty-four.

By an old rule of the church a man might not marry after being ordained a deacon or priest or bishop, though married men could be ordained. There was, however, a strong feeling in the west that the higher clergy should, if married, be continent, and the popes from Siricius (385–99) tried to enforce this rule—Pope Leo (446–61) included subdeacons in the ban—and councils in Africa, Gaul and Spain followed suit. To judge by its frequent reiteration the rule was not well kept. In the east some leading theologians, like Eusebius of Caesarea and Epiphanius of Salamis, advocated it, but the council of Nicaea expressly rejected it and no subsequent council enacted it. According to Socrates it was still in the mid-fifth century normal in the east for all the clergy, including bishops, to cohabit with their wives. Justinian forbade married men to be consecrated, declaring that bishops ought not to be distracted by family cares but devote themselves to their spiritual duties. Pope Pelagius I (551–61) ventured to break this law by consecrating a married man bishop of Syracuse, but extracted from him a guarantee that he would not alienate the property of the church to his family.

Clerical stipends varied enormously. Bishops were paid many times what their priests or deacons received and—in the west at any rate—the greater the see the greater the disparity: at Ravenna the bishop got 3,000 *solidi* and in addition 880 fowls, 266 chickens, 8,800 eggs, 3,760 pounds of pork, 3,450 pounds of honey, and unknown quantities of geese and milk 'on account of the expenses of his household and the presents which are offered to many persons and the banquets which he has to give either for the honour and dignity of his see or for the reception of visitors';[1] while his priests and deacons drew between 50 and 100 *solidi*. But there were vast differences between bishops of different sees. When Musonius, bishop of Meloe, a little Isaurian hill town, was accused of usury, he indignantly retorted: 'My God, what do you care, you who receive the stipends of Antioch, while I have nothing in my city, not so much as six *solidi*?'[2] Musonius in these words compared himself unfavourably to a priest of Antioch, and probably with justice. Gregory, a priest of Ravenna, who was compelled by his bishop to accept the see of Mutina, demanded and received in compensation the tenure for life of an estate of the Ravennate church worth 30 *solidi* a year.

The *cardinales* of the cathedral churches were normally, it would

[1] Agnellus, *Liber Pontif. Eccl. Ravenn.* 60.
[2] *The Select Letters of Severus of Antioch*, I. 4.

seem, better paid than the parochial clergy, and were unwilling to accept parishes unless they could keep at least part of their emoluments as *cardinales*. The rural clergy were often miserably paid. Pope Gregory licensed the consecration of parish churches whose endowment amounted to as little as three or six *solidi* a year, and of this a third went to lights and repairs, while the priests had to pay two *solidi* a year to the bishop as *cathedraticum*. The rural clergy must have relied largely on the offerings of their parishioners. Some landlords in Spain in the sixth century built churches as a commercial speculation, going fifty-fifty with the priests on the offerings.

In the ordination and promotion of his clergy the bishop had, subject to the canonical rules, a fairly free hand. In parochial churches, however, he had to take account of the wishes of the founder or patron, and where the church was on an estate, of the landlord; for the priest was commonly a *colonus* of the estate and the landlord's permission was required for his ordination. Even with his own cathedral clergy the bishop was subject to heavy pressure from great men who demanded places for their poor relations and clients.

In the election of bishops there was a great variety of procedure and practice. In the electoral body the clergy might be represented by the *cardinales* only, or might include the parochial clergy, as Pope Gelasius ordered in one case. The people might be the whole population in a village bishopric, but in larger cities the effective voters were the decurions, or later the *honorati*, though the crowd often influenced them by demonstrations in favour of a popular candidate. The balance of power between the clergy and people on the one hand, and the consecrating bishops on the other, also varied greatly. Not infrequently the clergy and people could find no suitable candidate and asked the metropolitan to choose one for them. Sometimes the metropolitan and bishops tried to force their man on a city, not always with success; we know of several bishops who were consecrated but rejected by their cities and henceforth proved an embarrassing problem to their colleagues. We know of cases where the populace prevailed against the bishops; Martin was consecrated to the see of Tours despite the protest of the bishops that he was 'a contemptible person, unworthy of the episcopate, a man of despicable appearance, with dirty clothes and unbrushed hair'.[1]

More usually a compromise was reached, but a deadlock was always possible. To avoid this the Council of Arles in the middle of the fifth century enacted that the bishops should make a short list of three candi-

[1] Sulpicius Severus, *Vita S. Martini*, 9.

dates out of which the electors should choose; this rule does not seem to have proved popular and is never heard of again. In the east the rule was adopted, and confirmed by imperial legislation under Anastasius, that the clergy, decurions and *honorati* of the city should elect three candidates, of whom the metropolitan chose one.

Among the men chosen to be bishops there were three main types. There were safe and deserving men, usually priests or deacons of the cathedral church. It was these whom the popes and the hierarchy naturally favoured, and they were probably the commonest. The people, however, often preferred a really holy man, a monk or hermit, whose prayers would win them God's favour. Some of these, like Martin, proved very successful; others, like Theodore, could not cope with business; Theodore eventually got leave to resign his see of Anastasio-polis. Alternatively the people might prefer a prominent layman, an ex-provincial governor or a barrister, who could influence the imperial government on their behalf. Such elections were not unnaturally generally disliked by the clergy and bishops, but were often a great success; examples are Ambrose and Sidonius Apollinaris.

In times of doctrinal controversy the imperial government often lent its support to candidates who were from its point of view on the right side, especially in the great sees. At Alexandria Gregory and George, the candidates of the anti-Athanasian party, were installed by armed force in 339 and 356, and after the Council of Chalcedon few patriarchs who accepted its doctrine assumed their see without substantial military protection. But the emperors did not otherwise interfere in episcopal elections, except at Constantinople. Here Theodosius I instructed the Council of Constantinople in 381 to draw up a short list, and himself selected the last name on it, a senator called Nectarius. The great eunuch, Eutropius, selected Nectarius' successor, John Chrysostom, and Theodosius II chose Nestorius. But even in the capital free elections were not infrequently allowed until the late fifth or early sixth century. From the reign of Justinian, at any rate, it was the emperor who appointed the patriarch of Constantinople. As Pope Agapetus said of the election of Menas in 536: 'If the choice of the most serene emperors smiled upon him above the rest, yet such was the approval of all the clergy and the people that he may be believed to have been chosen by everyone.'[1] It was left to the kings of the Franks to issue *congés d'élire* for the election of their ministers and favourites, or whoever paid them most.

[1] *Acta Conc. Oec. III*, 135, 153.

XX

The Aristocracy

In a society in which official titles of rank counted for so much, it is inevitable that this criterion should govern any description of the social classification of the empire. It has, however, two disadvantages. Official rank did not always coincide with social status. There were always some who had no titles but ranked high; thus the great bishops came to be social equals of senators. On the other hand some relatively humble persons earned official rank. In the second place, there was a great inflation of honours in the later Roman empire, and titles which had been very select became widely diffused and sank in value. Under Diocletian to be *clarissimus* meant to belong to that very exclusive body, the Roman senate, which comprised perhaps the 500 best families of the empire. By the reign of Justinian there were many thousands of *clarissimi* and the title carried few privileges and not much prestige. In the time of Diocletian praetorian prefects were normally not senators and bore the highest equestrian title, *eminentissimus*, while the next equestrian grade, *perfectissimus*, was accorded to the ministers of the court, vicars, *duces* and provincial governors. By the latter part of the fourth century the perfectissimate was being granted to the financial chief clerks (*numerarii*) of provincial governors and to the quartermasters (*actuarii*) of regiments after five years blameless service, while the ranks of *ducenarius* and *centenarius* survived only for middle-grade clerks in the *largitiones*, and *egregius*, the lowest equestrian rank, is never mentioned after 324.

BIBLIOGRAPHY. Besides Chapter XV of my *Later Roman Empire* (Oxford, 1964) there is no comprehensive account of the later Roman aristocracy except the antiquated work of C. Lécrivain, *Le Sénat romain depuis Dioclétien à Rome et à Constantinople* (Paris, 1888). For their social life, literary activities and religion see Samuel Dill, *Roman Society in the last Century of the Western Empire* (London, 1910).

The main legal source is *Cod. Theod.* VI, *Cod. Just.* XII. i–xv, for the rules of rank and precedence. The letters of Symmachus and Sidonius Apollinaris lliustrate the social life of the aristocracy.

The *comitiva*, founded by Constantine, always had a wide range, being from the beginning awarded both to senators and commoners and being divided into three grades. The title of *comes primi ordinis* continued to be given to the highest ministers in the sixth century, but had been extended by then to relatively low-ranking persons, such as the retired *advocati fisci* of the superior courts and retired chief clerks of the praetorian prefecture; it retained, however, some distinction, being associated with the lower grades of the senatorial order. Third-class *comitivae* were by the end of the fourth century regularly given to senior decurions who had fulfilled all their duties, and by the early fifth to the heads of the Roman guilds of bakers and butchers.

Under Diocletian the senate enjoyed very little political power, and the effective aristocracy of the empire was formed by the equestrian order, whose members filled all the important administrative and military posts. It was very greatly expanded to fill the numerous new posts which Diocletian created, and it also grew by the admission of honorary members. Equestrian rank was held for life, and was accorded by imperial codicils. These might confer an office which carried with it one of the equestrian ranks, or might bestow a fictive past office, entitling the recipient to call himself former governor (*ex praesidibus*) or former *rationalis* (*ex rationalibus*) with the appropriate grading, or again might convey the simple title of *perfectissimus, ducenarius, centenarius* or *egregius*. The *comitiva* was also held for life, and was similarly conferred by a codicil, which either gave an active office or the mere title. Though these ranks were legally not hereditary, fathers who had been ennobled naturally sought to secure their sons' promotion, and the imperial government was often accommodating. Constantine originally ruled that sons of *comites*, provincial governors, *rationales* and *magistri rei privatae* of curial condition should be returned to their city councils, but later enacted that those suitable for imperial office should after performing their curial duties be promoted.

The persons promoted were often, especially under Diocletian, military men who had risen from the ranks; but to fill the civilian offices there was a demand for men who had received literary and rhetorical education, and especially for lawyers, and these were normally drawn from the curial class. It was naturally also chiefly the upper layer of the curial class who aspired to honorary rank. They had the birth, wealth and education which were the standard qualifications for rank; they had a strong motive for seeking it in that it freed them from curial duties; and they possessed the social connections to pull the necessary strings and the money to pay the necessary bribes. A long series of laws ranging down to the third quarter of the fourth century denounced the corrupt grant of honorary equestrian rank and honorary *comitivae*.

The Roman senate was still, it would seem, under Diocletian the small body of about 600 members which it had been since the late republic. Membership was in effect hereditary, since the sons of senators had the right to hold the quaestorship, which was the qualifying office, but as senatorial families had always tended to die out, it was steadily but slowly infiltrated by newcomers, who were either licensed by the emperor to hold the quaestorship or directly adlected into the senate with higher rank. The newcomers were often high equestrian officers—praetorian prefects were normally ennobled during or after their office—or their sons, and often also men of birth and wealth who had held no office. The senate comprised a number of families which claimed very ancient lineage, sometimes going back to the great republican families like the Gracchi and the Scipios. Their genealogies cannot be checked, but they may have inherited some ancient blood through the female line. The old families had by generations of accumulation acquired vast fortunes.

Constantine began to expand the senatorial order, partly by enrolling more equestrian magistrates and their sons, partly by increasing the number of administrative posts reserved for senators, and appointing commoners to them; in particular he upgraded many provincial governorships from the rank of *praeses* (which carried the perfectissi-mate) to that of *consularis* (which carried the clarissimate). These processes continued under his sons, who normally gave senatorial rank to praetorian prefects, *magistri militum*, the ministers of the *comitatus* and vicars, as well as to *consulares* of provinces, and by Valentinian and Valens, who made *duces clarissimi*. Constantius II also founded a new senate at Constantinople, recruiting it not only from Roman senators domiciled in the eastern parts and from holders of administrative posts, but also from the higher gentry of the eastern provinces, who had hitherto been underrepresented in the Roman senate. The Constanti-nopolitan senate was originally a small body of about 300 members, but had by the last quarter of the fourth century swelled to 2,000. The Roman senate no doubt swelled proportionately, and both bodies continued to grow at an increasing tempo.

The senatorial order was by now becoming not only very large but rather mixed, and Valentinian I laid down strict rules of precedence. The highest rank was accorded to holders and former holders of the ancient republican office of ordinary consul, by seniority of appointment, and next to patricians. This ancient title had been revived by Constantine as a personal honour, which was very sparingly bestowed; even under Zeno only ex-consuls, praetorian or urban prefects and *magistri militum* were eligible. Below the consuls and patricians came praetorian and urban prefects and *magistri militum*, with whom in 432 were graded *praepositi sacri cubiculi*. Senators of this grade came to be called *illustres* and from the middle of the fifth century *gloriosi*. Next came the principal palatine ministers, the quaestor, master of the offices, and *comites sacrarum largitionum* and *rei privatae* and *domesticorum*. These were at first styled *spectabiles* but before the end of the fourth century *illustres*. Next came proconsuls and then vicars, with whom were equated *comites rei militaris* and *duces* and some minor palatine ministers such as the *magistri scriniorum* and the second and third eunuchs. These grades acquired the rank of *spectabiles*. Below them again came ordinary *clarissimi*, who included consulars of provinces and senators who had held no official post, active or honorary. *Praesides* of provinces also became *clarissimi* at the end of the fourth century, and tribunes of regiments, it would seem, in the early fifth.

Within each group, senators who had actually held offices ranked above those with honorary codicils, and among the actual or honorary office-holders precedence went by seniority of appointment. There were, however, many complicating factors, and the rules became highly intricate. Difficulties were caused when those who had held lower offices obtained honorary codicils of higher. The grant of a *comitiva primi ordinis* disturbed the normal order of precedence, enhancing the rank of certain offices. In the early fifth century a further complication was introduced by the grant of offices which were in fact honorary but were styled *inter agentes*. Under Theodosius II *illustres* formed five groups, those who had really held illustrious offices, those who had personally received codicils *inter agentes* (also called *vacantes*), those who had received such codicils in absence, those who had received honorary codicils in person, and those who had been given honorary codicils in absence.

The senate was an ancient corporation and jealous of its privileges. Admission to it therefore was more complicated than the grant of equestrian rank or the *comitiva*. The sons and grandsons of a senator (after 364 those born after his admission) were *clarissimi* from birth, and could enter the senate by holding the quaestorship. Outsiders had first to obtain *codicilli clarissimatus* or some appropriate office from the emperor. They had then to submit this document to the prefect of the city and get three senators to make speeches on their behalf and three others to swear to their character. The senate then voted. The vote was not always a pure formality, for we know of one candidate who was rejected, Thalassius, a friend of Libanius, who was blackballed at Constantinople on the ground that he was a vulgar artisan; in reality, as Libanius explains, he owned a factory like the Athenian orator Demosthenes. Alternatively, candidates might receive imperial *adlectio*, which excused them from holding the ancient republican magistracies and giving the games associated with them.

The ancient republican magistracies were now pure forms, and those which did not give games are very rarely mentioned. The quaestors gave games at Rome and are frequently mentioned there, but not at Constantinople, where they did not give games. Aediles happen to be mentioned at Rome and tribunes of the plebs at Constantinople. Praetors gave games at both capitals and are often recorded. Suffect consuls are only mentioned at Rome.

The ordinary consulate, whose holders gave their names to the year, still retained its glamour. The office was often held by the emperors and their sons and was also accorded to praetorian prefects and *magistri militum*, occasionally to *magistri officiorum* of outstanding distinction. It was from time to time also given to imperial favourites, more regularly to representatives of the great senatorial families, even though they had held no office. When the empire was divided one consul was nominated by the emperor who controlled Rome and one by the emperor of Constantinople. When there ceased to be an emperor in the west Odoacer and Theoderic and Amalasuntha continued to appoint consuls, who were recognized in the east if they obtained codicils from the emperor, as they usually did. The last western consul, Paulinus, was nominated by Amalasuntha in 534, and the office did not survive much longer in the east. Its exclusive dignity had been undermined by Zeno, who had instituted honorary consuls, whose codicils cost far less then the games traditionally given by the real consuls, and it became increasingly difficult to find rich senators willing to undertake the office. The last was Basilius in 541; after this the consulate was held only by the successive emperors in the first year of their reign.

Membership of the senate, and the title of senator, were by Justinian's time restricted to *illustres*. When *spectabiles* and *clarissimi* were formally excluded is not known, but probably not earlier than the reign of Marcian (450–57), and, since the same rule prevailed in Ostrogothic

Italy, while there were still emperors in the west; Anthemius (467–72) or Julius Nepos (473–75), who were appointed by Leo, might have introduced the new rule in the west. This meant that senatorial rank was no longer legally hereditary, but depended entirely on imperial codicil. In fact, it tended to be hereditary. We know of a *vir gloriosus*, Hierius, whose son Constantine was only a *vir clarissimus* when Hierius made his will, but when he later added a codicil had become *gloriosus* like his father. His son, another Hierius, was at the time of the codicil only *clarissimus* but later became *gloriosus*, as did his son Constantine.

Senators enjoyed certain privileges. They could as defendants claim the jurisdiction of the prefect of the city, their estates were immune from extraordinary levies and *sordida munera*, and they were exempt from curial duties. All these privileges were whittled down for senators of lower degree and came to be confined to *illustres*. The fiscal privileges were confined to holders of the highest offices only by Gratian and Theodosius I, but extended to all *illustres* in 412. Immunity from curial duties was denied to all senators by Theodosius I, but allowed to holders or ex-holders of illustrious offices in 436, but restricted again to holders of offices which ranked as 'glorious'.

On the other hand senators had certain financial burdens. They had to contribute to the *aurum oblaticium* offered by the senate on festal occasions. From Constantine's time they paid a special graded surtax, the *follis*, until it was abolished in the east by Marcian in 451. But above all they had to celebrate games as quaestor and praetor (at Rome) or as praetor (at Constantinople).

The magistrates who gave games were elected by the senate. At Rome no details are known, but at Constantinople we have the rules laid down by Constantius II. A quorum of fifty was required drawn from those who had already held the praetorship, and including ten senators of the highest rank. Elections were made ten years in advance (this rule applied in Rome also), to allow candidates ample time to accumulate funds; later in 409, the waiting period was abolished in Constantinople, except in necessitous cases, where it was to be from two to five years at the senate's discretion. The election was a formal matter and nominations were in practice left to the *censuales*, the officials who kept the register of the senators and the returns of their property.

At Rome very high standards of expenditure were set by members of the immensely wealthy old families, who are recorded to have spent as much as 2,000 or even 4,000 pounds of gold on their games. This made it difficult for lesser senators, who did their best to evade their responsibilities, and often, it would seem, succeeded, especially if they resided overseas. At Constantinople, on the other hand, where there was no old tradition of munificence, Constantius II and his successors had to lay down schedules of expenditure, which were progressively reduced. The highest sum mentioned is 1,000 pounds of silver, equivalent to less than 60 pounds of gold, in 361, and later figures range from 500 to 100 pounds of silver (about 15 to 6 pounds of gold). As there were only eight praetorships a year to fill and thousands of senators to choose from, it ought to have been easy to find candidates for whom these modest sums would be no burden, but we have evidence that the praetorship was imposed on quite humble senators living far from Constantinople. Marcian remedied their grievance by exempting *spectabiles* and *clarissimi* resident in the provinces. He also reduced the number of praetorships to three, and left the amount of money they spent on their games to their discretion. The games of ordinary consuls were much more splendid and even in Constantinople cost 2,000 pounds of gold, but this office was reserved for the greatest, and there was only one consul, if that, each year.

The senatorial order was drawn from a great variety of geographical, racial and social origins. Every province was represented, and there were not a few barbarians, palace eunuchs originally imported from Persia, Armenia or Abasgia, and German, Alan, Sarmatian, Armenian and Persian generals and their descendants. Areobindus, master of the soldiers in the reign of Theodosius II, left a son Dagalaifus, who was consul in 461, and a grandson Areobindus Dagalaifus (consul in 506), who married Anicia Juliana of the ancient Roman house of the Anicii. Pusaeus, a Persian officer who deserted to Julian, founded a family which included Pusaeus, consul in 467.

The social structure of the senatorial order was rather different in east and west. In the west there was a core of ancient and very wealthy families, like the Anicii with their many branches, the Acilii Glabriones and the Petronii Probi, who claimed descent from senators of the principate and even the republic. This group, reinforced by some others of more recent distinction, such as the Aurelii Symmachi, regularly held the consulship and often the greater offices of state, and continued to do so under the Ostrogothic kings. While they did not hold a monopoly of the illustrious offices, they predominated in the top class of senators, which ultimately became the senate.

In the east there were no ancient noble families, and it was upstarts who achieved high office under Constantius II who founded the great families. Taurus, a low-born notary who became consul in 361, left a son Aurelian and a grandson Taurus who were both praetorian prefects and consuls (in 400 and 428). Philip, another notary and according to Libanius a sausage seller's son, consul in 348, left an even more distinguished family, which included Anthemius, praetorian prefect, patrician and virtual ruler of the east from 404 to 414, Isidore, consul in 436, Anthemius, emperor of the west (467–72), Marcian, who married a daughter of the emperor Leo, and Anthemius, consul in 515. These families did not, however, predominate in the eastern senate to the degree that the old Roman families did in the west, and many persons of lower degree achieved illustrious office and rank down to the sixth century.

It was always possible for a peasant to achieve the highest rank through the army. Examples are Arbetio, who rose from the ranks to be *magister militum* under Constantius II (consul in 355), and Justin, who became *comes excubitorum* and ultimately emperor. More became *comites rei militarii* or *duces*, like Gratian the father of Valentinian and Valens, and thus *spectabiles*, and many tribunes, and thus from the fifth century *clarissimi*. The urban working class had less chance, but we know of several who became notaries in the early fourth century and rose to the highest offices. Evagrius notes two Antiochiene artisans, one of whom became a senator under Zeno and the other held high offices under Tiberius Constantine.

The higher branches of the civil service provided regular access to the senate from the latter part of the fourth century. Already in 381 notaries were all senators, the senior being *spectabiles* and the junior *clarissimi*. The retired *proximi* of the *sacra scrinia* became *spectabiles* from 381, and from 410 all senior clerks became *clarissimi*. The *principes* of the *agentes in rebus* became *clarissimi* in 386 and *spectabiles* in 426. The decurions of the silentiaries became *spectabiles* in 415. Between 414 and 427 the ten seniors of the *domestici* and of the *protectores* became *clarissimi*. Outside the palatine ministries senatorial rank was more sparingly awarded. It was not until the reign of Anastasius that the chief clerks of the praetorian prefecture became *clarissimi*. These civil servants were men of modest fortune and were for the most part adlected to the senate and thus excused the production of games. Some were also excused the *follis*. The chief clerks of the *largitiones* and *res privata*, who were not given the latter privilege when they were accorded the clarissimate in 408 and 425, renounced the expensive honour in 428.

Higher civil servants were not infrequently given provincial governorships on retirement and a few achieved high office and thus rose to the illustrate.

Distinguished members of the liberal professions were often ennobled. Doctors could become court physicians (*archiatri sacri palatii*), thus achieving the *comitiva primi ordinis*. Emeritus professors of Constantinople were rewarded with the same rank, which made them *spectabiles*, and outstanding rhetoricians often became quaestors of the sacred palace, or were given honorary quaestorships or even prefectures; so too were distinguished jurisconsults and professors of law. Architects engaged on imperial works were often also given senatorial rank.

The legal profession contributed many members to the senate. Barristers were frequently appointed to provincial governorships and might rise to higher offices. More distinguished lawyers were appointed directly to the quaestorship or the praetorian prefecture; this was regular under Anastasius. Barristers of the higher courts who did not aspire to office retired, if they lived long enough to become *advocati fisci*, as *spectabiles* or *clarissimi* in the later fifth and sixth centuries.

The great majority of entrants to the senate were decurions of the superior sort, landowners of substance, of respectable pedigree and with a liberal education. It was such men who by the favour of influential friends, or by paying for the requisite *suffragia*, secured provincial governorships or obtained honorary codicils. Despite the efforts of the imperial government men of this class continued to filter into the senate from the middle of the fourth century onwards. Even in the sixth century they were still obtaining codicils of illustrious rank.

No senators could be called poor, but a good many of them were men of modest means, retired civil servants or tribunes who had risen from the ranks, who grumbled at paying the *follis* even on the minimum scale of seven *solidi* a year. Some senators on the other hand were immensely rich. At Rome, according to Olympiodorus, the wealthiest had incomes of 4,000 pounds of gold from their estates with a third as much again in kind, while families of the second order had 1,500 or 1,000 pounds gold a year. These figures are borne out by the biography of Melania, whose income is stated to have been 120,000 *solidi*. At Constantinople there seem to have been no such millionaires. John Lydus tells how Paulus, son of Vibianus, praetorian prefect and consul (463), who himself in 498 celebrated his consulship with unexampled splendour, got into financial difficulties and borrowed 1,000 pounds of gold from another senator, Zenodotus, who was an honorary consul. Both men were hard pressed by their creditors, when Anastasius gave Paulus 2,000 pounds of gold to repay Zenodotus and put him on his feet again. A wealthy Constantinopolitan senator, then, might be worth about 1,000 pounds of gold in capital. The Apions, a very wealthy Egyptian family, which produced one of the last consuls in 539, are known to have owned about 120 square miles in Oxyrhynchus, which would have brought them in about 300 pounds of gold a year. They also owned land in some adjacent cities, but their income can hardly have exceeded 500 pounds.

All senators, great and small, derived the bulk of their income from agricultural rents. Most had started with inherited land and those who made their way by the bar or the civil service or the higher administration invested their surplus income in land. Those who pursued an administrative career added to their income from the profits, legal and illegal, of office, and those who formed the inner court circle could make very large sums by *suffragia*, and add to their estates by petitioning for grants of crown lands. No senator is known to have engaged in trade, though some seem to have owned ships, which they chartered to entrepreneurs (*exercitores*), who paid a fixed charter fee and took the risks and kept the profits.

Senators were legally supposed to reside at Rome or Constantinople and had to obtain leave (*commeatus*) to go elsewhere. In point of fact it is quite clear that very many senators lived permanently in the provinces and never visited the capitals unless they had to give games—and often did this *in absentia*; Marcian relieved *spectabiles* and *clarissimi* from the formality of *commeatus*.

Most senators seem to have led an idle life. It was a small minority only that pursued an active political career, holding any considerable number of offices or attending the consistory regularly. The majority were content to hold the minimum number of offices to keep up or enhance their precedence. Symmachus, who served as *corrector* of Lucania, proconsul of Africa and urban prefect, thus devoting less than three years of his life to the public service, is typical of the fourth-century great noble. In the fifth century many Roman nobles jumped straight to an illustrious office, the prefecture of the city or the praetorian prefecture, often at a very early age; Petronius Maximus was urban prefect when still under twenty-five. The greatest of all disdained administrative posts and relied on securing the patriciate or an ordinary consulship to give them their due precedence.

Some senators practised at the bar, but generally in a rather desultory fashion; Floridus, who was twice assessor at Rome, and ended up as professor of law was an exception. Others obtained or bought posts in the fashionable regiments of the *scholares* or *protectores* and *domestici*, or in the silentiaries or the tribunes and notaries, whose duties, if any, were ceremonial only. Most seem to have spent their time going to the baths, hunting, paying and receiving calls, entertaining and being entertained, and writing countless elegant letters about nothing in particular to a wide circle of acquaintances. Many who had literary pretensions wrote orations and occasional verse and recited them to their friends, and listened to their friends' effusions. Quite a number, including some of the bluest blood, were serious scholars. Agorius Praetextatus in the fourth century and Boethius in the sixth, both of the best Roman families, translated Greek philosophical works, and many of the Symmachi edited texts of the classics. Such men were not however typical if we are to believe Ammianus, who declared that Roman senators' libraries were 'perpetually closed like mausolea' and that they read nothing but the satires of Juvenal and the scandalous biographies of Marius Maximus.

It may be asked why there was so strong a pressure among the middle classes to enter the senate. The fiscal privileges were not great and were from the last quarter of the fourth century limited to the holders of high offices or to *illustres*. At first *curiales* could escape their local duties, but this privilege was also from the last quarter of the fourth century legally limited to holders of the highest offices. Senators, moreover, down to the middle of the fifth century had their peculiar financial burdens, the *follis* and the praetorian games. Between 390 and 450 decurions became legally worse off by becoming senators, being subject to both curial and senatorial charges, and apart from this they had to spend very large sums in *suffragia* to achieve senatorial rank. Yet during these very years the government had to pass several stringent measures to prevent *curiales* from entering the senate.

Some no doubt had political ambitions, but these were few, and did not include the vast majority who held a single office or obtained honorary codicils. Some again merely wanted a handle to their names and were prepared to pay for it. The great majority expected to get more substantial gains. The position is well put in the preamble of a law issued by Theodosius II in 439.[1]

We have learned from a report from the illustrious and magnificent praetorian prefect of the East and ex-consul Florentius that some

[1] Theod. II, *Novel* 15 §1.

curiales, wishing to protect themselves from ill treatment by provincial governors, take refuge in the privileges of senatorial rank. There is no doubt that this weakens the city councils, since the burden of the praetorship imposed on *curiales* compels them, their fortunes being exhausted in this way, to refuse their ancestral obligations to their several cities. But you must also observe that it is detrimental to the public interest that owing to the respect accorded to their rank they flout the orders of governors; the collection of arrears stops if the collecting officer owes deference to the debtor.

There is ample evidence elsewhere for these statements. Decurions were legally *honestiores*, immune from flogging, but governors increasingly ignored their privileges. Libanius declared that physical ill-treatment of decurions was a major cause of the decline of the councils.

It is this that has chiefly emptied the council chambers. There are perhaps other causes, but this especially, lashes and subjection to such corporal injuries as not even the most criminal slaves endure. . . . In many a city, your majesty, after these floggings, this is what the few surviving decurions say: 'Goodbye house, goodbye lands! Let one and the other be sold, and with their price let us buy liberty.'[1]

Senatorial rank gave liberty, for no governor would dare to flog his equal or superior in official precedence. As senators, moreover, decurions could in fact, whatever the law might say, ignore the protests of their colleagues and refuse to perform their curial duties. They could, as many laws reveal, postpone the payment of their taxes, whether the collectors were their former colleagues on the council or the governor's officials. Official rank carried not only prestige but vast intangible privileges.

The later Roman empire is often depicted as a rigid hierarchy, in which a man's position was fixed from birth. This description certainly does not apply to the aristocracy. If one takes as a test the ordinary consulship, the highest honour that a subject could attain, of the hundred men who became consuls—apart from members of the imperial family—in the century following 325, twelve were barbarians from without the empire, three barristers of modest origin, one a professor of a provincial university, one a private soldier; five are said to have been sons of artisans; and one was a slave. These are minimum figures, for many of the praetorian prefects and *magistri militum* honoured with the consulship were men of unknown origin who may well have started as barristers or common soldiers.

[1] Libanius, *Oration* XXVIII. 21–2.

XXI

The Middle and Lower Classes

The middle classes may be roughly equated with the legal term *honestiores*—less the *honorati*, the official aristocracy. The term *honestiores*, though it carried useful privileges, is nowhere exactly defined, but it certainly included decurions, civil servants and soldiers, and may be taken to have also covered the clergy and the liberal professions. The range of wealth and social status covered was very wide and overlapped at one end of the *honorati* and the other with the *plebeii* or commoners.

The army was the largest group, numbering about 650,000 at the end of the fourth century. Its recruitment and conditions have been described in an earlier chapter; it may be sufficient to note that many soldiers owned a little land, and that sons of veterans were substantial enough to become decurions if they did not join the army. With soldiers may be classed the armourers (*fabricenses* and *barbaricarii*) who worked in the forty or so state armament factories scattered throughout the empire. They were a legally hereditary class like soldiers, and advanced to the usual N.C.O. grades up to *primicerius fabricae*. They appear to have been men of some substance and some decurions tried to join their body.

Decurions were the most important and, apart from the army, the largest class. In the 900 cities of the eastern parts, there must have been, if we allow an average of 300 members for each council, about a quarter of a million when the councils were up to strength. In the west there

BIBLIOGRAPHY. The colonate is exhaustively discussed, with a full summary of the earlier literature, by R. Clausing, *The Roman Colonate* (New York, 1925). Later contributions to this subject include C. Saumagne, *Byzantion* XII (1937), F. L. Ganshof, *Antiquité Classique* XIV (1945), 261–77, A. Ségré, *Traditio* V (1958), 1–13.

For the various social classes see my *Later Roman Empire* (Oxford, 1964), pp. 510–15 (lawyers), 737–39, 752–54 (decurions), 773–81, 792–812 (peasants) 851–55 (slaves), 858–64 (craftsmen and labourers), 864–72 (traders), 920–27 (clergy), 1001–02 (teachers), 1012–14 (doctors and architects).

were considerably more cities, but most were very small places and normally had councils of only one hundred, so that the total number of decurions was probably smaller. As decurions went off into other walks of life and were not replaced, membership shrank very greatly, but we have no figures.

There were immense variations in wealth within the group. A law of 342 speaks of decurions, probably in Arabia, who might own less than 25 *iugera* (15 acres), and Augustine mentions 'a man called Curma, a poor *curialis* of the Municipium Tullense near Hippo, just a former duumvir of the place, a simple peasant'. Decurions who joined the army must have fallen into this class, and those who became bailiffs or tenants of great landlords and married peasant women and even slaves.

On the other hand there were in Libanius' day rich decurions of Antioch, who sent agents to Spain to buy racehorses, and imported wild beasts from Mount Ida in the Troad. As the richer decurions percolated into the senate, the general level of wealth sank, but in 444 Valerian, a decurion of Emisa, having obtained codicils of illustrious rank, 'burst into the provincial governor's court, surrounded with a great crowd of barbarians, and claimed precedence for himself, seated himself on the right hand of him to whom we had committed the laws and entrusted the fortunes of the provincials, drove out all his staff and left everything desolate'.[1] He also used his barbarian slaves to protect his fellow decurions from the tax collectors. Valerian must have been a rich man to do this and get off with losing his illustrious codicils. Even under Justinian, the daughter and heiress of Anatolius, a leading decurion of Ascalon, regarded herself as very ill-used when Justinian confiscated her fortune and allowed her a pittance of 365 *solidi* a year.

Decurions were almost by definition landowners. In Alexandria we hear of wealthy merchants, whose fortunes lay in cash and ships, being leading men in the city, and in very poor cities, those of Moesia for instance, owners of slaves—probably master craftsmen who used slave labour—were admitted to the council. Caecilian, duumvir of the little African town of Aptungi in 303, the year of the great persecution, was probably such a man. 'I had gone to Zama to buy linen yarn with Saturninus', he later deposed, on the day when the edict was posted; and again, 'he came to me at my house, I was having dinner with my workmen'.[2] But the laws always assume that decurions own land, whether they are great landlords or peasant farmers, and in any sizeable city they were absentee landlords, for they were obliged to reside in

[1] Theod. II, *Novel* 15.　　　　[2] Optatus of Mileve, *Appendix* II.

town, and landlords of some substance. At Tralles Critias owned seven farms, assessed at $20\frac{1}{2}$ *iuga*, Latron four farms (over 17 *iuga*) and Tatian fourteen farms ($57\frac{1}{2}$ *iuga*); the last is also assessed at 70 *capita* of free tenants, slaves and cattle. Unfortunately we do not know the acreage of a *iugum* in Asia, but a plausible guess is about 60 acres of arable or 15 acres of vineyard; a *caput* probably represented one man or two women.

Decurions were legally a hereditary class, but outsiders could be and were enrolled if they possessed the requisite property qualification; such enrolments seem to have become very rare after the middle of the fourth century, probably because most qualified persons had either been enrolled or acquired a status which gave them exemption.

Decurions might legally work as supernumerary clerks in the provincial office or practice at the bar, if they concurrently fulfilled their curial duties. This concession in the nature of things could apply only to decurions of the capital cities of provinces. Some humble members of the order practised as private notaries, but if so lost their privileges as *honestiores*. Some were doctors or teachers of rhetoric or grammar, becoming immune from curial duties if they received an official appointment. Many took orders in the church, joined the civil service, practised at the bars of the high courts, or obtained administrative posts, and were lost to the order.

The next most important group were civil servants, who as we have seen numbered between 30,000 and 40,000. Here again there were vast contrasts in wealth and standing between the highest and the lowest grades. The members of the most select palatine ministries, such as the notaries, the silentiaries and the *sacra scrinia*, were by the late fourth and early fifth centuries *ex officio* senators, at any rate in the latter part of their career, and were often recruited from sons of the aristocracy. At the other extreme subclerical officers of the provincial offices were working men with little or no property; Flavius Pousi, a messenger of a provincial *officium*, owned only his house, furniture and clothes.

It is impossible to say much about the income of the civil servants, as their salaries, which are known in some cases, formed a small part of their earnings, and they lived mostly on fees. There were considerable differences in salary. A palace barber (a *castrensianus*, not one of the superior palatine offices) in Julian's day received 20 *annonae* and 20 *capitus* (equivalent to 180 *solidi*) and a large money salary, while provincial officials got 4 *solidi* or less. The fees also varied greatly in different offices and between different grades. In the praetorian prefecture of the east a fairly senior clerk on the judicial side could earn as much as 1,000 *solidi* in some years and the senior clerk received nearly 2,000, but fees in the diocesan and provincial offices were much lower.

Provincial officials (*cohortales*) were from Constantine's time legally a hereditary class, neither they nor their sons being allowed to enter any other ministry or an outside career; needless to say they regularly eluded the law. Service in the higher ministries was to some extent hereditary by voluntary choice; in some of the best offices the sons of the chief clerks had by the fifth century acquired a preferential claim to a vacancy. In the highest ministries such as the notaries, the silentiaries, the *sacra scrinia* and the praetorian prefecture, vacancies were by this time purchased from the retiring seniors or from the heirs of those who had died before reaching the top. Apart from the sons of officials, including those of *cohortales*, who wormed themselves into superior ministries, the clerical grades of the civil service seem to have been largely recruited from decurions and their sons. We hear also of sons of veterans, and of merchants and superior shopkeepers, jewellers, clothiers, and the like, securing admission to provincial offices. The subclerical grades were drawn from the urban working class, or even from the peasantry.

Most officials of the clerical grades, and some even of the subclerical, owned some landed property, which they had inherited or bought from their earnings. We know of ten clerks of the provincial *officium* of the Thebaid who in the fourth century owned farms ranging from 30 to 180 *arurae* (20 to 120 acres). Flavius Theodore, a clerk in the ducal *officium* of the Thebaid in the sixth century (who was incidentally the son of a barrister at the provincial bar) owned land in the territories of three cities and house property in two, as well as quite a number of slaves. In the fifth century *cohortales* detected in higher ministries were made decurions of their native cities, which proves that they must have normally possessed fairly substantial landed property.

There were about 2,500 barristers practising in the ordinary courts of the provincial governors, vicars and urban and praetorian prefects in the eastern parts in the sixth century, or would have been if the imperial government had achieved its object of keeping down the number of barristers to fixed establishments—and probably under 1,000 in the military, financial and other special courts. It is impossible to gauge the average earnings of barristers, which differed widely according to their ability and the court in which they practised. Some clue is given by the salaries of assessors, which must have borne some relation to the earnings of young rising barristers. They ranged from 56 *solidi* for assessors of *duces* to 180 for those of the Augustal prefect of Egypt; those of the praetorian prefect of Africa got 720, but these would be more senior men. A clue to the earnings of senior counsel is afforded by the salaries of *advocati fisci*, who received 600 *solidi* in the court of the urban prefecture and over 2,000 in that of the praetorian prefecture of the East.

The preparation for the profession was rather expensive, and became more so with the passage of time. All barristers had to spend two or three years on a rhetorical training, and from the late fourth century another four years on their legal course at Berytus or Constantinople (or in the west Rome). By the late fifth century they had also to buy their admission to the bar. Some senators practised, and we hear of odd cases of very poor men winning through, but the great majority of barristers, to judge by the laws, came from the *curiales* or the *cohortales*, who had sufficient means to start, and for whom the career offered the chance of ample promotion, even to a praetorian prefecture. By the middle of the fifth century the profession was tending to become hereditary; sons of barristers could claim priority over outsiders for admission to the bar, and did not have to pay for it. Most lawyers were hereditary landowners, and they bought more land from their earnings —and sometimes received it (illegally) as their fee. Retired barristers were regularly privileged to continue to plead for their tenants.

Teachers of literature and rhetoric were widespread if not very numerous. Apart from the major university towns, Rome, Constantinople (which had twenty-eight chairs besides two in law and one in philosophy), Athens, Alexandria and Berytus, all the larger towns, such as capitals of provinces, had two or more salaried professors, and there were many more free-lance teachers both in the big cities and in minor towns. The scale of salaries laid down by Gratian in Gaul was 24 *annonae* (96 *solidi*) for a rhetorician and half as much for a grammarian, with higher rates (120 and 80 *solidi*) for the imperial residence of Trier. Justinian allotted 70 *solidi* to the professors of Carthage. The official salary was however a small part of a professor's earnings, for they charged fees, which varied according to their reputation and the purses of their pupils. Most professors seem to have come from the curial class and to have been men of property, for the training was expensive. It was almost essential to study at one of the major towns which possessed a celebrated professor, and to spend a long time in study; Libanius took ten years. We know of one poor boy, Aetius, son of a bankrupt *cohortalis*, who got his higher education by becoming the personal servant of a professor. Augustine, son of a modest decurion of a little African town, could not have gone to Carthage to complete his training, had not a wealthy fellow townsman, who recognized his talent, given his father financial help.

Elementary schoolmasters, who taught reading, writing and arithmetic, were humble folk who enjoyed neither official salaries nor privileges. Their fees were fixed in the Diocletianic tariff at a quarter or a fifth of those of grammarians and rhetors.

Doctors came in the same social bracket as professors. Cities maintained public doctors; at Antinopolis in the sixth century the salary was 60 *solidi*, at Carthage, where there were five public doctors, the senior got 99 *solidi*, the second 70 and the others 50. They also took fees, and there were private practitioners who lived on fees.

Architects came from the same class; of the four brothers of Anthemius of Tralles, who built S. Sophia, one was a barrister, one a professor and two doctors. They normally took a liberal education in grammar and rhetoric before their professional training. Sculptors and painters, on the other hand, were superior craftsmen; figure painters (*pictores imaginarii*) were entitled under the Diocletianic tariff to only twice the pay of an ordinary wall painter, and in a law of Valentinian I are definitely classed as *plebeii*. Actors and actresses were also *plebeii*, though stars lived very comfortably from the gifts of their admirers and lovers.

The number of the clergy increased phenomenally from the conversion of Constantine, and must have been very large, even if we take into account only the full-time salaried staff, by the fifth and sixth centuries. By then the cathedral of Constantinople (without the numerous parish churches and charitable institutions of the city) had a staff of 525; the great city of Carthage over 500 urban clergy; and Edessa, a lesser metropolis, 200, while an ordinary provincial city like Cyrrhus had at least 800 rural clergy (more than one to every two square miles). The very varying emoluments of the clergy have been discussed in a previous chapter. It may suffice to say here that they varied from the princely income of the patriarchs, which were on a par with the salaries of praetorian prefects, to the wretched pittances of rural priests, who ranked with the peasantry.

The clergy were drawn from every social class. Senators, it is true, rarely deigned to take holy orders, and were normally consecrated bishops straight away if they did so; Paulinus, a wealthy Aquitanian senator who sold all his goods and gave to the poor and became a priest, is not typical. The first known senator to become a bishop was Ambrose, son of a praetorian prefect, elected by popular acclamation to the see of Milan in 374, while consular of Aemilia. Next came Nectarius, selected for Constantinople by Theodosius I in 381; his brother Arsacius, elected to the same see in 404, was doubtless also a senator. By this time lesser senators, ex-provincial governors, must have been not uncommon candidates, for Pope Siricius (385–99) objected when 'those who, after they have gloried in secular pomp and preferred to take service under the state and undertaken the care of worldly affairs, get together a group of people and, supported by the favour of their friends, are dinned into my ears as possible bishops'.[1] Nevertheless we know of few actual cases, even in the fifth and sixth centuries—Germanus, an ex-provincial governor, and Sidonius Apollinaris, ex-prefect of the city, in Gaul, and in the east Nemesius, an ex-provincial governor, Chrysanthus, former vicar of Britain, Thalassius, former praetorian prefect of Illyricum, and Ephraem, *comes Orientis*.

The popes from Siricius (385–99) to Symmachus (498–514) disapproved of the ordination of ex-officials, 'who in obedience to the authorities had perforce executed cruel judgments',[2] and Justinian on similar grounds would only allow the sons of *cohortales* to be ordained if they entered a monastery in early youth. Nevertheless we know of many retired officials who became priests or bishops, from *memoriales* and *agentes in rebus* to Stephen, elected bishop of Larissa, who 'in my previous secular life was a provincial official and in this modest career passed my life humbly'.[3]

Pope Innocent (401–17) had a strong objection to barristers being ordained, but he appears to have been alone in this, and we know of many who became bishops. Professors are rarer; Augustine is a famous case. Soldiers are very rare; we know in fact of only one ex-officer, the tribune Mamertinus, and two common soldiers, Martin and Victricius, bishops of Tours and Rouen in the late fourth and early fifth centuries.

The bulk of the higher clergy would seem to have come from the *curiales*. They possessed the necessary education, and they had the worldly incentive of escaping from their curial duties, even if they had to surrender two-thirds of their property, a rule which large numbers evaded. Pope Innocent disliked the ordination of *curiales*, ostensibly on the grounds that 'they have in obedience to the authorities executed

---

[1] Siricius, *Epist.* 6 §1.   [2] Innocent I, *Epist.* 3 §4.
[3] *Stephani ad Bonifacium libellus* (Migne, *Patr. Lat.* LXV. 34).

orders given to them' and that 'in the actual course of their public duties they produced theatrical shows, which are without doubt inventions of the devil',[1] but really because they were always liable to be recalled to their curial duties. Later popes acquiesced in the exclusion of decurions for the latter reason: Justinian, as we have seen, made it very difficult for them to take orders on the high moral ground that they were unfitted by their official duties to preach the gospel of loving kindness.

Members of the urban working class served in the minor unpaid orders, and as funeral attendants and hospital orderlies, but we hear of few who became deacons or priests. The peasantry were normally ordained to rural parishes, but we do not know of any who became bishops. From the early fifth century tied tenants (*coloni adscripticii* or *originales*) might not be ordained without their landlords' consent, even to serve the estate to which they were attached. This was a secular law, relaxed by Justinian, and was accepted by the popes.

Slaves could not legally be ordained; they had to be manumitted by their masters first. Pope Leo (440–61) thoroughly approved of this rule.

'Persons whom the merit neither of their birth nor of their character recommends are being freely admitted to holy orders, and those who have not been able to obtain their freedom from their owners are raised to the dignity of the priesthood, as if servile vileness could lawfully receive this honour . . . there is a double wrong in this matter, that the sacred ministry is polluted by such vile company, and that the rights of owners are violated in so far as an audacious and illicit usurpation is involved.'[2]

Justinian took a more liberal view, allowing slaves to be ordained with their master's consent, and forbidding owners to reclaim slaves who had been ordained without their knowledge after the lapse of a year.

Very few persons engaged in trade or industry ranked as *honestiores*. Exceptional were the *navicularii* or state shippers, who carried the corn from Egypt and Africa to feed Constantinople and Rome and other cargoes destined for the army to the ports of supply. They were organized in guilds, normally one for each diocese, and when the guilds of Oriens and Egypt were increased in 371, new members were designated from ex-provincial governors and other *honorati* (even senators might volunteer), *curiales* and senior provincial officials. Normally membership of the guilds was obligatory on all who inherited or otherwise acquired

---

[1] Innocent I, *Epist.* 3 §4.   [2] Leo I, *Epist.* 4 §1.

land burdened with the *navicularia functio*. *Navicularii* were in fact not masters, but owners of ships, obliged to repair or replace them and to pay for their running costs. Towards the latter charge they received freight for the cargoes which they carried (at well below commercial rates); towards the former immunity from land tax, on the scale of 50 *iuga* excused for each 10,000 *modii* of ship's capacity. They also enjoyed immunity from customs duties and various other privileges.

There were some rich merchants in Alexandria. We hear of one who having lost all his capital was put on his feet again by a gift of 50 pounds of gold (3,600 *solidi*), of another worth 5,000 *solidi* and of a third who is said to have left 20,000 *solidi*. These are substantial sums but hardly compare with the 1,000 pounds of gold (72,000 *solidi*) which contemporary senators of Constantinople enjoyed. The silk merchants and the so-called silversmiths (*argentarii*) of Constantinople, who were actually rudimentary bankers, seem also to have been men of substance. They made a practice of buying sinecures in the palatine ministries for themselves and their sons. We know of one, an imperial butler (*castrensianus sacrae mensae*), who in 541 made a loan to two Egyptians of 20 *solidi* at 8 per cent repayable at four months to his agent in Alexandria. The bakers of Rome were also substantial men, owning land in addition to their mills; some are known to have become provincial governors or even senators.

The great mass of merchants, shopkeepers and craftsmen were however *humiliores*. They are definitely classed with or among *plebeii* in the laws; they were only very exceptionally elected to the city council, and in the poorest towns; when the richest of them, the jewellers and clothiers, got posts in the provincial offices, they were expelled with ignominy. Merchants, of course, varied considerably in wealth; there were substantial sea captains who owned a big ship of 20,000 *modii*, which must have cost about 1,000 *solidi*, and had some working capital as well, though they mostly operated on nautical loans. There were also itinerant pedlars with a capital of fifteen or ten *solidi* or less, who if veterans or clergy were exempted from the *chrysargyron*. Craftsmen also ranged from those who had a number of slaves or paid hands to men who owned nothing but their tools. The grievous hardship inflicted by the *chrysargyron*, so far as we can tell a moderate tax, shows that the majority of craftsmen and shopkeepers were very poor. Lowest among the urban poor were the casual labourers who worked in the building trade and earned a carat or half a carat (one-twenty-fourth or one-forty-eighth *solidus* a day)—when in work.

Urban craftsmen were enrolled in guilds, through which the city council fixed prices, regulated trade practices and organized *corvées*. Membership of the guilds appears to have been voluntary in the east, and in the west down to the end of the fourth century, when the massive migration of craftsmen to the countryside stimulated the government to enact that they must be brought back to their own cities with their children.

There were rural merchants who frequented the village fairs, and village shopkeepers and craftsmen, weavers, smiths, potters and the like, but the great majority of the rural population worked on the land. There were in the first place peasant proprietors, a slowly dwindling class, reinforced only by government grants of farms to veterans (which apparently ceased after the fourth century) and eroded by constant economic pressure. At first sight freeholders, who paid taxes only, would seem to have been better off than tenants, who paid rent and taxes, or a rent which included and exceeded the tax. But smallholders were very liable to be over-assessed and otherwise exploited fiscally, and moreover their holdings were probably on average smaller than the parcels (*colonicae*) let to tenants. A landlord had no reason to alter the size of his *colonicae*, whereas a peasant's holding was normally divided between his sons, and thus tended to grow smaller from generation to generation. But the weakest point of the peasant proprietor was that, living from hand to mouth, he had no reserves to fall back upon if the harvest failed or was destroyed by invaders, or his cattle died, or were carried off by barbarian raiders.

In such circumstances he had to borrow to pay his taxes, often at exorbitant rates of interest; Justinian found it necessary to give special protection to the peasants of Thrace and Illyricum against money-lenders, limiting the rate of interest to 5 per cent and compelling lenders to return the land or stock which they had seized. Many peasants thus lost their land by the foreclosure of mortgages. Others abandoned their holdings, leaving their fellow villagers to cope with their tax liability, and took up tenancies on the estates.

Very many sought the patronage or protection of a great man. In the late fourth century in Syria we find villages paying a regular douceur to the *dux* of the province, who in return stationed troops in the village and drove the tax collectors off, and when the latter sued the villagers claimed the case for his military court and found in the villagers' favour. Similar practices are alluded to in the laws in Egypt and other provinces of the eastern parts; the patrons are normally military commanders of all grades, but also proconsuls and vicars. This kind of bargain was doubtless profitable to villagers, but when the patron, as normally was the case, was a neighbouring great landlord, he insisted on the peasants' making over their land to him by a deed of gift or fictitious sale or by will. The eastern government made periodical attempts to fight patronage, which was bad for the revenue, in 360, 368, 395, 399, 415, and still under Marcian and Leo. In the west no attempt was made to curb it, and it is described as rampant in the mid-fifth century by Salvian. Many peasant holdings and whole villages were thus swallowed up in the great estates.

Only in Egypt can we approximately measure the change. In the territory of Hermopolis it can be calculated that only about one-sixth of the area was owned by urban landlords in the mid-fourth century. In the comparable territory of Oxyrhynchus in the sixth century the Apion family alone, without counting other lesser landlords, owned two-fifths of the area. In Egypt peasant proprietors were exceptionally numerous, but there were still substantial numbers in Illyricum, Thrace and eastern Asia Minor under Justinian, who recruited them extensively into his armies. In the west we have little evidence, but great estates seem to have covered most of the country in Italy, Africa, Spain and Gaul.

Diocletian appears to have enacted that all the rural population must remain in the places in which they were registered in the census: as infants were registered, the effect was to tie the peasantry hereditarily to their places of registration. The object of the law was, it would seem, to simplify the collection of the *capitatio* or poll tax, and ensure that the land was cultivated and could pay the land tax, the *iugatio*. The system of registration varied in different provinces. In Egypt, and probably Palestine and some other provinces, all the population, both freeholders and tenants (*coloni*) were registered by villages. In Asiana, and it would seem most provinces, freeholders were registered in their villages, tenants who lived on the estates which they cultivated under the land-lord's name on their several farms; freeholders who also rented land were registered in their villages.

The law was only very occasionally enforced against peasant pro-prietors, who rarely abandoned their holdings; there was moreover no one interested in enforcing it except the fellow villagers of the refugees, who had little chance of effective action. Landlords, on the other hand, perennially short of labour, welcomed a rule which prevented their tenants from moving elsewhere, and vigorously enforced the law and exercised pressure on the government for its extension and reinforcement. The tied tenancy was preserved even when the *capitatio*, its main *raison d'être*, was abolished by Valentinian I in Illyricum and by Theodosius I in Thrace.

> Throughout the whole diocese of Thrace the *capitatio* of persons is abolished and only the *iugatio* of land is to be paid, and lest it may appear that licence has been given to tenants, freed from the tie of taxation, to wander and go off where they wish, they shall be bound by the rule of origin, and though they appear to be free-born by condition, shall nevertheless be considered as slaves of the land itself to which they are born, and shall have no right of going off where they like or of changing their place, but the landowner shall enjoy his right over them with the care of a patron and the power of a master.[1]

In provinces, moreover, like Palestine, where tenants were not—probably owing to the system of registration—tied to individual farms and landowners, the stricter rule was introduced:

> Whereas in other provinces which are subject to the rule of our serenity a law instituted by our ancestors holds tenants down by a kind of eternal right, so that they are not allowed to leave the places by whose crops they are nurtured or desert the fields which they have once undertaken to cultivate, but the landlords of Palestine do not enjoy this advantage: we ordain that in Palestine also no tenant whatever be free to wander at his own choice, but as in other provinces be tied to the owner of the farm.[2]

The condition of tied tenants was progressively degraded. Constantine in 332 allowed landlords to chain *coloni* who were suspected of planning to leave; Valens enacted that they could not alienate their own property without their landlord's consent, and that the landlord should collect their taxes; Arcadius ruled that they might not sue their landlords except for increasing their rents. In the early fifth century they were declared ineligible for military service, and were forbidden to take holy orders without their landlord's consent.

How far landlords were successful in reclaiming tenants who absconded is hard to say, but it is clear from the heavy penalties frequently imposed that they were often willing to accept other landlords' *coloni* without asking awkward questions. Many tenants thus freed themselves

---

[1] *Cod. Just.* XI. lii. 1. [2] *Cod. Just.* XI. li. 1.

and their descendants; for it was only descendants of the original registered tenants who were tied, and newcomers were free. There thus grew up a considerable class of free tenants, comprising not only free-holders who also rented land, who had always been free, but tied tenants from elsewhere who had evaded detection, and also landless men who had lost their holdings through debt, or sold or abandoned them, and taken up vacant tenancies. In the late fourth century the laws begin to distinguish between ordinary *coloni* and tied *coloni*, who came to be styled either *originales* in the west or *censibus adscripti* and finally *adscripticii* in the east.

In 419 it was enacted that an *originalis* became legally free by pre-scription if he was absent from his farm for more than thirty years. In the west this rule was changed; he became the *originalis* of the landlord whose tenant he was when his thirty years absence was completed. In the east Anastasius enacted a different rule: any *colonus*, whether originally an *adscripticius* or a free tenant, if he stayed on the same farm for thirty years, became tied to it with his descendants, but did not suffer the other disabilities of an *adscripticius*. Justinian made the status of an *adscripticius* imprescriptable by any length of absence.

Justinian also made an important change in the rules governing adscript status. Hitherto the children of mixed marriages had been *adscripticii* if either parent was of that status. Justinian, on the legalistic ground that *adscripticii* were virtually slaves, applied the servile rule that the children of a free mother were free, even if the father was *adscripticius*. From the violent protests of landlords in Illyricum and Africa under Justinian himself and Justin II and Tiberius Constantine, it would appear that in these areas at any rate there was a large class of free peasants, either tenants or freeholders.

On the economic condition of the peasantry it is impossible to generalize, as conditions varied greatly. Peasants' freeholds differed widely in size; in one Egyptian village some held as much as $58\frac{3}{4}$ and $47\frac{1}{2}$ *arurae* (40 and 32 acres), some as little as $3\frac{1}{8}$ (2 acres) or even $1\frac{1}{4}$ (under 1 acre). *Colonicae* were of a more uniform size, but were some-times farmed by one family, sometimes by several in common. We know of thriving peasants, like the Egyptian Aurelius Sacaon, who owned 20 *arurae*, but leased much other land and also leased flocks of sheep and built up a considerable flock of his own. Some *coloni* owned a slave or two, and a law speaks of *coloni* of the *res privata* buying their holdings from the crown.

On the other hand, the rate of taxation had by the sixth century become crushing, equivalent to about a third of the crop on arable land, and rents—in Egypt, where alone we know them—were larger, usually half the crop or the equivalent in corn or gold (including tax). Rents were frozen by a law of Constantine, which remained on the statute book under Justinian, but the rule did not apply to short-term leases of one to seven years, such as were common in Egypt, nor probably when a new tenant was taken on from outside. It was in general evaded by various standard devices, such as making a surcharge on gold rents for lightweight coin, or using an outsize 'estate receipt measure' for rents in kind—Gregory the Great found *modius* measures of 25 *sextarii* (instead of the correct 16), being used on the papal estates and enacted that none larger than 18 *sextarii* should be used, and the Apions reckoned to gain 15 per cent on their corn rents by their estate measures. It also became increasingly common in the fifth and sixth centuries to add to the regular rent 'presents' in pork, geese, fowls, eggs, fruit, honey, etc.; such presents incidentally prove that *coloni* did keep pigs, poultry, bees, etc., and thus supplemented their main crop.

The clearest evidence of the poverty of the peasantry is given by a number of circumstantial stories of famines in Syria, Mesopotamia and Italy, in which the starving peasants flocked to the great towns for bread, and were fed from the state granaries or those of rich landlords. As the Roman world in general lived from hand to mouth, and very rarely carried over stocks from one season to another, this meant that even in a famine year taxes and rents were exacted from the peasants, though they might have nothing left to eat.

The above account exhausts Roman citizens. Since A.D. 212 when all free inhabitants of the empire were granted citizenship, their descendants had naturally been citizens, and the only aliens were barbarians settled since that date within the empire, such as *foederati* and *laeti*. Barbarians enlisted as soldiers seem to have received citizenship, and inhabitants of newly acquired areas, such as the Armenian satrapies, became Roman citizens by annexation. Slaves, if manumitted in proper legal form by will, before a provincial governor, or from Constantine's reign before a bishop, became Roman citizens, though they suffered from certain disabilities, such as ineligibility for the army, the civil service and the city councils. Informally manumitted slaves became what were called Latins, who differed from Romans only in that their patrons retained extensive rights over the succession to their property.

There remain slaves, a legal category which has very little social or economic content. We have no statistics of the absolute number of slaves or of their relative number to the free population; it can only be said that they were proportionally few. In the peaceful and orderly days of the first and second centuries, when there were few wars even on the frontiers, and piracy and kidnapping were well controlled, slaves became very dear (about 500 to 600 *denarii* for an unskilled adult, man or woman). The result was that most owners who could bred their slaves, and that for many purposes free labour was substituted for servile. On many estates, which had been stocked with slaves in the late republic or in the early decades of the principate, when slaves were still plentiful and cheap, the stock was maintained by breeding; on others the landlords went over to leasing their land in small holdings to free tenants. In the mines and quarries the contractors or managers ceased to use slaves (who in the conditions prevailing could not breed) and either turned over to free indentured labour or to convicts, or leased individual shafts to free tenants. Slavery thus survived in the main in domestic service, for which there was no alternative source of supply, as freeborn persons had a strong objection to it; in agriculture on some estates where it was already established; and for skilled jobs, whether manual or clerical, and posts of confidence, such as those of bailiffs or commercial agents. On the one hand it was not worth while to pay a high price for a slave unless one trained him to do remunerative work, and on the other masters preferred to entrust their affairs to slaves, whom they could keep indefinitely, thus profiting from their experience, and could punish more easily if they betrayed their interests.

In the later empire slave prices, owing to the more disturbed conditions, dropped to about half the rate prevailing in the second century; 20 *solidi* was the average price for an unskilled adult, 30 for a skilled craftsman, 50 for a trained clerk, while children up to ten cost about a *solidus* for each year of their age. Even so, however, slaves remained very dear, as compared with the great days of slavery in the second and first centuries B.C., and they were employed in the same range of avocations as under the principate. On the land they were employed as bailiffs (*vilici*) or agents (*actores, procuratores*) or even head tenants (*conductores*) of an estate or group of estates; as skilled hands, especially as vinedressers; and on some estates for ordinary agricultural labour. They do not seem to have worked in gangs, but leased holdings as *quasi coloni*. There were great regional variations in this matter: agricultural slaves were unknown in Egypt, but, it would seem, fairly common in Italy, where wealthy senators and equestrians had stocked their estates in republican days. Agricultural slaves were practically always hereditary, and we scarcely ever hear of landowners buying them. From the reign of Valentinian I they could not be sold apart from the land which they cultivated, and their position was for most practical purposes indistinguishable from *coloni adscripticii*. They *de facto* owned personal property (their *peculium*), and some are known to have made wills; their owner could quash such instruments (which were of course legally null) but usually did so only to prevent their property passing to outsiders off his estates.

In industry the only large blocks of slaves were those in the mints and the state dyeing and weaving establishments. The workers in the mints had always been state slaves, and Diocletian seems to have stocked the factories with convicts. These groups became hereditary, and ceased to differ in any significant point from the workmen in the state arms factories, who were legally soldiers. The ostlers, wheelwrights, and vets in the public post were also hereditary state slaves, as were the maintenance staff of the Roman aqueducts. We very rarely hear of private slave factories, and most industrial slaves were probably apprentices and assistants of more prosperous craftsmen. From the preservation of the complicated rules governing it in Justinian's Digest, it would appear that the system of *institores* was not uncommon. These were slaves who ran a shop or workshop on their own, paying their owner a fixed income, and keeping the surplus profit and being responsible for the debts. Slaves were also used as clerks and commercial agents, and, it would appear, sometimes as skippers of ships.

It is probable that the majority of slaves were domestic servants. Domestic slaves were a status symbol, and no one with any pretensions to gentility could dispense with at least one, even if he could not really afford it. Non-commissioned officers (and even privates in the guards) commonly had one or two. Libanius draws a pitiful picture of his assistant lecturers, who could not afford to marry, lived in lodgings and owed money to the baker, and, supreme degradation, could only afford two or three slaves. Rich senators kept hundreds, if not thousands, if the moralists are to be believed.

Apart from breeding the main source of slaves was persons captured in war, and for this reason prices were lower in the frontier provinces. Barbarian prisoners of war were not always sold by the government, which often preferred to enrol them in the army, settle them as *laeti*, or sell or grant them to landlords as *coloni*, so that they and their descendants would remain liable to conscription. There were occasional gluts, as when Radagaesus' men were sold off at a *solidus* apiece, but the normal intake cannot have been very large. Barbarians also sold their fellow countrymen captured in intertribal wars, and Roman citizens captured in their raids. The latter in strict law automatically regained their liberty and property as soon as they set foot on Roman soil, but they had to serve their purchasers until they could pay off their price, until Honorius in 408 introduced the more merciful rule that they were free after five years' service. Despite the law many ignorant persons, especially children, must have remained slaves through ignorance of their rights or because they could not establish their identity. On the other hand many Roman prisoners were redeemed by the churches, which, especially in the frontier provinces, regarded this work as a primary duty, and spent much of their funds on it; they were allowed to alienate plate and even land for the purpose.

Other sources of slaves were foundlings (until Justinian declared them free); newborn children of poor parents, who could be legally sold from Diocletian's reign; and older children sold or given as security for loans; both practices were illegal but common. Adults could also collusively allow themselves to be sold, and if they shared in the price, legally forfeited their freedom. Humble persons found guilty of crimes or misdemeanours could also be condemned to penal servitude in the mines, quarries and the Roman bakeries.

XXII

Agriculture

The principal cereal crop of the Roman empire was wheat, the next largest was barley, which was mainly used for animal fodder, and also brewed into beer in Egypt, northern Gaul and Illyricum. Peas and beans were also extensively grown, and onions and cabbages and other vegetables. Flax was commonly raised for manufacture into linen; a peculiar crop was papyrus in Egypt, which supplied paper for the whole empire. Viticulture was very widespread, and had extended into northern Gaul; wine was the staple drink of all classes in Mediterranean lands, and of the upper classes everywhere. Olives were very important, providing not only the principal edible fat used in the Mediterranean area, but also soap and lamp oil. Olives were cultivated as far north as they would grow, and in desert areas in Africa and Syria, where they have now ceased to exist or been recently reintroduced; in some areas, notably the desert parts of Syria, there was a marked advance in olive growing in the fifth and sixth centuries. Various fruit and nut trees were also cultivated, often in now arid zones.

Cattle, sheep and goats, donkeys, mules and horses, pigs and poultry were raised throughout the empire. Cattle were used mainly as draught animals, though some cows were kept for milk and cheese, usually, it would seem, on water meadows, and their skins were an important source of leather. The ubiquitous goat was valued for its milk, meat,

BIBLIOGRAPHY. There is an excellent survey of later Roman agriculture, especially on the technical side, by C. E. Stevens in *The Cambridge Economic History*, vol. I, ch. ii. E. R. Hardy, *The Large Estates of Byzantine Egypt* (New York, 1931), gives a good account, based on the papyri, of the management of large estates, especially those of the Apion family. An analytic list of Egyptian land leases from Diocletian to the Arab conquest is given in Johnson and West, *Byzantine Egypt; Economic Studies*, 80–93. The system of estate management of the Roman See is described in Holmes Dudden, *Gregory the Great* (London, 1905), on the basis of Gregory's letters. On the whole subject of agriculture see also Chapter x of my *Later Roman Empire*.

skin and hair. Some mutton was eaten but sheep were generally raised for their wool; they also supplied milk. Pigs were the main meat producers. Many animals were kept on mixed farms, but some areas specialized in breeding various species. Pigs were for instance, raised in large numbers for the Roman market in the mountains of south Italy, which were well forested. The best sheep were grazed on the uplands of Spain and central Asia Minor and in northern Gaul and south-east Italy; wool called Asturian, Laodicene, Tarentine and Atrebatic, fetched high prices (100, 150 and 175 and 200 *denarii* the pound respectively, as against 50 for 'best medium wool' and 25 for 'other wool'). Donkeys and mules were the ordinary transport animals, but horses were used by the upper classes and in the army; some areas, such as Spain and Cappadocia, were famous for their racehorses. Camels were also bred in the deserts of Syria and Africa, and used extensively as pack animals in most parts of the empire, including Gaul.

We know very little of the methods of tillage except in Mediterranean lands, for which the contemporary agricultural handbook of Palladius was written. To judge by this work there were no technical advances and no retrogression from the practice of the republic and the early empire. For cereals land was fallowed in alternate years (except in Egypt where the annual flood refertilized the soil with silt), and a laborious technique of dry farming was followed, with frequent ploughing and hoeing to break up the soil and keep down weeds and conserve moisture.

What little we know of yields is confined to wheat, and it is not very much. In Egypt one *artaba* was sown to the *arura* and a tenfold yield was expected every year on flooded land. This is equivalent in modern terms to about $7\frac{1}{2}$ quintals per hectare, which compares very badly with the 20 quintals which Egypt today produces with modern seed and fertilizers and perennial irrigation; but it compares favourably with modern Syria, Iraq and Tunisia, which produce only 5 to 7 quintals. If we may use figures from an earlier period, as we probably may, since conditions and techniques were unchanged, Cicero states that in Sicily land was sown nearly twice as thick as in Egypt and normally yielded eightfold, and Varro gives rather higher yields, tenfold or even fifteenfold, for Etruria. These figures are equivalent to 11 quintals per hectare for Sicily (as compared with the modern $10\frac{1}{2}$) and from 11 to 17 quintals for Italy (as compared with the modern Italian average of 18). But it must be remembered that in antiquity only half the land was utilized in any year. Egypt thus yielded more per annum ($7\frac{1}{2}$ quintals) for the same area than did Sicily ($5\frac{1}{2}$ quintals).

All we can say of viticulture was that it was much more profitable than arable cultivation. For taxation 5 *iugera* of vineyard were assessed as equal to 20 *iugera* of best arable in Syria, and in metayage leases in Egypt the tenant kept only a third or a quarter of the crop in vineyards as against a half on arable land. One *iugerum* of olive-yard was assessed at the same figure as 5 *iugera* of vineyard or 20 of the best arable land.

Agriculture was far and away the major industry of the Roman empire. The land tax (including the clothing levy), levied on agricultural land, stock and the rural population, seems to have yielded about twenty times as much as the *chrysargyron*, levied on merchants and craftsmen and their capital assets. Of the other forms of revenue, the *aurum oblaticium, aurum coronarium, follis* and *aurum tironicum* were all surtaxes on various classes of landowners, and the *res privata* was fed by rents, almost entirely of agricultural land. Customs were probably not a significant item in the revenue, and in any case fell on all classes alike.

Agriculture also provided the overwhelming bulk of the national income of the empire. The incomes of senators and *honorati* and decurions were almost entirely derived from rents. The revenues of cities came mainly from the same source, and those of the churches from rents and offerings which were normally first fruits. All these rents came predominantly from agricultural land; in the rent roll of the Roman church nearly 90 per cent was agricultural and a little over 10 per cent came from house property, baths, bakeries, warehouses and so forth. Most professional men—civil servants, lawyers, doctors, clergy— supplemented their earnings with the rents of land which they owned, and soldiers often owned a little land, as did many merchants and craftsmen. Millions of peasants derived their living from the land.

The ownership of land was very widely dispersed. We know from Egyptian census records and from deeds from Ravenna that quite humble urban shopkeepers and craftsmen often owned a piece or two of land. The clergy were also quite often, if not normally, landowners. They asked for, and failed to get, immunity from taxation on their private lands, and we have many individual records, from the estates of Remigius of Rheims, set out in detail in his will, to the statements of Augustine on his priests and deacons, whom he required to sell their land. One reason for this state of affairs was the law of intestate succession and the testamentary habits of the age, whereby all sons shared more or less equally in the estate (and daughters too unless they had already been dowered). This meant that when one brother of a land-owning family went into the civil service, the army, the church or trade, he kept his share of the land. Another reason was that land was the only permanent investment, and those who made money in the professions or trade or manufacture bought land. There was in fact an always unsatisfied land hunger of the well-to-do.

The physical pattern of landowning was for the same reason highly complicated, most landlords from the greatest to the smallest owning a number of scattered parcels. Great senators possessed estates in many provinces. Melania, who belonged to the ancient Roman senatorial aristocracy, owned land in various parts of Italy, Sicily, Africa, Numidia, Mauretania, Spain and Britain. Paulinus of Pella, a lesser senator, had estates near Bordeaux and in many cities of Achaea and Old and New Epirus. The church of Rome held patrimonies in every province of Italy, Sicily, Africa, Gaul and Dalmatia. The estate office of the Great Church of Constantinople had departments for Thrace, Asiana, Pontica and Oriens (including Egypt). Both the churches of Milan and Ravenna held land in Sicily. Cities also sometimes possessed estates outside their own territories; Nicaea for instance in the territory of Apanea. Lesser landlords, such as decurions, owned many farms—Tatian of Tralles had fourteen and his lesser colleagues Critias and Latron seven and four —and they were not always in the city territory. Even the humblest landowners often owned several parcels; we know of a Hermopolitan who owned three holdings, each leased to a different tenant, totalling 9 *arurae* (6 acres).

The basic unit of ownership in the west was the estate or *fundus*, which was a fairly stable unit, usually named after some long-past owner, the Fundus Cornelianus, Claudianus and so forth. It was normally divided into a home farm and a number of tenancies (*colonicae*); we know of two *fundi* at Padua one of which was divided into nine holdings (total rent roll 38½ *solidi*), the other into ten (rent roll over 44 *solidi*). *Fundi* naturally varied in size, but a rental value of from 60 to 40 *solidi* was the mean in Italy. They could be subdivided; we know of many landlords who owned half, a third or even an eighth of a *fundus*. On the other hand they could be grouped in *massae*, with rentals usually in the range of 600 to 300 *solidi*, but sometimes much larger; we know of one *massa* which comprised over 30 *fundi*, and another with a rental of 1,650 *solidi*. *Massae* were not necessarily solid blocks of land, but large landowners tended to hold large blocks, because they had less occasion to divide them between their heirs and had often pursued a policy of rounding off their estates for generations. The newly rich family of the Apions owned a great deal of land in Egypt, but all in moderate-sized farms and even small holdings interspersed with peasant freeholders. Melania owned huge blocks of land; one *massa* is said to have comprised sixty-two hamlets.

Landowners managed their land in a variety of ways. The Apion family were perhaps exceptional in leasing their land directly to the working tenants in small lots. They employed a hierarchy of agents to collect the rents in gold, corn and wine, to build cisterns, maintain canals, distribute irrigation machinery to the tenants, and to plant vineyards and otherwise improve the estate. At the head was the 'deputy owner', under him 'administrators', and under them 'supervisors'. A supervisor was quite a humble person, who looked after one or two hamlets, and scattered peasant holdings in the same area; we have the contract of one Serenus, a deacon, who was paid 2 *solidi* and 24 *artabae* of wheat (worth 2½ *solidi*) per annum, but evidently made more in perquisites, as he paid 12 *solidi* for one year's appointment.

Most great landlords were much more passive. They employed agents of various grades (*procuratores* and *actores*), but leased their estates in large blocks to head tenants or contractors (*conductores*), usually for short terms. These *conductores* collected the rents of the working tenants or *coloni*. Thus Lauricius, formerly *praepositus sacri cubiculi* of Honorius, had a head agent, the tribune Pyrrhus, and several *actores* in Sicily, but leased his land, which consisted of three *massae* (rents 445, 500 and 756 *solidi*) and a *fundus* (rent 147 *solidi*) and part of a *fundus* (52 *solidi*) to five *conductores*. The Roman church employed a similar system, but its *conductores* were apparently smaller men. Each patrimony, which generally comprised the lands in one province, had a *rector*, who was usually a deacon, subdeacon, *defensor* or notary of the Roman church, and under him *actores* or *actionarii*, and under them *conductores*; there were 400 *conductores* in Sicily, which exceptionally formed two patrimonies, the districts of Syracuse and of Palermo.

Procuratores and *actores* were commonly slaves of the owner, and so curiously enough were *conductores* occasionally. But landlords sometimes preferred to employ local men of substance and position, who would be able to stand up to the government. We find bishops active in these capacities, a practice which church councils condemned, and military officers and high-grade civil servants (absentees from their regiments and offices). The government objected to these practices, as such agents made use of their judicial privileges to evade the payment of taxes on the estates which they managed.

Some private owners let estates on emphyteutic leases, that is long-term leases, for life, several lives or in perpetuity, at a fixed rent, with an obligation to ameliorate the land, which was normally in a bad state initially; such leases could be inherited, bequeathed or sold. The practice was rare with private landlords, but common with corporate owners, who wished to avoid administrative trouble and possible losses, and receive a safe if reduced income. Emphyteutic or perpetual leases became standard for crown lands, and very common for church lands. The emperors of the fourth and fifth centuries imposed various restrictions on church leases of this type, which sometimes degenerated into virtual alienation of the land, either limiting their length to twenty years or three lives (those of the original lessee and his children and grandchildren), or insisting that the rent must be not substantially below the rack rent.

The condition of the *coloni*, whether free, adscript or servile, has been described in the previous chapter. Most farmers employed supplementary casual labour in the peak periods of the harvest and vintage; these labourers might be townsmen, and in Egypt were often monks and hermits, who thus made enough to live on for the rest of the year. On some estates regular weekly labour services were exacted from the *coloni* for the cultivation of the home farm of the *fundus*, but the practice appears to have been rare.

There can be little doubt that from the middle of the third century, if not earlier, down to the end of the sixth, there was a significant and progressive shrinkage in the area cultivated. The principal evidence is the imperial legislation on deserted lands. The government frequently utilized such lands for the settlement of veterans and barbarian prisoners or immigrants, but its primary objective was fiscal, to maintain the land tax, and it adopted a variety of means to achieve this end. It sometimes tried to induce the owner or a new owner to bring the land under cultivation again by temporary remission or reduction of tax, or in the case of crown lands the grant of a more secure title to the lessee with reduction of rent. It tried to compel owners of mixed land, part profitable, part deserted, to pay the taxes of the deserted land out of the profits of the better farms. It went yet further and allocated waste land to owners of good land, or to a village or city corporately, making them pay the tax, and leaving them, if they thought it worth while, to cultivate the land or find tenants who would do so. It might make the city financially responsible, imposing a general extra levy on all landowners to make up for the deficit arising on deserted lands in the territory. Only as a last resort did it write off deserted lands.

On crown lands the administrative problem was simple. Lands which had deteriorated were let on emphyteutic or perpetual leases, with initial remissions of rent. Care was taken to mix profitable and unprofitable lands in all leases, and to ensure that lessees of bad land had good private land of their own. On private land the problem was complicated by the rights of owners. They were encouraged to resume possession by cancellation of arrears and temporary remission of tax; if they failed to do so, the lands were auctioned or given away on similar terms, but the original owner was often allowed to reclaim his land within a short period (usually two years), provided that he compensated the new owner for improvements. If no willing tenant could be found deserted lands were compulsorily allocated.

The allocation was based on two main principles. The owner (or heir) of any aggregate of lands had to accept the tax responsibility for all the land, good or bad; at the most he might claim a reassessment by a *peraequator*, who would balance the losses on the bad against the gains on the good. This principle was extended to any aggregate of lands which had once been under common ownership. Thus, to cite an example given in an edict of Demosthenes, praetorian prefect of the East in 521 and 529, A having sold one estate to an outsider X, left the rest to his heirs, B, C and D, and D later sold part of his share to another outsider Y, who subsequently defaulted. On whom do the taxes of this estate fall? First on D the vendor, then on his coheirs B and C, and finally on X, the purchaser of an estate once owned by A. This form of allocation was known as ἐπιβολὴ ὁμοδούλων. Secondly deserted lands might be allocated, especially in a *peraequatio* of a city territory, to any suitable owner in the same fiscal area; this was known as ἐπιβολὴ ὁμοκήνσων. A third principle, of minor importance, was that any landowner who received runaway slaves (in Justinian's reign *coloni* also) from a deserted estate, or even legally petitioned the crown for slaves left on a deserted estate, had to accept responsibility for the taxes of that estate.

We have some figures which give clues to the magnitude of the problem. Julian assigned 3,000 *iuga* of uncultivated land to the council of Antioch, remitting the taxes; as the total assessment of Antioch cannot have been under 60,000 *iuga*, the proportion of deserted land was less than 5 per cent. Under Valens of the confiscated civic estates of the province of Asia 6,736½ *iuga* were in good condition, and 703, less than 10 per cent, 'deserted and in bad condition and sterile'. In 395 Honorius wrote off 528,042 *iugera* in the province of Campania; this would be about 10 per cent. In Proconsular Africa and Byzacena in 422 the figures were much more alarming. Of the imperial land in the former province 5,700 *centuriae* 144½ *iugera* were deserted and 9,002 *centuriae* and 141 *iugera* in good condition, while in the latter the figures were 7,615 *centuriae* 3½ *iugera* and 7,560 *centuriae* 180 *iugera*; that is a third of the land was deserted in Proconsularis, and half in Byzacena. In 451 Valentinian III allocated to refugee landowners from Africa and Byzacena the 13,000 deserted *centuriae* of Numidia. Finally in 451 of the 62,000 *iuga* of the Syrian city of Cyrrhus 15,000 *iuga* paid their tax in gold, and of these 2,500, a sixth, were deserted.

In assessing the causes of this phenomenon it must be remembered that the great bulk of the land not only continued to be cultivated, but to pay a heavy tax, amounting in the sixth century to about a third of the gross product, and in most cases a rent which included and exceeded the tax. Many landowners still continued in the sixth century to draw enormous rents from their estates, and there continued to be a keen demand for land, as is demonstrated by the perennial petitions for crown lands, and the constant pressure to buy or secure emphyteutic leases of church lands.

It has been suggested that the main cause was exhaustion of the soil. This would account for many individual cases, where hard-pressed farmers had not been able to cope with the laborious technique of cultivation needed in Mediterranean lands, or had been tempted to omit fallow years. Such land could, however, be put into good condition again; it is noticeable that landowners were very liable to reclaim their lands when improved by the new owners who had bought them or received them from the crown—former owners often reasserted their title even to lands granted to veterans. Exhaustion of the soil is moreover not a complete explanation; for deserted lands were not uncommon in Egypt, where the fertility of the soil was annually renewed by the flood. There is in fact no evidence for progressive or permanent exhaustion of the soil, and clearly much land continued to be in good heart.

Denudation may account for part of the loss. In most Mediterranean lands denudation has now gone very far. The forests which originally covered the mountains have been felled, and grazing, particularly by goats, has prevented new growth; the soil on the uplands has as a result been washed away; and perennial streams have become occasional torrents, whose floods often wash away the good soil of the plains. The ancients cut timber recklessly for roofing buildings and constructing ships, and checked new growth by cutting brushwood for fuel—the thousands of baths must have consumed enormous quantities —and by grazing goats. It is nevertheless improbable that denudation had gone very far even by the sixth century. It is evident that there was then still plenty of forest in areas now completely treeless, for thousands of churches of the basilican form, which requires long roof timbers, were built in the fourth, fifth and sixth centuries. In inland towns this timber must have been cut locally, for the cost of transporting big timber by land was prohibitive. In the second place archaeological remains show that many areas now desert were densely inhabited in the sixth century. A curious test case is the peninsula of Mount Athos, where timber has been cut in moderation and all animals, including goats, excluded since about A.D. 900. It presents a complete contrast to the rest of Greece, being well wooded, with plenty of soil on the hills and perennial streams.

Another possible explanation is declining security. This of course mainly affected the northern frontier provinces along the Rhine and the Danube, where barbarian raiders constantly carried off the crops and killed or drove away the cattle and other stock. Many farmers, if they were not themselves killed or enslaved, must have lost heart, and in fact deserted lands seem to have been common in the frontier areas. Similar conditions prevailed on some desert frontiers, where the bedouin—the Moors, Blemmyes, Saracens and so forth—became more aggressive and were no longer effectively controlled, and in some inland areas where large-scale brigandage prevailed; the Isaurians regularly raided eastern Asia Minor and northern Syria in the fourth and fifth centuries, until they were finally quelled by Anastasius.

Another explanation which has been strongly urged is declining manpower. This, in the absence of any statistics, is difficult to prove or to disprove. There was a great plague under Marcus Aurelius, which recurred at intervals down to the third quarter of the third century. No other major epidemic is recorded until the bubonic plague which swept over the empire from 542 onwards, recurring frequently in the next thirty years. This great plague undoubtedly did, as Procopius declares, cause the abandonment of many estates for lack of cultivators, but there is not much sign that shortage of manpower was important before Justinian's reign. The great plague of Marcus Aurelius had caused a similar crisis—he had to settle barbarian prisoners on the land in large numbers and Pertinax (A.D. 193) is the first emperor known to have legislated on deserted lands.

It is probable that the rural population was permanently reduced and that agricultural labour remained in general in short supply. What figures there are—and they are very tenuous and doubtful—suggest that on various estates of western Asia Minor of which we possess census records, the slaves and *coloni* in the fourth century were well under half the optimum number recommended by the agricultural experts of the second century B.C. and the first century A.D., Cato and Columella. Landlords were most reluctant to surrender their tenants as recruits to the army and preferred to pay 25 *solidi* a man (more than what an unskilled slave cost). They also, despite the penalties, welcomed runaway slaves and *coloni*, and miners and urban workmen. There was no flight from the land to the towns, but rather the reverse. There is however very little evidence until Justinian's reign that shortage of labour caused the abandonment of land. In one law it is envisaged that a new owner or lessee, having taken over a deteriorated farm, might supplement the labour force with slaves; but on the other hand, other laws suggest that some owners abandoned estates with their slaves or tenants on them.

Contemporaries from Lactantius onwards attribute the abandonment of land to high taxation, and what figures there are support their contention. By Justinian's reign the rate of tax on arable land in Egypt was equivalent to $7\frac{2}{3}$ carats per *arura* and the normal rent to about 12 carats on average land, but often less on inferior land. At the same period in Italy out of a gross rental of $2,171\frac{1}{2}$ *solidi* 1,239 (57 per cent) went in taxation, and, as the estates in question belonged to the church and did not therefore pay supplementary dues, the normal rate of taxation must have been even higher. This meant that, as the land tax rose, more and more marginal land, whose rent was below average, ceased to yield any profit to the landlord and might involve him in loss; in which case he abandoned it, no doubt usually withdrawing the labour to more profitable farms.

It may be noted that deserted lands were almost entirely rented farms. We very rarely hear of peasants abandoning their freeholds, and then usually for special reasons. In the Egyptian village of Theadelphia the three surviving villagers complained in 332 that the other twenty-two had all made off to neighbouring landlords or villages; but this was because Theadelphia depended upon a canal and other villages had for two years past intercepted their water. A case at another Egyptian village, Caranis, in 340, is suggestive.[1] 'The father of the defendants . . . cultivated them well and got profits from them and at the same time paid the public taxes on them to the most sacred treasury . . . and it

[1] F. Preisigke, *Sammelbuch griechischer Urkunden aus Aegypten*, 8246.

appears, to make a long story short, that the father of the defendants died leaving as his heirs his daughters, i.e. the defendants, and they, not being able to stand up against the taxes demanded for the same lands, fled.' It seems likely that the daughters had to lease the land, and on this basis it ceased to pay.

If the taxes were the main factor in the abandonment of land, it obviously made a great difference if they were equitably assessed or not. The accuracy of the assessment varied very greatly in different provinces. In some, like Syria, the land was valued according to its use and quality, in others, like Egypt and Asiana, by its use only—olives, vines, arable and pasture—without any account of quality; in others, like south Italy and Africa, by area, without regard to use or quality. Marginal land was thus in Africa taxed as heavily as good land, and this is probably the principal reason for the enormous figures of abandoned land in Numidia, Proconsularis and Byzacena; for much land in Tunisia is marginal. Other special contributory factors may have been incipient erosion and Moorish raids and sabotage by Donatist peasants.

The average loss would seem to have been in the range of 10 to 15 per cent in area, and less in produce, since the lands abandoned were marginal. This was a serious loss but not catastrophic.

XXIII

Trade and Industry

The external trade of the empire was not important. From the northern barbarians little was imported but slaves, and the account was probably balanced by the export of manufactured goods. From Armenia, Persia and the Caucasian lands came very highly priced slaves, eunuchs. The other principal imports were highly priced luxury goods which came from the east either by long sea or by caravan across central Asia; incense from the Yemen, pepper from Malabar, sundry other spices and perfumes, and above all silk from China. The sea trade was shared by Alexandrian and Arab shippers; goods that came overland had to be bought on the Persian frontier, and their price was vastly augmented by numerous tolls en route. Hence Justinian's attempts to establish friendly relations with the kingdoms of the Axumites and Himyarites, who controlled the southern extremity of the Red Sea, and thus to facilitate direct sea voyages to India and Ceylon to buy silk. These imports were apparently paid for almost entirely in gold coin, but the drain on the empire's currency was not noticeable. On the contrary, the amount of gold in circulation in the empire seems to have risen from the fourth century onwards, mainly in all probability by the release of demonetized hoards.

Foreign trade was charged a high duty ($12\frac{1}{2}$ per cent), and strictly controlled, being allowed only at a few licensed places, Clysma (Suez) or Iotabe (in the gulf of Aqaba) for the sea-borne eastern trade, Hieron on the Bosphorus for the Black Sea, Nisibis, later Callinicum, for overland trade with Persia, and two or three towns on the Danube. Here the government *commerciarii* tried to prevent the passage of certain articles

BIBLIOGRAPHY. See Chapter XXI of my *Later Roman Empire* (Oxford, 1964).
The principal primary sources are Diocletian's *Edict on Prices* and the laws in *Cod. Theod.* XIII. v-ix, *Cod. Just.* XI. i-v (*navicularii*), *Cod. Theod.* VIII. v, vi, *Cod. Just.* XII, li, lii (*cursus publicus*), *Cod. Theod.* X. xix, xx, xxii, *Cod. Just.* XI. vi-ix (mines and factories).

whose export was prohibited for security reasons, such as iron, bronze, arms and armour, and bought up certain imports, notably silk, in which the state had a monopoly.

For internal trade conditions were in some ways very favourable. The Roman empire formed a vast common market, with negligible internal tolls (of 2 or 2½ per cent), and a common currency which was abundant and, so far as the gold coins were concerned, stable and of excellent quality. The state of the small change was deplorable until Anastasius' reign, but this only affected minor transactions. Within the Mediterranean piracy was kept under control and did not seriously affect sea-borne trade, even during the fifth century, when the Vandals conducted raids from Africa. On land there was extensive brigandage in some areas, notably by the Isaurians in eastern Asia Minor and northern Syria, but again not on a scale to impede commerce. Roads and bridges were quite well maintained, and so were canals and harbours.

There were, however, a number of factors which limited trade. In the first place transport by land was very expensive and slow, and by sea erratic and somewhat risky. Secondly, the largest single consumer, the state, made virtually no use of private traders, obtaining most of its multifarious needs—food and clothing for the army, civil service and its other employees, weapons and horses for the army, draught animals for the post, timber and stone for public works—by levies in kind, or sometimes producing them in its own establishments; transporting them by its own shipping and wagon services; and distributing them through its administrative machine. Thirdly, and probably most important of all, the market was very confined, since the vast majority of the population, the peasants, produced their own food and had very little surplus to buy anything, and bought the cheapest goods from local craftsmen.

The normal means of land transport were pack donkeys or camels and for heavier loads ox wagons. The average pace of a donkey or camel is three miles per hour and of an ox about two miles per hour. We have in Diocletian's tariff exact figures for transport charges; the rate was 4 *denarii* per mile for a donkey, 8 *denarii* for a camel (load 600 pounds) and 20 *denarii* for a wagon (load 1,200 pounds). This works out that a load of wheat would be doubled in price by a journey of 300 miles by wagon, 375 miles by camel. Sea charges were very much lower, especially for long journeys. The charge per *modius* from Alexandria to Rome, some 1,250 miles, was 16 *denarii*, from Syria to Lusitania 26 *denarii*. It was thus cheaper to transport wheat from one end of the empire to the other by sea than to cart it seventy-five miles.

In these circumstances inland water transport was of great importance. This accounts for the predominance of ports like Arles, Marseilles, Ephesus or Alexandria, which lay at or near the mouth of extensive river systems. One reason for the value of Egypt as a source of corn was that practically no place in Egypt is over ten miles from the Nile or a navigable canal. In Africa too most of the corn land is within easy reach of the sea or of the navigable Bagradas river. It was logistic reasons also which mainly dictated the adoption of the Rhine and Danube as frontiers. In the fourth century the Rhine army was largely fed by sea from Britain, and in the sixth the army of the lower Danube was supplied by sea from the maritime provinces of Caria, Cyprus and the Aegean Islands. The upper Danube army presented a problem which imposed great strain on the road transport system.

Roughly speaking it may be said that it did not pay commercially to cart corn for more than about fifty miles. When there was a famine at Antioch Julian had to use the *cursus publicus* to move corn from Hierapolis, 100 miles away, and Chalcis, not much over fifty. At Caesarea of Cappadocia, as Gregory of Nazianzus explains, famines were disastrous; 'coastal cities support such shortages without much difficulty, as they can dispose of their own products and receive supplies by sea; for us inland our surpluses are unprofitable and our scarcities irremediable, as we have no means of disposing of what we have or of importing what we lack'. The corn trade did not pay although the normal price of corn was much higher in big towns, at Antioch 15 *modii* to the *solidus* according to Julian, against a general average of about 30 *modii*; hence the common practice of subsidizing the corn supply of large cities.

Sea transport, though infinitely cheaper, had its drawbacks. The sailing season was limited to the six summer months—the *navicularii* were not expected to accept cargoes between 10 October and 31 March, and the dates recorded in the Codes show that even imperial couriers did not risk the voyage from Italy to Africa in winter. As the ancients could not beat against the wind, ships were held up for long periods not only by calms or storms but by contrary winds. In favourable circumstances voyages could be very quick—Narbonne to Carthage in five days, twelve or thirteen days from Ascalon to Thessalonica and vice versa, ten days from Constantinople to Gaza (but twenty in the reverse direction), Alexandria to Marseilles in thirty days; but we also hear of long waits for bad weather.

Ships were mostly small and not very seaworthy. The largest ship of which we have record was of 50,000 *modii* (about 330 tons deadweight) and one of 35,000 *modii* is spoken of as exceptional. The normal capacity for corn ships was 20,000 to 10,000 *modii* (130 to 60 tons) and little ships of 2,000 *modii* (15 tons) were common and might be chartered by the government for the transport of corn. Shipwrecks were evidently quite common even in the summer; the apportionment of loss in the case of *navicularii* was the subject of many petitions and much legislation. Cargoes were also often spoilt by sea water or had to be jettisoned; there is a large body of the law on the rules of average to be applied in such cases.

The government transported all its cargoes by sea, not only the corn from Africa to Rome and Egypt to Constantinople, but supplies for the army, through the guilds of state shippers (*navicularii*). These were, as explained earlier, substantial landowners who in return for rebate of land tax, immunity from curial duties and sundry other privileges, built, maintained and operated ships. They were paid freight at about half the commercial rate, and were frankly expected to make up the deficit from their lands. We know much less about inland water transport, but there were state-controlled guilds of bargees on the Tiber to carry corn up from Ostia to Rome, and to collect fuel for the Roman baths; there was also a state boat service on the Po from Pavia to Ravenna. On the Nile there was a mixed service of government and municipal and private ships, organized by the state.

For land transport there was an elaborate and comprehensive state-operated service, the *cursus publicus*. It consisted of two divisions, the express post (*cursus velox*), which provided saddle horses, pack horses, light two-wheeled carriages drawn by three mules and four-wheeled carriages (eight to ten mules); and the wagon post (*cursus clabularis*), which provided ox wagons with two pairs of oxen for heavy goods. The *cursus velox* provided transport mainly for imperial couriers and other officials travelling on public business, but also carried light and valuable goods, such as gold and silver and superior clothing—and the bibles provided by Eusebius, bishop of Caesarea, for the churches of Constantinople. The *cursus clabularis* handled foodstuffs, clothing, arms, stone and timber, and the baggage of troops in transit.

The service consisted of major and minor posting stations (*mansiones* and *mutationes*), placed at intervals of ten or a dozen miles along all the major roads. From Bordeaux via northern Italy to Constantinople there were 208 stations, and from Chalcedon to Jerusalem 102: the service included out-of-the-way areas like Sardinia. At each station were kept an appropriate number of animals—according to Procopius as many as forty horses, but this was probably only on trunk roads—carriages and wagons, and veterinary surgeons, cartwrights and ostlers (the last on the scale of one to three animals): these were hereditary public slaves paid in rations and clothing. The buildings were maintained from the provincial taxes by the governor; beasts were provided by a regular levy (animals had an average useful life of four years, and a quarter were therefore annually replaced; in an emergency extra animals could be requisitioned temporarily); fodder was supplied from local taxation in kind. Each station, or sometimes group of stations, was managed by a *manceps*, who was usually a decurion, sometimes a retired official, who served for five years. Inspectors (*curiosi*), one or two per province, drawn from the *agentes in rebus*, kept a check on the service, especially on its unauthorized use by private persons. The use of the post was controlled by travel warrants (*evectiones* for the express post, *tractoriae* for the wagon post), issued by the praetorian prefects and the masters of the offices, and doled out in limited numbers to other office-holders down to provincial governors, who had two only, one for communication with the central government and one for local use. Warrants were often given to private persons, such as bishops attending councils and senators for their agents buying horses and wild beasts for the games.

The post was, in some sections at any rate, heavily overloaded. There are numerous regulations fixing the maximum number of horses, carriages and carts which a station might despatch on any day, and the maximum loads (30 pounds for a rider, 200 pounds for a two-wheeled carriage, 1,000 pounds for a four-wheeled carriage, 1,500 pounds for an ox wagon). The service was also enormously expensive, and economical emperors cut it down. Julian abolished the express post in Sardinia; Leo the wagon post throughout Oriens, making use of private carters; John the Cappadocian abolished both services in large areas, such as Asiana. According to Procopius and John Lydus, the landowners of this diocese, who had hitherto paid the bulk of their taxes in fodder, were ruined by this move, since being inland they could not dispose of their crops; this gives some idea of the consumption of barley by the *cursus publicus*.

The state manufactured all arms and armour required for the army in about forty state factories (*fabricae*), including those of the *barbaricarii*, who made ornamental parade armour for officers. It also manufactured a proportion of the clothing required for the army and the civil service in state linen mills (*linyphia*), woollen mills (*gynaecia*) and dye works (*baphia*). In the western parts there were two *linyphia*, fourteen *gynaecia* and nine *baphia*; no figures are available for the eastern parts. The *fabricae* were originally under the general management of praetorian prefects, from the late fourth century of the master of the offices, the other factories were under the *comes sacrarum largitionum*. Each had a manager and they were staffed by hereditary groups of workers who received rations, technically soldiers in the *fabricae*, and public slaves in the clothing factories. The system was apparently that each factory was expected to produce an annual quota of its products, the raw materials being provided by the government from taxation in kind. The provision of charcoal for the arms factories was a *sordidum munus* on landowners. The dyeworks produced their own dyes, fishing for the murex. The factories were quite large establishments; the armament workers of Adrianople and Caesarea of Cappadocia are spoken of as a major element in the city population, and so are the woollen workers at Caesarea, and the woollen workers and the employees in the mint at Cyzicus.

The state also had its own quarries; in the east the marble quarries of Proconnesus (an island in the sea of Marmora), Alexandria Troas, and Docimium (in Phrygia) were famous, and were regularly worked by convict labour. Other quarries were worked as need occurred by *corvée* labour. The government also owned many mines, and levied taxes in gold, silver, copper and iron from the owners of private mines.

In the fourth century the government requisitioned and distributed most of its other requirements, foodstuffs and more clothes for the army and civil service (including the industrial grades mentioned above), and timber and lime for public works, not to speak of craftsmen and labourers, through its ordinary administrative machinery. When from the late fourth century onwards, it began to commute rations and clothing for gold, it gave more scope to the private trader, who supplied soldiers and civil servants with food and clothing. But a large part of the army continued to draw rations, and these were supplied either by taxation in kind, or by compulsory purchase, normally from the taxpayers against a rebate of the gold tax, sometimes from merchants. In the fifth century building labour was no longer raised by a *corvée*, but hired, but the management of building projects remained in official hands; contractors were not employed.

The state thus bypassed the private trader almost entirely in the fourth century and to a large extent in the fifth and sixth. It also produced a substantial amount of its requirements in its own establishments. Wealthy landowners (including bishops) did the same to some extent. Most took part of their rents in foodstuffs, with which they fed their large households; Lauricius wrote to his agent in Sicily, 'if a ship can be found which is by good luck sailing for the port of Ravenna at a suitable date, despatch the produce for the requirements of our house there, and if it happens that you do not find one which is coming to Ravenna, it should be sent to the city (Rome) and stored in our granary'. They also apparently used their domestic slaves to weave clothing for the household; when a group of slaves was bequeathed partly to the Roman church and partly to another beneficiary Pope Pelagius instructed his agent that domestic servants and craftsmen, 'men perhaps who could be useful for wool weaving' were to be rejected in favour of agricultural slaves.

The private trader was thus virtually restricted to a few raw materials, such as iron, copper, timber and high-grade wool and flax; clothing for all classes (except the households of the wealthy and soldiers and civil servants whose uniform was supplied by the state); furniture and domestic utensils for all classes; tools for agricultural and industrial workers; food for the urban poor (except in Rome, Constantinople and other big cities, where it was provided by the state), and for the middle classes, in so far as they did not receive rations or rents in kind; slaves; and luxury goods for the upper and middle classes, such as silk and other high-grade fabrics, plate and jewellery, exotic perfumes and spices, vintage wines. The private manufacturer was restricted to a similar range of products, naturally excluding food, and to a similar market, except that private weavers produced the bulk of the clothing requisitioned by the state for uniforms, selling it to the taxpayers from whom it was levied, or to the tax collectors who theoretically levied it, actually taking money instead.

We know most about the clothing industry. There were certain cities which produced highly priced fabrics which commanded an empire-wide market. Silk manufacture was concentrated at Berytus and Tyre. Tarsus, Byblus, Laodicea of Syria, Scythopolis and Alexandria were centres of high-class linen manufacture; Antinopolis, Tralles and Damascus specialized in linen mattresses and bolsters. High-class woollens were produced in other cities and regions, Amiens, Tournai, Bourges, Trier, Laodicea of Phrygia, Noricum and Raetia. Middle-range garments, suitable for army uniforms, were produced in many places, and so were cheap clothes 'for the use of commoners and slaves' at half the price of uniforms. In fact the weaving of middling and cheap clothes seems to have been very widely dispersed, even in villages; this is strongly suggested by the clothing levy, which was assessed on agricultural land throughout the empire, and is proved by papyrological records in Egypt. There was perhaps some mass production of cheap clothes in certain towns and regions; we hear of 'Antiochenes' as cheap clothing at Rome, and African garments carry very low prices.

Spinning was not done by professionals (except for silk), but by women in their spare time, as in the Middle East today. Weaving, fulling and dyeing were on the other hand professional and even the poorest bought their clothes ready made. Augustine tells how Florentius, a poor cobbler of Hippo, lost his one and only *casula*. He prayed to the Twenty Martyrs to succour him, and small boys jeered at him, 'as if he had asked the Martyrs for 50 *folles* each wherewith to buy clothes'. He was not granted the 1,000 *folles* which a *casula* would have cost him, but on the seashore he found a large fish which he sold for 300 *folles*. With the money he planned 'to buy wool so that his wife could make up something for him to wear as best she could'.

All the weavers of whom we know, makers of ordinary middling and cheap fabrics, were independent craftsmen, employing perhaps a few slaves or indentured hands, who bought their yarn and sold their cloth either direct to their customers or to merchants. In the silk and high-grade linen and woollen trades, where the raw material was very dear, it is possible that merchants employed the spinners and weavers on a task-work basis, supplying the raw wool, flax and silk.

Most other industries seem to have been dominated by the independent craftsman; we very rarely hear of factories owned by rich men. The same applies to the building trade; there were no large-scale contractors, but independent masons and carpenters who undertook jobs on contract or for daily pay, often working in gangs. We possess an interesting agreement between the *defensor* of Sardis and the local builders' guild, which specified amongst other things that builders will complete their contracts, and that if they abandon them for other reasons than sickness, other members of the guild will finish the work. Jewellers, who had to carry a stock of valuable goods, tended to be the élite of craftsmen; but they often worked gold or silver provided by the customer.

Any substantial village had its own craftsmen—smiths, potters, weavers—who supplied most local needs; dealers in local produce who bought and marketed its crops; and carriers and carters. At Aphrodito, an exceptionally large village, there were in the sixth century guilds of smiths, carpenters, weavers, fullers and boatbuilders, a dyer, three tailors, some shoemakers, five goldsmiths, nine bakers, six butchers, five greengrocers, two millers, three beekeepers, and a potter (in a big way of business—he paid 2,400 wine jars as rent for one-third of his premises). According to Libanius there were in the territory of Antioch 'many large populous villages with larger populations than not a few cities, which have craftsmen as in towns, and exchange their products with one another through fairs'. We often hear of such rural fairs, frequented by small itinerant merchants.

Smaller cities were, as Libanius said, not very different from large villages, but had more shopkeepers who dealt in foodstuffs, and some superior craftsmen who catered for the decurions and the higher clergy. Large cities, like metropoleis of provinces, where there were also lawyers and officials, had more superior craftsmen and dealers in imported luxury goods, such as high-class clothing. Craftsmen and shopkeepers were always in the cities organized in guilds, whose head men were responsible to the city for seeing that agreed trade practices were observed and maximum prices, when fixed, were enforced; for collecting the *chrysargyron*; for supplying nightwatchmen; and for organizing *corvées* for public works, the service of the local posting station and its resthouse, and similar tasks.

For luxury articles well-to-do families residing in provincial towns had to rely on travelling merchants, who hawked their goods from city to city selling direct to their customers. Synesius of Cyrene apparently relied for his clothes on an Athenian merchant who made an annual call at Ptolemais, a neighbouring seaport; he writes urgently to his brother to seize the opportunity to buy him three Attic cloaks, and to do so quickly before the merchant has sold his best stock. In the early seventh century we know of Jacob, a Jew, who was employed by a Constantinopalitan clothier and put on a ship sailing for Africa and Gaul with a bale of clothes, which he sold to individual customers at ports of call.

Alternatively the provincial *honorati* did their shopping when they attended the annual assemblies at the provincial or diocesan metropolis; bishops made similar use of the annual church congresses. Honorius, in confirming the revival of the annual council of the Seven Provinces at Arles, suggests that a visit to' this great city, where the products of all the provinces were on sale, might not be unwelcome to *honorati* and decurions. In such great cities there were shopkeepers who dealt in all kinds of superior goods. In the west they were generally orientals, Syrians, Jews or Egyptians, who no doubt had personal or family ties with the centres of production in the eastern parts and with the importers of oriental goods in Alexandria and Mesopotamia.

The organization of sea-borne trade was complex. There were rich men who owned ships and chartered them to entrepreneurs (*exercitores*), who in turn employed skippers (*magistri navis*) to navigate them; in this case the owner received the fixed charter fee and the *exercitor* took the profits and stood the risks. Or again the shipowner might employ skippers to navigate his ships, himself taking the risks and profits. The commonest figure was the owner skipper, who had to be a fairly substantial man, since a ship of 10,000 *modii* cost about 500 *solidi*; but many tramp skippers owned much smaller ships of only 2,000 *modii* or less. Skippers normally carried passengers, who paid fares, providing their own food, and these included merchants and agents of merchants who paid freight for their cargoes. Skippers also normally carried cargo on their own account, raising the money to buy it, in part at least, through nautical loans. These loans carried a high rate of interest, but the lender lost his money if the cargo was lost at sea. Justinian virtually abolished them by fixing the maximum rate of interest at 12 per cent for all loans, and we hear subsequently of several unfortunate captains who after shipwreck were imprisoned for debt.

Traders by land seem all to have been in a very small way. In the fourth century Antonius, described as a wealthy merchant of Mesopotamia, presumably in the far eastern trade, bettered himself by becoming an official in the office of the *dux* and rose to be a *protector*. In the sixth century two commercial agents in Mesopotamia, employed in the far eastern trade, were paid 5 *solidi* a year each, rising after twenty years' service to 30 *solidi*.

Maritime merchants were more substantial men, but many operated on a capital of 200 *solidi* or so, including their ships. A great merchant of Alexandria needed no more capital than 50 pounds of gold (3,600 *solidi*).

XXIV

Religion and Morals

The third, fourth, fifth and sixth centuries were a profoundly religious age. The lower classes had probably always been religious; now all classes were so without exception—rationalists and free thinkers were practically unknown, and Epicureanism, the materialist school of philosophy, had virtually died out. Everyone believed that there were supernatural powers, who would be angered by neglect of their worship, by moral offences and, in the case of Christians, by wrong beliefs about their nature, and who on the other hand could be placated by certain rites and would be pleased by good moral behaviour.

The interest of the higher powers extended both to the individual

BIBLIOGRAPHY. For religion and morals see Chapter XXIII of my *Later Roman Empire* (Oxford, 1964). For the survival of paganism see Gaston Boissier, *La fin du Paganisme* (Paris, 1898). Legislation on this subject is contained in *Cod. Theod.* XVI. x, *Cod. Just.* I. xi, and that on the Jews in *Cod. Theod.* XVI. viii, ix, *Cod. Just.* I. ix, x.

The principal works on heresies are Epiphanius, *Panarium*, Philastrius Brixiensis, *Liber de haeresibus*, Augustine, *de haeresibus ad Quodvultdeum*, and Theodoret, *Compendium Haereticarum Fabularum*. The longest official list of heresies is in *Cod. Theod.* XVI. v. 65 (= *Cod. Just.* I, v. 5) 428. The laws against them are in *Cod. Theod.* XVI. v. For the significance of heresies see my article in *Journal of Theological Studies* x (1959), 280–97.

For the cult of the martyrs see H. Delehaye, *Les origines du culte des martyres* (Brussels, 1933). There are curious catalogues of miracles in *de miraculis S. Stephani protomartyris* (PL. XLI. 833–54), Aug. *Civ. Dei*, XXII. viii.

On the early eremitic and monastic movements in Egypt and Palestine see D. J. Chitty, *The Desert a City* (Oxford, 1966). There is a good general account of the movement by P. de Labriolle in *Histoire de l'église*, vol. III, pp. 299–369. The main primary sources are Athanasius' *Life of Antony*, Jerome's *Life of Hilarion*, *The Life of Pachomius*, the Pachomian rule in Jerome, Rufinus' *Historia Monachorum* and its Greek original, Sulpicius Severus, *Dialogi*, Palladius' *Lausiac History*, John Cassian's *Institutes* and *Collations*, Theodoret's *Historia Religiosa*, John Moschus' *Spiritual Meadow*, and Basil's and Benedict's *Regulae*.

and to the community. It was problematical how far individuals could expect the divine favour in return for due respect to God or the gods, but they hoped that special petitions would be granted, and most if not all anticipated bliss or punishment beyond the grave according to whether they had pleased the heavenly powers or no. It was universally believed that the prosperity of the state depended on a right relation with God or the gods. It was for this reason that pagan emperors persecuted the Christians, who were in their view contumacious atheists, who neglected and insulted the gods, and thereby provoked them to send plagues and famines and barbarian invaders to punish the empire. Diocletian, in a law redolent with religious feeling, imposed heavy penalties on incest, because it gravely offended the immortal gods, who had hitherto always favoured Rome. Constantine expressed the fear that the quarrels of the African church might move the Highest Divinity to wrath against the human race and the emperor himself. The pagans regarded the sack of Rome in 410 as clear evidence that the gods were offended by the imperial ban on their worship twenty years before. Justinian regarded the reconquest of Africa and Italy as God's reward for his suppression of heresy and, on the ground that the purity of life of the clergy 'brings great favour and increase to our commonwealth, whereby it is granted to us to subdue the barbarians', forbade clerics to play dice or go to the theatre or the races.

The age was also superstitious. Throughout antiquity there was a general belief in magic, the inducement by incantations, rites or charms of a desired natural event, such as rain, the death of an enemy or, very commonly, the defeat of a chariot in the races. There was also a general belief in various forms of divination and the pseudo-science of astrology was popular. Maleficent magic, private divination and astrology were all crimes, but commonly practised. The lower classes also believed readily in miracles, but the educated do not seem to have shared this belief; there is a remarkable lack of the miraculous element in the literature of the first three centuries of our era, both pagan and Christian. A change begins with the fourth century. The philosophers Plotinus and Porphyry had been sceptical of miracles; the latter's successor Iamblichus defended them and is reported to have performed them. Henceforth the greatest philosophers were famed for their 'theurgy' as it was called, and it was his miracles rather than his doctrines that made Maximus the idol of Julian. In Christian circles similarly there was in the mid-fourth century a great outburst of miracles, and they were accepted and indeed welcomed by the major intellectual figures of the church.

When Constantine was converted in 312 Christians were an insignificant minority in the empire; when Phocas died in 610 pagans were an insignificant minority. Beyond this it is difficult to go statistically, but the advance was probably most rapid in the century following Constantine's conversion. The advance was uneven and patchy. In the early fourth century the great majority of Christians belonged to the urban lower classes, though they included some decurions and even some *honorati*; the peasantry, except in Africa and Egypt, were almost entirely pagan.

As Christianity became not only secure but fashionable and a passport to official advancement, it went up in the social scale, and this movement was assisted by the fact that fair numbers of humble persons, who were already Christians, advanced into the official aristocracy. The educated classes, brought up on pagan literature, found the new faith with its uncouth scriptures rather unpalatable, and adopted it more slowly; the academic profession was particularly resistant and many professors remained pagan down to the sixth century. The high Roman aristocracy, in whose minds the pagan gods were closely linked with the traditions of the Roman state, remained pagan until the early fifth century. The peasantry, innately conservative, clung stubbornly to their old cults, unless they were uprooted from their environment and put into the army, in which case they adopted the official religion, whatever it might be at the time: the army was Christian under Constantius II, pagan under Julian, Christian again under Valentinian and Valens. There were still 80,000 rural pagans for John of Ephesus to convert in 542 in the provinces of Asia, Caria, Lydia and Phrygia, one of the first homelands of Christianity, and at the end of the sixth century Pope Gregory found pagans at Tarracina in Italy, and Tyndaris in Sicily, and in large numbers in Sardinia, where they paid an annual douceur to the provincial governor for his connivance at their cult. In Spain the council of Toledo in 589 declared that 'the sacrilege of idolatry is rooted in almost the whole of Gaul and Spain', and the allusion is, as other documents prove, to peasants who still venerated sacred trees and fountains, and kept Thursday, the day of Jupiter, as their weekly holiday.

There were curious local contrasts. In Africa, which had become predominantly Christian by the end of the third century, the cities of Calama, Madaura and Sufes were still pagan more than a century later. In Mesopotamia, Edessa had been converted in the early third century, but its neighbour Carrhae remained faithful to its old gods even after the Arab conquest. Antioch was already under Julian a Christian city; its neighbour Apamea still defended its temples under Theodosius I. Maiuma, the port of Gaza, petitioned Constantine for a city charter and got it because it was Christian. In Gaza itself the Christian community amounted to 280 persons, men, women and children in 396, and the pagan cult was openly celebrated in all the temples despite Theodosius I's penal laws.

The conversion of the neighbouring peoples was very spasmodic. King Tiridates, restored to the Armenian throne in 298, became a Christian and imposed his religion on his subjects, anticipating the Roman empire in the official adoption of Christianity. In Constantine's reign a Roman woman, carried as a slave to the Iberian kingdom, preached the Christian faith there and thus founded the Georgian church; and Frumentius, a young man from Tyre, shipwrecked on the coast of the Axumite kingdom, was made the king's secretary and converted him, thus founding the Abyssinian church. On the other hand the Nobades and Blemmyes of Nubia enjoyed until Justinian's day the right of worshipping in the temple of Isis at Philae, and many of the Saracen and Moorish tribes on the frontiers of Syria and Africa were still pagan in the sixth century. The Goths were converted in the middle of the fourth century, and passed the brand of Christianity which they had learned, which was unfortunately Arian, to the Vandals, Burgundians and other east German tribes; but the Franks in the west remained pagan until Clovis was converted in 496.

There was practically no organized missionary activity; bishops were usually content to demolish pagan temples. Pagan sacrifice was officially banned by Constantine at the end of his reign, but again tolerated from Julian's accession in 361 until 391, when Theodosius forbade all forms of pagan cult. The law was laxly enforced and had to be repeated in 407 and 415 in the west, and in 423, 435, 451 and 472 in the east; even later Anastasius prohibited bequests for the maintenance of pagan cults. Pagans also suffered increasing disabilities. Honorius and Theodosius II excluded them from governmental posts, Leo from the legal profession, Justinian from academic chairs. In 529 he even ordered all pagans to receive instruction and be baptized on pain of confiscation and exile.

Paganism was not so much a religion as an amalgam of cults of very various kinds, united by mutual tolerance and respect and by syncretism, whereby the local gods were equated with those of the Greek and Roman pantheon. The cults were normally local. Carthage worshipped the Heavenly Goddess (Caelestis), identified with Juno,

Ephesus her peculiar many-breasted Artemis; the Syrian towns had their several Baals, usually dubbed Zeus, but sometimes like Marnas of Gaza or Elagabal, the black stone of Emisa, retaining their native names; each Egyptian city had its patron, Hermes (Thoth), Aphrodite (Hathor) and the rest. There were also some gods and goddesses, like Mithras or Isis, who had achieved an international reputation, and were worshipped by congregations all over the empire. They generally promised a blissful future life to their devotees, if they kept certain rules and performed certain rites; the cult of Mithras was particularly objectionable to Christians because it so closely resembled their own, and seemed to be a parody of it. Animal sacrifice was fairly general, but there were many peculiar rites, from the *taurobolium* of the Great Mother, in which the initiate was literally bathed in the blood of a bull, to the ritual prostitution practised at Heliopolis and Apheca in Phoenicia.

Educated pagans were mostly monotheists or pantheists, adoring one god, the ineffable Monad of the Neoplatonists or the Unconquered Sun, and regarding the other gods as subordinates or emanations of the One. They combined a lofty philosophy, normally Neoplatonist, with a deep respect for the pagan myths, which they interpreted allegorically, and for pagan cult practices, which they regarded as divinely enacted symbols of esoteric truths.

Paganism had no theology beyond Neoplatonic philosophy and the amalgam of myths belonging to the various cults, which were very imperfectly synthesized. It possessed a fairly generally accepted moral code, which differed only in emphasis from the Christian code. It had no organization, cults being conducted by cities, villages or private societies. This was felt as a weakness by Maximin and Julian, who appointed high priests, analogous to bishops, in each city, and a high priest of superior rank, analogous to the metropolitan, in each province. Except in Egypt there was no professional clergy, priesthoods being in general held by laymen, sometimes annually, sometimes for life; those of the civic cults were usually elected by the city council.

The strength of paganism was that it was all things to all men. It gave to the peasants rites to promote fertility and ward off pests; to serious men and women, anxious about their welfare beyond the grave, the mystery cults; to intellectuals a profound if rather nebulous philosophy. Its temples and ceremonials had a strong aesthetic appeal. Its myths and ritual were inextricably intertwined with the great literary heritage of Greece and Rome, which was dear to all educated men, and with the glorious traditions of the Roman state.

Paganism was not a heroic religion. Some pagans fought for their temples, but there were few pagan martyrs, and most were content to bribe the authorities to connive at their worship or to carry it on secretly. Nevertheless paganism kept up a tenacious rearguard action against Christianity; pagans still hoped that the old gods would come into their own again not only under Julian (361–63), but under Eugenius (392–94) in the west, and even during the rebellion of Illus in Zeno's reign (484) in the east. On all these occasions the Christians were fearful that the dream of the pagans might come true. Relapses from Christianity to paganism were still sufficiently common in 425 to provoke a renewal of the penal laws against apostates.

The austere monotheism of early Christianity did not long survive the great influx of converts which began in the early fourth century. The memory of holy men of the past, and in particular of martyrs, had always been cherished by Christians, their tombs venerated and the anniversaries of their death commemorated by special services. In the fourth century chapels were built over their tombs and anniversaries became popular festivals. It came to be believed that, having intimate access to God, they could press their devotees' petitions on him, and it was soon popularly believed that they could answer petitions themselves. For all practical purposes they came to be worshipped as minor gods. Their bodies were believed to have magical powers and a vast number of miracles were performed at their tombs.

Genuine martyrs' bodies were far too few to satisfy public demand and, usually with the aid of visions, many more were found. Pope Damasus (366–84) discovered many at Rome, Ambrose unearthed two saints, Gervasius and Protasius, at Milan, another pair, Vitalis and Agricola at Bologna, and yet a third pair at Milan. In 415 Lucian, the priest at Caphargamala in Palestine, discovered the bodies of Gamaliel, his son Nicodemus and, most precious of all, the protomartyr Stephen; we possess the circular letter in which Lucian described his discoveries to the churches of the empire, and the body of S. Stephen was soon dissected, and portions of it reached Africa and the Balearic Isles. The bodies of contemporary holy men, especially hermits, were also much sought after, and there were sometimes bitter battles for the corpse.

There was some uneasiness about bogus relics. Martin of Tours visited a martyr's shrine which had been consecrated by his predecessor in a place near Tours. The saint's name was unknown and there was no firm tradition about his passion; Martin, with a critical sense unusual for his age, had doubts. He prayed for a revelation and there appeared a sinister wraith, which confessed he had in fact been a brigand executed for his crimes and reverenced by a vulgar error. An African council in 401 condemned 'the altars which have been established everywhere through the dreams or vain so-called revelations of anybody and everybody'. But in principle the new cult went unchallenged and was indeed welcomed by the hierarchy.

The only Christian who is known to have raised his voice against it was an obscure Aquitanian priest named Vigilantius, who wrote: 'We almost see the rites of the pagans introduced into the churches under the pretext of religion, ranks of candles are lit in full daylight, and everywhere people kiss and adore some bit of dust in a little pot, wrapped in a precious fabric.'[1] His pamphlet was crushingly refuted by the greatest intellectual figure of the church, Jerome.

Another of the church's intellectual luminaries, Augustine, set enormous store on miracles, and organized their systematic record at Hippo and two neighbouring towns, Uzalis and Calama. The beneficiary wrote a brief narrative (*libellus*), and these *libelli* were read in church and filed. We possess one actual *libellus*, and a catalogue of the miracles filed at Uzalis. Miracles were extraordinarily common; seventy were recorded at Hippo in less than two years. Most were cures of illness, with a few resurrections from the dead. What is most noticeable about them is their triviality and their mechanically magical character. A typical one was as follows. A proprietor of a vineyard at Uzalis, going to his cellar, finds that his entire vintage, 200 jars of wine, is utterly undrinkable. He tells his slave to draw a little wine from each jar into a flagon and leave it for the night in S. Stephen's shrine. Next day the flagon is brought back and a little poured from it into each jar, and the entire contents of the cellar forthwith acquire a superb quality.

Saints and martyrs, as Theodoret boasts, replaced the pagan gods and heroes; their churches superseded the temples, their commemorations the old festivals. They performed the same functions, curing the sick, giving children to barren women, detecting perjurers, and issuing oracles. Some became protectors and patrons of particular cities; S. Martin became for Tours what Artemis had been for Ephesus. Others developed specialized functions. S. Felix of Nola was well known for revealing perjury, and Augustine sent two of his clergy all the way from Africa to find out which was a liar. The shrines of Saints Cyrus and John, the doctors who charged no fee, at Canopus, replaced the temple of Asclepius at Aegae, which Constantine had demolished.

[1] Jerome, *contra Vigilantium*, 4.

This is not to say that pagan gods were actually transformed into martyrs. Christians regarded the old gods as maleficent demons and shunned their temples as haunted places. A martyr's body was sometimes buried in an abandoned temple to exorcize it, and a martyr thus took over a god's abode. Commemorations seem sometimes to have been put on the same day as a pagan festival as a counter-attraction. Occasionally a pagan myth became attached to the martyr who had succeeded a local god or hero; S. George thus acquired the story of Perseus and Andromeda.

Theological controversies of the most abstruse kind excited vehement and widespread passion. Not only did theologians bombard each other with venomous pamphlets and monks demonstrate in their thousands, but city mobs rioted and had to be quelled by massive military action, and peasants formed marauding gangs that kidnapped their theological opponents and harried their farms. This phenomenon has surprised modern historians, who have postulated that such passion cannot have been engendered by theological disputes, but must have been the product of latent national or class animosities. It is not in fact surprising when one realizes that religion was the major interest of the age, and that right or wrong belief entailed not only individual salvation or damnation, but prosperity or disaster to the empire. 'Give me the earth purified of heretics, your Majesty,' proclaimed Nestorius to Theodosius II, 'and I will give you heaven in return. Subdue the heretics with me and I will subdue the Persians with you.'[1]

Nearly all emperors therefore felt it their duty to get the churches to define what was the correct doctrine, or failing this to define it themselves, and then to suppress all variant beliefs by penal measures. The first Christian emperor took this line. 'What higher duty have I', wrote Constantine, 'in virtue of my imperial office and policy than to dissipate errors and repress rash indiscretions, and so to cause all to offer to Almighty God true religion, honest concord and due worship.'[2] In accordance with this principle, when the Council of Nicaea had defined the truth, Constantine forthwith issued a constitution confiscating the churches of all dissidents and forbidding them to hold meetings. Valentinian I was the only emperor who refused to intervene in theological controversies. 'It is not right for me a layman', he said, 'to meddle in such things. Let the bishops whose business it is meet by themselves wherever they like.'[3] It followed that he granted toleration to all sects

[1] Socrates, *Hist. Eccl.* VII. 29.   [2] Optatus of Mileve, *Appendix* VII.
[3] Sozomen, *Hist. Eccl.* VI. 7.

(except Manichees). Some emperors, faced by the enormous practical difficulties of enforcing unanimity, seem to have tried to hedge. In view of the intransigent attitude of both sides on the Monophysite issue Zeno by his Henotikon tried to annul the Council of Chalcedon, which had brought the issue to a head, and Justinian tried to effect a compromise by condemning the Three Chapters. But there is no reason to doubt that these emperors thought the formula which they proposed to be theologically sound.

The leaders of the church and indeed all Christians shared the government's view, and unanimously supported and demanded state action to suppress heretics—except of course when they were heretics themselves in the government's view. Athanasius and Hilary talked a lot about liberty of belief when Constantius II was enforcing Arianism, but the Catholics rejoiced when Theodosius I banned all opinions but their own. The Donatists indignantly asked 'What has the emperor to do with the church?' when Constantine persecuted them, but they had previously asked for Constantine's decision on their dispute with the Catholics. Martin of Tours courageously opposed his fellow bishops and the emperor Magnus Maximus, urging that the Priscillianists ought, having been condemned by an episcopal council, to be excommunicated, but should not be tried by a secular court and subjected to death and exile. But he stands almost alone. Augustine at first deprecated the exercise of the penal laws against the Donatists, hoping to convert them by persuasion, but he soon advocated the use of the secular arm. Socrates expressed disapproval of Nestorius' heresy hunting, but he was probably a Novatian himself—his sympathy with that sect is marked. Procopius in the *Secret History* condemned Justinian's persecution of heretics, but in his eyes nothing that Justinian did was right.

Theologians sometimes endeavoured to inform the general public of their side of the controversies by composing popular expositions of their views, usually in verse and intended to be sung. Arius composed his *Thaleia* in a vulgar metre, but to judge by the few verses which we possess, he did not try to talk down to his audience. 'God himself therefore is ineffable to all. He alone has no equal, none like him or of the same glory. We call him ingenerate because of him that is generate by nature; we hymn him as without beginning because of him who has a beginning; we revere him as everlasting because of him that is born in time.'[1] Such indoctrination seems to have been fairly successful. Ordinary people at least learned the stock arguments and catchwords and enjoyed

[1] Athanasius, *de Synodis*, 15.

argumentation. At Constantinople during the Arian controversy Gregory of Nyssa writes: 'If you ask about your change, the shopkeeper philosophizes to you about the begotten and the unbegotten; if you enquire the price of a loaf, the reply is: "The Father is greater and the Son inferior", and if you say, Is the bath ready? the attendant affirms that the Son is of nothing.'[1] Those who could not understand the issue at all could at least learn slogans. The most ignorant Monophysite knew that by shouting: 'Holy, Holy, Holy, Lord God Almighty, who was crucified for us', he expressed his own faith and roused Dyophysites to fury.

The ordinary man did not of course adopt a theological position because he was intellectually convinced by it. He was swayed by the example of hermits and holy men, often as theologically ignorant as himself, or by the pronouncements of church leaders, the occupants of great sees whose authority he venerated. This was particularly so in the west, where the level of theological knowledge was low, and what the pope said was usually accepted. This was why the west was unanimously in favour of the Nicene dogma which the pope had blessed, and of the Chalcedonian view, which was based on Pope Leo's Tome. In Egypt too there was always monolithic support for the doctrines enunciated by the genuine (as opposed to the intruded) bishops of Alexandria, the Nicene doctrine under Athanasius and his successors, the Monophysite under Cyril and his successors. The east German tribes clung stubbornly to Arianism, because that was the faith of Ulfilas, who first converted the Goths. This does not mean that they did not genuinely believe that Arianism was the correct doctrine. Their clergy delighted in confuting their Catholic Roman *confrères* in theological debates, and King Euric of the Visigoths persecuted his Catholic Roman subjects because 'he believes that success is vouchsafed to him in his plans and policies in virtue of his religion'.[2] The Armenians became Monophysite by a historical accident. They did not hear of the controversy until the beginning of the sixth century, when Zeno's Henotikon, which implicitly condemns Chalcedon, was the orthodoxy of the day, and they accepted and persevered in that view.

It is often alleged that the Donatist schism, which rent Africa for three centuries, was the expression of the national sentiment of the Punic- and Berber-speaking population against the Roman empire, and of the animosity of the peasants against their landlords, who were

---

[1] Gregory of Nyssa, *de Deitate Filii et Spiritus Sancti* (Migne, *Patr. Gr.* XLVI. 557).

[2] Sidonius Apollinaris, *Epist.* VII. 6 §6.

Romans by culture, if not by birth. The facts are not quite so simple. Most humble Donatists spoke Punic or Berber, but so did most humble Catholics, and Latin was the liturgical and theological language of the Donatist church. The Donatist church, being a mass movement, included a high proportion of the peasantry, but its leaders were men of rank and wealth and Roman culture. The Donatists gave their support to two Moorish chieftains, who were also Roman officers of high rank, Firmus and Gildo, when they made a bid for the empire, but this was probably only because they were persecuted by the legitimate emperors and hoped for better treatment under these pretenders. There is no evidence that they welcomed or supported the Vandal invaders. The Circumcellions, the peasant shock troops of the movement, burnt mortgages, liberated slaves and personally insulted and maltreated landowners and moneylenders, but they apparently confined their activities to Catholic landowners and moneylenders, and beat up the humble Catholic clergy even more unmercifully. There can be no doubt that the movement was by origin doctrinal. The Donatists believed that they were the only true Catholics, because their adversaries had allowed clergy who had surrendered the scriptures in Diocletian's persecution to retain their positions in the church, and that the orders of all the so-called Catholic clergy were therefore null and their sacraments invalid. The movement may have later acquired national and social overtones. The Donatists were rather proud that the true Catholic church had survived only in Africa, and quoted scriptural prophecies which foreshadowed this event; and Circumcellions no doubt took pleasure in beating up landlords and moneylenders as such. But the movement always remained basically theological.

A pagan when he became a catechumen was told that he was a sinner (and had indeed been born in sin), and would be punished eternally unless he repented and underwent the rite of baptism, which washed away all sin up to date. But he was also instructed that unless after baptism he conformed very strictly to an ethical code which was considerably more severe, especially in sexual matters, than what he was used to, he would be damned. He had only one further chance; he could perform penance, a public and humiliating ceremony, involving much previous prayer and fasting. But penance could be performed once and once only: if he sinned thereafter the church could offer him no assurance of salvation.

The Christian moral code was severe. A man was forbidden not only to commit adultery (which pagans agreed was wrong, and was anyhow a crime) but also to commit fornication (which was tolerated by most

pagans, and was legal, so long as the other party was a registered prosti-
tute). Homosexual relations were also condemned, as they were by better
pagan opinion. What was more difficult, men and women were forbidden to divorce their wives and husbands, or at any rate to remarry
while their partner was still living, although according to the pagan code
and the civil law divorce was fully accepted. According to some Christian
teachers a man might not keep a concubine, even if he were a bachelor,
but this view was not universally accepted. The theatre, gladiatorial
shows, wild beast fights, and even horse racing were all sinful, and the
baths were deprecated as an indulgence liable to stimulate the carnal
appetites. Murder was very rigorously interpreted. Some severe moralists
like Basil held that a soldier who killed an enemy in battle was a murderer, but this extreme view was uncommon. It was felt by some that a
magistrate who condemned a criminal to death and an official who executed the sentence were murderers; Ambrose hedged on this point, but
Pope Innocent pronounced that the secular sword was of God. But
Innocent apparently held that a prosecuting barrister in a criminal case
was guilty of murder. Similar views were held on the judicial use of
torture.

In these circumstances it was clearly very difficult for the ordinary
man, who had his living to earn, to avoid sin. John Chrysostom does
indeed in one passage deprecate this attitude. 'Where now are those who
say that it is impossible for a man to preserve his virtue living in the
midst of a city, and that withdrawal and life in the mountains is essential, and the man who is head of a household, has a wife and looks after
his children and slaves, cannot be virtuous?'[1] But this is not his usual
tone, nor that of Christian moralists generally. Most careers were
regarded as, if not in themselves sinful, so fraught with temptation as to
be very dangerous. An early papal letter declares:

It is manifest that those who have acquired secular power and administered secular justice cannot be free from sin. For when the
sword is unsheathed or an unjust sentence is pronounced, or torture is
applied for the requirements of the cases, or they devote their care to
preparing games, or attend games prepared for them, they are making
a large claim not if they aspire to a bishopric, but if having undergone
penance for all this they are allowed after a certain time has elapsed to
approach the altar.[2]

[1] John Chrysostom, *Homilia in Genesim*, xliii. 1.
[2] *Epistula ad Gallos*, 10 (Migne, *Patr. Lat.* XIII. 1181).

In a similar spirit the popes debarred from holy orders all who after baptism had held administrative posts, served in the army or the civil service or even practised at the bar. Decurions were in as perilous a case, for in the course of their official duties they gave games and could hardly avoid extortion and cruelty in collecting the taxes. Even more striking evidence is accorded by the precautionary rules laid down for those who had done their penance and whose future sins were irredeemable. They might not engage in trade, serve in the army or the civil service, marry (except for youths who might otherwise be tempted to worse things), or go to law or attend the theatre.

The result of these strict rules was that in the fourth century most Christians lived as catechumens all their lives, not enjoying the sacraments of the church, and were not baptized until their deathbeds, or at any rate until they had retired and could concentrate on living a holy life. This is proved by innumerable tombstones of persons who died newly baptized at all ages from infancy to late middle age, and by many individual cases. Not only the convert Constantine, but his son Constantius II also, brought up from infancy as a Christian and a very pious man, was baptized during his final illness. Ambrose was not baptized until he became a bishop, and his brother Satyrus not until many years later, shortly before his death. It was not only nominal Christians but serious and pious men who adopted this course.

Many were of course like Theodosius I baptized owing to illness, and then recovered. Anxious parents often baptized children as infants to make sure that they did not go to hell through sudden death. In the latter part of the fourth century several bishops including Basil and the two Gregories preached against deathbed baptism, and early baptism seems to have become general in the fifth century, though not necessarily infant baptism. In Pamphylia it was customary to be baptized on reaching man's estate. This left penance as the only safeguard, and people normally postponed penance till their deathbeds. Augustine and Caesarius of Arles preached against this practice, but even they do not seem to have advocated penance before old age.

During the greater part of his life then the ordinary Christian did not make much effort to practise the Christian virtues, pleading that the flesh is weak and man by nature sinful, and relying on divine grace, mechanically interpreted as the sacraments of baptism and penance. It was this general attitude which at the end of the fourth century aroused a British layman, probably a lawyer, Pelagius, to preach the doctrine that a man could achieve sinlessness by his own efforts, and that it was his duty to strive to do so. While admitting the necessity of baptism and penance to wash away sins which, despite all one's efforts, one might commit, he regarded grace as something given to all men, equating it with conscience, which enabled a man to distinguish the good, and with free will, which enabled a man to choose it. His teaching excited no interest at all in the east, and in the west was condemned as heretical through the influence of Augustine, who insisted on the utter sinfulness of man without divine grace.

Another reaction to the stern moral code of the church was the eremitic or monastic movement. Some people went into the desert to seek, through mortification of the flesh and prayer and meditation, a more intimate union with God than was possible to the worldly man. There exist several handbooks of progressive exercises to be followed to achieve such spiritual insight. But such persons were rare, and most people became monks and hermits to avoid the ordinary temptations of life, and thus keep themselves free from sin. For this reason the imperial government very rarely dared to forbid anyone, whatever his status, to enter a monastery. Marcian urged the council of Chalcedon to ban the reception of slaves or *adscripticii* into monasteries; the council yielded on slaves but not on *adscripticii*. Both classes were later excluded (except by their master's leave) by Valentinian III in the west and by Zeno in the east. Justinian ordained that they should undergo a three years' probation, during which their masters might claim them, but should after this be finally admitted. Maurice forbade serving soldiers and civil servants who owed money to the treasury to be admitted to monasteries. Pope Gregory[1] vehemently resisted this law. 'I am terribly frightened by this constitution, I confess to your majesty, for by it the way of heaven is closed to many, and what has hitherto been lawful is now prohibited. For there are many who can live a religious life even in a secular garb, but there are some who unless they leave everything can in no way be saved before God.'

The eremitic movement was started by Antony, an Egyptian peasant who retired into the desert of the Thebaid in the 270s, and about 305–06 organized the group of disciples which had grown up around him into a loose community. Such loose communities, where the hermits or monks lived in separate cells, meeting only for weekly worship, were known as *laurae*. The monastic movement proper was founded by Pachomius, another Egyptian peasant, who in the 320s formed the first *coenobium*, where the monks lived in common under a strict discipline,

[1] *Epist.* III. 61.

performing manual work under the direction of the abbot and the foremen whom he appointed from the seniors. The eremitic life soon spread to Palestine, where Hilarion built up a *laura* near Gaza in about 330. It seems to have sprung up independently in Syria rather earlier. In eastern Asia Minor it was introduced by Eustathius of Sebaste and Basil of Caesarea in the middle of the fourth century; the latter favoured the coenobitic life, but not, it would seem, in so rigorously disciplined a form as the Pachomian rule. One Isaac came from the east to Constantinople and founded a monastery in the 380s, but the movement did not catch on in this area until the early fifth century.

In the west the movement began later than in the east and spread more slowly. Martin founded the first monastery in Gaul at Tours in about 375, but it remained isolated until the early fifth century, when Honoratus and Cassian founded three houses in the south, one at Lérins, the other two near Marseilles. Ambrose appears to have introduced monastic life into Italy and Augustine into Africa.

Many thousands of men became hermits or monks and many thousands of women nuns. It is impossible to estimate the total figure, but Pachomius' original house came to number about 1,300, and by the beginning of the fifth century the Pachomian group of monasteries had 7,000 inmates. Nitria and Scetis, two famous groups of *laurae* in the western desert of Egypt, had at this period 5,000 and 3,500 monks respectively. By 518 there were eighty-five monasteries in and about Constantinople and thirty-nine across the Bosphorus at Chalcedon.

Hermits, monks and nuns were all celibate and lived with varying degrees of austerity. Many scarcely credible stories are told of the minute quantities of bread on which Egyptian hermits existed; Gauls regretted that they had heartier appetites and could not compete. Many oriental hermits trained themselves to live with incredibly short hours of sleep. In Syria in particular hermits imposed fantastic self-torments on themselves, such as wearing loads of chains weighing many hundredweight. The most famous case is that of Symeon Stylites, who lived for forty years (*c.* 420–59) near Antioch on a column, whose height he progressively increased from 10 to 60 feet. This had a practical purpose, to avoid the crowds of pilgrims who pestered him for his blessing or advice, but probably contained an element of exhibitionism. He found many imitators, some of them in more rigorous climates, like Daniel, who lived on a pillar near Constantinople for thirty-three years (460–93), and was once nearly frozen to death in a snowstorm, after which the emperor Leo insisted on his having a little hut on top of his column. We even know of a stylite who lived on a pillar near Trier in the late sixth century and likewise suffered severely from frostbite; he was a Lombard who had settled in Gaul.

Not all monks of course lived up to the rigorous standards of discipline and austerity set by the pioneers of the movement. We hear of hordes of vagrant monks, who were virtually tramps. The rule of celibacy was not always kept, especially in houses which contained communities of both monks and nuns. Justinian enacted that monasteries and nunneries must be separated, and that all monks must sleep in common dormitories. As endowments accumulated many monks led idle and comfortable lives, as Cassian laments in Gaul. The ideal of labour, rigorously enforced in the Pachomian houses of Egypt, does not seem to have been kept in other provinces, where a few individual abbots are praised for introducing a regime of regular productive work, until Benedict revived it in Italy in the sixth century.

Among ordinary laymen who did not become monks or hermits, but hoped to be absolved of their sins by baptism or penance when death was approaching, Christian moral teaching seems to have had little effect. Despite the church's disapproval, everyone went to the baths, including the clergy; a Novatian bishop of Constantinople, when asked by one of his puritanical congregation why he took two baths a day, replied, 'Because I have not got time for a third.' Despite the thunders of the church even clerics frequented the games. The severe teaching of the church on sexual conduct was little observed. Prostitution continued to flourish openly. In 439 a pious layman, Florentius, praetorian prefect of the East, inspired a law freeing all prostitutes in Constantinople and expelling the brothel keepers, compensating the government for its loss of revenue out of his own pocket. Nearly a century later in 529 the empress Theodora bought up all the prostitutes in Constantinople and installed them in a disused imperial palace which she converted into the Nunnery of Repentance. Six years later Justinian instituted an enquiry by the praetor of the people, the chief of the Constantinople police, and found that prostitution was again rampant.

More striking is the history of divorce. Under the civil law either spouse could divorce the other at will, and the husband might remarry forthwith, the wife after a year. Constantine, clearly under clerical influence, enacted that a wife could divorce her husband only for murder or tomb robbery, and a husband could divorce his wife only for adultery, poisoning or procuring. In 421 Honorius relaxed this law, distinguishing three kinds of divorce; for a crime, in which case the innocent party could remarry, a husband forthwith, a wife after five years; for bad character, in which case the guilty husband could remarry after two years but the guilty wife was debarred from a second marriage; for no reason, in which case the husband who divorced his wife was debarred from a second marriage, the wife who divorced her husband was deported. None of these rules affected the dissolution of marriage by mutual consent.

This remained the law in the west. In the east Theodosius II in 439 restored the old rules of the civil law; in 449 he repented of such extreme liberality, but at the same time greatly extended the grounds of divorce for both sexes, including in the case of a man wife-beating, and in the case of a woman, going to the theatre without her husband's leave; in such cases the husband could remarry forthwith, the wife after a year. Moreover, divorces without cause were allowed; in such cases a divorcing wife could not remarry for five years. Justinian made a drastic change by forbidding divorce without cause even by consent of the other party, relegating the divorcing party to a nunnery or monastery. This rule caused such widespread complaint that Justin II revoked it, restoring divorce by consent.

This is the record of legislation by a succession of Christian governments for a Christian population; for there is no reason to believe that the emperors paid any regard to the feelings of the dwindling remnant of pagans. It indicates that the average churchman regarded the church's teaching on divorce as a counsel of perfection; sermons also indicate that people who went to church quite frequently divorced each other and remarried. We possess a contract of divorce dating from immediately after Justin II's repeal of Justinian's law; the preamble runs

> We were in time past joined to one another in marriage and community of life in fair hopes and with a view to the procreation of legitimate children, thinking to maintain a peaceful and seemly married life with one another for the whole time of our joint lives; but on the contrary we have suffered from a sinister and wicked demon which attacked us unexpectedly from we know not whence, with a view to our being separated from one another.[1]

This is all the more remarkable because among the pious there was an overpowering, not to say morbid, interest in sexual morality. Celibacy was preached as the ideal, marriage was grudgingly condoned as a

---

[1] L. Mitteis, *Chrestomathie*, 297.

second best, and the temptations of the flesh occupied a predominant part in the struggles of ascetics for spiritual purity.

On one major issue the teaching of the church was powerful and effective, on charity, in the sense of giving money to good causes. In the pagan ideal the rich man distributed doles to a circle of clients, who gave him a *quid pro quo* in sundry services, and gave liberally to his fellow citizens, in the form of public buildings, distributions of largesse, and above all games: a few rather exceptional benefactors founded free schools, or established schemes for feeding poor children. The church had always urged all, whatever their means, to give to the poor and the helpless, and the call was widely answered. Most rich Christians did not, it is true, sell all their goods and give to the poor, though some like Paulinus of Nola and Melania did. To judge by the sermons of John Chrysostom and others, very few rich Christians gave as much as the tenth of their income that the scriptures suggested, but some poor men did. All classes practised the least painful form of charity and remembered the church in their wills. A good deal of Christian charity went to the building and endowing of churches and monasteries, but ample was left over for supporting orphans, widows, the aged, the sick, the deserving poor and vagrants, and for redeeming prisoners of war. These were fields of social work which were almost entirely neglected by the government and by the old pagan upper class. Julian was much impressed by the superiority of Christians to pagans in this matter, and gave state grants for charitable purposes to the pagan high priests, and instructed them to urge pagan landlords and villagers to emulate the Christians.

Although it did much to alleviate the lot of the poor, the church never questioned the social system as it found it. To judge by the surviving literature, especially sermons, there was no great interest in social problems. John Chrysostom was genuinely moved by the plight of the poor, and preached many eloquent sermons urging his wealthy congregation to alleviate it. Salvian in his great denunciation of the wickedness of the age, the *de Gubernatione Dei*, lays about equal emphasis on exploitation of the poor, sexual morals and theatre-going, and his rhetoric does not ring true. Pelagius, defining riches as 'a superfluous affluence of unnecessary possessions', questions whether extremes of wealth were 'of God, whom we must believe the fount of equity and justice', and thought that God had created the good things of this world 'not in order that one man should become rich with an infinite affluence of possession and another be afflicted with excessive poverty, but that all should possess them with an equal balance and like right'. But Pelagius was condemned for heresy (on doctrinal grounds), and most Christians preferred the text, 'The poor ye have always with you.'

In the sphere of charity there was marked progress. In most others there is no discernible change. In some there was regression. There was increasing cruelty and brutality, at any rate in the public administration; torture and flogging were more and more commonly used, and cruel forms of execution, such as burning alive, were more and more often prescribed. The lower orders had perhaps always been rather brutally handled, but their treatment became worse, and the middle class was progressively subjected to the same kind of treatment. There are very few protests against this development, and the most eloquent come from a pagan, Libanius of Antioch, who pled not only for decurions but for bakers and peasants.

In the second place there was a marked decline in political and administrative probity. It is possible to paint too rosy a picture of the principate; there was not a little graft, bribery and extortion in the imperial service then. But it is probably true to say that the general tone of the public service was sound, and that such abuses were generally reprobated and exceptional. In the later empire, on the other hand, offices were habitually bought and sold, there was endemic corruption in the courts of justice, and extortion was normal. This appears not only from the countless laws denouncing these abuses and endeavouring to reform them, but in the terms in which good administrators are habitually praised—it is a standard compliment to a good governor to say that he left office as poor as when he entered it.

The church of course denounced those who gave unjust judgments and oppressed the poor and helpless, but this negative teaching was singularly ineffective. In the pagan scheme of things the service of the state was a noble activity, to which even philosophers should condescend, and it attracted the best types. In the eyes of the church the public service was at best a worldly occupation, to be avoided by the good Christian, and was in fact generally regarded as a dirty business. The Council of Arles enacted in 314: 'About governors who being of the faithful advance to a governorship, it was resolved that when they are promoted they shall receive ecclesiastical letters of communion, with the reservation that wherever they administer, the bishop of the place shall keep an eye on them, and when they begin to act contrary to the rules of the church, then they shall be excluded from communion.'[1] A fourth-

---

[1] *Conc. Arelat.* canon 7.

century pope declared: 'It is manifest that those who acquire secular power and administer secular justice cannot be free from sin.'[1] Augustine is exceptional in urging an imperial administrator not to postpone his baptism: 'As if the faithful, the more faithful and the better they are, cannot administer the state the more faithfully and the better.'[2] Paulinus of Nola is more typical in urging his friends to abandon their official careers: 'Ye cannot serve two masters, that is the one God and Mammon, in other words Christ and Caesar.'[3]

In these circumstances it is not surprising that earnest Christians tended to avoid the public service and that those who took it up were nominal Christians, who, knowing that they had undertaken a sinful career, acted accordingly; they could always be saved by baptism or penance when they retired.

From the reign of Constantine heretics were practically always forbidden to own churches or hold services elsewhere. They were from the reign of Theodosius I generally debarred from the public service, and from that of Leo from the bar. Some sects suffered from civil disabilities, such as incapacity to make wills or to inherit. More drastic measures were rarely used. Recusant Donatists were in 412 subjected to heavy fines, and Manichees and other particularly detested sectaries were from the reign of Theodosius I sometimes liable to the death penalty.

This legislation was intermittently and on the whole laxly enforced, and despite it heresies were extraordinarily long-lived. The Melitians in Egypt and the Donatists in Africa, whose schisms dated from the great persecution of Diocletian, still subsisted down to the Arab conquest. The Novatians, whose schism went back to the persecution of Decius in 250, were still flourishing in the sixth century. Even earlier heresies, like that of the Marcionites, whose founder lived under Hadrian, survived at the same period.

The sects included every variety of belief. Some had broken off on questions of discipline rather than doctrine. The Novatians, Melitians and Donatists all held that the rest of the church had erred in having received back Christians, especially clergy, who had lapsed in the persecutions, and that its orders and sacraments were thereby vitiated. The Quartodecimans held that Easter ought to be celebrated on the 14th of the Jewish month Nisan—this dispute went back to the second century. Others differed on points of theology, the Arians, the Macedonians, the Nestorians, the Monophysites; the Pelagians held that works were more

---

[1] *Epist. ad Gallos*, 10.   [2] Augustine, *Epist.* 151 §14.
[3] Paulinus of Nola, *Epist.* 25.

important than grace. The Manichees, the most hated sect, were really a different religion, but were generally regarded as heretical Christians, and seem to have so regarded themselves. Their founder, Mani, a Persian who lived in the third century, adopted the Zoroastrian thesis of dualism—there were two powers, Good and Evil, which contended in the world—and proclaimed himself a prophet whose message completed and superseded that of Christ. The Manichees were a very secretive sect, and for that reason excited exaggerated fears and hatred; it is impossible to say how numerous they were, but they were certainly widespread in east and west alike. There were also a large number of minor sects, having no historical connection with Manicheism, and often older than it, which held similar dualist views; they mostly identified the evil principle with matter, and were commonly total abstainers and vegetarians, and deprecated or even forbade sexual intercourse. Some of this lunatic fringe of Christianity went to extraordinary lengths. Theodoret met an aged Marcionite who had always washed his face with his own spittle, because water was the creation of the evil principle, the Demiurge. Augustine knew a village of Abelonii, who held that both marriage and continence were obligatory on all: each pair of 'parents' adopted a boy and a girl from neighbouring villages—there was never a lack of children for this purpose, for every adoptee was sure of a farm. There were even more curious sects, the Ophitae, who kept a snake in a box on the altar and released it during the mass, and the Adamites, who worshipped naked—in heated churches.

At times of doctrinal controversy substantial portions of the Christian population were heretics—cases are the Arians and allied sects in the fourth century and the Monophysites in the late fifth and sixth, both in the eastern parts only. Here there was at first no schism, each party trying to capture the hierarchy of the church. The German Arians later formed substantial groups, with their own hierarchy, and the Donatists were a rival church in Africa which often outnumbered the Catholics. Other sects seem to have been insignificant minorities, little dissenting groups in the towns, isolated villages in the countryside, but these groups seem mostly to have had their own ecclesiastical hierarchy. Many were regional—the Montanists, for instance, the followers of a Christian prophet who preached in Phrygia in the second century, were still in the sixth century mainly confined to Phrygia.

Almost all the literature on heretics comes from their adversaries, and we have as a result little knowledge of the inner life of the sects. An exception are the Novatians, of whom Socrates, who was a sympathizer if not an adherent of the sect, has much to say. They were by his day, it would seem, confined to north-west Asia Minor, and were mostly peasants, puritanical folk who, because they never went to the theatre, unhesitatingly condemned it. These rural Novatians in the reign of Valens adopted the fundamentalist Quartodeciman view about the date of Easter. This move was opposed by the four chief Novatian bishops, of Constantinople, Nicaea, Nicomedia and Cotyaeum, whose congregations were more educated, but the two parties finally agreed to differ. The Novatian bishops of Constantinople were mostly highly cultivated men, grammarians and rhetoricians, and one was a highly placed senator.

Apart from the pagans and heretics the only substantial religious minority was the Jews, with whom may be classed the Samaritans, still at this period a substantial community. The Jews had been nearly exterminated in Judaea proper by Hadrian, but they still formed the overwhelming majority of the population in Galilee, as did the Samaritans in Samaria around Neapolis, their national shrine. There were also Jews and Samaritans scattered in every province. We hear mostly of merchants, but there were Jewish agricultural tenants in Syria and even in Sicily in the sixth century. In some towns, such as Mago in the Balearic Isles, they were the dominant element; in the early fifth century the rabbi Theodore had held all the local magistracies and finally become *defensor civitatis*, in which office he was succeeded by the father of the synagogue. In most cities Jews avoided office and the decurionate, which was liable to involve ritual pollution, and they made an unsuccessful claim to immunity from curial duties. On the other hand many Jews seem to have entered the imperial civil service and the army, and one is known to have become a provincial governor.

Spiritually the Jews throughout the empire were governed by a hereditary patriarch, who resided at Tiberias; the line died out and the office lapsed in 429. The patriarch was usually honoured by the government with the rank of *illustris* and recognized as head of the Jewish community. He appointed all synagogue clergy (who were up to a given number exempt from curial duties), and collected dues from all synagogues through a body of itinerant inspectors, who were also his chief advisers, the apostles; these dues were in 429 diverted to the imperial treasury. In the sixth century many synagogues apparently used a Greek or Latin rite: those who favoured Hebrew put the case to Justinian, who, hoping that the Jews, if they listened to the scriptures in the vulgar tongue, would be converted, authorized the use of Latin and Greek (preferably according to the Septuagint version) and also forbade the teaching of the Talmud.

The Jews had always held an ambivalent position in the empire. On the one hand there was, and had been since the first century B.C., widespread popular antisemitism; on the other hand the imperial government had since Caesar's day consistently protected Jewish worship, and even exempted the Jews from the normal obligations of citizens when these conflicted with their religious laws. The triumph of Christianity intensified antisemitism amongst the masses, and inspired the imperial government to some anti-Jewish measures; Theodosius I for instance banned marriage between Jews and Christians, and from Constantine's reign successive laws forbade Jews to circumcise their slaves, to buy Christian slaves, or finally to own such slaves. They were in the early fifth century excluded from the civil service and under Leo from the bar. Justinian subjected them to the same civil disabilities that he imposed on pagans and heretics, incapacity to make wills, receive inheritances, give testimony in a court of law, and so forth.

The imperial government, however, consistently maintained and enforced their religious liberty. They might repair their synagogues (but not build new ones), and if their enemies destroyed them, the aggressors had to compensate them. Synagogues were immune from billeting and their clergy from curial duties. It was illegal to serve a summons on a Jew on the sabbath, and their clergy exercised a voluntary jurisdiction between Jews analogous to that of bishops.

Most responsible bishops supported governmental policy. Some firebrands invited their congregations to burn down synagogues and forcibly baptize their congregations, but the church councils and the popes condemned such actions. Ambrose was exceptional in bullying Theodosius I into reversing his decision when he condemned the bishop of Callinicum to rebuild a synagogue which he had burnt down.

Justinian not only inflicted civil disabilities on the Jews but confiscated their synagogues in reconquered Africa, and also seized those of the Samaritans, who were after all schismatics from the Chosen People. It was left to Heraclius to order the baptism of all Jews in the empire.

The Jews and the Samaritans seem to have been the only religious minorities which nursed strong animosity against the Roman empire. There was a serious Jewish rebellion in Galilee under the Caesar Gallus (351–54), a Samaritan uprising in 451, a more serious rising (after the seizure of the synagogues) in 529, and a combined Jewish and Samaritan revolt towards the end of Justinian's reign. The Jews of Naples supported that city's resistance to Belisarius, and the eastern Jews seem to have welcomed the Persian invaders under Phocas and Heraclius, and rejoiced in the first victories of the Arabs.

Other minorities, such as the Donatists in Africa and the Monophysites in the east, though they naturally had bitter feelings about the emperors who persecuted them, do not seem to have felt any animosity against the empire as such, and there is no sign that they collaborated with its enemies. The Monophysite Copts of Egypt certainly regarded the Persians and the Arabs as scourges of God, sent by him to chastise the empire for its heretical Dyophysite doctrine and its suppression of the orthodox, that is themselves; but they had no love for these scourges.

XXV

Education, Culture and Art

Linguistically the empire fell into two halves. In the Asiatic provinces, in Egypt and Cyrenaica, and in Greece, Epirus, Macedonia and the four provinces of Thrace south of the Haemus range, Greek was the *lingua franca* and the language of polite society. In the European provinces, with the exceptions named above, and in Africa up to Tripolitania inclusive, Latin fulfilled a corresponding role. The line was remarkably sharp. In Africa the boundary was the long stretch of desert between Tripolitania and Cyrenaica. In Europe there was a slight overlap; Scythia, at the mouth of the Danube, was bilingual, and there were mixed areas along the frontiers of Epirus and Macedonia. The linguistic line did not, it may be noted, correspond to political or ecclesiastical boundaries in Europe. The eastern emperors from 395 ruled the Latin-speaking diocese of Dacia, the popes exercised jurisdiction in the Greek-speaking diocese of Macedonia.

The Greeks never ceased to regard the Romans as barbarians, and it is broadly true to say that no Greek ever learned Latin except for a practical purpose, to be a lawyer or a civil servant or a military officer, or to make his way into high Roman society. Two Greeks, Claudian of Alexandria and Ammianus of Antioch, wrote poetry and history respec-

BIBLIOGRAPHY. For education and culture see Chapter XXIV of my *Later Roman Empire* (Oxford, 1964). For education see H. I. Marrou, *A History of Education in Antiquity* (London, 1956), and *Saint Augustin et la fin de la culture antique* (Paris, 1958), and for the survival of Greek studies in the west P. Courcelle, *Les lettres Grecs en Occident de Macrobe à Cassiodore*. For Syriac and Coptic literature see A. Baumstark, *Geschichte der Syrischen Literatur* (Bonn, 1922), J. Leipoldt, *Geschichte der Koptischen Literatur* (Leipzig, 1907).

For late Roman art and architecture see O. M. Dalton, *Byzantine Art and Archaeology* (Oxford, 1911), J. Arnott Hamilton, *Byzantine Architecture and Decoration*[2] (London, 1956), D. Talbot Rice, *The Beginnings of Christian Art* (London, 1957), *The Art of Byzantium* (London, 1959), *Art of the Byzantine Era* (London, 1963).

tively in Latin with a view to reaching a western aristocratic public, but no Greek would want to read Latin literature.

Under the principate all cultivated Romans learnt Greek at school, and to many it became a second language scarcely less familiar than Latin: Marcus Aurelius wrote his intimate memoirs in Greek. From the fourth century onwards the knowledge of Greek in the west waned. Upper-class boys learnt it at school, and there were a few professors of Greek literature and rhetoric available at Rome and the larger provincial cities. But even such cultivated men as Symmachus and Sidonius Apollinaris had to rub up their schoolboy Greek to help their sons with their lessons, and Augustine, a professor of rhetoric, never managed to learn Greek properly, but could only, it would seem, construe a piece painfully with a dictionary.

Intellectual contact was thus largely broken between east and west. Some Latin works were translated into Greek, many Greek works, especially philosophical and theological treatises, were translated into Latin. The work was mainly done by a few scholars, like the pagan Agorius Praetextatus, a great Roman senator of the late fourth century, or the Christians Rufinus and Jerome. Several of the translators, including Cassian and Dionysius Exiguus, came from the bilingual province of Scythia. But argument and the free play of ideas was difficult, and doctrinal controversies were exacerbated by this fact. In the last phase of the Arian controversy agreement between the schools of Basil and of Ambrose was long held up because the latter could not understand the difference between οὐσία and ὑπόστασις, both rendered substantia in the dictionaries. Pope Leo's delegates at the Council of Ephesus had to use a Greek bishop as interpreter, and could contribute nothing except an occasional 'contradicitur' to the debate.

Greek was—and had always been—used for most official purposes in the eastern provinces. Imperial constitutions and rescripts were issued with a Greek translation, legal proceedings were conducted in Greek, and in the provincial offices the administrative language was Greek. This might cause difficulties when the provincial governor was, as sometimes happened, a westerner who knew no Greek. On the other hand the language of the army was Latin; words of command were presumably given in Latin, and army records were kept in Latin down to the end of the fifth century at least. This required a supply of military clerks who knew enough Latin to write formal documents. The administrative language of the praetorian prefecture of the East was also Latin until Cyrus substituted Greek in 439-41. In the sacra scrinia Latin was required still longer, as the clerks had to draft constitutions in Latin; in the sixth century the Greek version was clearly the master copy and the Latin a not always accurate translation. Most important of all, Latin was required for a serious study of law, for the sources were nearly all in Latin and legal education was conducted in Latin. Libanius frequently and bitterly laments that Greek literature and rhetoric were being abandoned by ambitious young men for Latin and the law. But his fears proved groundless: to practise in the courts a Greek rhetorical training was essential, and eventually the legal literature was translated; two professors of Berytus are known to have written Greek textbooks and commentaries in the early fifth century.

In the fourth century Latin was also useful to a man of higher ambitions. The emperors during that period were mostly more at home in Latin than in Greek—Constantine preferred to read his theology in Latin translations, and used the bilingual Strategius to conduct his ecclesiastical negotiations, while Valens knew no Greek, and Theodosius probably very little. Their chief ministers were often also westerners, like Rufinus or Cynegius, whose Greek was non-existent or scanty. To men in court circles Latin was therefore very useful, if not essential. But from 395 the emperors and their ministers were all Greek speaking (though the native language of several, including Justinian, was Latin).

Elementary teaching in Latin for aspiring clerks seems to have been fairly common in the east; many Greco-Latin *abecedaria* and word-for-word cribs of Virgil and Cicero are preserved in the Egyptian papyri. Higher teaching was rarer. It was given regularly at Constantinople and probably at Berytus, but at Antioch the appointment of a Latin professor was a rare event. The professors were sometimes distinguished Latinists imported from the west, like Lactantius at the imperial capita of Nicomedia under Diocletian, and the famous grammarian Priscian at Constantinople under Justinian. Sometimes they were native scholars like John Lydus, whose knowledge of Latin was, to judge by his surviving works, rather schoolboyish.

Owing to the predominance of Latin in the legal and administrative field civil service and legal Greek became replete with Latinisms like σπορτοῦλα or φιδεικόμμισσον and many Latin words, like *comes, dux, iugum*, became assimilated in ordinary spoken Greek, and in the less pretentious literature. No stylist, however, would sully his page with such Latinisms, and Libanius and Procopius use synonyms culled from Demosthenes and Thucydides.

With a few minor exceptions Greek and Latin were the only written languages of the empire. Syriac maintained itself as a literary language in Mesopotamia, and was taught at the grammatical and rhetorical levels at Nisibis, across the Persian frontier, and perhaps in Roman territory too; it was later used for popular Christian literature in Syria and Palestine. The Egyptian language was provided with an alphabet (mostly Greek with a few demotic letters) in the fourth century, and used for popular Christian literature. Gothic was also provided with an alphabet (based on Greek) in the mid-fourth century and used for the scriptures and theological works. Not only were Greek and Latin with these exceptions the only literary languages, they were the normal and often the sole language of the middle and upper classes. But in most provinces the peasantry, and many of the urban proletariat, continued to speak their indigenous tongues. Latin was of course indigenous in Italy, and had probably long superseded the native languages in southern Gaul and eastern and southern Spain. Greek was indigenous in Greece, Epirus and Macedonia and in Cyprus, Pamphylia and Cilicia, and had conquered the Lydian, Carian and Lycian tongues in western Asia Minor in the Hellenistic age.

The evidence for the existence of spoken native languages is of necessity tenuous, depending partly on anecdotes and casual remarks, partly on the survival to this day of pre-Roman and pre-Greek tongues. Thus, in Britain there is the fact that Welsh is derived from Celtic, not from Latin, and there is the survival of Basque, once spoken in a large area of northern Spain and southern France. In northern Gaul we have the evidence of Jerome on the Celtic dialect spoken in his day near Trier, and a joking remark of a character in one of Sulpicius Severus' dialogues to a north Gallic friend, 'talk in Celtic or Gallic if you prefer, so long as you talk about Martin'. In Africa Augustine makes it plain that many peasants and humble folk knew only Punic, and Berber has survived through Carthaginian, Roman and Arab rule. Albanian is undoubtedly the old native language of the Illyrians, and further east Thracian is attested by John Chrysostom and Gregory of Nyssa as a living language in their day.

Many native languages survived in the interior of Asia Minor. We happen to know of Isaurian and Lycaonian from hagiographical anecdotes of the sixth century, and in a sermon Basil of Caesarea alludes to Cappadocian as a language known to his congregation. We know from Jerome that the Galatians still spoke a Celtic language in his day. For the general prevalence of Syriac in Mesopotamia, Syria and Palestine the evidence is overwhelming. Of Palestine a fourth-century pilgrim writes: 'Since in that province part of the people know both Greek and Syriac, another part too Greek by itself, some part too Syriac only, so, since the bishop, though he may know Syriac, nevertheless always speaks in Greek and never in Syriac, there is always a priest who translates into Syriac as the bishop speaks in Greek.' In Egypt the papyri at first sight give the impression that Greek was the universal language, since not only administrative and business documents, but the private letters of the humblest persons are nearly all written in Greek. But the letters are mostly the work of professional letterwriters, and when villagers appear in court they plead through an interpreter, and in the sixth century even government notices were posted in Coptic as well as Greek.

Elementary schools, in which Latin or Greek reading and writing and arithmetic were taught, were fairly common, existing even in villages; the children of the upper classes usually received this stage of their education from a tutor at home. Some schools also taught shorthand, a necessary qualification for a government clerkship. Elementary schools were all private, the teacher living from the fees of his pupils, which were moderate. Upper and middle-class boys next went to a professor of grammar, that is literature. Such professors existed in all cities of any consequence, either occupying official chairs, appointed and salaried by the civic authorities, or living on fees as freelance teachers; official professors also charged fees, which were four or five times as high as those of an elementary schoolmaster.

The courses were based on a rather limited range of authors, Virgil and Terence, Sallust and Cicero being the standard texts in Latin; Homer, selected plays of the Attic tragedians and comedians, Thucydides, Demosthenes and selections from the other Attic orators in Greek. Other authors were not read *in extenso*, but only extracts from them in anthologies. The aim was to teach correct classical diction and appreciation of the form and content of classical literature. The method was to make the pupils learn by rote declensions, paradigms, and grammatical rules, set them exercises involving the application of these rules, and illustrate them by a minute analysis of the classical texts word by word. It must be remembered that vulgar spoken Latin and Greek were by this time rather different from the classical languages, and the object of education was to enable the pupil to express himself using no words or idioms not certified as correct by their occurrence in classical texts. Literary appreciation of the classics meant in practice the memorization of the recognized poetical and rhetorical tropes, reinforced by a close analysis of the texts. Appreciation of their content meant a commentary on the mythological, historical and geographical allusions in the texts, and this was all the history and geography that most people learned.

Boys or young men next went to a professor of rhetoric; these were not quite so common as grammarians, but existed in most considerable cities. Under him the course became more interesting, after the grind of grammar, which most pupils found tedious. Further study was given to rhetorical techniques, ancient orators were more thoroughly studied, and the pupil began to write compositions, speeches on set themes. These themes fell into various classes, panegyrics, laments, political and forensic speeches. The topics were curiously unreal, culled from mythology or ancient history. Typical are: 'Menelaus addresses the Trojans, reclaiming Helen', or 'After Chaeronea Philip sends promising to give back 2,000 prisoners if Demosthenes is surrendered to him; Demosthenes asks to be surrendered.'

This was the standard course for a gentleman. Those who aspired to higher learning or wished to prepare themselves for the professions usually went on to one of the centres of higher learning. There were no universities in the medieval or modern sense, but there were certain cities, notably Rome, Constantinople, Athens, Alexandria and Berytus, where there were groups of professors, appointed and salaried by the state or by the municipality, and which had an established reputation for superior teaching in grammar and rhetoric, and offered other courses, philosophy at Rome, Constantinople and Athens, mathematics and medicine at Alexandria, law at Rome, Constantinople and Berytus. Other major cities such as Bordeaux, Milan, Carthage or Antioch also enjoyed some reputation, especially when the municipal chair was occupied by a famous scholar; Libanius at Antioch attracted pupils from Asia Minor and from Palestine.

There were no fixed curricula and no degrees, except at Berytus in law, where there was a regular four-year course with prescribed books, and students received a certificate of satisfactory study from their professors at the end. The length of courses elsewhere was indeterminate. The average student took two or three years over his rhetorical course. Libanius spent ten years at Antioch and at Athens. There was great competition between cities to secure professors of high reputation, and great competition between professors, the freelance teachers trying to build up their classes at the expense of the occupants of the official chairs, and the latter competing with each other and their unestablished rivals. At Athens the students of the several professors formed gangs and tried to kidnap freshmen, and the resultant brawls often called for the intervention of the proconsul of Achaea.

This system of education had its obvious defects. It included no systematic study of history, geography, or, except for a few specialists, of higher mathematics, philosophy or the physical sciences. On the other hand it produced a large and widely distributed class of cultivated gentlemen, who read and appreciated classical and contemporary literature, and could write an elegant letter, compose a well-constructed speech and turn out passable verse.

Education was entirely based on the pagan classics, and necessarily involved a thorough study of pagan mythology. Some Christians felt qualms about this. There was a rigorist school of thought, exemplified by the *Constitutions of the Apostles*, a fourth-century document widely regarded as authoritative in the east, which commanded Christians to abstain from all pagan books, and content themselves with the scriptures. 'Do you want history? There is the Book of Kings. Eloquence and poetry? The Prophets. Lyrics? The Psalms. Cosmology? Genesis. Law and Ethics? The glorious law of God.'[1] Such sentiments survived in the west down to the end of the sixth century and beyond. Pope Gregory the Great severely reprimanded a Gallic bishop for teaching grammar: 'One mouth cannot contain the praise of Christ together with the praise of Jupiter.'[2]

Even the severest fundamentalists, however, who held that adult Christians ought not to read the classics, still less teach them, had to admit that boys had no choice. As Jerome[3] says, priests who 'abandon the gospels and prophets and read comedies, sing the amatory words of bucolic verse and cling to Virgil, make what is for boys a necessity a deliberate sin for themselves'. The vast majority of enlightened Christians, including such holy men as Basil and Gregory of Nyssa, held that a classical education was perfectly acceptable, and that Christians could teach the classics; Julian's prohibition against Christians being appointed professors excited widespread indignation, loudly voiced by Gregory of Nazianzus.

This prohibition had a curious by-product. Two Christians named Apollinarius, father and son, the former a grammarian and the latter a rhetorician, transposed the scriptures into classical forms, the Penta-

[1] *Const. Apost.* I. 6. [2] Gregory the Great, *Epist.* XIII. 34.
[3] *Epist.* 21 §13.

teuch into a Homeric epic, the historical books into tragedies, the New
Testament into Platonic dialogues. When Julian died these works,
though their literary elegance was impeccable, were immediately forgotten, 'by the divine providence', says Socrates.

> But someone will sharply retort to me, 'Why do you say this hap-
> pened by the divine providence ? It is plain that the emperor's speedy
> death was beneficial to Christianity, but that the Christian composi-
> tions of the Apollinarii were thrown aside, and Christians once again
> began to follow Greek education, was not for the interests of Chris-
> tianity. For Greek education is dangerous and harmful, teaching
> polytheism.' To this I will reply to the best of my ability. Greek
> education was not received as inspired or condemned as harmful by
> Christ and his disciples. And this I think they did with providence.
> For many Greek philosophers were not far from knowing God . . .
> in the second place the divinely inspired scriptures teach admirable
> and indeed divine doctrines and inspire their readers with much piety
> and a good life, providing for their students a fate acceptable to God.
> But they do not teach the art of speaking, to enable us to refute those
> who wish to attack the truth; for our adversaries are well and truly
> defeated when we use their own weapons against them. And this
> resource would not have been available to Christians from the works
> of the Apollinarii.[1]

In fact what the Christians wanted their children to learn was not the
bogus classics of the Apollinarii but the real thing.

The church never developed any Christian form of education. At
Nisibis in Persian Mesopotamia there was a rhetorical school in which
instruction was based on the Syriac version of the scriptures, but
Augustine's blueprint for a similar Latin course was never put into
practice, and Cassiodorus' similar attempt soon petered out. There were
monastic schools which gave elementary education to illiterate postulants and boy oblates and, when literacy waned in the sixth century in
Spain and Italy, bishops and parish priests were instructed to keep
schools for educating future clergy: but no Christian education was
ever provided for laymen.

The literature of the age was, as one might expect from its educational
system, imitative and rhetorical. Symmachus and Sidonius Apollinaris
wrote letters closely modelled on those of the younger Pliny. Not that
they could not sometimes write well. Symmachus' official despatches

[1] Socrates, *Hist. Eccl.* III. 16.

are clear and dignified, his plea for the Altar of Victory is deeply moving. Sidonius has a gift for vivid description and narrative and paints lively pictures of a dinner with the emperor Majorian, contested episcopal elections, or a day in the life of the Gothic king Theoderic. It is only when, as too often, they have nothing to say that their eloquence becomes frigid and dreary. Libanius wrote speeches in the manner and style of Demosthenes, and to avoid any jarring note will not call a vicar a vicar but 'a ruler of several peoples'; he even avoided modern-sounding proper names and prefers to call Valens 'the younger of the two Paeonian brothers' (actually Valentinian and Valens were Pannonians, but Demosthenes had not heard of Pannonians and does speak of Paeonians). But Libanius can tell a story well and can write forcibly and movingly on questions on which he felt strongly—such as the decay of the curial class, the ill-treatment of the urban poor and the peasants and the corruption of justice by the influence of the great. Ammianus adopted a Tacitean idiom in his history, but is none the less a very great historian; Procopius imitated Thucydidean diction in his history of the wars of Justinian, but he too writes clearly and accurately.

Rhetoric invaded poetry, and even the language of the law. Claudian's poems must be judged as rhetorical panegyrics and diatribes, and as such they have indubitable power. It is less easy to be indulgent to the successive quaestors who veiled the plain meaning of imperial constitutions in rhetorical bombast, or to the preachers who blew up the simple lives of saints into lengthy high-falutin' orations.

In prose the main types of literary production were speeches, history and letters. The speeches are too often vapid panegyrics or diatribes, but some discuss serious topics of the day. With them may be classed sermons, which take the form of moral exhortations, exegesis of scripture or doctrinal controversy; some sermons are, like those of John Chrysostom, highly polished rhetorical pieces, others deliberately simple and plain spoken. Historiography was very popular in the Greek east, which produced a whole series of contemporary historians, both secular and ecclesiastical, some of the highest order and mostly competent. The west was on the contrary very sterile, producing only brief compendia for the benefit of those who wanted an elegantly written summary of events. With history may be classed biography; some, like Eunapius' lives of the Sophists or Sulpicius Severus' life of S. Martin, ranked as literature, but there was also a large body of popular lives of saints. Epistolography was highly esteemed, and most men of education seem to have spent much of their time in penning elegant letters about nothing in particular to a wide circle of acquaintances. Many collections of letters were edited for publication.

In poetry the epic, Homeric or Virgilian, still flourished, whether on mythological themes, like the *Dionysiaca* of Nonnus of Panopolis, or on contemporary events, like the *Johannis* which Corippus wrote on the exploits of John, *magister militum* of Africa under Justinian. Verse panegyrics and diatribes were common, like those of Claudian and Sidonius Apollinaris, and much occasional verse and epigram were written. Very little of the poetry of the age appeals to modern taste, but there are some good pieces, like Ausonius' *Mosella*, a sensitive description of a voyage down the Moselle, and some of the Christian hymns are moving and dignified.

Literary productivity was far more widespread geographically than under the principate. Most authors then came from the most Hellenized or Romanized provinces, or from cities with a long Roman or Hellenic tradition. Now once backward provinces and minor cities produced their orators, historians, theologians and poets. Britain, it is true, gave birth to only one figure of note, Pelagius, and he was probably educated in Rome; but Egypt, where hitherto only the old Greek cities of Alexandria, Ptolemais and Naucratis had produced literary men, could now boast of the historian Olympiodorus of Thebes and the poets Cyrus and Nonnus of Panopolis. In backward Cappadocia, where only Caesarea and Tyana had been islands of Hellenism, the remote little city of Nazianzus gave birth to Gregory, the Christian poet and theologian.

In philosophy, mathematics and the physical sciences there was little creative work. In the west little except translation from Greek into Latin was achieved. In the east most of the work was commentaries on the great Greek and Hellenistic thinkers. Such commentaries were not however entirely sterile. Plato and Aristotle were not regarded as sacrosanct, but subjected to searching criticism, and in the sixth century John Philoponus anticipated Galileo by a millennium in observing that heavier objects do not fall faster than lighter, and corrected Aristotle's theory of motion on this point.

In the field of philology much useful work was done in collating and correcting texts. Donatus and Priscian wrote Latin grammars which remained standard works until the eighteenth century, and scholars such as Servius produced commentaries on the classics which were read throughout the Middle Ages. The greatest volume of philological work was done on the scriptures, but with the outstanding exception of

Jerome, who took the trouble to master Greek and Hebrew and was by any standards a great scholar, much of this work was superficial and repetitive. Commentators on the scriptures followed too faithfully in the footsteps of the secular grammarians, and wrote philological and historical and geographical notes on each word and sentence, adding allegorical interpretations of difficult passages, and drawing doctrinal conclusions and moral lessons.

The greatest intellectual achievements of the age were in theology. The main problem was to state Christian beliefs in the philosophical language of the day, and in particular to reconcile the apparently contradictory thesis that there was one God, and that not only the Father, but the Son was God. The Holy Spirit attracted little interest at this period, and only one heresy, that of the Macedonians, was concerned with his divinity and position in the Trinity. One solution, that the Father, Son and Holy Spirit were merely aspects or names of the one God, had been propounded in the mid-third century by the Cyrenaican priest Sabellius, but condemned. It was revived by Marcellus, bishop of Ancyra, in Constantine's reign, but again condemned. Arius, also a Cyrenaican, and a priest of Alexandria, attempted a new solution. He was a disciple of Lucian of Antioch, who was martyred in Diocletian's persecution, and like him a follower of Origen, who had first in the third century tried to synthesize Neoplatonism with Christianity. His central thesis was that God the Father was the eternal and unknowable Monad of the Neoplatonists, and that the Son therefore could not be in the same sense God. He was posterior logically, though not in time, to the Father; 'there was when He was not' was his thesis, not as his enemies alleged, 'there was a time when He was not'; for the Son was created or begotten (on this issue Arius was vague) before all ages. He further argued that since the Monad was indivisible, God must have created or begotten the Son out of nothing.

This doctrine was attractive to intellectuals, but deeply shocking to ordinary Christians, who passionately upheld the full divinity of Christ. The formula, probably western in origin, imposed by Constantine on the Council of Nicaea, that the Son was of one substance with the Father, satisfied simple Christians, since it affirmed the equal divinity of the Son and the Father, but shocked educated theologians, since it meant in effect that the Father and Son were identical, substance ($o\dot{v}\sigma\acute{\iota}a$) in philosophical language meaning something like individuality, and therefore revived the condemned doctrine of Sabellius. The deadlock took a long while to resolve, since the west clung obstinately to *con-*

substantialis, and would not accept such compromises as 'of like substance'. Eventually οὐσία was accepted in the east as meaning something like nature, and another term was introduced to describe the individuality of the persons of the Trinity, ὑπόστασις (which is a literal translation of *substantia*). Westerners long failed to understand what the Greeks meant by one οὐσία in three ὑποστάσεις, since the words seemed to them identical in meaning, but they eventually accepted the formula and both parties were satisfied.

The next difficulty arose over the question of how Christ could be both God and man. Nestorius taught that Christ was truly and spontaneously human with an intellectual and moral development like other men and that at the same time he was 'perfect in his Godhead'. To safeguard the reality of Christ's humanity he deplored the growing tendency to pay extreme reverence to the Virgin Mary by calling her 'mother of God'. His opponents were able to represent him as teaching that in Christ there are two separate persons, divine and human, without any effective principle of unity, or even as reducing Christ to the level of an inspired prophet. This rather rationalistic view shocked ordinary pious opinion, which was beginning to pay extreme reverence to the Virgin Mary, and, what was more important, felt that Nestorius' doctrine derogated from the full divinity of Christ and reduced him to a major prophet. Nestorius' view was condemned by the Council of Ephesus in 431, and never achieved any substantial following in the Roman empire, though it prevailed in Persia. The contrary doctrine of Cyril, bishop of Alexandria, as developed by his successor Dioscorus, in its turn aroused opposition. Their view was that the humanity of Christ was absorbed in His divinity, and their slogan was that God was crucified for us. This view was affirmed at the Council of Ephesus in 449 and condemned at the Council of Chalcedon in 451, which declared that Christ was one person in two natures, human and divine, in a fundamental union which did not prejudice their distinctness. There were many shades of Monophysitism, ranging from the moderate view of Severus of Antioch, which differed only in emphasis from the Dyophysite position, to such extremes as Aphthartodocetism, according to which Christ had not a human body but a divine and imperishable simulacrum. The division between Monophysites and Dyophysites has never been healed, the Coptic, Ethiopian, Jacobite, Armenian and Indian Christians still adhering to the Monophysite position, while the Catholic and Orthodox churches and all protestant sects are Dyophysites.

The Trinitarian and Christological theology of the fourth and fifth centuries, which has satisfied all Christians ever since, was entirely the product of the Greek east. In the west there were two original thinkers only. Pelagius, whose views on works and grace have already been discussed, and Augustine. Augustine was not a systematic theologian, but developed his original views in the course of the various controversies in which he engaged. Against the Donatists he developed and refined the doctrine that the validity of a sacrament is independent of the character or beliefs of him who administers it. Against the Manichean doctrine of the two equal principles of good and evil he worked out the theory that all nature *qua* nature is good, and that evil is man's disobedience to the divine will, the necessary concomitant of man's free will. Against Pelagius he insisted on man's congenital sinfulness, which involved the conclusion that he could be saved only by divine grace, and went on to evolve the doctrine that God's grace was arbitrarily granted to a select few. Against the pagans, who claimed that the fall of Rome was due to the anger of the gods, he wrote his most famous work, *The City of God*. It was composed at intervals over a period of thirteen years and is as a result a very rambling work, which deals with almost every problem from original sin to contemporary miracles. His greatest contribution to Christian thought was the concept of the two cities, the *civitas terrena* and the *civitas Dei*. The former, though evil and of the devil, being based on self-love, developed, he admitted, earthly virtues such as justice and courage. The latter, based on the love of God, was not identical with the Christian empire or the church, but existed in the minds of its spiritual citizens on earth, and would prevail in the world to come.

Unlike the literature, and, it must be admitted, the theology of the later Roman empire, which excites little interest today, its art is highly appreciated, and its art history is the subject of active debate. In sculpture and painting classical realism gave way to a formalistic treatment, in which balance and pattern are more important than verisimilitude, and the bold use of gorgeous colour is preferred to delicate light and shade. In architecture the rather rigid rules of the classical orders, which had already been to some extent broken down in the baroque of the second century, gave way to an architecture which delighted in curves, and for decoration preferred to sculpture the enrichment of surfaces by patterns or formal iconography, mainly executed in marble revetment and mosaic.

For about fifty years in the middle of the third century monumental building virtually ceased in the provinces, and was greatly reduced at Rome itself. At the same time the demand for statues abruptly ceased. Private building of course went on, and masons and carpenters and ordinary painters and mosaicists, who could decorate room walls and lay simple pavements, found plenty of employment. But stone and wood carvers, sculptors and architects, went out of business, and so did the higher grade of painters and mosaicists. By the time that monumental building was revived under Diocletian and Constantine, mainly in the capitals and the other great cities of the empire, architects and skilled craftsmen were very hard to find. 'There is a demand for as many architects as possible, but none exist', proclaimed Constantine,[1] and instituted a system of state scholarships to train them. With a similar object he gave sundry immunities to a variety of skilled craftsmen, including painters, sculptors, mosaicists, wood and stone carvers, to encourage them 'to increase their own skill and teach their sons'. By this time the highly sophisticated techniques of Roman painting and sculpture, which were handed on by apprenticeship, had largely been lost. The break in architecture was less catastrophic, since architecture was a science enshrined in books, but here too the practical tradition whereby the theoretical rules were applied was largely broken.

In carving the result can be seen in the arch of Constantine at Rome, where the sculptured panels are either old pieces, filched from classical monuments, or the crude productions of monumental masons ordered to execute large and elaborate scenes. These masons produced what can only be called child or peasant art, with rigid frontal figures arranged in symmetrical rows. The same kind of thing can be seen in mosaics, where the craftsmen eschew large figure designs and prefer geometrical patterns or formalized floral designs, with crude little figures in the intervening panels. In architecture the designers pay very little attention to the rigid classical rules of proportion, and get over such difficulties as the placing of the springs of arches on the narrow tops of classical capitals not by the classical device of superimposing a section of entablature on the capital, but by using amorphous impost blocks. Architectural carving virtually died out for a long period, since it was simpler and cheaper to re-use columns, entablatures and other architectural members rifled from derelict buildings. Even in the great imperial churches the architects were singularly slapdash in the use of old materials, using columns of different sizes in one colonnade, and propping up the smaller ones on higher bases.

[1] *Cod. Theod.* XIII. iv. I.

357

The apparent disaster proved a blessing in disguise. Freed from a tradition which had run dry, artists were able to develop a new style and, as their skill increased, to refine it. Statuary in the round never recovered its vogue, but in bas-relief, painting and mosaic the formal, frontal and symmetrical designs of the simple masons, painters and mosaicists of Constantine's day evidently pleased contemporary taste and caught the imagination of artists. Henceforth there were two streams in design which sometimes commingled, while sometimes one or the other prevailed. The old traditions of Hellenistic and Roman art, with its use of perspective and shading, did not die out; no doubt some few schools or families of artists maintained their hereditary traditions, and there were always old works or pattern books to copy. Some mosaics in the fifth and sixth centuries, those for instance of the floors of the imperial palace at Constantinople, are highly skilled work in the full Hellenistic tradition. But for the most part mosaicists, particularly in wall and vault mosaics, preferred hieratic figures in formal rows or symmetrical groups, and flat masses of colour, in particular gold backgrounds, combined with rich bands of geometrical or stylized floral patterns; though some, like the designers of the mosaics of S. George's church at Thessalonica, preferred to set their figures in the fantastic architectural frames of the Pompeian tradition.

Civic buildings, such as theatres, baths, street colonnades and palaces and mansions, continued to be built in the traditional manner, but for churches new forms were invented. By far the commonest was the basilica. This was a long oblong hall lit by clerestory windows and flanked by two, or rarely four, lower aisles. The central hall terminated in an apse, the aisles sometimes in smaller apses, sometimes in square rooms, sometimes with a plain wall. The roof was of timber, often concealed by a coffered ceiling, except for the apse, which was vaulted with a semi-dome. The aisles were separated from the nave either by colonnades with a flat entablature or by arcades. At the end opposite the apse three or five doors opened on to the narthex, a high colonnade, and thence into a square colonnaded court, the atrium. There were many regional variations in such matters as the orientation of the building, and the arrangement of the apse or apses, and sometimes a transverse hall or transept was introduced between the main body of the basilica and the apse. Larger churches had baptisteries, administrative offices and side chapels flanking them.

Externally a basilica is a dull building except as seen from the atrium. Internally it is spacious and dignified and well adapted for its purpose, congregational worship. The altar usually stood in the centre of the apse and the clergy sat on a semicircular stone bench behind the altar along the apse wall. In front of the altar on either side were pulpits for reading the epistle and gospel and preaching, and the clergy were separated from the people by a waist-high stone screen.

The architectural members of these buildings were practically always re-used antiques, and the new work was confined to the coffered ceilings, the mosaics of the apse and sometimes of the upper walls, the marble revetment of the lower walls, the mosaic or patterned marble floor and the screens. The marble revetment and paving were generally made from slices of antique columns. Architectural carving seems to have been almost entirely confined to the great imperial marble quarries of Proconnesus, Alexandria Troas and Docimium, which supplied imperial buildings, and, by imperial grant, favoured cities and churches. Here generations of craftsmen worked out a new style of decorative carving which superseded the Corinthian and Ionic capitals and friezes, evolving the lovely basket capitals of S. Sophia from the crude impost blocks of the Constantinian age.

More interesting than basilicas were the circular, polygonal or quatrefoil buildings, inspired by the similar rooms in the great baths, but greatly elaborated, particularly by the use of annular colonnades or arcades. The form was particularly favoured for baptisteries and martyrs' chapels, but was also used for big churches occasionally. Outstanding examples which survive are S. Constanza and S. Stefano Rotondo at Rome, S. Vitale at Ravenna, S. George at Thessalonica and SS. Sergius and Bacchus at Constantinople. These churches were sometimes roofed in timber, like S. Stefano Rotondo, but were more commonly, following the tradition of the baths, vaulted, and the intricate problems of combining domes, semi-domes and barrel and cross vaults were ingeniously solved.

The supreme masterpiece of late Roman architecture, Justinian's S. Sophia, is a conflation, on a vast scale, of the basilican and centralized plans. A great central hall is covered by a huge dome, abutted east and west by two semi-domes, and is flanked by cross-vaulted aisles with galleries above them, opening into the central hall by arcades. The spaciousness of the basilica and its dignified arcades are here combined with the soaring domes and interesting curvilinear structure of a circular church. Little is known of Isidore of Miletus, but the other architect, Anthemius of Tralles, was a brilliant and learned *mechanicus* (structural engineer). His calculations were perhaps too bold, for the crown of the central dome, which was low, being continuous with the pendentives, fell as the result of an earthquake twenty years after it was built. The solution of Isidore the Younger, son of Anthemius' colleague, was brilliant. He left the pendentives in the corners, and built on them a dome of steeper pitch, lit by a ring of windows, thus increasing the height of the building and greatly improving its lighting.

Textiles survive only in Egypt. They are of course provincial work and somewhat unsophisticated, but many are beautiful pieces. Many are still in the Hellenistic tradition, but the figures are rather childish; most have geometrical or formalized floral patterns. From Egypt too comes the only surviving furniture. The more elaborate pieces are inlaid with Hellenistic mythological figures, but the drawing is crude. We still possess and treasure many specimens of silver plate, glassware, jewellery and ivory carving; notable among the last are the diptychs sent out as invitation cards by the consuls to their games, usually depicting the donor starting the races. These pieces were produced at Constantinople or one of the other great artistic centres, and are of superb craftsmanship and design; they exemplify both the naturalistic traditions of Hellenistic art and the formal style which we call Byzantine.

The culture of the Roman world was extraordinarily uniform. The upper and middle classes all received the same type of education, and read the same literature, Latin in the west, and Greek in the east, and applied the same canons of taste in its appreciation, and wrote in the same style. Except for odd pockets of heretics and surviving coteries of pagans they all practised the same religion, attended similar church services, heard similar sermons and read the same devotional literature. They all spent much of their day in the ritual of the baths, and watched the same mimes, chariot races and wild beast fights; there was a slight difference in the matter of sports between the east, where athletic competitions were more popular and lasted longer, and the west, where gladiatorial shows were common and survived till the early fifth century. They all wore the same kind of clothes, often produced in the same centres, and used the same kind of table ware. In architecture there were, of course, regional variations in the humbler class of buildings, mostly due to local building materials. Timber was more used in the forested north, brick in some areas; in Africa walls were built with vertical stone beams and rubble fillings between, and in Arabia, where there were no trees at all and the only stone was basalt, roofs and ceilings were constructed of stone beams and doors and windows of stone slabs. But the architectural appearance of any city from York to Gaza was basically similar, and it is very difficult to distinguish a mosaic pavement on the Rhine frontier from one in Africa or Palestine.

Corresponding to this there was a general uniformity of sentiment, at any rate among the upper and middle classes, who have alone recorded their opinions. They had legally been Romans since A.D. 212 and they now felt themselves to be Romans. They were of course also Britons, Africans or Egyptians, but these names had no great emotive force. There were supposed to be provincial characteristics—Gauls were gluttonous, Cappadocians boorish, Cretans liars; but these distinctions were on a par with the differences between a Cockney and a Yorkshireman. Of the lower classes we can say little, but, though they spoke different languages, there is nothing to show that they too did not think themselves Romans. The German kings certainly called all their provincial subjects *Romani*, and the Arabs styled all the inhabitants of the areas that they conquered Rumi.

XXVI

Why did the Western Empire Fall?

The causes of the fall of the western empire in the fifth century have been endlessly debated since Augustine's day, but those who have debated the question have all been westerners, and have tended to forget that the eastern empire did not fall till many centuries later. Many of the causes alleged for the fall of the west were common to the east, and therefore cannot be complete and self-sufficient causes. If, as the pagans said in 410, it was the gods, incensed by the apostasy of the empire, who struck it down, why did they not strike down the equally Christian eastern parts? If, as Salvian argues, it was God who sent the barbarians to chastize the sinful Romans, why did He not send barbarians to chastize the equally sinful Constantinopolitans? If Christianity, as Gibbon thought, sapped the empire's morale and weakened it by internal schisms, why did not the more Christian east, with its much more virulent theological disputes, fall first?

We must look then for points in which the two halves of the empire differed. In the first place the western provinces were much more exposed to barbarian attack. The western emperor had to guard the long fronts of the Rhine and the upper Danube, the eastern emperor only the lower Danube. For on the eastern front his neighbour was the Persian empire, a civilized power which was not on the whole aggressive and kept its treaties. If a Persian war broke out, it was a more serious affair than a barbarian invasion, but wars were rare until the sixth century, and they then tested the Roman empire very severely. Moreover, if the western emperor failed to hold any part of the Rhine and Danube fronts, he had no second line of defence; the invaders could penetrate straight into Italy and Gaul, and even into Spain. The eastern emperor, if he failed, as he often did, to hold the lower Danube, only lost control temporarily of the European dioceses; for no enemy could force the Bosphorus and the Hellespont, guarded by Constantinople itself. Asia Minor, Syria and Egypt thus remained sealed off from invasion.

The barbarian invaders soon grasped the strategical position and, even if they first crossed the lower Danube and ravaged Thrace and Illyricum, soon tired of these exhausted lands and, unable to penetrate into the rich lands of Asia Minor, trekked westwards to Italy. This path was successively followed by the Visigoths under Alaric and the Ostrogoths under Theoderic.

In the second place the eastern parts were probably more populous, more intensively cultivated and richer than the western. This is hard to prove and difficult to believe nowadays, when the Balkans, Asia Minor and Syria are poor and thinly peopled, and only Egypt is rich and populous, whereas in the west Italy, France, Britain and the Low Countries are wealthy and densely populated, and only north Africa is poor. But many lines of argument suggest that the reverse was true in Roman times. The population of Egypt was about 8 million, that of Gaul (which included besides modern France the Low Countries and Germany west of the Rhine) can be estimated at about $2\frac{1}{2}$ million. The diocese of Egypt yielded perhaps three times as much revenue as that of Africa. Archaeological evidence proves that many areas now desert or waste in Syria and Asia Minor were inhabited and cultivated in late Roman times, and suggest that much of the most fertile soil in northern Gaul and Britain was still uncleared forest. It is moreover possible to estimate the wealth of different areas in the Roman empire from the number and scale of the public buildings of the cities, since the rich put much of their surplus wealth into such buildings. On this test the Mediterranean lands, eastern and southern Spain, southern Gaul, Italy, Africa, the southern Balkans, Asia Minor, Syria and Egypt were all wealthy, and Asia Minor and Syria the wealthiest of all, whereas Britain, northern Gaul and the Danubian lands were miserably poor. This analysis is borne out by literary testimonies. In the west Sardinia, Sicily and above all Africa, were regarded as the richest provinces, the granaries of the empire, and Aquitania as more fertile than northern Gaul. This implies that the potential fertility of the northern plains had not yet been exploited to the full.

In some other ways the east was superior to the west. It enjoyed much greater political stability and less of its resources were wasted in civil wars. From the accession of Diocletian in 284 to the death of Maurice in 602 there were only five attempted usurpations, those of Domitius Domitianus under Diocletian, of Procopius under Valens, of Basiliscus, Marcian and Leontius under Zeno, and all were quickly subdued without many casualties. In the west there were rebellions or usurpations by Carausius, Maxentius, Alexander, Magnentius, Firmus, Magnus Maximus, Gildo, Constantine, Jovinus and John, most of which involved heavy fighting, and after the death of Valentinian III a succession of ephemeral emperors.

The social and economic structure of the east was healthier than that of the west. In the east more of the land was owned by peasant proprietors, who paid taxes only, and thus a larger proportion of the total yield of agriculture went to the peasantry. In the west a much higher proportion of the land was owned by great landlords, whose tenants had to pay rents in excess of their taxes, and the general condition of the peasantry was therefore poorer. This is reflected in the recurrent revolts of the Bacaudae in Gaul and Spain, which at times contained troops urgently needed elsewhere.

Another result of this difference in social structure was that the landed aristocracy in the west obtained a stranglehold on the administration, with two deleterious results. They were inefficient administrators, and allowed the bureaucracy to add a very appreciable sum to the burden of taxation by their exorbitant fees. They were over-indulgent to their own class, and slack in curbing grants of immunity and reductions and remissions of taxes. In the east the administrative machine remained in the hands of men of middle-class origin, who owed their advancement to the imperial government; they kept the expenses of tax collection down to a very reasonable figure, and periodically cancelled reductions of tax granted to landowners. A higher proportion of the total yield of agriculture thus reached the imperial treasury, and less was absorbed by the bureaucracy and by landlords.

Another question may be asked. When the western empire had stood firm for two-and-a-half centuries from the reign of Augustus, and had surmounted the crisis of the mid-third century, and, reorganized by Diocletian, had maintained itself intact for another three generations, why did it so rapidly collapse in the fifth century? Was the collapse primarily due to increased outside pressure or to internal decay or to a mixture of both?

One can only approximately gauge the external pressure on the empire. If one compares two historians who wrote on a similar scale of the first and of the fourth centuries A.D., Tacitus and Ammianus, one gains the impression that in the former period there was no heavy pressure on the frontiers, but in general peace, with only occasional border wars, whereas in the latter the emperors were constantly engaged in checking a breakthrough here and another breakthrough there.

The first serious attack on the Roman frontier was under Marcus Aurelius, and in the mid-third century the migrations of the Goths and other east German tribes set up a general movement along the Danube, while the west German tribes grouped in the Frankish and Alamannic federation became more aggressive. The emperors of the late third century managed to restore the line, but it was henceforth held with far more effort than before. In the third quarter of the fourth century the westward movement of the Huns set all the German tribes in motion, and their pressure on the empire was redoubled. The tremendous losses incurred by the western Roman army during this period, amounting it would seem to two-thirds of its effectives, are striking evidence of the severity of the barbarian attacks.

One cause of weakness to the western parts was their administrative separation from the east. Formerly the emperors had been able to draw freely on the wealth of the east to finance the defence of the west. From the time of Diocletian the relatively poor western parts had to make do on their own resources with only occasional aid from the east.

To meet the increased barbarian pressure both halves of the empire enormously increased their armed forces, probably doubling their numbers. How far the high standard of military efficiency established in the principate was kept up, it is difficult to say, but it is unlikely that there was any significant decline. As any reader of Tacitus knows, the army of the early principate was not perfect. In peaceful times discipline became very slack, and the men spent their days on their private avocations and rarely attended a parade. Troops could get out of hand and plunder the provinces they were supposed to protect, and could panic in the face of the enemy. The officers were not professional soldiers and were often incompetent. These and other weaknesses appear in the later Roman empire, but the officers were on the whole of better quality, being experienced professionals. Small bodies of Roman troops still could and did defeat very much larger barbarian hordes in the fourth, fifth and sixth centuries.

The heavy economic burden imposed by the increased size of the army overstrained the resources of the empire and produced a number of weaknesses. It may seem an exaggeration to say that the resources of so large an area as the Roman empire could be overstrained by feeding, clothing and arming an extra 300,000 men, but it must be remembered that the empire was technologically even more backward than Europe of the Middle Ages. With primitive methods of agriculture, industrial production and transport it took very many more man-hours than today to produce the food for rations, to weave the fabrics for uniforms, to hammer out the arms and armour and to transport all this material by barge and wagon to the frontiers. Taxation had to be enormously increased, and to assess and collect the increased taxes, the civil service had to be expanded, thus increasing the taxation load again.

The heavy burden of taxation was probably the root cause of the economic decline of the empire. Marginal lands, which could not yield a profit to the landlord over and above the taxes, ceased to be cultivated. The population seems also to have shrunk. This is a highly disputable point, but there are distinct signs of a chronic shortage of agricultural manpower, notably the reluctance of landlords to surrender their tenants as recruits, the legislation tying tenants to their farms, the constant attempts of landlords to filch tenants from their neighbours, and the large-scale settlement of barbarians on the land. The shortage was not due to a flight from the land to the towns—the movement was rather in the opposite direction. It was exacerbated by the demands of conscription, but it is difficult to resist the suggestion that the peasant population failed to maintain its numbers. The decline in the cultivated area, though not primarily due to manpower shortage, implies that the rural population did decline. The reason for this was that the peasantry, after paying their taxes, and the tenants their rent, did not retain enough food to rear large families, and many died of malnutrition or of actual starvation in bad seasons or after enemy devastations.

Ideally speaking the empire could of course have reduced the economic burden by rigid efficiency and drastic pruning of superfluities. It maintained large numbers of idle or nominal soldiers and sinecurist civil servants. According to old custom it fed 120,000 citizens of Rome, and added to these 80,000 citizens of Constantinople. These were a direct burden on the treasury. It also tolerated, and indeed encouraged, the growth of other classes of idle mouths, notably the clergy. Paganism had cost very little, its priests, except in Egypt, receiving no remuneration except portions of sacrifices. The churches, with their many thousands of clergy, maintained from agricultural rents and first fruits, constituted a new and substantial burden on the economy. The emperors moreover did nothing to curb the growth of the official aristocracy in numbers and wealth, and thus tolerated and encouraged the increase of another unproductive class.

The basic cause of the economic decline of the empire was in fact the increasing number of (economically speaking) idle mouths—senators with their vast households, decurions, civil servants, lawyers, soldiers, clergy, citizens of the capitals—as compared with the number of producers. The resultant burden of taxation and rents proved too much for the peasantry, who slowly dwindled in numbers.

It has been argued that the empire was weakened by the decay of its trade and industry. It is in fact very doubtful if trade and industry did decay; the production and distribution of high-grade and luxury goods for the rich certainly continued to flourish down to the sixth century, and the bulk of industrial and commercial activity had probably always been devoted to such goods. In any event industry and trade had at all times made so small a contribution to the national income that their decay, if it did occur, was economically unimportant.

This economic pressure was, it must be remembered, as severe in the eastern as in the western parts. The east maintained as large an army and a civil service, and had an even larger and richer body of clergy, if a less wealthy aristocracy, than the west. Its rate of taxation was very high, its marginal lands fell out of cultivation, and its population probably sank. But it had greater reserves of agricultural wealth and manpower on which to draw.

No one who reads the scanty records of the collapse of the western empire can fail to be struck by the apathy of the Roman population from the highest to the lowest. The only instance of concerted self help by the provincials is the action of the cities of Britain and Armorica in 408, when, failing to receive aid from the usurper Constantine, they organized their own defence against the barbarians, with the subsequent approval of Honorius. In 471–75 Sidonius Apollinaris, the bishop of their city, inspired the Arverni to defend themselves against the Visigoths. In 532 Pudentius raised his province of Tripolitania against the Vandals and, with the aid of a small imperial force, ejected them. In 546 Tullianus, a landlord of Lucania and Bruttium, organized a large body of peasants, which assisted the imperial forces against Totila. These are the only resistance movements of which we know. Elsewhere the upper classes either fled—there is ample evidence for Spain in 409, when the barbarians first broke in, and for the African provinces in 437 and 442, when the Vandals invaded them—or stayed put and collaborated with the barbarian kings. Not that they were active traitors, with one or two notorious exceptions, but they passively accepted their lot. They were very pleased in Africa and

Italy when Justinian's armies arrived, but they did very little to help them.

The lower classes were just as inert. Townsmen would generally man the walls, but their object was to avoid a sack, and if guaranteed security they would usually surrender. Peasants, like their betters, sometimes fled in panic, but more often accepted their fate passively. They would fight if given a lead, as by Tullianus, but they would fight on either side. Totila subsequently ordered the landlords under his control to recall their peasants from Tullianus' force, and they meekly obeyed. Later Totila raised his own force of Italian peasants and they fought their fellow-citizens under Tullianus in bloody battles. Among the lower classes again there is very little evidence of active co-operation with the barbarians. In fact only one case is known; in 376 some Thracian miners joined the Goths and guided them to rich villas where stores of food were available. Having recently been recalled to their work from agriculture, they may have had a special grievance. It is alleged by Salvian that some peasants in Gaul fled to the barbarians to escape the oppression of landlords and tax collectors; this is no doubt true, but Salvian is a biased witness and perhaps exaggerates.

This apathy was not peculiar to the western parts; instances of self help are as rare in the east. Nor was it, so far as we know, anything new. There had been less occasion for civilian resistance to the enemy under the principate, when the armies on the whole held the invaders at the frontier, but no civilian action is recorded when a breakthrough did occur. For many centuries the provincials had been used to being protected by a professional army, and they had indeed, ever since the reign of Augustus, been prohibited by the *lex Iulia de vi* from bearing arms; this law was in force and more or less observed in the fifth century, and Justinian stiffened it by making the manufacture of arms a strict government monopoly. It was only on the rarest occasions that the government appealed to the civil population (including slaves) to take up arms to defend the empire; in 406 when Radagaesus with his horde had broken into Italy, the government appealed for volunteers 'for love of peace and country', and in 440, when Gaiseric was threatening to invade Italy, it authorized the provincials to arm themselves to resist Vandal landing parties. It is not known whether either appeal was fruitful; in earlier crises Augustus and Marcus Aurelius had been obliged to apply conscription in Italy.

The general attitude of the provincials to the empire was, and always had been, passive. This is well illustrated under the principate by such panegyrics on the Roman empire as that of Aelius Aristides, and by the provincial cult of Rome and Augustus. Provincials were profoundly grateful to the empire for protecting them from the barbarians and maintaining internal security, and thus enabling them to enjoy and develop the amenities of civilized life in peace. But they felt no active loyalty, no obligation to help the emperor in his task. He was a god, whom they delighted to worship, but who needed no aid from his mortal subjects.

It has been argued that the regimentation of the population into hereditary castes led to inertia and discontent. It is true that many members of the classes affected tried to evade their hereditary obligations, but this does not prove that all were discontented. In any society, however free, most people are content to carry on in their parents' vocation, and it is only an enterprising few who strike out a new line and rise in the social scale. So far as we can tell the enterprising few in the later Roman empire normally succeeded in flouting or evading the law, which was very inefficiently enforced. The extent and the rigidity of the caste system have in any case been exaggerated, and it was, it may be noted, common to both east and west.

There was undoubtedly a decline in public spirit in the later Roman empire, both in the east and in the west. Under the principate there had existed a strong sense of civic patriotism among the gentry, and they had given freely of their time and money not only to improve the amenities of their cities, but to perform many administrative tasks, such as collecting the taxes and levying recruits, delegated to the cities by the imperial government. From the third century onwards this civic patriotism faded, and the imperial government had to rely more and more on its own administrators and civil servants. Under the principate the service of the state had been regarded as a high duty, incumbent on the imperial aristocracy, and on the whole, the government service being small and select, high standards were maintained. Under the later empire the old pagan idea of public service waned and the church taught good Christians to regard the imperial service as dirty work, if not sinful, while the ranks of the administration were greatly expanded and its quality inevitably diluted. Hence the growth of corruption and extortion, leading to popular discontent and waste of the limited resources of the empire. Over a wider field the teaching of the church that salvation was only to be found in the world to come and that the things of this world did not matter may have encouraged apathy and defeatism.

It must however be emphasized that the eastern empire shared to the full these various weaknesses, economic, social and moral, and that it nevertheless survived for centuries as a great power. It was the increasing pressure of the barbarians, concentrated on the weaker western half of the empire, that caused the collapse.

Appendix I

GENERAL BIBLIOGRAPHY

The most readable history of the later Roman Empire is Edward Gibbon's *Decline and Fall of the Roman Empire*; the few factual errors are corrected in J. B. Bury's edition (1897–1900). Readers may also consult O. Seeck, *Geschichte des untergangs der antiken Welt* (Berlin, 1897–1921), for the period A.D. 284–476; J. B. Bury, *A History of the Later Roman Empire* (London, 1923), for A.D. 395–565; A. Piganiol, *L'empire chrétien (325–95)*, (Paris, 1947); E. Stein, *Histoire du Bas-empire*, vol. I *(284–476)*, (Paris, 1959, translation and revision by J. R. Palanque); vol. II *(476–565)*, (Paris, 1949). For church history the most important book is *Histoire de l'église* (A. Fliche, B. Martin), vol. III, *De la paix Constantinienne à la mort de Théodose* (by J. R. Palanque, G. Bardy, P. de Labriolle, Paris, 1947), vol. IV, *De la mort de Théodose à l'avénement de Grégoire le Grand* (by P. de Labriolle, G. Bardy, L. Bréhier, G. de Plinval, Paris, 1945).

My own *Later Roman Empire* (Oxford, 1964) contains a narrative, but is mainly devoted to an administrative, economic and social survey of the empire.

It is appropriate to mention here those sources that extend over the whole period. They include the *Codex Theodosianus* with the *Novels*, now available in an English translation, C. Pharr, *The Theodosian Code and Novels and the Sirmondian Constitutions*, Princeton, 1952; the *Codex Justinianus*; the letters of the popes, from Siricius to Boniface in Migne, *Patrologia Latina*, from Hilarus to Hormisdas in A. Thiel, *Epistulae Pontificum Romanorum*, and the later popes in Migne, *Patrologia Latina*, again, except for Pelagius I, P. M. Gasso and C. M. Batti, *Pelagii I Papae Epistulae quae supersunt* (Montserrat, 1956) and Gregory the Great, *Monumenta Germaniae Historica, Epistolae*, I, II. Also the canons of councils in Mansi, *Concilia*, and the *Liber Pontificalis* (acts of the popes and endowments of the Roman Church). The secular authors are mostly available in English in the Loeb series, and the ecclesiastical in the Nicene and post-Nicene Fathers. Nearly all editions of the papyri have English, French or German translations.

371

Appendix II

EMPERORS, POPES AND BISHOPS

EMPERORS

West	East
Maximian C. 285–86	Diocletian A. 284–305
A. 286–305, 307–10	
Constantius I C. 293–305	Galerius C. 293–305
A. 305–06	A. 305–11
[1]Constantine C. 306–08	Maximin C. 305–08
A. 308–37	A. 308–13
Severus A. 306–07	
Maxentius A. 307–12	Licinius A. 308–24
(Alexander A. 308–11)	Licinianus C. 317–23
Crispus C. 317–25	Martinianus C. 324
	[1] Constantine A. 324–37
Constantine II C. 317–37	[2] Constantius II C. 324–37
A. 337–40	A. 337–61
Constans C. 333–37	
A. 337–50	
Dalmatius C. 335–37	
(Magnentius A. 350–3)	
(Vetranio A. 350)	Gallus C. 350–54
(Nepotianus A. 350)	
[2] Constantius II A. 351–61	
[3] Julian C. 355–60	
A. 360–63	[3] Julian A. 361–63
[4] Jovian A. 363–64	[4] Jovian A. 363–64
Valentinian I A. 364–75	Valens A. 364–78
(Firmus, 372)	(Procopius A. 365)
Gratian A. 375–83	
Maximus A. 383–87	[5] Theodosius I A. 379–95

[1] Constantine was ruler of the whole empire (with his sons as Caesars of different areas) 324–37.

[2] Constantius II was ruler of the whole empire 351–60 (with Gallus and Julian Caesars of certain areas).

[3] Julian was sole emperor 361–63.

[4] Jovian was sole emperor 363–64.

[5] Theodosius I was *de facto* ruler of the whole empire 388–94 and sole emperor 394–95.

POPES	BISHOPS OF ALEXANDRIA	BISHOPS OF CONSTANTINOPLE
Gaius 283–96	Theonas 282–300	
Marcellinus 296–304	Peter I 300–11	
Marcellus 307–09		Metrophanes 306–14
Miltiades 310–14	Achillas 311–12	
Silvester 314–35	Alexander 312–28	Alexander 314–37
Marcus 336	Athanasius 328–73	
Julius 337–52	(Gregory 339–45)	Paul 337–39
		Eusebius 339–41
		Paul (bis) 341–42
		Macedonius 342–46
		Paul (ter) 346–51
Liberius 352–66	(George 356–62)	Macedonius (bis) 351–60
Damasus 366–85		Eudoxius 360–70
	Peter II 373–80	Demophilus 370–80
	Timothy I 380–85	Gregory 380–81
		Nectarius 381–97

Note. A. = Augustus: C. = Caesar. Names in brackets = usurpers. The dates of the Augusti are those of their independent rule, and do not include the years when they merely bore the title or ruled as viceregents. Many of the earlier emperors (down to 395) ruled only parts of the West or the East.

EMPERORS

West	East
Valentinian II A. 383–92	
(Eugenius A. 392–94)	
[5] Theodosius I A. 394–95	
Honorius A. 395–423	Arcadius A. 395–408
(Gildo, 397)	
(Constantine A. 407–11)	Theodosius II A. 408–50
(Constans C. 408–10)	
(Attalus A. 408–10)	
(Jovinus A. 412–13)	
Constantius III A. 421	
(John A. 423–25)	
Valentinian III A. 425–55	Marcian A. 450–57
Petronius Maximus A. 455	
Avitus A. 455–56	
Majorian A. 457–61	Leo I A. 457–74
Libius Severus A. 461–65	
Anthemius A. 467–72	
Olybrius A. 472	
Glycerius A. 473	
Julius Nepos A. 473–80	Leo II A. 474
Romulus A. 475–76	Zeno A. 474–91
	(Basiliscus A. 475–76)
	(Marcian A. 479)
	(Leontius A. 483)
	Anastasius A. 491–518
	Justin I A. 518–27
	[6] Justinian A. 527–65
	[7] Justin II A. 565–78
	Tiberius Constantine C. 574–78
	A. 578–82
	Maurice A. 582–602

Justinian and his successors also ruled Africa, Italy (or parts of it) and part of Spain.

[7] Justin II went mad in 574, and the effective reign of Tiberius Constantine began in that year.

POPES	BISHOPS OF ALEXANDRIA	BISHOPS OF CONSTANTINOPLE
Siricius 385–99	Theophilus 385–412	
Anastasius 399–401		John I (Chrysostom) 398–404
Innocent I 401–17		Arsacius 404–05
Zosimus 417–18	Cyril 412–44	Atticus 406–25
Boniface I 418–22		
		Sisinnius 426–27
Celestine I 422–32		Nestorius 428–31
Sixtus III 432–40		Maximian 431–34
		Proclus 434–47
Leo I 440–61	Dioscorus 444–51	Flavian 447–49
	Proterius 452–57	Anatolius 449–58
	Timothy II (the Cat) 457–60	Gennadius 458–71
Hilary 461–68	Timothy III (White Hat) 460–75	
Simplicius 468–83	Timothy II 475–77	Acacius 471–89
	Timothy III 477–82	
Felix III 483–92	John I (Talaias) 482	
	Peter III (Mongus) 482–89	Fravitta 489
		Euphemius 489–95
Gelasius I 492–96	Athanasius II 490–96	
Anastasius II 496–98	John II 496–505	Macedonius II 496–511
Symmachus 498–514	John III 506–16	Timothy 511–18
Hormisdas 514–23	Dioscorus II 516–17	John II 518–20
	Timothy IV 517–35	
John I 523–26		Epiphanius 520–35
Felix IV 526–30		
Boniface II 530–32		
John II 532–35	Gaian 535	
Agapetus I 535–36	Theodosius 535–36	Anthimus 535–36
Silverius 536–37	Paul 537–42	Menas 536–52
Vigilius 537–55	Zoilus 542–51	
Pelagius I 555–61	Apollinarius 551–70	Eutychius 552–65
John III 561–74		John III 565–77
Benedictus I 574–78	John IV 570–80	
Pelagius II 578–90	Eulogius 580–607	Eutychius (bis) 577–582
		John IV 582–95
Gregory I 590–604		Cyriacus 596–606

Appendix III

NOTE ON WEIGHTS, MEASURES AND CURRENCY

I use Roman weights and measures throughout. The modern equivalents are approximately as follows:

12 inches (*unciae*) = 1 foot (*pes*) = 11⅔ inches = 29·6 centimetres
1 mile (*mille passus*) = 4,855 feet = 1,480 metres
1 *iugerum* = ⅝ acre = 0·25 hectares
1 *arura* = ⅔ acre = 0·27 hectares
1 *centuria* = 200 iugera = 125 acres = 50 hectares
1 *millena* = 12½ iugera = 7¾ acres = 3·25 hectares
24 scruples (*scripuli*) = 1 ounce (*uncia*)
12 ounces (*unciae*) = 1 pound (*libra*) = 11½ ounces = 321 grammes
1 *sextarius* = 1 pint = 0·57 litres
16 *sextarii* = 1 *modius*
1 *modius* = 1 peck = 9 litres
1 *artaba* = 3⅓ pecks = 30 litres

For the currency see pp. 165–68, and for the purchasing power of the *solidus* see p. 8.

In gold the following denominations were used:

24 carats (*siliquae*) = 3 *tremisses* = 2 *semisses* = 1 *solidus*
72 *solidi* = 1 lb gold (*libra auri*)
7,200 solidi = 1 cwt gold (*centenarium auri*)

Appendix IV

GLOSSARY OF TECHNICAL TERMS

A

a libellis, judicial official (p. 17)

a secretis, clerks of the consistory (p. 203)

ab actis, judicial officials (p. 207)

actores, agents of estates (p. 303)

actuarii, quartermasters of regiments (p. 222)

adaeratio, commutation of levies and issues in kind into gold (p. 173)

adiutores, assistants (rank of official) (p. 207)

adlectio, enrolment in the senate (p. 274)

administrationes, offices of state, also called *dignitates* or *honores* (p. 199)

adoratio, imperial audience (p. 29)

adscripticii, tied tenants of land (p. 294)

advocatus fisci, counsel to the crown (p. 196)

aediles, Roman magistrates (p. 274)

aerikon, tax (p. 114)

agentes in rebus, imperial couriers (p. 205)

ager publicus, public land (p. 155)

alae, cavalry regiments (p. 212)

annona (1) rations of soldiers and officials (p. 169)
         (2) corn supply of Rome and Constantinople (p. 233)

Antoninianus, coin (p. 22)

aphthartodocetism, heresy (p. 111)

arca vinaria, treasury at Rome (p. 167)

archiatri sacri palatii, court physicians (p. 278)

argentarii, silversmiths or money-changers (p. 290)

artaba, Egyptian measure of corn (p. 376)

arura, Egyptian unit of land measurement (p. 376)

Augustal prefect, governor of the Egyptian diocese (p. 143)

aureus, coin (p. 33)

aurum coronarium, tax on decurions (p. 161)

aurum oblaticium, tax on senators (p. 161)

aurum tironicum, tax in lieu of recruits (p. 163)
auxilia, infantry regiments (p. 213)
auxilia palatina, infantry regiments (p. 214)

B

baphia, state dye works (p. 315)
barbaricarii, smiths who made officers' armour (p. 314)
beneficiarii, grade of official (p. 200)
biarchus, N.C.O. grade in the army (p. 224)
bona caduca, property illegally bequeathed (p. 155)
bona damnatorum, property of felons (p. 155)
bona vacantia, property of which there was no heir (p. 155)
breves, official returns (p. 177)
bucellarii, military bodyguards (p. 217)

C

Caesariani, imperial slaves and freedmen (p. 200)
campidoctores, drill sergeants (p. 228)
cancellarii, palatine officials (p. 206)
canon praefectorum, taxation controlled by the praetorian prefects (p. 163)
canonicarii, financial officials (p. 207)
canonici, clergy of an episcopal church (p. 253)
canons, decrees of church councils
capita, units of population for taxation purposes (p. 34)
capitatio, tax on units of population (p. 169)
capitula, groups of taxpayers responsible for furnishing recruits, also called *temones* (p. 219)
capitus, fodder (p. 169)
cardinales, clergy of an episcopal church (p. 253)
castrenses, see *limitanei*
castrensiani, domestic servants of the palace (p. 202)
castrensiani sacrae mensae, palace waiters (p. 290)
castrensis, eunuch, major domo of the palace (p. 201)
castrum, fort or town (p. 237)
casula, garment (p. 317)
catabolenses, carters (p. 235)
catechumen, unbaptized Christian
cathedraticum, fee payable by parish priests to their bishop (p. 268)

caudicarii, bargees (p. 235)

cellaria, special rations for officers (p. 96)

censibus adscripti, see *adscripticii*

censitor, reviser of the tax assessments (p. 176)

censuales, officials of the city prefect (p. 275)

centenarium, 100 pounds (p. 376)

centenarius (1) grade of the equestrian order (p. 270)

             (2) N.C.O. grade in the army (p. 224)

centuria, unit of land measurement (p. 376)

centurion, army officer (p. 19)

chartularii, minor officials (p. 207)

chorepiscopi, rural bishops (p. 256)

chrysargyron, see *collatio lustralis*

circitor, N.C.O. grade in the army (p. 224)

clari, rank of councillors of Constantinople (p. 49)

clarissimi, grade of senatorial order (p. 270)

codicils, imperial letters conferring an office or title (p. 271)

coemptio, compulsory purchase (p. 173)

coenobia, monasteries (p. 333)

cohort, infantry regiment (p. 212)

cohortales, officials of provincial governors (p. 208)

collatio aeraria, levy of copper (p. 165)

collatio auraria, levy of gold (p. 165)

collatio lustralis, tax on traders (p. 162)

collectarii, money-changers (p. 167)

college, group of co-ordinate emperors (p. 125)

collegia, guilds (p. 318)

coloni adscripticii, tied tenants of land (p. 294)

colonicae, holdings of tenants (p. 302)

colonus, tenant (p. 292)

comes or *comites:*

c. *Africae,* military commander of Africa (p. 52)

c. *civitatis,* military commandant of a city (p. 96)

c. *commerciorum,* controller of external trade (p.161)

c. *consistorianus,* member of the consistory (p. 194)

c. *domesticorum,* commander of the corps of officer cadets (p. 140)

c. *domorum,* controller of the imperial estates which supplied the palace (p. 201)

c. *excubitorum,* commander of the imperial bodyguard (p. 218)

c. *foederatorum,* commander of the foreign troops (p. 94)

c. Gildoniaci patrimonii, controller of the confiscated property of Gildo (p. 156)

c. Gothorum per singulas civitates, commanders of the Goths in the Italian cities (p. 98)

c. largitionum Italicianarum, high financial official (p. 193)

c. metallorum, controller of the mines (p. 161)

c. Orientis, governor of the diocese of Oriens (p. 48)

c. patrimonii or *vice dominus*, minister in charge of the royal lands in Italy and Spain (p. 98)

c. portus Romae, governor of the port of Rome (p. 232)

c. primi (secundi, tertii) ordinis, member of the imperial order of Companions (1st, 2nd or 3rd grade) (p. 271)

c. provinciarum, imperial commissioner for a group of provinces (p. 48)

c. rei militaris, military commander (p. 48)

c. rei privatae, minister in charge of imperial lands (p. 156)

c. sacrae vestis, head of the imperial wardrobe (p. 201)

c. sacrarum largitionum, financial minister (p. 161)

c. stabuli, controller of the imperial stable and of military remounts (p. 141)

c. titulorum largitionalium, high financial official (p. 161)

comitatenses, soldiers of the field army (p. 214)

comitatus (1) the imperial court (p. 31)
          (2) the field army (p. 213)

comitiva, the office of *comes* (p. 271)

commeatus, leave of absence (p. 279)

commentarienses, judicial officials (p. 207)

commerciarii, controllers of external trade (p. 310)

compulsores, collectors of arrears of tax (p. 207)

concilium principis, the imperial council (p. 15)

conductores, contractors or lessees of land or taxes (p. 156)

confessor, a Christian who has suffered for the faith

consistorium, the imperial council (p. 129)

constitutiones, imperial enactments (p. 181)

consularis, governor of a province (p. 143)

consultationes, form of judicial appeal (p. 182)

copiatae, grave-diggers (p. 265)

cornicularius, judicial official (p. 207)

corrector, governor of a province (p. 143)

cubiculariae, ladies-in-waiting of the empress (p. 201)

cubicularii, eunuchs of the palace (p. 201)

cunei equitum, cavalry regiments (p. 214)

cura epistolarum, official in charge of financial correspondence (p. 207)

cura palatii, controller of the palace (p. 141)

curator, manager of a group of imperial estates (p. 160)

curator civitatis, financial controller of a city (p. 241)

curia, city council (p. 240)

curiales, members of a city council and their families (p. 243)

curiosi, inspectors of the imperial post (p. 205)

cursores, runners or messengers (p. 206)

cursus clabularis, the wagon post for heavy goods (p. 313)

cursus publicus, the imperial post (p. 313)

cursus velox, the quick post for passengers and light goods (p. 313)

D

decani, officials of the palace (p. 206)

decemprimi, the first ten (p. 225)

decreta, judicial decisions (p. 182)

decurions, members of city councils (p. 243)

defensor civitatis (*plebis*), local judge (p. 241)

defensores (ecclesiastical), legal and police officers of the church (p. 266)

delatores, informers (p. 159)

delegatoriae, warrants for rations (p. 172)

denarius, coin (p. 22)

deportatio, penal exile with loss of property (p. 198)

dignitates, offices of state, also called *honores* (p. 199)

dioceses, groups of provinces (p. 143)

dioceses (ecclesiastical), parishes (p. 253)

diptychs, list of deceased bishops for whom prayers were made

discussores, auditors (p. 207)

domestici (1) see *protectores*

        (2) personal assistants of officers of state (p. 87)

domus, group of imperial estates (p. 160)

domus divina, imperial estates, the income of which was allocated to the maintenance of the palace (p. 160)

domus fiscales, imperial estates (p. 96)

donative, bounty given to soldiers on the accession of an emperor and thereafter at intervals of five years (p. 222) *ducenarius* (1) grade of equestrian order (p. 270)

(2) N.C.O. grade in the army (p. 224)

duces, military commanders of frontier districts (p. 144)

duoviri, chief magistrates of a city (p. 240)

dux, see *duces*

E

egregius, grade of equestrian order (p. 270)

eirenarchs, police officers of cities (p. 249)

eminentissimus, grade of equestrian order (p. 270)

emphyteutic lease, (p. 156)

encyclical, circular letter

epistolae (*scrinium* of), department of the imperial secretariat (p. 203)

epistolares, clerks of the *scrinium epistolarum* (p. 204)

equestrian order, second order of aristocracy, i.e. below senators (p. 16)

equites promoti, legionary cavalry (p. 32)

evectiones, postal warrants (p. 314)

exactor civitatis, controller of imperial taxation in a city (p. 241)

exarch, military governor general (p. 118)

exceptores, shorthand writers (p. 206)

excubitors, imperial guards (p. 218)

exercitores, charterers of ships (p. 319)

extraordinaria or *superindictions*, additional land taxes over and above the indiction (p. 172)

F

fabricae, state arms factories (p. 314)

fabricenses, workers in the above (p. 315)

fasti, list of consuls

foederati (1) contingents of client tribes (p. 215)

(2) foreign legions (p. 217)

follis (1) monetary unit (p. 33)

(2) coin (p. 168)

(3) tax on senators, also called *gleba* (p. 162)

forma, grade of lower officials (p. 200)

fossores, grave-diggers (p. 265)

fundi iuris rei publicae, estates of the cities, later imperial (p. 155)

fundi iuris templorum, estates of the temples, later imperial (p. 155)

fundus, estate or farm (p. 302)

G

gentiles, foreigners (p. 218)

gleba, tax on senators, also called *follis* (p. 162)

gloriosi, grade of senatorial order (p. 273)

gradus, steps on which bread was distributed at Rome and Constantinople (p. 233)

gynaecia, state woollen mills (p. 315)

H

homoiousios, of like substance (p. 55)

homoousios, of the same substance (p. 43)

honestiores, upper-class citizens (p. 23)

honorati, holders of *honores*, actual or honorary, present or past (p. 177)

honores, offices of state, also called *dignitates* (p. 199)

hospitalitas, billeting, assignment of land to barbarians (p. 99)

humiliores, lower-class citizens (p. 23)

I

illustres, grade of senatorial order (p. 273)

incolae, residents of a city who are not citizens (p. 237)

indiction, annual budget, fiscal year (p. 169)

insinuativa, admission fee paid by clergy (p. 263)

institores, commercial agents (p. 297)

insulae, flats (p. 232)

iudices pedanei, delegate judges (p. 193)

iugatio, tax on or assessment of land (p. 169)

iugerum, units of land measurement (p. 376)

iugum, fiscal unit of land (p. 34)

iuridicus, judge (p. 186)

ius privatum salvo canone, freehold subject to rent charge (p. 157)

L

laeti, barbarian settlers (p. 221)

lampadarii, palatine officials (p. 206)

largitionales, officials of the *largitiones* (p. 206)

largitionales urbium singularum, officials of the *largitiones* stationed in the cities (p. 161)

largitiones, financial ministry (p. 161)

laterculum maius, register of imperial offices, also called *Notitia Dignitatum* (p. 203)

laterculum minus, register of minor military commissions (p. 204)
laura, group of hermits (p. 333)
leges generales, laws of general application (p. 182)
libellenses, clerks of the *scrinium libellorum* (p. 204)
libelli (*scrinium* of), department of the imperial secretariat (p. 203)
limitanei, frontier troops, also called *ripenses*, *riparienses* (p. 214)
linyphia, imperial linen works (p. 315)

M

magister:
  m. epistolarum, secretary of state for correspondence (p. 140)
  m. equitum, commander-in-chief of the cavalry (p. 47)
  m. libellorum, secretary of state for judicial petitions (p. 140)
  m. memoriae, secretary of state for general petitions (p. 140)
  m. militum, commander-in-chief, also called *magister utriusque militiae*
    (p. 52)
  m. navis, master of a ship (p. 319)
  m. officiorum, imperial minister (p. 140)
  m. peditum, commander-in-chief of the infantry (p. 47)
  m. rei privatae, minister of imperial lands (p. 31)
  m. scrinii, head of an imperial secretariat (p. 140)
  m. utriusque militiae, see *m. militum*
manceps, manager of posting station (p. 314)
mandata, instructions to officers of state (p. 107)
mansiones, posting stations (p. 313)
massa, group of *fundi* (p. 302)
mechanicus, civil engineer or architect (p. 359)
melloproximus, official of the *sacra scrinia* (p. 204)
memoria (*scrinium* of), department of the imperial secretariat (p. 203)
memoriales, clerks of the *scrinium memoriae* (p. 204)
mensores (1) billeting officers (p. 206)
       (2) tally clerks (p. 235)
metata, billeting (p. 99)
militia, government service (p. 199)
militia armata, military service (p. 200)
militia officialis, civil service (p. 200)
millena, unit of land measurement (p. 376)
milliarensis, coin (p. 166)
mimes, ballet
mittendarii, messengers (p. 150)

modius, measure of corn (p. 376)
monetarii, mint workers (p. 164)
more consultationum, type of judicial appeal (p. 191)
mutationes, posting stations (p. 313)

N

navicularii, state shippers (p. 289)
nobilissimus puer, child heir-apparent (p. 79)
notary, official of the consistory (p. 202)
Notitia Dignitatum, see *laterculum maius*
novel, a new law
numerarius, financial official (p. 170)
numerus, regiment
nummus, coin (p. 33)

O

oblationes, offerings in church (p. 261)
octavae, customs dues (p. 161)
oeconomus, financial manager of a church (p. 266)
officium, ministry
officium admissionum, department dealing with imperial audiences (p. 140)
officium dispositionum, department dealing with the imperial timetable (p. 140)
opinator, regimental quartermaster (p. 223)
originales, tied tenants of land (p. 294)

P

pagus, district of a city territory (p. 241)
palatini (1) soldiers of the central field armies (p. 214)
       (2) officials of the central ministries (pp. 201–6)
       (3) officials of the *largitiones* and *res privata* (p. 138)
panes gradiles, loaves issued free at Rome and Constantinople (p. 234)
panes Ostienses, loaves issued cheap at Rome (p. 234)
parabalani, hospital attendants (p. 265)
parochiae, parishes (p. 253)
patrician, title of honour (p. 273)
patricius praesentalis, commander-in-chief (p. 98)
peculium, quasi property of a slave (p. 297)
peraequator, reviser of tax assessments (p. 176)

perfectissimus, grade of equestrian order (p. 270)

periodeutae, rural deans (p. 256)

petitio, petition for grant of state lands (p. 159)

phylarch, paramount chief of Saracens (p. 215)

plebeii, the lower classes (p. 282)

postulatio simplex, legal statement of claim (p. 192)

praefectus annonae, director of the corn supply at Rome and Constantinople (p. 17)

praefectus vigilum, chief of the police at Rome and Constantinople (p. 17)

praepositi pagorum, civic magistrates in charge of *pagi* (p. 241)

praepositus regni, chief minister of Vandal kingdom (p. 96)

praepositus sacri cubiculi, the chief eunuch of the palace (p. 201)

praesental armies, central field armies, also called *palatini* (p. 52)

praesentalis, at the imperial court (p. 52)

praeses, governor of a province (p. 143)

praetor plebis, chief of police at Constantinople (p. 108)

praetorian prefect, chief imperial minister (p. 141)

praetors, Roman and Constantinopolitan magistrates (p. 274)

pragmaticae, laws issued to communities or individuals (p. 182)

primicerius, senior clerk or N.C.O. (pp. 203, 224)

primipili pastus, military purveyance (p. 172)

princeps, chief clerk of a ministry (p. 200)

principales, leading decurions (p. 243)

principatus, post of chief clerk (p. 205)

privatiani, officials of the *res privata* (p. 206)

probatoria, enlistment certificate (p. 199)

proceres palatii, imperial ministers (p. 129)

proconsul, governor of a province (p. 142)

procurator (1) imperial financial official (p. 16)

          (2) private agent of an estate (p. 303)

protector (*domesticus*), officer cadet (p. 224)

proximus, senior clerk of a *scrinium* (p. 204)

Q

quadrimenstrui breves, four-monthly returns (p. 170)

quaesitor, police officer of Constantinople (p. 232)

quaestor, Roman and Constantinopolitan magistracy (p. 273)

quaestor exercitus, title of praetorian prefect on lower Danube (p. 108)

quaestor sacri palatii, legal minister (p. 140)

R

rationalis, financial officer (pp. 156, 161)

rationalis rei summae (*summarum*), minister of finance (p. 31)

rector provinciae, governor of a province (p. 96)

rectores (of the Roman church), district managers of papal estates (p. 303)

regendarius, official of the praetorian prefecture (p. 207)

regiones, districts of imperial land (p. 238)

relationes, reference of legal issues by a judge to the emperor (p. 182)

res privata, ministry of imperial lands (p. 154)

res summa, ministry of finance (p. 154)

rescripts, replies to petitions (p. 182)

riparienses, see *limitanei*

riparii, civic police officers (p. 249)

ripenses, see *limitanei*

S

sacellarius, eunuch keeper of the privy purse (p. 201)

sacerdotes, high priests of provincial imperial cult (p. 136)

sacra scrinia, the imperial secretariats (*memoria*, *epistolae*, *libelli*) (p. 203)

sacrae largitiones, finance ministry (p. 161)

saiones, royal messengers in the Gothic kingdom (p. 98)

saltus, districts of imperial land (p. 238)

satrapy, Persian word for a province (p. 30)

scholae, regiments of the imperial guard (p. 218)

scholares, soldiers of the *scholae* (p. 227)

scribones, officers of the excubitors (p. 218)

scriniarii, financial clerks (p. 207)

scrinium, department of a ministry (p. 206)

semissis, coin (p. 376)

senator (1) member of the senate

(2) N.C.O. grade in the army (p. 224)

senatus consultum, decree of the senate (p. 121)

sextarius, pint (p. 376)

silentiary, usher of the consistory (p. 202)

siliqua, carat (p. 376)

siliquaticum, tax on sales (p. 81)

solidus, coin (p. 376)

sordida munera, *corvées* falling on land owners (p. 275 cf. 165, 315) *sortes Vandalorum*, lots of land given to the Vandals (p. 99)

spatharius, eunuch bodyguard (p. 201)

spectabilis, grade of the senatorial order (p. 273)

speculatores, judicial officials (p. 200)

sportulae, tips or fees to officials (p. 192)

stellatura, perquisite of army officers (p. 226)

stipendium, pay (in the army and civil service) (p. 167)

strator, groom (p. 222)

subadiuvae, deputy assistants (p. 205)

Suburbicarian diocese, the provinces of southern Italy, Sicily, Sardinia and Corsica (p. 143)

suffragium, bribe to obtain an imperial office (p. 148)

superindiction, see *extraordinaria*

supplicatio, judicial appeal from the praetorian prefect to the emperor (p. 187)

susceptores, tax collectors (p. 170)

T

tabelliones, legal notaries (p. 197)

tabularii, financial officials (p. 200)

temones, see *capitula*

tertiae, Ostrogothic tax in lieu of *hospitalitas* (p. 99)

terunciani, coins (p. 168)

tesserae, bread tickets (p. 233)

thesaurenses, officials of the *thesauri* (p. 208)

thesauri, diocesan treasuries of the *largitiones* (p. 161)

tituli largitionales, taxes under the *largitiones* (p. 163)

tractatores, financial officials (p. 170)

tractoriae, postal warrants for wagons (p. 314)

tractus, districts of imperial land (p. 238)

traditio, surrender of the scriptures in the persecution (p. 41)

traditor, one guilty of *traditio* (p. 40)

tremissis, coin (p. 376)

tribunes, regimental commanders (p. 225)

tribunes of the plebs, Roman and Constantinopolitan magistrates (p. 274)

tributum capitis, poll tax (p. 21)

tuitio, protection (p. 102)

U

urban prefect, governor of the city of Rome or Constantinople (p. 232)

V

vexillatio, cavalry regiment (p. 213)

vicar, governor of a diocese (p. 143)

vice sacra iudicantes, judges of appeal (p. 187)

vicedominus, see *comes patrimonii*

vicomagistri, head of the wards of Rome (p. 233)

vigiles, nightwatchmen at Rome (p. 17)

vilici, bailiffs (p. 296)

vindex, director of imperial taxation in a city (p. 171)

Index

Abasgi, eunuchs from, 201
Ablabius, praetorian prefect, 46, 51
Abyssinian church, 323
Acacius, patriarch of Constantinople, 94
Achaea, 31, 64, 143, 173
Acilius Glabrio, praetorian prefect, 82
Acilli Glabriones, the, 276
Adamites, 340
Adrianople, battle of (378), 1, 68, 128, 221; Council at (342/3), 55; armaments factory, 315
Aegean islands, 312
Aegidius, commander-in-chief, 92
Aelafius, 41
Aelius Aristides, 369
Aemilia, 69, 116, 288
Aetius, commander-in-chief to Galla Placidia, 79, 80, 81, 145; murder of, 89; ruler of western empire, 132; his bodyguard, 217
Africa, north, 17, 31, 236; archaeological evidence, 6; annexation, 10, 228; senators from, 14, 142; the army in, 19, 75, 216, 218; spoken dialect, 23, 347; religion, 23; diocese of, 31, 143; fiscal unit of land, 34, 176; poll tax, 35; Christian martyrdoms, 38; Donatist schism, 40–2, 329–30; its prefecture, 48, 106, 111, 142, 206–7, 286; Vandal acquisitions, 79, 92, 98, 260, 357; and Pelagianism, 83; allotted to German tribesmen, 98–9; mutiny of Roman troops, 106–7, 111; army recruitment from, 114; Moorish rebellions, 116, 118; proconsulate, 145, 208; imperial land ownership, 155, 160; financial control, 161; copper coinage, 168; provincial revenues, 178; rate of taxation, 179; appointment of Roman prefects, 215; number of cities in the diocese, 239; civic government, 242; rival bishoprics, 253; congresses of bishops, 256; and papal jurisdiction, 258, 260; agriculture in, 299; land valuation, 309; survival of paganism, 322; monasticism, 334; *lingua franca*, 344; architecture, 360, 363

Africa Proconsularis, 79, 81, 118, 146; revenue from, 178; area of deserted land, 306, 308
Agapetus, Pope, 109, 269
Agathias, 2, 218
Agorius Praetextatus, proconsul of Achaea, 64, 280, 345
Agricola, St, 325
Agriculture, tax burden and, 32, 35, 178, 301, 308, 366; caste system and, 36; use of slaves, 296–7, 303, 308; principal crops, 299; livestock, 299–300; methods of tillage, 300; yields, 300; main source of national income, 301; clothing levy, 317
Alamans, the, raids by, 12, 30, 66; in the army, 218
Alans, the, invasions by, 76, 77, 78, 80, 216; settlements, 81; become federated, 215
Alaric, king of the Visigoths, 75, 126; invades Italy, 76, 216, 363; sacks Rome, 77
Alaric II, king of the Visigoths, codification of the law, 185
Alboin, king of the Lombards, 116, 117
Alexander, bishop of Alexandria, and Arianism, 42, 44, 45
Alexander, vicar of Africa, proclaims himself Augustus, 29–30, 364
Alexandria, its population, 7, 238; and foundations of Christian theology, 26; authority of its bishop, 44, 70, 238, 256–7, 258; Athanasius and, 55; and bishop George, 60; paganism in, 71; jealousy of see of Constantinople, 84–6, 260–1; patriarchal control, 88–9, 252, 261; its mint, 164, educational reputation,

Alexandria—*cont.*
231, 349, third city of the empire,
238; riots in, 242; customs income,
248; free bread distribution, 249;
parochial churches, 253; its merchants, 290; as a port, 310, 312;
manufactures, 316
Alexandria Troas, marble quarries,
315, 359
Allectus, revolt against Diocletian, 28,
30
Amalasuntha, mother of Athalaric,
106, 274
Ambrose, St, bishop of Milan, 3, 65,
121, 201, 269, 331, 334, 342, 345;
dominating role in church and
state, 69, 70–1; ex-senator, 288;
unearths saints, 325; baptism, 332
Ammianus Marcellinus, historian, 60–
1, 66, 159, 280, 344–5, 352, 364;
career, 1; and the consistory, 129;
on Eutherius, 202; and the Roman
army, 218, 220, 221; his poetry,
344–5
Amoricans, the, 80
Anastasius, emperor of the East, 4,
94, 96, 126, 133, 143, 210, 250; and
Monophysites, 94–5; and imperial
finances, 95, 130, 134, 135, 162,
173, 176, 227, 247; and the prefecture, 134; and the coinage, 168; and
tax collection, 171, 177; legal reforms, 189; Persian campaign, 228;
religious policy, 261, 263, 269; and
tied tenants, 294; and paganism,
323
Anatolius, decurion, 283
Ancyra, 63; Council of (358), and
Arianism, 42
Anicia Juliana, 276
Antaeopolis, tax register under Justinian, 179
Anthemius, emperor of the west, 5,
90, 91, 125, 127, 275, 277
Anthemius, patriarch of Constantinople, 109
Anthemius, praetorian prefect, 76, 78,
82, 277; ruler of eastern empire,
130, 132, 143
Anthemius of Tralles, architect of S.
Sophia, 232, 287, 359–60
Anthony, St, hermit, 333
Antinopolis, 316
Antioch, 52, 56, 67, 109, 123, 240,
283; historians of, 1, 2, 4; its
population, 7; position of its bishop
(patriarch), 44, 88–9, 231, 257,
258, 261; its churches, 46; the
emperors and, 139; ecclesiastical
capital, 239; riots in, 242; city

services, 248, 249, 251; church in-
come, 262; village craftsmen, 318;
reputation for scholarship, 349
Council of (268), 43
Antiochus, quaestor and praetorian
prefect, 83; and codification of the
law, 184
'house' of, 160
Antoninus, bishop of Ephesus, 260
Anullinus, proconsul of Africa, 40
Apamea, 117, 240, 265; paganism,
323
Apheca, 47, 324
Aphrodito, village documents, 6,
317–18
Aphthartodocetism, 111, 355
Apiarus, priest, 84
Apion family, 6, 279, 292; land owner-
ship, 302, 303
Apodemus, 57
Apollinarii, the, 350–1
Aquileia, 239
Aquitania, 78, 81, 99, 133, 215, 363
Arabia, Roman army in, 19; para-
mount chiefs, 215; its cities, 240;
architecture, 360
Arabs, 6, 343; united by Islam, 10;
occupy Palestine and Egypt, 120
Arbetio, commander-in-chief, 277
Arbetio, senator, 53
Arbogast, 71, 127; and Valentinian II,
69, 131, 226
Arcadius, emperor of the east, 3, 69,
74, 76, 85, 130, 132, 202; and
Honorius, 126; his successor, 127;
and tied tenants, 293
Architecture, 356–9; its uniformity,
360–1
Ardaburius, Alan general, 79, 82, 90,
133
Areobindus, general, 82, 276
Ariadne, empress of Zeno, 90, 91,
94, 126
Arians and Arianism, 328, 329, 340;
its dogmas, 42, 339; Constantine
and, 42–3, 45; and Council of
Nicaea, 43–4; division in, 55;
dwindling importance, 70; barbarians and, 102, 105, 325; language
difficulties, 345
Ariminum, Council of (359), 54, 58, 64,
134, 136
Aristius Optatus, prefect of Egypt, on
Diocletian's tax reforms, 33–4
Aristocracy, and Rome, 230–1; and
games, 251; rank and precedence,
270, 272–3; position of the *comitiva*,
271; and religion, 322; and Dona-
tism, 330; comparison between east
and west, 364; a burden on the

Nepotianus, emperor of the west
(usurper), 56
Nero, emperor, 13, 25; Jewish rising
against, 26–7
Nerva, emperor, and the succession, 14
Nestorius, bishop of Constantinople,
85, 260, 327, 328; doctrines of, 93,
94, 110, 339, 355; his opponents,
355
Nicaea, 260, 302
Nicaea, First Council of (325); and
Arianism, 43, 45; and Melitian–
Novatian schism, 44; settles points
of church discipline, 44–5; its
creed, 55, 65, 70, 84, 93, 354–5;
imposition of creed on eastern
church, 134, 355; and the bishops,
253, 256, 257; and the movement of
clergy, 266; rejects continence
among married clergy, 267; western
church and, 329
Nichomachus Flavianus, prefect of
Italy, 71
Nicomedia, 42, 46; Diocletian and, 36,
37, 50, 346
Nika rebellion, 104, 105
Nisibis, 63, 94, 310, 347; rhetorical
school, 351
Nitria, monasteries, 334
Nobades, the, 323
Nomus, master of the offices, 80, 86,
88, 132, 134, 140, 202
Nonnus of Panopolis, *Dionysiaca*,
353
Noricum, 92, 217
Notaries, 203, 284; and senatorship,
277
Notitia Dignitatum, 5, 7, 32, 74n, 81,
144, 164, 205, 216, 218, 221, 223
Novatianism, 44, 45, 328, 339; its
tenets, 340–1
Nubia, paganism in, 323
Numidia, 8, 38, 173, 192; church dis-
putes, 40; Vandal invasion, 79;
restored to the empire, 81; army
recruits from, 114; revenue, 178;
rate of taxation, 179; legal fees,
196; area of deserted land, 306, 309
Nunneries, 334, 335

Odoacer, king, 92, 93; administration
of Italy, 96, 97–8, 99; and post of
patrician, 132; and prefecture of
Italy, 142; appoints consuls, 274
Olybrius, emperor, 91, 127
Olympiodorus of Thebes, 2, 278, 350
Olympius, and Alaric, 76–7
Ophitae, the, 340
Optatus, 3, 51
Orcistus, 47

Orestes, patrician, 92, 99, 128, 131
Oriens, diocese of, 31, 48, 51, 89, 143,
163, 329; its census, 34; and primacy of Antioch, 44, 239, 257;
reorganization, 108; diocesan governorship, 143; revenue, 179; appointment of local judge, 186; its
cities, 240; guilds, 289
Origen, 27, 354
Orléans, 81
Orosius, 3, 68, 83
Ostrogoths, 70, 75, 96, 97, 142, 162,
274–5; Valens and, 67–8; expelled
from the empire, 68; Theodoric
Strabo and, 91; and the army, 98;
land allotments, 99; legal code, 185
Ostrys, 91
Oxyrhynchus, 279, 292; minutes of a
council meeting, 243

Pachomius, St, founder of monasticism, 264–5, 333–4, 335
Paganism, 23–5, 39, 50, 70–1, 362;
Maximin and, 37; Constantine and,
47, 134, 323; Julian and, 59–61,
62, 134, 323; hopes of a revival, 62,
325; Valentinian and Valens and,
64; Theodosius and, 71, 323;
Justinian and, 108; position of the
emperor, 123; penal laws against,
152, 323, 325; and sack of Rome,
321; professional classes and, 322; its
survival, 322–3, 325; its cults, 323–
4; universal appeal, 324; moral
code compared with Christianity,
330–1; and charity, 337; service of
the state, 338; its small cost, 366
Palace, the, its membership, 129; the
emperor and, 129–30; eunuchs and,
201–2; domestic staff, 202; corps of
notaries, 202–3; secretariats, 203–4;
establishment of couriers, 205;
financial ministries, 205–6; minor
offices, 206–9; imperial guard,
218–19
Palestine, 5, 6, 43, 83, 89; Roman
army in, 19; Christian martyrs,
38; the plague in, 114; invaded by
Chosroes II, 120; diocese of, 143;
paramount chiefs, 215; estates,
238; under patriarch of Antioch,
261; introduction of tied tenancies,
293; monasticism, 334; languages,
347–8
Palladius, manual on agriculture, 4,
300; *Lausiac History*, 4
Pamphylia, 257, 332
Pannonia, 14, 52, 63, 98, 133; annexation, 10; diocese of, 31, 69, 143;
Ostrogoth settlement, 91